THE COLLECTION

THE
COLLECTION

edited by Mark Elsdon-Dew

HTB PUBLICATIONS
LONDON

ISBN 1-898838-29-1

Front cover illustration by Charlie Mackesy

Editor's Acknowledgements

I am profoundly grateful to all this book's contributors, who never
expected their spoken words to be put into print, but have given me
immense encouragement with this project. I would also like to thank
Gil Rea, Tanya Ivas and Linda Williams for all their help with typing,
editing and honing the final manuscript.

Designed and produced by Bookprint Creative Services
P.O. Box 827, BN21 3YJ, England for
HTB PUBLICATIONS
Brompton Road, London, SW7 1JA
Printed in Great Britain.

CONTENTS

3. Faith's challenges

4. The mission of the Church

5. The power of the Spirit

The teachings of the wise are a fountain of life...

Proverbs 13 v14

BIOGRAPHIES

John Arnott
Senior pastor of the Toronto Airport Christian Fellowship, a church which has seen a remarkable move of the Holy Spirit in recent years, attracting visitors from all over the world.

Michael Cassidy
The founder of African Enterprise and one of the most influential Christian leaders in southern Africa, Michael Cassidy is author of several books including *Bursting the Wineskins* and *A Witness For Ever.*

Steve Chalke
International Director of Oasis Trust, a charitable trust involved in church and social work in Britain and abroad, Steve Chalke is a Baptist minister who presents regularly on television.

Pastor David Yonggi Cho
Leader of the world's largest church in Seoul, Korea, Pastor Cho is a leading authority on prayer and has written several books on the subject.

Michael Coates
A former headmaster of Monkton Combe Junior School and Secretary of the Incorporated Association of Preparatory Schools, Michael Coates is a lay reader in the Anglican church.

John Collins

Former Vicar of St Mark's, Gillingham, Canford and Holy Trinity Brompton. John Collins is retired and lives in Oxford.

Ken Costa

Chairman of the Investment Banking Board of merchant bankers SBC Warburg, Ken Costa is a senior financier in the city. He is also the founder of the READY vision to inspire and equip young Christians.

Gordon Fee

Professor of New Testament at Regent College, Vancouver, in Canada, Gordon Fee is author of numerous theological works, including a much-heralded commentary of 1 Corinthians. He has recently published a comprehensive book on Paul's treatment of the Holy Spirit in his epistles entitled *God's Empowering Presence* (Paternoster Press).

Richard Foster

Bestselling author of *Prayer: Finding the Heart's True Home* and *Celebration of Discipline*, Richard Foster is the founder of *RENOVARÉ*, a movement commited to spiritual renewal.

Tom Gillum

A former Chaplain to the Royal Brompton Hospital, Tom Gillum is Priest-in-Charge of St Stephen's Church, Westbourne Park, which was 'planted' from Holy Trinity Brompton in 1994.

Jeremy Jennings

Pastoral Director of Holy Trinity Brompton for the last ten years, Jeremy Jennings has led the growth of corporate prayer in the church for the past six years.

J. John

One of the most popular evangelists in Britain today, with a cross-denominational acceptability, J. John travels all over the country and the world speaking about Jesus Christ. He is author of several books including *Dead Sure?*, *Natural Evangelism* and the best-selling *What's the Point of Christmas?*

John McClure
John McClure is Senior Pastor of the Vineyard Christian Fellowship in Newport Beach, California.

Sandy Millar
A former barrister, Sandy Millar has been Vicar of Holy Trinity Brompton for 11 years. He has considerable experience of church planting and has led a large number of Alpha and church leadership conferences.

Paul Negrut
Persecuted under the Ceausescu regime, Paul Negrut is pastor of the Second Baptist Church in Oradea, Romania, and President of the Romanian Evangelical Alliance.

Lesslie Newbigin
Lesslie Newbigin served as a missionary in India from 1936 to 1974 with a break of six years from '59 to '65 when he was Secretary of the International Missionary Council and then Associate Secretary of the World Council of Churches. He was one of the Bishops consecrated in 1947 at the inauguration of the Church of South India. He is the author of several books including *The Gospel in a Pluralist Society*.

Steve Nicholson
Steve Nicholson is Senior Pastor of the Vineyard Christian Fellowship, Evanston, Illinois, USA.

James Odgers
James Odgers is a merchant banker and founder of the Besom Foundation, which provides a bridge between those who want to give money, time or skills, and those who are in need.

Nick and Jane Oundjian
Three years after the tragic death of their 13-month-old-son Jeremy 17 years ago from a sudden illness, Nick and Jane Oundjian became

committed Christians. They run a bereavement course at Holy Trinity
Brompton and Jane Oundjian is a trained counsellor with the national
bereavement agency CRUSE.

David Parker
David Parker is Senior Pastor of the Vineyard Christian Fellowship in
Lancaster, California.

Jackie Pullinger-To
Jackie Pullinger-To has been a missionary in Hong Kong since 1966
and is the founder of the St Stephen's Society. Her work with heroin
addicts in the colony's notorious Walled City has brought recognition
throughout the world and is described in her best-selling book
Chasing the Dragon.

Glenda Waddell
Glenda Waddell is a member of the staff of Holy Trinity Brompton,
where she is actively involved in the church's prayer ministry.

John Wimber
Leader and founder of the Association of Vineyard Churches, John
Wimber is one of the foremost authorities on church growth in the
world. He has led numerous conferences worldwide on a variety of
topics including healing, the gifts of the Holy Spirit, church growth,
signs and wonders, prayer and power evangelism. He has received
treatment for cancer in recent years and is now recovering.

Chris Woods
Chris Woods is Vicar of Holy Trinity, Parr Mount, St Helens,
Merseyside, an urban priority area in the north of England.

FOREWORD

by Sandy Millar

The Collection is an unusual book. Mark Elsdon-Dew has taken teaching from many different sources (most of those whose teaching is included here would almost certainly be unknown to one another) but all speak of the same eternal, unchangingly faithful, generous and loving God who has chosen to reveal himself to us through his Son Jesus Christ. Not in super success-stories as the world would see them, but in the realities of relationship and day-to-day life, difficulties and persecution, sadness, sickness and bereavement.

All those who have contributed to this book are personal friends of ours here at Holy Trinity Brompton. They each in their different ways bring their own experience and giftedness to their teaching. They each have a passion for Jesus Christ and it is this rather than the attempt to make the immediacy of their spoken teaching look like polished prose that, in my view, holds it all so powerfully together. I hope you will find it as helpful and inspiring as I have.

INTRODUCTION

by Mark Elsdon-Dew

Whether by virtue of its unique situation in the centre of London, its large congregation, or its position as a resourcing church and the home of the popular 'Alpha Course', a large variety of well-known teachers and speakers have accepted invitations to speak at Holy Trinity Brompton or at one of its events.

During the last five years, I have published edited extracts of some of the material in the church's monthly newspaper *Focus*. Although some talks were reproduced at length, my intention was mainly to select bits and pieces which I had found personally most moving and helpful.

This book is a collection of those extracts and I must acknowledge my gratitude to all the contributors for giving me permission not only to 'pick and choose', but to go ahead and print their words which, when delivered, were never intended for publication.

The result, I hope you will agree, is a book which is not only a fascinating and stimulating collection of teaching material, but a medley which can be dipped into time and again to encourage us in what Paul refers to as the 'good fight of the faith'.

Walking in Faith

"We have been drawn... to a sincere and pure devotion to Christ."

Sandy Millar *on living the Christian life*

> I am afraid that ... your minds may somehow be led astray from your sincere and pure devotion to Christ. (2 Corinthians 11:3)

The call of God is a strange thing. You start to analyse it and you get lost. You try to describe it to an old friend who is outside the kingdom of God and he looks blank and suggests a game of golf next Sunday. Nevertheless, it is a real and precious thing. It is the stirring in every part of us – mind, body, soul and spirit – in response to the overwhelming love of God.

Jesus spoke to Nicodemus about the wind, "blowing wherever it pleases. You hear its sound but you cannot tell where it comes from or where it is going. So it is with everyone born of the Spirit." Nicodemus looked blank too because until then it hadn't happened to him and he couldn't therefore see the kingdom of God.

For some it is a gradual realisation; for some quite a sudden thing (there are examples in the Bible of both) but in all of us who have been born from above, something distinctive has happened. Paul describes it beautifully in this part of his letter to the people whom he loved so deeply in Corinth. We have been drawn, he says, to a sincere and pure devotion to Christ.

The problem that Paul faced in Corinth was that there were

strong voices within the Church there that were seeking to seduce it. They were doubtless very 'modern' and 'liberal', but they were preaching their own version of Christianity and the beguiling subtlety with which they were unsettling the Christians there, drew from Paul some of his most anguished teaching yet.

For the call of God was then, and still is, a call to a sincere and pure devotion to Christ. The difficulty faced by those who have heard that call and responded to it, is that those outside the kingdom of God simply do not – and Jesus said 'cannot' – understand why devotion to Christ carries with it a passion for Jesus Christ himself, for his honour, for everything that he said and a desire to respond to his slightest wish.

That is simply another way of saying that to be brought within sound of the voice of God is to be profoundly altered. It is to have one's centre of gravity radically changed, all because we have begun to understand the true implications of redemption; not only the horror of the cross but also the dawning realisation that what God the Father was doing (and Jesus Christ with him) was something so wonderfully sacrificial and unconditionally generous that it draws from us the desire to be what he wants us to be and do what he wants us to do.

We have seen through supernatural eyes that he alone is real, and have begun also increasingly to see the grubbiness and inadequacy of so many aspects of the old life from which Jesus died to save us.

To you, the church of Christ here, I want to provide these reflections.

Life in the kingdom of God is always going to be different from the life of the world. We ought not expect people outside the kingdom of God to be able to live up to the standards of morality, sexuality or honesty that are set before those in the kingdom of God. Our call from God is to tell them about Jesus Christ, to show them by our lives a better way and serve them as servants of Christ for his sake, in any way we can. He loves them and wants all to be saved.

The Church has always been called to purity for God's nature is to be pure. That means purity of thought and deed; relationships that are open and honest. Sexual activity (hetero or homo) outside marriage destroys that precious 'sincere and pure devotion to Christ', and marriage is one man, one woman, for life. In our hearts we know that and in our hearts we are right.

Jesus set a standard that even condemned lustful thoughts but we have been subjected in recent times to so many confusing arguments – a sort of drip feed of a different brand of so-called Christianity, a 'Christianity' without the cross, in which self-denial plays no part, an anaemic unsatisfying brand of Christ-less religion in which 'I' am at the centre and God on the fringe – that we have lost sight of the pursuit of holiness. But we are committed to God's point of view, and sympathy for God's point of view is what seems to be lacking in many parts of Christ's church today. Church leaders are called to lead and any attempt to buy off any party with specious sub-biblical or heretical views can only lead, in the long run to the deep discouragement and ultimate disaffection of the loyal flock who are trying to lead a biblically Christian life against fierce opposition from the world, the flesh and the devil.

That is why it is serious, as well as sad, when leaders fall and when they do they must lay down their leadership responsibility. That too is why leaders must teach clearly and unambiguously. Of course practising homosexuals should not be ordained. Of course those in Christian leadership who are involved in immoral relationships (hetero or homo) should resign or be removed. It can sadly happen all too easily but it is inconsistent with Christian leadership. This is nothing to do with homophobia – it is to do with a proper phobia of sin. A so-called 'stable relationship' that is immoral is, after all, only one that has gone on for longer than any other one.

All of that leads me to this: sometime, in some place, there has to be a body of people who are committed to living out the life of Christ, in sincere and pure devotion to him, reaching out to the people of the world in his name to offer them not criticism, but a better way of life and an unconditional love through an incomparable Saviour. They have traditionally been called the Church. In this generation why shouldn't they be us?

"The tiniest bit of faith in the right object is sufficient."

John McClure *on biblical faith*

I think some people feel that if they just had enough faith that would get them through. But it's not a question of having a massive quantity of faith. You can have massive faith in a rickety chair that will not support you and go over. Sit on it and it will crash down. But you need only the tiniest wit of faith in a concrete floor – if you put out your toe and try it and find that it will support you, then walk on it, pretty soon you realise you can run and jump on it. Just a little bit of faith in a concrete floor is sufficient.

You can stand on top of a building ten stories up, convince yourself that you can fly, and say, "Well, here I go" and dive off, flapping your arms. I tell you, you'll just drop like a brick! It doesn't matter how much faith you have – you can be loaded with faith – you will just make a terrible mess.

But on the other hand you need only the tiniest bit of faith in a 747 – if you can just muscle up the faith to get in the door and buckle yourself in, you can go all the way to London and you'll be fine. The tiniest bit of faith in the right object is sufficient.

Biblical faith is just taking the tiniest bit of faith and putting it in the right object – that is Jesus Christ – and saying, "I trust you!"

"He had a big piece of straw in the corner of his mouth and he was leaning back and just floating down the river!"

John McClure *on faith in times of trouble*

As a kid, our family used to take vacations at the end of summer when we went to Yellowstone National Park in Wyoming. It was always a wonderful trip for us. We would pull a trailer and have a boat on top of the car, and the whole family would have a wonderful two weeks.

I remember one time on the road, along the Snake River which is in Idaho – a vast beautiful river about 100 yards across – we were driving when a great electrical storm struck. After a while, we became afraid of going on, so my dad pulled into a sheltered area and we all went back and sat in the trailer. We began counting the strikes of lightning, and then of course the thunder that would come along afterwards. I remember we counted over 100 as we watched the lightning striking everywhere. There was such violence all around us, it was really quite frightening.

We glanced over to the river and we saw a little object that looked very strange out there. As it got closer we realised it was a massive inner tube from the tyre of an airplane, floating slowly down the river. As it got nearer to us, we finally realised there was a huge fat man sitting on this airplane inner tube.

He must have been wearing swimming trunks because otherwise he was just out there large as life. It was a warm summer day and I remember he was wearing a great big hat and he had a big piece of straw in the corner of his mouth and he was leaning back and just floating down the river!

I'll never forget that sight. With lightning striking everywhere and thunder peals all over, here was this man floating by – he looked over and saw us and he just waved, and all of us waved back to him. He just floated on by!

I've never forgotten that picture, because that's what your life is supposed to be like in the midst of all the trauma, all the lightning and all the stress, pressure and struggle. Your life is supposed to have that bit of grass coming out of your mouth and that hat on your head, and you are literally flowing along in the stream of the Spirit of God.

"But I will never forget... the look on the face of Jesus – that marvellous, sympathetic look of absolute power and yet such pathos, such tenderness..."

John McClure *describes how God revealed to him that David Watson, the British evangelist, was going to die*

I will never forget seeing the throne of grace in December of 1983. David Watson was dying of cancer and he flew over to

Los Angeles. I remember getting a phone call in the morning from John Wimber saying, "John, I want you to come up and join me. David has come over for prayer and I wonder if you could set this day aside." So I did. I changed my plans, drove over and I remember we spent the day in John's office with David just praying over him.

At about 3 o'clock in the afternoon when someone was praying, I had a vision. It is one of the privileges of my life that I have the occasional, often very vivid vision. But this was certainly the most vivid vision I had ever had in my life.

Suddenly I was taken up out of the room and I found myself in a great ante-room. It was a magnificent room and it seemed to have a glass floor, as though we were standing on clouds. It was just a beautiful, beautiful room. We were all together waiting there.

David was there and John, and several of the others who were praying for him. We were all standing chatting with each other and at the end of the room, there were two great doors. After a while the doors opened and two great angels walked in and beckoned us to come. We turned and went with them through the doors and suddenly, we were in a room that was so massive I couldn't tell you the dimensions of it. It seemed like 100 miles across except somehow, you could see the whole room. It was a vast amphitheatre, a theatre on all sides and it looked like millions of people were inside worshipping and praising the Lord. There were angels above and in the centre was this magnificent throne. Over it was a great rainbow of glory, just radiant. It didn't matter where you were, it looked the same from every side.

There was one seated on this throne that you could hardly look at. But it seemed like 50 miles away and I remember just glancing at it. Suddenly, these angels took us and we were there in front of the throne of grace! It was absolutely awesome – beyond words to describe.

I remember that we carried David up the stairs of this throne and Jesus stood up, came down the stairs and met us half way. We lifted David into his arms and he turned and walked back, and we walked down. Suddenly, we were in the ante-room again and then I was back in the prayer room. It was a couple of days later that I woke in the middle of the night and realised that we had left David there.

I picked up the phone and called John the next day and said, "You know in that vision, I realise that the Lord was telling me that David was going to be going home." On February 18, 1984, he passed into the presence of the Lord.

I will never forget that throne, or the look on the face of Jesus – that marvellous, sympathetic look of absolute power and yet such pathos, such tenderness – so completely engaged in the struggle that David was in.

"The well meaning people were saying, 'You've got to normalise. You've got to put more devotional time in with the kids.' I never was good at devotions. I mean I was devoted but I was never good at organising devotions."

John Wimber *on faith and his family*

I was converted out of the pagan pool and had very little understanding of church life. For four generations, we had nobody in my family with any identification with a church. As a new Christian, I found that other Christians would come to me and say, "You're spending too much time with the unsaved. You're spending night after night winning people to Christ. You must raise your children," and I said, "Well, I agree with that but I thought I was."

You see, I was spending time with the unsaved but I was doing it in my living room with my children on my lap. We never said, "Now, children, go out of the room. We have something important to talk about here." We talked about it and over them to the visitor. If we had to cast out a demon, or pray for the sick, lend money to someone who needed it, or take someone in, we did it.

We had people living with us for 20 years. Our children never resented that. They still refer to those people as 'aunts' and 'uncles' and friends and loved ones. They still tell stories: "Dad, do you remember when we went out and started that church in that garage and how funny it was? Remember that time when we went to the mission and that man came up who was drunk and you talked to him and he got sober? Remember when we went to the jail and they wouldn't let me in and you wouldn't go in unless I could go in. They let us both in and you prayed for those people and they became Christians? Do you remember those Bible studies?"

You know, my kids never ever saw a difference between the way we were publicly and the way we were privately. We were never very 'religious' if religious means affected. We were always broke, always trusting God and always in trouble and somebody always hated us.

The well meaning people were saying, "You've got to normalise. You've got to put more devotional time in with the kids." I never was good at devotions. I mean I was devoted but I was never good at organising devotions. I would try to tell the Bible stories and the kids would get bored. I would try to read the booklets and they didn't like those either.

But they loved seeing illustrations – the living illustrations of the same thing. They remember when the demons came out of 'that man'. They were young but they remember watching it and praying with me. One of them remembers in the midst of a long deliverance session, there was a big bag of potato chips and I was hungry, so I was casting the demons out and eating the potato chips at the same time. They thought it was funny. I didn't know you weren't supposed to do that. It doesn't say anything about it in the Bible.

If we didn't have any money we said so. If we didn't have any faith we said so. But we said it first to God and then he would give it to us. If we didn't have the money for a vacation or holiday, we just said so: "Hey kids, we're not going to go anywhere unless God does something for us," and when he did something for us we were all very grateful. He did it over and over again.

We didn't go out and tell anybody, "Oh, we're living by faith and it just isn't working out too well. Pray for us, brother." God told us not to do that. That's manipulative. So we didn't do that. But what we did do is we never told anyone a lie. We never pretended that things were different from what they were. We never quit doing it and we never will until Jesus comes.

"When children ask us if they may do something, there are only two answers: either 'No' or 'Yes, willingly'. The answer we are so tempted to give, but which we should never give is: 'Yes, grudgingly.'"

Michael Coates *on parenting*

There's a mistake that we commonly make which is to confuse two things: compromise on the one hand and balance on the other. Compromise is a quality which is traditionally highly regarded by our nation. 'A good British compromise' we say. In matters of policy, compromise is right and admirable. It's not however suitable in matters of ethics or morality or behaviour or belief.

In education, upbringing and other aspects of our lives we need not compromise but balance, where we hold in tension two points that may seem opposite and even contradictory and, without attempting to reconcile them, we find a way between the two.

We teach our children to play games. On the one hand, they must play flat out to win, with no half-heartedness. On the other, they must be sportsmanlike, with no ruthlessness. No half-heartedness, no ruthlessness – that is a difficult concept, difficult enough for adults as you can see sometimes from your television screens, very difficult for children. You are refereeing a rugby match and a voice comes out of the scrum,"Go on, kill him." You blow the whistle, disentangle the players, identify the culprit, and you are met with an expression of innocent blankness: "But you said I was to be whole-hearted." Another time, as you watch from the touch-line the vital moment of a match, one of the three-quarters stands aside as if to say to the other side, "Go on – your turn." Afterwards you remonstrate. Again the blank look: "But you said I was to be sportsmanlike." The answer is that it's both. Not a mixture of the two, which is the worst of both worlds – but both. We want them to be wholly committed and wholly sportsmanlike.

Now may I follow this on to some other examples. Take love and firmness. Before I was a parent myself, I thought it was a sensible question to ask parents which child they loved the most. Once I became a parent I realised that the question is meaningless. Parents love all their children totally. If we have two children, it doesn't mean that each child has half our love, or that four children have a quarter each. All our children have all our love – which incidentally, is a picture of God's love for us.

Then what about firmness? What do we do when we have to deny our children something that love would like to give to them? Or we have to treat them as love would not wish to treat them? The answer is not to dilute our love with a little firmness and make a mixture, but to cling to both our love and our firmness.

A long time ago, I came across an expression which has helped me on this – stern love. Indulgent love says, "Do as you like." When you come to think about it, indulgent love is not love at all. Why is it that children nearly always prefer the teacher who is strict? There may be several reasons, but I'll tell you one: a strict teacher pays them a compliment – the compliment of saying to them,"You could be very good at this and I'm going to see that you become good at it." Whereas the indulgent person is saying in effect, "I don't mind how you turn out." God's love is stern, not indulgent.

Then there is care and trust. We take great care of our

children, rightly protecting them from danger – physical and moral. So what do we do when they want to climb a tree? Or ride a motorbike? Or go off on holiday with their friends. Again, compromise isn't the answer. We've got to find a way between the two.

Judy and I have learned one thing as parents. When children ask if they may do something, there are only two answers: either 'no' or 'yes, willingly'. The answer we are tempted to give, but which we should never give is, 'yes, grudgingly'. "Well, yes, I suppose so. Your mother and I don't want you to do this at all. We think it is a bad idea, but if you must I suppose you'd better…." That takes all the fun out of it and they don't ask you any more.

Our son David announced three years ago that he was intending to bicycle to Athens. Judy and I gasped. Mind you, he was grown up and it would have been difficult to say no. Fortunately we didn't try. We said, "What a good idea! What a marvellous thing to do!" Well, then he knew he had our approval and support. So he could talk about it and he would even ask our advice. "Dad says I should wear a helmet."

Here is another: participation and perfection. We say to our children, "Come on, have a go. Never mind if it's not perfect." Then a little later we say, "You know, that wasn't good enough." They reply, 'But you said it didn't matter if it wasn't perfect." Both are right. In our desire to encourage participation we must not let them think that that 'near enough is good enough'.

Finally, what about prayer and work? We're told that things happen when we pray and that, if we don't pray, things don't happen. So, "Let's pray", we say, "and leave the rest." But things also happen when we make them happen. Well then, why pray? I can't tell you why but I do like the little saying, "You should pray as if there's no such thing as work and work as if there is no such thing as prayer." Charles Simeon, vicar of Holy Trinity Cambridge, in the 18th century, made a famous remark which really sums up all I am saying. "The truth," he said, "lies neither at one end nor the other, nor even in the middle, but at both ends at the same time."

"In the kingdom anything you want to keep, you've got to learn to give."

Sandy Millar *on some principles of giving*

O ne of the things that I think the church has to learn all over again is that it belongs to Jesus. We are Jesus's people. We were brought into existence for him. He is the head of the church. We are the body of the church. We are his body and we exist for him and not the other way round. We are intended to reflect him and his nature in the world. We are intended to be him and do the things that he does, to think the way he thinks.

For some of us, it's quite a shock because we've come from a world that's been teaching us exactly the opposite because the world has not been programmed by Jesus but by the enemies of Jesus. In Matthew 6:21, Jesus says one of the profoundest things we can ever hear: "For where your treasure is, there your heart will be also." There is a completely different sort of standard in the kingdom of God when we come from the dominion of darkness or the world.

The world has a number of preconceived axioms that we've been brought up on. One is that we are entitled to possessions, a certain degree of money, a certain degree of comfort, a certain degree of safety against the events of the world; so we have to make provision for ourselves and protect ourselves and get what we can. I'm not actually saying any of that is fatal, I'm just observing the principles.

So presumably if we're earning 'x' thousand a year and somebody offers us 'y' thousand a year, and 'y' is greater than 'x', it doesn't take us very long to think in terms of moving from x to y – what you get you keep. But what I want to observe is that when we come into the kingdom of God, a wholly different dynamic begins to operate. The dynamic in the kingdom of God is almost the exact opposite. It's what you give you keep. It's a giving mentality, a giving currency. It's so different from what, at one level, we hope to hear.

We have a feeling, somewhere at the back of our minds that anything we give, we've lost. I'm not just talking about money. In the kingdom, anything you want to keep, you've got to learn to give.

In Philippians 4:12, Paul says, "I have learnt ..." In that context he's saying, "I have learnt how to have plenty of things and I have learnt how to have nothing." I think there is a wealth of experience behind that expression, "I have learnt." It wasn't easy. I don't think Paul was any happier to be poor than any of us but he learnt how to abound and how to be abased.

We have to learn to be in the giving economy. Somebody said to me again the other day, "I'm so lonely," and I said it almost without really thinking, "You know if you're lonely, you've got to give friendship." That's cruel, isn't it? No, it isn't. If you want love back, you've got to start learning to give it. I'm not saying you can do that overnight because many of us have been so battered by the world we don't know how to give anything except abuse.

But we come into the kingdom and suddenly discover that in the kingdom, there are people in the world who care about you. They seem to like you. They want to give things to you. They want to love you and pray for you, to sit up half the night ministering to you. It surprises you because you haven't seen that kind of thing outside the kingdom of God.

If you want friendship, you have to give it. If you want to keep your healing, you have to give it and pray for it. If you want salvation, you have to learn to give it. If you want to enjoy money, you have to learn to give it. This is the dynamic in the kingdom of God.

Let me attempt to persuade you in some other way. Do you know that every part of our service is designed around the concept that we come through those doors longing to give? In the old days we used to sing a big hymn of praise when we started. Why? Because the understanding is that we all come through the door so full of praise and love to God that we'd just burst if we were not given a chance to give him thanks and praise.

Somehow it got twisted along the way so that in many churches, you'll see the poor organist pumping away trying to get more volume, more steam, more excitement, more thrill, in order to get the congregation to sing more and get this hymn of praise out. That's what the Bible would call worship in the flesh. The Bible doesn't seem to think much of that.

Worship in the Spirit is when the congregation is so full of love, excitement and buzz, they come to church because it's the only building big enough for them all and they can't wait to sing their praises to God .... giving, giving. We give worship to God. In Matthew 6:4, Jesus says, "Then your Father, who sees what is done in secret, will reward you." What's the point of that? The point is that giving is done not primarily for anyone on this earth. Giving is primarily done for God.

I was asked to subscribe to something the other day. I couldn't because it was more money than I could have afforded to give and what was offered to me, done very nicely and very discreetly with beautiful print and glossy paper, was a chance to have my name included. But I don't want my name included here. I want my name included there, in heaven. The only way to get my name included there is if I don't get my name included here. I've got to make up my mind which I want because both are very tempting.

It's nice to feel that people think you're very generous, isn't it? But Jesus is saying that there is a reward in giving. In those days, word went out from the temple that they needed money and the trumpets would be blown and the messengers would go down the street. The godly man sitting in his stall in the bazaar somewhere, would put up the shutters and shut the door and hurry off to the temple. Everybody would nudge their neighbour and say, "You know where he's going? He's going to the temple because they've just sent a message saying they need money." Jesus was saying, "Don't do that. That's what the hypocrites do because they hope that you will have noticed."

From time to time, people ask me whether I teach on tithing. Tithing is a reference to the Old Testament where one of the offerings that the Jews were told to give was a tenth of their income as a free will offering. It was only one of the offerings they had to do. They had offerings for sin, offerings for the temple, offerings for the government, offerings for this and that.The free will offering was on top of that and it was a tenth.

I don't teach tithing because I think that in the Sermon on the Mount, Jesus is making a number of distinctions between the Old Testament emphasis which is on the activity, and the New Testament emphasis which is on the heart. I want us here to catch the New Testament spirit of giving.

The expression 'a tithe' or 'a tenth' is not a helpful one because the New Testament spirit of giving is that we give to God because he gave us everything. I cannot imagine God in heaven working out a tenth in order to give that to us, can you? I think he thought, "What can I give them? I'll give them my Son. I've only got one. I'll give them my Son. Jesus, would you go and get them, and rescue them and save them and die for them?"

Can you imagine Jesus saying, "What? Why should I go when I'm rich and I've got glory?" Can you see how foreign it is to the nature of God? Jesus didn't say that. Jesus said, "I'll go and Lord, how can we make it easier for them? I'll go simply and give up everything I've got." He who was rich became poor for our sakes, the New Testament tells us.

Paul says at the beginning of his letter to the Philippians that it was in response to that attitude that God said, "That is my man. I will now give him everything because he can be trusted." He was rich but he became poor.

In Matthew 6:19, Jesus goes on in that vein, "Don't store up treasures on earth, where moth and rust destroy, and where thieves break in and steal. But store up for yourselves treasures in heaven…"

William Law, commenting on that passage several hundred years ago, said it was as if a man had hands and eyes and feet which he could give to those who needed them, but instead of giving them to his blind or lame brethren, he locked them up in a chest. We would think he was rather selfish and inhuman, wouldn't we? But if he chose to amuse himself with hoarding them up rather than entitle himself to an eternal reward by giving them to those who needed them, might we not justly reckon him to be mad?

"A servant serves! That's how we know he is a servant."

Sandy Millar *on the importance of being servants*

One of the reasons that Paul's letter to the Ephesians is such an important part of the New Testament is that it speaks so much about God's intentions in bringing the church into existence, his love for the church, the grace that he has and continues to lavish upon her, the resources of his love and power that are available to her and – the bit we so often skip

over in our excitement about the rest – his purposes for her here
on earth.

> ... for it is by grace you have been saved, through faith – and this is
> not from yourselves, it is the gift of God – not by works, so that no
> one can boast. For we are God's workmanship, created in Christ
> Jesus to do good works, which God prepared in advance for us to
> do. (Ephesians 2: 8-10)

I have often referred to the marks of the end-time church as
generous, loving, obedient, worshipping – GLOW.

Obedience means doing what God tells us to do. It doesn't
mean delegating what God's told us to do to someone else. Nor
does it mean reverently explaining to God why what he has
told us to do is impractical, impossible or more likely ought to
wait for a more suitable time! We have been ".. created to do
good works." I want to suggest that in practice, if we are to
fulfil our calling in this way, we shall have to keep constantly
under review two areas of our lives.

Our attitude. Paul writes to the Philippian church:

> "Your attitude should be the same as that of Christ Jesus who being
> in very nature God... made himself nothing taking the very nature
> of a servant, being made in human likeness... He humbled himself
> and became obedient to death..." (Philippians 2:5-8).

The Christian calling is to serve, to be obedient, to do good
works, and to see that not as part of the rather unpleasant
aspects of struggling along but as the highest possible calling,
with rewards of their own on earth as well as later in heaven.
That is why the world has never had any time for the true
Christian attitude (but admires it deeply when it sees it) for the
world recognises only power that seeks to rule. Jesus and his
followers exercise a power that seeks to serve and such power
is misnamed 'weakness' by the world.

It is obvious in public life that with the diminishing

influence of the Christian faith, the desire to serve has been correspondingly lost and the desire to rule, which is always at the heart of unredeemed human affairs, has correspondingly emerged more obviously. Paradoxically, as the desire to rule has become more obvious, so has the influence of those in public life diminished.

More seriously, the same worldly attitude is becoming more deeply embedded in the heart of the church and unless we see what is happening and turn from it, we shall not be able or willing to fulfil this high purpose for which God has called us.

Do we see ourselves as servants, ready to do what God tells us? In the words of the old prayer, 'to spend and be spent' in God's service, to him and to others? Narrowing it down perhaps more uncomfortably – do we see our education, training, 'social skills', position, possessions and money as qualifying us to rule, as the world does, or as having been given to us in order to serve as Christ does and did?

Human nature has always been the same. You may remember when Solomon died, his son Rehoboam became king. The Israelites got up a petition and sent Jeroboam (one of Solomon's officials who had had to flee when Solomon tried to kill him) to ask on behalf of all the Israelites if they could look forward to an easier life under the new king, in return for which they promised to be loyal to him and to serve him.

Rehoboam very sensibly consulted his father's advisers who told him: "If today you will be a servant to these people and serve them and give them a favourable answer, they will always by your servants." But their advice was unacceptable to Rehoboam, presumably because he thought it was inconsistent to be a king and a servant. As a result he was overthrown and the kingdom was divided. (1 Kings 12)

Jesus, by contrast, was a king who came to serve and his followers, who share some aspects of his kingship, can most obviously be seen to be his followers by their willingness to serve. That too was the message of what must have been an incredibly embarrassing incident for them, when James and John came to Jesus and asked to be given the seats of honour on his left and right when he came in his glory (Mark 10).

It provoked such trouble amongst the disciples that Jesus got them together to sort it out and teach them the lesson that each generation has to learn for themselves:

> You know that those who are regarded as rulers of the Gentiles lord it over them and their high officials exercise authority over them. Not so with you. Instead, whoever wants to become great among you must be a servant, and whoever wants to be first must be slave of all. For even the Son of Man did not come to be served, but to serve and to give his life as a ransom for many (Mark 10: 42-45).

Activity. A servant serves! That's how we know he is a servant. Good works will include things we do for God inside and outside the context of the church building. A church like ours can only function because people come with the desire to do something – anything – and allow God to tell them what it might be, visible or not very visible, apparently important or very humble. The ideal servant sees or hears what needs to be done, and does it! If we want to catch the attention of the world for Jesus, and we do, it will be through not just what we say but what we do and how we do it.

I appeal to you to join me in reviewing honestly, on your own with God and with your family – if you have one – your own priorities and attitudes and activities, not as an exercise in guilt but as a means of fulfilling the call that God has on your life. I can't think of a more important issue for us as a church today or a more fulfilling one.

One final word: Paul's opening words to the Ephesians are a reminder to them of who they are in Christ, and of their importance to God and the place they have in his heart. The test of spiritual maturity is not the ability to speak in tongues, prophesy, memorise or expound Scripture. It is the ability and willingness to serve God and others through good works, learning to love the unlovely and serve them, to value those whom the world has discarded.

But Paul's point is this: it is only as we know who we are in Christ and all the resources of heaven that are ours, that we shall have the power, love and victory that is needed to serve and change the lives of those whom, for God and with God, we are seeking to serve.

"Commitment is not a dirty word, is it? It's actually a wonderfully secure word."

Sandy Millar *on commitment*

> Then Joshua assembled all the tribes of Israel at Shechem. He summoned the elders, leaders, judges and officials of Israel, and they presented themselves before God. (Joshua 24:1)

I'd love to feel that is what we are doing. We've allowed the Spirit of God to speak to us, to encourage us, to touch us, to communicate with us – as we present ourselves before God. Then we come to the verse where God calls his people through Joshua to what we would call commitment. Joshua said to the people:

> This is what the Lord, the God of Israel, says…Now fear the Lord and serve him with all faithfulness. Throw away the gods your forefathers worshipped beyond the River and in Egypt, and serve the Lord. But if serving the Lord seems undesirable to you, then choose for yourselves this day whom you will serve, whether the

gods your forefathers served beyond the River, or the gods of the
Amorites, in whose land you are living. But as for me and my
household, we will serve the Lord. (Joshua 24:14-15)

Commitment is not a dirty word, is it? It's actually a wonderfully secure word. We get a hint of that in that it is so rarely
valued in our present culture. The people said to Joshua, "We
will serve the Lord our God and obey him," and he made a
covenant for the people.

I want to earth this into our activities – a commitment to
Christ, a commitment to live as disciples of Christ and to be of
use to the world where we are, whether as Christian bus
drivers, bankers, dustmen, doctors, lawyers, professional
people, unprofessional people. We want to bring back into
equality of recognition within the kingdom of God, that every
job and every person doing a job has a value. We pledge
ourselves to build up the local Christian community and make
it as near to heaven as we can.

We commit ourselves to love one another, to have unity with
one another and to plant churches. Then there is a commitment
to resourcing the vision – such a thrilling vision. It's a much
bigger vision than any one of us but the issue which faces us,
faced Joshua's people. We can't do it on our own. The question
is: are we ready for the cost?

Let me suggest a couple of challenges to our faith and
commitment: firstly it seems to me just conceivably possible
that, in the interest of a home group or church plant, you may
be asked by the Lord to move job or house and secondly, you
may have to risk looking foolish. That's what the writer to
Hebrews said: 'scorning the shame'. The shame of the cross.
I've often thought the most agonising aspect of Jesus on the
cross was seeing his mother, and the disappointment that he
wasn't able to explain to her and help her to see why it was
necessary that her son should die on the cross. We may have to
scorn shame.

We have to resist contemporary culture. We have to go for a Christian view of sex. The ingenuity with which the world at the moment – the unbelievers, the liberal elements in the church – are attempting to redraft the Christian manifesto is breathtaking because they want to look like Christians but not bear the shame of the cross. We want a community that is worth planting. A community that is going to have purity in relationships and love. A community that is able to have relationships in an uncluttered way, free from innuendo, suggestion, any hint of impropriety.

It isn't 'cool', I am told, to want purity in relationships – but morality is of vital importance. Purity in relationships is important. God hates divorce – hates it. If you're divorced, God bless you. We want to be sympathetic and minister and to do everything that we can to help, but I am only saying what you want me to say. I've spoken to many people who have been through divorces. It's the most agonising thing and we have to say, "God hates it." That's what the Bible tells us. It's not a Christian option.

We may just have to risk the shame in countering too the modern cultural attitude towards children. Children in the Bible are a tremendous blessing. They are hard work but they are worth every ounce of that hard work. There is no higher calling recognised by God than the patient, loving, caring, home-bound attitude towards bringing up children.

Mothers, if you have children that you're bringing up, you are fulfilling in that job alone your ministry to the church. Husbands, your primary ministry is to your wife. Wives, your primary ministry is to your husband and family – and children are the key in that. The pressure from the modern culture is: "When are you coming back to work Jean?" "Oh, I'm not." "Not? What you going to do? Look after babies all day?" "Yes, my babies and I'm going to bring them up and pray for them and teach them."

Thirdly, we risk 'not looking cool' in our attitude to giving, but this needs resourcing. I'm not talking about everyday giving. We're all called to give to the church but there will be some people whose ministry to the church is giving.

Everyone gets a prize as they come into line with Jesus Christ. "May our attitude be that of Christ, who being in himself God, counted not equality with God as something to be grasped..." What is it going to cost you? I know that it cost him everything.

"The 'New Morality' is the old immorality by another name."

Sandy Millar *on how sex can be enjoyed to the full – God's perfect way*

The secular world has changed since I was at school. It's been a process, a steady drip feed of poison. It's in the culture – in the literature, the books, the films, the television programmes, the magazines – because steadily, over that period of 30 years we've been living off and steadily running out of Christian capital. So those things which when I was at school, I would have had to make a furtive and serious expedition to the centre of Soho to find, are now in most newsagents and outside on the pavement. Whether it's hard porn, soft porn or just offensive and indecent, the Bible knows no distinction. They are man-made, secular distinctions in order to justify a trend.

The point is that they know where we are weakest and you and I are being manipulated by commercial interests fed by the devil himself, whose main interest is in separating us from God. Over those 30 years or so, they have steadily moved the goalposts so that what is acceptable now to talk about, to look at and to do would have been unthinkable at that time.

That is one aspect of the issue, but that attitude is creeping into the church, where it never used to be and there's confusion, hurt and damage being done to people we don't want to damage, to hurt and to see confused.

So the overall question is, "I am a Christian. What do I do about sex?" I want to look at Genesis 2 because sex after all was God's invention. You'd really think nowadays that it was an invention of the world's and that God was looking down from heaven, thinking, "Oh my goodness, whatever will they think of next?" He actually thought of sex before we were born. He must have done, mustn't he!

Here's the Christian doctrine of marriage:

> For this reason a man will leave his father and mother and be united to his wife and they will become one flesh. The man and his wife were both naked, and they felt no shame. (Genesis 2: 24-25)

The Christian doctrine of marriage is the most exciting, thrilling and positive doctrine that there is in the Bible, because what it sets before us is God's perfect plan. That doesn't mean that if you're not married, you're not part of God's perfect plan – you are. But his doctrine so far as sex is concerned, is contained in his doctrine of marriage which is that in the ideal world, a man will leave a perfect happy family; his fiancee will leave her perfect happy family and they will be joined together by God and from that union, they will be united and become one flesh.

On the day Annette and I got married we went into the church at Stoke Poges with two heads, two bodies and, notionally speaking, the Bible describes that we came out with one head and one body. We were united. We hadn't become one flesh up until then but we were united. Springing from that unity, enhancing that unity, recreating and reminding us of that unity, we came together physically in sex which was the consummation and the completion of the marriage.

Now Paul says – and you can't get a higher doctrine than this

– that the relationship between a husband and a wife is the nearest thing you can get on earth to the relationship that exists between Christ and the church. There is a unity between Christ and the church which is indivisible, inseparable – a total unity. The unity between a husband and a wife reflects that spiritual unity between Christ and the church.

In due course, through the physical union of the man and the wife which comes after the pre-existent spiritual union, a child is born and he is the perfect evidence of the pre-existent unity, both physical obviously, but equally importantly spirit-ual unity of his parents. As you know, people spend hours trying to work out if he is like his daddy or his mummy; the fact is that he's like both of them. Why? Because God ordained it that way. That's why it is such a devastating thing for a child if his parents come unstuck because subconsciously, it puts a question mark, a threat over his or her very existence until he or she re-finds their existence again in Jesus Christ and the Spirit of God ministers to them.

It is for that reason that it is not possible to have a physical sexual relationship which does not affect you spiritually. It's bound to, indeed it was intended to. In 1 Corinthians 6, Paul writes:

The body is not meant for sexual immorality, but for the Lord, and the Lord for the body. By his power God raised the Lord from the dead, and he will raise us also. Do you not know that your bodies are members of Christ himself? Shall I then take the members of Christ and unite them with a prostitute? Never! Do you not know that he who unites himself with a prostitute is one with her in body? For it is said: 'the two will become one flesh'. But he who unites himself with the Lord is one with him in spirit. Flee from sexual immorality. All other sins a man commits are outside his body, but he who sins sexually sins against his own body. Do you not know that your body is a temple of the Holy Spirit, who is in you, whom you have received from God? You are not your own; you were bought at a price. Therefore honour God with your body. (1 Cor 6:13-20)

What Paul is saying of course is that sex is not a casual thing. It matters who you sleep with. It affects you because in the giving of yourself in sex, you cannot give yourself to A on one day, to B on another day, to C on another day – however far apart A, B, or C may be spaced – and then tear yourself away from A and give yourself entirely to B and tear yourself away from B and give yourself entirely to C, without being affected by it.

So God's idea in sex is that it is the fulfilment of a unity for life that he has created, reflecting the unity between Christ and you. As with everything God is involved in, it is a creative union. The Bible is against everything else because the Bible is for sex in marriage. Anything else is a corruption or a perversion at worst of what God has created as the perfect relationship for his people.

Homosexual practising relationships are sterile, uncreative and not of God. Masturbation is solo, getting rather than giving – not of God. Fornication between unmarried people is coming together without commitment for life – not of God. There is no total, complete giving of oneself in fornication.

But what if you say to me, "I am a girl in this fellowship and I've met this guy; he really loves me and I really love him. We are totally committed to each other. What about that – can we sleep together?" The only way of total commitment is to get married. Why don't you get married? If you're not ready to be totally sure, don't sleep together. God is calling into existence a people who are, intend and want to be holy. That's what is going on. That is why there is such attack about it.

Don't be conned by this 'New Morality'. There is nothing new about the so-called 'New Morality'. Sometimes younger people suggest that the biblical view seems out of touch and old-fashioned. If I may say so, if you have fallen for the 'New Morality', it's you that's old fashioned. Because the 'New Morality' is the old immorality by another name. The people of God were always tempted to pervert God's will, and immorality and godlessness have always gone together. So it's

no coincidence that with the lessening of the impact of the
Christian faith over the last 25-30 years, and the growth of a
rather arrogant paganism that seems to think it can exist
without God's love, protection, power and grace, the
brazenness of the new immorality has increased.

Is purity possible? In Hebrews 12:14, the author says,
"Make every effort to live in peace with all men and to be holy;
without holiness no-one will see the Lord." The author is
determined that we are to be holy because if we're not holy, we
won't see God. It makes sense. Heaven wouldn't be heaven if
we got there in the state most of us were in before we were
saved. The justification, the saving of us, is in order to set us
apart from that stuff and bring us into the sanctity of a family in
which these things are unthinkable.

Holiness is a process. It consists of steps in the right
direction. Every time we say yes to the Spirit of God, every time
we say no to the enemy, we have made another step in the right
direction and we will wake up one day and find that our
transformation is complete by the Spirit of God. It's not complete yet, but – God willing – one day it will be. So it is possible.

The $64,000 question: how do I stay pure? How are we to
achieve this standard? Firstly, be honest. I think we would
admit that most of our dealings with God never took on a
reality until we were honest with him. Jacob had to go through
that; we have to go through that. Admit where we're weak,
admit where we're sinful and repent.

I remember John Collins, my predecessor, saying that if
you're a burglar, you don't gradually give up burgling when
you come to Christ. You stop NOW – no more burgling.
I remember watching this rather cultured congregation
and I could see straight away the resolve on the faces of each
one of them: 'No more burgling'. But it hasn't got to be
burgling. It is repenting of anything which is spoiling our life.
Turn from it. Throw away those magazines. Stop taking the
paper if it means you have to go and collect it and look at

those magazines every time. Stop it or it will destroy you.

Temptations go on and on. You people who are unmarried think that we who are married are never tempted and ought not to be. I quite agree. But we are, so whatever it is that is causing trouble, STOP IT! Deal with it just as you would if someone offered you poison with a label on it because of course the enemy never shows you a picture of what you will be if you consistently give in to that temptation.

Secondly, marry! Paul says it's much better. For some of us, it is inconceivable that we could go through life unmarried. Well, then marry. Some of you – I am talking to men now – are in a position to marry; you're quite well off, you can afford it. Think about it. I'm not one to speak because I took seven years to propose to my wife. If you are married, cultivate faithfulness within marriage and chuck out everything within your marriage that springs more from lust than from love. Why do you think the author to the Hebrews says that marriage should be held honourable by all and 'the marriage bed undefiled'. What do you think he means by that? How do you defile a marriage bed? By bringing into it lust.

I was talking to a couple the other day who have a tremendous ministry in deliverance. He said something to me that I found surprising. "Many of the people I've ministered to recently", he said, "have got into spiritual oppression through oral sex, even in marriage." It's unproductive, it's uncreative so chuck it! Stop it, in or out of marriage.

So, fellers, marry or put sex out of your minds. Now I recognise that in saying that, it's hard on those who are longing to get married. So, thirdly, if you are not married and not in a position to get married, Paul suggests that in some ways you may be better off.

I want to tell you of St Augustine's confessions. He was in absolute agonies because he was a sensual man; he lived with a girl who was below him in his social station – which is what prevented him from marrying her – and he couldn't see how he could ever live a holy life. He said; "For I felt my past to have a grip on me. It uttered wretched cries: How long? How long is it to be? Tomorrow, tomorrow." "But why not now?" I said. "Why not an end to my impure life in this very hour?"

He was in a bitter agony, weeping and crying out to God because he knew there was something better but he'd never found it. Then he heard the voice of a boy or girl – he doesn't know which it was – in the next door garden. They were playing a game of some kind which involved saying, "Pick it up and read, pick it up and read."

These are his words:

> At once my countenance changed and I began to think intently whether there might be some sort of children's game in which such a chant is used, but I couldn't remember having heard of one. I checked the flood of tears and stood up. I interpreted it solely as a divine command to me to open the book and read the first chapter I might find... So I hurried back to the place where...I'd put the book of the apostle when I'd got up. I seized it, opened it and in silence I read the first passage on which my eyes lit: "Not in riots and drunken parties; not in eroticism and indecencies; not in strife and rivalry; but put on the Lord Jesus Christ and make no provision for the flesh in its lusts." [Romans 13:13-14] I neither wished nor needed to read further. At once, with the last words of this sentence, it was as if a light of relief from all anxiety flooded into my heart. All the shadows of doubt were dispelled. The effect of your converting me to yourself was that I did not now seek a wife and had no ambition for success in this world.

Augustine began on the course of life which led to us now calling him Saint Augustine. He was no saint before that. After he'd lived with a girl for 12 or 13 years, as he had, he didn't say, "Oh it's hard." He said, "Oh God, I've found something better." By God's grace.

"There we are at the bottom of the ocean going: 'Bubble, bubble, glug, glug.'"

David Parker *on a dependent relationship with God*

I think of so many things in terms of pictures and my picture of what our life is like from the fall onwards, is a parable of deep sea diving. You and I were created underwater – at the bottom of the ocean. We all had lifelines to the surface where we could breathe air. There we were in the garden, all walking around on the bottom of the ocean saying, "This is good" and the presence of the Lord was there. But we decided it was a little encumbering to be hooked up to this lifeline. Wouldn't it be better to cut it off and just go on our own? So we rejected God's provision and we rejected relationship with him. We cut ourselves off through sin and the fall.

There we are at the bottom of the ocean going, "Bubble, bubble, glug, glug." But God told us, "If you do this, you will surely die." So the only question that remains now is, how long can you hold your breath? Some people, amazingly, can hold their breath for 80 or 90 years. They just hold their breath, never acknowledging that they were made dependent on God. You and I were made, as Jesus said, to live by every word that comes out of the mouth of God. We were not made independent. We derive our life from our connection, our relationship with God. He sent his Son through the surface of the waters to the very bottom of the ocean, to reconnect us with the lifeline and it cost the Son his life to do that. He came to reconnect you to the surface, to bring back the breath of God into your life.

"The choice is between life ... and death."

David Parker *on a matter of life and death*

For some time, I found myself making these excruciating decisions to do what God wanted, instead of what I wanted and I thought of myself as so heroic. Then, one day the Lord graciously came to me and said, "Son, you think the choice is between life on my terms and life on your terms." I said, "Yes. That's it, Lord. That's the choice I've got." He said, "That's not the choice. The choice is between life ... and death."

Prayer

"I start by going out into the garden – if it's not raining – and singing a loud song of praise."

Bishop Lesslie Newbigin *on personal prayer*

We will not learn to pray without ceasing unless we also set aside times which are particularly for prayer, when our whole attention is focused on prayer and on nothing else. Now there are many guidebooks about how one should spend these times and I suppose that everybody in the end has to find his or her own way. I think we ought to be growing in our prayer life. We ought to be reviewing our practice and seeing whether we are becoming stale, or are in a rut, but I will simply tell you what I do. I don't think that I am a model but it's useful to say something. I am sure there are many people who are far ahead of me in these matters.

I make sure that I have a clear half hour before breakfast, absolutely undisturbed. I start by going out into the garden – if it's not raining – and singing a loud song of praise. It was the great William Laud in his book about a devout and holy life, who said you should always begin by singing a hymn of praise (not just thinking it or mumbling it but singing it) and anyone who has heard my voice will understand why I go into the garden if I can. Then I think about those acts of God which especially concern that day.

Sunday: the creation of light, the separation of light from darkness, and all that it means; the resurrection of Jesus on the first day and the gift of the Spirit on the first day. Sunday is a very rich day for the first part of my prayers.

Monday: the creation of the firmament, the rain, the snow, the clouds, the mist; all the mysterious powers, the invisible powers which exist, although it's hard for us to visualise them; the unseen realities which we can only dimly grasp but which we know are God's servants and obey his command.

Tuesday: the day he separated the water from the land. I think about the dry land, the rocks that underlie it, the soil that covers it, the ploughed fields, the meadows, the trees, the mountains, the trees and the flowers and the grass, and all the particular bits of the world that I love very specially and I thank God for them.

Wednesday: the creation of the sun and the moon and the stars, and therefore the times and seasons; the rich variety that we have as we move from winter into spring, into summer then autumn, and back into winter – all the joy that we get from the varying of the seasons.

Thursday: the fishes and the birds, and all their magnificent multitude; and of course, the ascension of Jesus on that Thursday and his seating at the right hand of the Father, reigning with the Father over all things.

Friday: the cross; the creation of the human family; the fall and the story of God's patient dealing with his erring family, leading up to the cross and the passion of Jesus.

Saturday: that mysterious day when Jesus lies in the tomb and when we remember those who have fallen asleep in Christ. It is a time when I specially remember my own parents and all who have been very dear to me, who have died. I remember them name by name, and I thank God for them. And so we come again to Sunday.

This gives one a distinct subject matter for praise at the beginning of the morning's prayer. Then I read a psalm, an Old Testament passage and a New Testament passage, and I try to place each passage within the whole context of God's story of creation and redemption.

After this I say the Lord's prayer – often saying it two or three times over because every phrase in it needs to be said with all one's heart and mind. Then I say the collect of the day, I take out my diary and I look at the day's agenda – at the things that are coming up, the people I am going to meet, the crises that may come, the decisions that have to be made – and I pray for God's grace for that day.

Then I turn to intercession. Our intercessory prayer needs to be serious. Everyone makes their own arrangements. I have three 'schedules': those things and people for whom I pray every day; those for whom I pray weekly; those for whom I pray monthly. You cannot hold more than a certain amount in one time of prayer.

My wife and I always have our evening prayer together in which we read a portion of the New Testament, thank God for the day, ask forgiveness for our sin, lay before God any very special concerns, and pray for our family. We finish with a prayer for the night. That is my particular pattern of prayer at this point in my journey.

"Go on faithfully, even if it seems as dry as dust."

Bishop Lesslie Newbigin *on praying through dry times*

What about those periods when everything is dry? There are days, thank God, when our hearts are deeply touched and we feel it's all so real that we want to run out and shout to the world, "This is the reality." But there are other days when the same words seem to mean almost nothing. What do we do about that?

Well, the first thing is to remember that all serious praying people know that experience. God gives us times of comfort and joy and he gives us times of darkness when only faith can hold us on. But that is part of his training – that we learn to walk even when we cannot see.

For me, the great model is something that I've learned from climbing in the Alps. You set out on a wonderful morning and against the blue sky, there is the white peak of the mountain you're setting out to climb. You go up and up and then you come into the mist and you can see nothing. Everything is blotted out. The one thing that you have is the track and you can go on putting one foot in front of the other on it, trusting that the track is reliable. Thank God, in Switzerland they generally are! Eventually, you come out and see the mountain again.

That's the model for our periods of darkness and dryness. Keep to your discipline of prayer. Go on faithfully even if it seems as dry as dust. Because God, who knows what he's doing and doesn't fool around with us, is teaching us what we need. He gives us everything we need to learn to walk by faith and not by sight. So, above all, don't give up your regular discipline of prayer but know that God is leading you in his own way.

"I think that the whole Bible teaches us that God does... change his mind."

Bishop Lesslie Newbigin *on intercession*

Intercession is something about which people have puzzled. If God knows already what we need and what we want, what is the good of it? He knows best. There is a phrase that William

Temple used which I have come to question. He said that the idea that we pray in order to change God's mind would be an enterprise blasphemous in the attempt and calamitous in the accomplishment.

Well yes, in a sense. But that sounds a little like the thought that God is a kind of implacable, immovable, unshakeable power to which we simply have to submit, and why bother him with our ideas when he will do what he knows best in the end. That is much more like a Moslem concept of prayer than a Christian concept.

Jesus lays tremendous stress upon intercessory, petitionary prayer – battering at the gates of God's house to ask him for what we need. One cannot escape from that – it is so central in Jesus's teaching. I think that the whole Bible teaches us that God does, if you like, change his mind. Over and over again, there is the story of stubborn rebellion and then repentance. Repentance – honest returning to God – does lead him to turn to us.

The relationship that God has with us, however hard it may be for us to understand it metaphysically, certainly in the context of the Bible and of all Jesus's teaching, is such that God desires our prayer because it is precisely in our praying that we are brought more fully into the mind of God.

I think that we have to take as our model, as so often, the prayer of Jesus in Gethsemane. That prayer has two parts.

The first part is, "If it be thy will, let this cup pass from me." Jesus prays to be delivered from the appalling agony and dereliction of the cross. Then the second part, "Nevertheless, not my will, but thine be done." Now I don't think we should use the second part simply to obliterate the first part. I think both parts are an essential part of our praying – that God wants us to bring our desires, our needs, our longings to him. And that has one important consequence – it means that we should be serious in our praying.

I have, for a long time, made it a custom that when I

undertake to pray for some particular outcome, group or person, I write this down and I go on praying until I know, or hope I know, how God has answered that prayer. There is a tick and that becomes an item for thanksgiving. Surely it would not be taking God seriously if we simply tossed off a petition and then forgot that we had asked it, so that we were not ready to listen for God's answer?

"It's all part of our training."

Bishop Lesslie Newbigin *on wandering thoughts in prayer*

You can't talk about prayer without talking about wandering thoughts. You set out to pray and suddenly wake up to find you're thinking about something quite different. Everybody has that problem. What do you do about it? I think the answer is quite simple – you pray for the thing or person that you were wanderingly thinking about and then you quietly come back to your prayers.

Don't worry. Everybody has that problem. Just raise up that person or situation and ask God for what is appropriate. Then return to the central line of your prayers. And even if you have to do that 10 or 20 times during your prayers, don't worry. It's all part of our training.

"The battle was not decided on the battlefield. The battle was decided on the praying field."

Pastor David Yonggi Cho *on praying for victory*

Korean people love Great Britain because the first missionary to Korea was from Great Britain. His name was Reverend Thomas. As soon as he arrived 120 years ago, he was executed by the Korean government. The blood of his martrydom cried to the throne of God and, as a result, now more than thirty percent of the population is Christian. Whenever we think of Great Britain, we think of Reverend Thomas who died for the salvation of Korea. The Bible says, "Cast your breath into the water and lo, afterwards you shall regain." So he cast his breath into the Korean water and, as the breath, I am returning to Great Britain to become a blessing to you.

I am deeply moved in my Spirit because I am already seeing revival here. I think the presence of the kingdom of God is so powerful in this place. You are a holy nation. Here is a scripture reading from Exodus 17:8-13.

> The Amalekites came and attacked the Israelites at Rephidim. Moses said to Joshua, 'Choose some of our men and go out to fight the Amalekites. Tomorrow I will stand on top of the hill with the staff of God in my hands.' So Joshua fought the Amalekites as Moses had ordered, and Moses, Aaron and Hur went to the top of the hill. As long as Moses held up his hands, the Israelites were winning, but whenever he lowered his hands the Amalekites were winning. When Moses' hands grew tired, they took a stone and put it under him and he sat on it. Aaron and Hur held his hands up – one on one side, one on the other – so that his hands remained

steady till sunset. So Joshua overcame the Amalekite army with the sword.

The Amalekites were so powerful. The Israelites were losing the battle. It was a desperate situation. Moses was on top of the hill, giving up intercessory prayer for Joshua and his army in the battlefield. Then they prevailed over the Amalekites. When Moses got tired, put his arms down and stopped intercessory prayer, then the power stopped flowing and the Amalekites got stronger. But Moses continued intercessory prayer until the going down of the sun. Joshua was enabled to smite the Amalekites completely and they had a tremendous victory that day.

We can see from this story that the battle was not decided on the battlefield. The battle was decided on the praying field. Many people think that the battle is being fought on the battlefield and that victory or defeat will be decided there. But as we see, the decisive battle was fought on the hill through intercessory prayer.

Christians are out there in the battleground and politicians also. People are fighting every day in the battlefield. Sin, corruption, hatred, unrighteousness, filthiness, sickness, disease, obsession, possession, oppression, depression, failure, hunger, curse, death and hell are all out to attack people, to destroy churches, to destroy the Christians, to destroy society.

We can't just stand back and criticise. By criticising we can't accomplish anything. We are fighting a losing battle. Who can relieve us from this predicament? Can education prevail against sin? Can politics prevail against this enemy? Could revolution/evolution of the society prevail against this enemy? Throughout human history, we tried everything but we found that we were lacking power. The Amalekites have been victorious in every place. But now God is raising 20th century Moseses. You are in the place of Moses, Aaron and Hur.

We have come together to carry out intercessory prayer for

the church of Great Britain, for the politicians, for the civilians, for the British people. We have not gathered together to pass criticism. We are here to pray for the nation and to release the power of God for this nation. Politicians can't solve the problem. Science can't solve the problem. Only the power of God can overcome this enemy.

My Bible says God never changes. My Bible says Jesus is the same yesterday, today and forever. We see the sin. We see the suffering. We see the corruption. We see the poverty but the power of God is only to be released when the Christian church comes together and prays. When you pray, God releases power but when you stop praying, God's power stops. God is omnipotent, omniscient and omnipresent but still God works through your prayers. You say, "God can perform a miracle without me," but that's your idea not God's idea. We are working together to bring this nation back to the Heavenly Father. To carry out a very effective intercessory prayer we must prepare our lives.

Firstly, our intercessory prayer should be **founded on the redemption of our Lord Jesus Christ.** We must stand upon the blood of Jesus Christ to enter the presence of God. Without the blood, we wouldn't have any access to the throne of God. His blood still prevails, still speaks, so when we carry out intercessory prayer we must know that the blood of Jesus Christ purchased us from sin. The blood of Jesus Christ reconciled us to the Heavenly Father so that we might have the love of God and the sanctification of God. The blood of Jesus Christ purchased us spirit, soul and body.

My Bible says Christ has redeemed us from the curse of the Law, so that the blessing of Abraham might come upon the Gentiles. Through the blood of Jesus, God destroyed death and hell. So when we stand on the blood, no enemy can stand against us. When we carry out intercessory prayer, we must not forget that we should pray through the blood of Jesus Christ.

Secondly, when we want to carry out victorious intercessory

prayer **we must repent of all the sins in our lives.** If we hide our sin, God cannot listen to us. One of our sisters in the church came to be healed from a facial paralysis and I prayed for her many times but nothing ever happened. She went to the hospital and received treatment but was not healed. She went to the Chinese doctors and received acupuncture but nothing happened. Finally, she became very discouraged. She came to my office and she was crying. And I lost my confidence because I had prayed for her many times and she was not healed.

Then after a while, I was praying and the Spirit spoke into my heart, "I can't heal her while she keeps enmity in her spirit." So I said, "Sister, do you hate anybody?" She said, "Yes, my in-laws. I hate my father-in-law, my mother-in-law, my brother-in-law and sister-in-law. I work like a horse in their house but they don't appreciate me. They always criticise me. There is bitterness in my soul." I said that if there was bitterness in her soul, then God could not heal her. She was crying. She said, "I can't love them. If you were in my position, you would know my situation. I can't love them."

Then, I was listening to the voice of the Holy Spirit. He said to me, "Don't force her to love. Just ask her to forgive. After forgiving them, if there is some power left over, then start to love." So I told her this. She nodded her head and said that she could forgive them. So we called each of the members of her family's name to forgive them. Then she said, "I have forgiven them all. Will you pray for me?" I laid my hands upon her and I was praying, and out of curiosity I peeped open my eyes to see. I was amazed because right in front of my eyes, her paralysis was disappearing and she was getting healed. I experienced the power of the forgiveness. God never sees the outside of you. He looks inside you. Once you hide sin in your heart, he won't listen to your prayer.

So when praying, we must confess all the known sin in our lives. We should confess unrighteousness, our hatred, our faithlessness, our pride, our inhumility. We should cleanse our lives from these things. Then God will hear our prayer.

Thirdly, **you have to depend on the Holy Spirit.** Say to him, "We do not know how to pray but you are here to help me so, help me to pray, Holy Spirit. I recognise you. I depend upon you." Then the Spirit will intervene and will help you to carry out victorious intercessory prayer. When you pray, God intervenes so ask the Holy Spirit to help. He's here to help you. God is on the throne. Jesus Christ is seated at his right hand but the Spirit of God is here on earth. He is working together with you.

Fourthly, **you must study the Bible.** You must stand on the word of God. The heavens shall pass away but the word of God shall never pass away. Ask the Holy Spirit to teach you the word of God. When you stand on the word of God and you carry out intercessory prayer then your prayer will be riding the power.

When you pray, the devil will come and put all kinds of hindrances on to you. You will see so many impossible things happen in your lives. When you stand upon the Word, then whether you can see, hear or feel, you will not be swayed by the situation and circumstances. Then you can prevail and carry out victorious intercessory prayer.

Fifthly, when you pray, **you must pray for the glory of God.** If we have any ulterior motive in our hearts then God won't listen. Whatever we do, we should do for the glory of God. We have all gathered together to see the glory of God and so God is ready to accept our prayers because we are praying for the glory of God. And that is very necessary.

The real fight is going on in your intercessory prayer. The devil will bring all kind of hindrances to the praying people or church. He won't let you study the Bible. He won't let you in the fellowship. He will try to stop you praying because the battle is won at the prayer meeting. Many look at the TV and read newspapers. You see that very important issues are being discussed in the political circle. And you will say, "I'm power-less." Prayer is the answer for this nation. Prayer is the answer for your problem. Prayer is the answer for your business.

Once when Billy Graham visited Korea I asked him, "If you wanted to leave a word to Christian people in the world before you die, what word would you like to leave?" He looked at me, smiled and said, "Brother Cho, I would say to the Christians of the world – number one, pray; number two, pray; number three, pray."

I already see revival here. I already see the power of prayer in your lives. You are the answer to this nation. You are the catalyst of a great revival in this nation. And so let us make this a turning point in the history of Great Britain. God will give a decisive victory over the Amalekites in your country because you are here on the hill, in the place of Moses, Aaron and Hur. And since you have prayed, there will be victory after victory.

"I think my Christian life has gained so much more from being part of this."

Glenda Waddell *on intercession*

I had felt uncomfortable for quite a while about the fact that I wasn't interceding. I didn't regard myself as an intercessory sort of person. I was much more a receiving sort of person. I was quite good at praising and reading the Bible, and generally letting God minister to me. I was quite scathing of people who went to God with long shopping lists. I didn't think it was for me.

Then I sat through a service at the end of which Jeremy

Jennings, Pastoral Director of Holy Trinity Brompton, asked people to stand and commit themselves to intercede. As the service had gone on, I had felt more and more uncomfortable and thought I heard God saying, "I've given you so much. Won't you do this thing for me?"

All the time, another voice was saying, "You couldn't do that. You'd never keep it up. It would be doomed to failure from the beginning. You're not the intercessory type. Let someone else do it who's got more time." At that time, I think I was probably busier than I'd ever been in my life. I was under more stress than I'd ever been and I was really tired. I couldn't believe that God would ask me to do this. But in the end, I did stand and I said, "Lord if you really want me to do this, will you wake me?"

I went to bed and I set the alarm, fully expecting to sleep through it as I had been doing. To my horror, I found myself sitting bolt upright the next morning at 5am! I said, "Oh no! I really can't face this!" Anyway, I went downstairs, sat in a chair with a cup of coffee and said, "Lord, I honestly don't know what to do. I don't know what intercession is. I don't know how you do intercession but if you want me to do it, I'll do it."

I sat there for a bit and then I think I started to pray in tongues. Almost immediately I had two pictures. One was of a dove flying and carrying what seemed to be a message. I understood that to mean that the prayers were being carried to the throne room. The other one was of a huge mountain made of wax – there was a light on a candle set into the mountain. I got the words from Psalm 97 that in the presence of the Lord, the mountains melt like wax. God said, "This is intercession. Go for it."

So I started to pray and I didn't find it easy. I got up fairly regularly – not every day – but when I did get up, I didn't actually know what I was praying for; it was either in the Spirit or sometimes it seemed to be in silence. Sometimes there were actions, which I thought were a bit silly but that's what God seemed to require of me. I remember one day thinking that it might be more effective and helpful if I actually knew what I was praying, rather than praying in tongues. I said, "Lord, wouldn't it be better for me to know more about this, to know what I'm actually praying for, rather than so much of it being in tongues – wouldn't that be better?" The answer was immediate: "I need people who are just prepared to pray – I'll do the rest."

One thing I had to do was to pray that God would change my heart because I am by nature a very apathetic person. I had often thought, "Well, God's got it all in control anyway. What's the point in going on and on about it to him? He knows it. He's got the answers. He must get pretty bored with us asking." So I had to pray that he would change my heart; that he would remove my apathy; that he would make me care.

Slowly he did this and I began to have a heart for the things that he put there, to see things that I hadn't seen before. I actually began to see things supernaturally in a way that I hadn't done before. I had pictures and sometimes prophetic words which I'd not had before. In my personal life, in ministry, in praying for people, I felt a new kind of authority. The power of God was more evident. It was nothing that I did. It all came out of the intercession.

If you're someone who thinks you could never do it, that you'd never keep it up; if the enemy says to you, "Don't bother. You'd give up before you'd start" – be encouraged. It is now five years since I became 'seriously' involved in personal and corporate intercessory prayer. I fail often – not getting up, not doing it at home, not getting to the prayer meeting, but God's not there with a great big stick. You get out of it far more than you give. I think my Christian life has gained so much more from intercession. I would really say, "Go for it."

"At least when we hit rock bottom, can't we thank him that we've got a rock to hit?"

James Odgers *on praying in bad times*

How should we pray when we hit rock bottom? Let's not fool about with prayers that we think are somehow 'all right'. Let's cry out and pray what we feel. Then, let's keep on praying in the way that we prayed before we felt forsaken. Let's remember to do that, however hollow it may feel. Let's continue in obedience to pray and praise and worship. It isn't a question of feeling at this stage – this is a question of obedience.

We need to know that when God is silent, he is silent for a purpose. We need to know that when we hit rock bottom, although God's view of rock bottom for us may be rockier and more bottomy than where we think it is, there is something to hold on to. At least when we hit rock bottom, can't we thank him that we've got a rock to hit?

In 2 Samuel 22:2, it says, "The Lord is my Rock, my fortress and my deliverer. My God is my Rock in whom I take refuge, he is my stronghold, my refuge and my saviour." And Psalm 26:5 says, "Trust in the Lord forever for the Lord is the Rock eternal." That's what we hit when we hit rock bottom.

If you pray in tongues, then I recommend that you pray in tongues all the time or for as much of the time as you can. Why? Because I have found at least, that it is a reminder that God has good gifts for his children. Also, let's prepare now for these times to come. Now that we know they are going to come because they do, they're part of God's plan which is perfect – let's prepare now.

How? Firstly, by saturating ourselves in the Word of God – Psalm 1 covers that. We are to meditate on the Bible day and night, immersing ourselves in the Word of God. Then, remember as many of the promises as we can for the dark, silent times. Here are some: "I came that you might have life, life in all its abundance." "Come unto me all you who are weary and heavy laden, and I will give you rest." "It is for freedom that Christ has set us free."

I find it useful as well, to keep a list of my answered prayers and every other answered prayer I can get a hold of, so that I can build a great wall like a wave, to flood into those desert times when they come. The other thing is to ensure that we are in a committed prayer relationship with at least one other person so that we can share those times. They are likely to be doing fine when we're hitting rock bottom. That's what Christian fellowship is about, isn't it? It is to share the tough times as well as the good times.

And as the saying goes, "Let us remember in the dark what we learned in the light."

"It's ... the place of deepest intimacy where we can know and be known to the fullest."

Richard Foster *on prayer as an act of grace*

In the summer of 1990 I was working furiously on a book on prayer[1]. Of course there wasn't a book then – just a thousand jumbled ideas in my head and scrawled notes on scraps of paper. The university where I was teaching gave me a room in their library for that summer. They gave me a key so I could come and go any time of the day or night.

Over those months, I suppose I worked my way through 300 or so books in the field of prayer – classical books and contemporary books. Books, books, books. My head was just swimming with all of the debates about prayer, all of the divisions of prayer, all of the discussions and definitions of prayer. I had read everything I could lay my hands on about formation prayer, covenant prayer, adoration prayer, healing prayer, authoritative prayer, sacramental prayer. At one time, I had identified 41 major forms of prayer in the great devotional writers. I had studied every jot about Aratio, Lexio, Meditatio, Contemplatio, Silencio ...!

I'll never forget a night in July 1990. There I was in that library all alone. Everybody had left hours before. I had studied too much. It was too late. I'd worked too hard. I was experiencing overload. How could anybody deal with all of the intricacies and all of the difficulties of prayer in one book? There was just no way. I threw up my hands ready to abandon

---

[1] *Prayer: Finding the Heart's True Home*, Hodder and Stoughton

the project. "Forget it," I said. "The task is too daunting. The intricacies are too much. I just won't write the book."

Then something happened to me that is hard for me to express to you. The only way I know to say it is that I saw something, and what I saw was the heart of God, and the heart of God was an open wound of love. As best I can discern it, I heard the voice of the true Shepherd, not outwardly but inwardly, saying:

> I don't want you to abandon the project. Instead, I want you to tell my children that my heart is broken. Tell them I hurt at their distance and their pre-occupation. Tell them I mourn that they do not draw near to me. Tell them I grieve that they have forgotten me. Tell them I weep over their obsession with muchness and manyness. Tell them that I long for their presence.

So I'm telling you as best I can. I'm telling you how very much God desires our company. God is inviting you – God is inviting me – to come home to where we belong, to that for which we were created. His arms are stretched out wide to receive us. His heart is enlarged to take us in. You see, for too long we've been in a far country. It's been a country of 'climb and push and shove', a country of noise and hurrying crowds. He's inviting us to come home to peace, serenity, wholeness, intimacy, affirmation and care. We don't have to be afraid.

He welcomes us into the living room of his heart where we can put on old slippers and share freely. God invites us into the kitchen of his friendship where there is chatter and batter, mix and good fun. God welcomes us into the dining room of his strength where we can feast to our heart's delight. God welcomes us into the study of his wisdom where we can grow and stretch and ask all of the questions that we want. God welcomes us into the workshop of his creativity where we can become 'co-labourers with God', as Paul put it, working together to determine the outcome of events. God welcomes us into the bedroom of his rest where we can be open and vulnerable and free. It's also the place of deepest intimacy where we can know and be known to the fullest.

It doesn't matter if we have little faith or none. It doesn't matter if we're bruised and broken by the pressures of life. It doesn't matter if prayer has become cold and brittle to us. It doesn't matter. You see, God's arms are stretched out wide. We're welcome. We're welcome to come home because God accepts us – fully, freely, totally. Prayer is an act of grace because in it we discover that wonderful, loving, caring acceptance of God.

"Sing it to me again Daddy. Sing it to me again."

Richard Foster *gives an illustration of experiencing God's love*

Let me tell you about a friend of mine – Lymen James. He's a radio disc jockey and has a three-year-old son called Zachary. One day he and Zachary were out for an afternoon doing a little shopping. It was one of those days when nothing went right. Zachary was fussing and fuming and Lymen was trying everything. He tried to discipline him, he tried to be nice to him, he tried to get him candy and the candy was sticky. I mean, just nothing worked.

Finally – maybe under some special inspiration – Lymen scooped up Zachary and held him close to his chest and he started to sing a love song to him. He just made it up. The words didn't rhyme and he sang off-key but he just tried to share his love for his son with him. "I love you Zachary," he'd sing. "I'm glad you're my boy. I like to play ball with you. It's fun to see you smile." Things like that.

Zachary began to calm down and put his head on his father's shoulder. They kept going from place to place and Lymen quietly kept singing with words that didn't rhyme and were sung off-key. Zachary kept listening to this strange and exotic song. Finally, when they had finished for the afternoon and Lymen went back to the car to put his son into the seat, Zachary lifted up his head and he said, "Sing it to me again, Daddy. Sing it to me again."

Now you see prayer is a little like that. With simplicity of heart, we allow the great God of the universe to scoop us up and draw us close. We come to experience the heart of God – his love, his acceptance, his availability.

"Honey, I feel good. I haven't said that for 26 years have I?"

Richard Foster *on confession*

Many years ago, a middle-aged man came up to me with tears in his eyes. He said, "I'd like to speak with you." I said, "Sure." I set a time to go see him on a Thursday night. This man began to share his need and his brokenness.

He described how he had been in a deep sadness and sorrow for 26 years. He would wake up in the middle of the night in a cold sweat, screaming. He described how, during the Second World War, he'd been a ranger in Italy in charge of 33 men on a mission. They got pinned down by the enemy. He had prayed desperately all day long that God would get them out of there, but it wasn't to be. He had to send his men out, two by two, and watch them get killed. Finally, in the early hours of the morning, he was able to escape with six men. Four of them were seriously wounded. All he had was a little flesh wound. He told me he had become an atheist out of that experience. He was mad at God, full of guilt and anger.

I listened to that little story and my heart just went out to him. I said, "Don't you know that Jesus Christ, the Son of God who died for you, can set you free from that deep sadness, that sorrow, that brokenness." He didn't know! For twenty-six years, he didn't know. I came and sat on the couch beside him and put my hand on his shoulder (that was my shy way of laying on of hands) and I prayed a child-like little prayer. I didn't know how else to do it.

I just asked Jesus to walk back those 26 years with that man, to walk through that day and let him know that he loved him, that he was there, that he cared for him and to draw out the guilt, the hurt and the anger, and to set him free. And I added – I just thought of it, I guess – "Lord, I would be so appreciative if one of the evidences of this healing work would be for him to be able to sleep all night long." After about a half an hour, he turned to his wife and said, "Do you know, Honey, I feel good. I haven't said that for 26 years, have I?" She said, "No, you haven't."

The next Sunday, there he was. It was the second time in 26 years that he'd been in a church building. He came down the aisle three feet off the ground. He got a hold of me, lifted me up and said, "I slept all night long for three nights straight and every morning, I woke up with a hymn on my mind." That's the way confession can work. God's grace, God's mercy. That's the discipline of confession.

"There is nothing new about prayer for revival."

Jeremy Jennings *on the importance of praying for revival*

There is nothing new about prayer for revival. Unfortunately, from time to time in the life of every people and nation we get to that situation where revival is the only way forward, the only way out.

It seems like God, in his infinite wisdom, knew that from the very beginning or at least from early days. This passage in 2 Chronicles 7 says it all:

> When I shut up the heavens so that there is no rain, or command locusts to devour the land or send a plague among my people, if my people, who are called by my name, will humble themselves and pray and seek my face and turn from their wicked ways, then will I hear from heaven and will forgive their sin and will heal their land. (vv 13-14)

What God requires of his people is addressed to us. Corporate intercessory prayer preceded the Day of Pentecost. We are told in Acts 1 that the risen Jesus gave his disciples this command, "Do not leave Jerusalem, but wait for the gift my father promised, which you have heard me speak about. For John baptised with water, but in a few days you will be baptised with the Holy Spirit." If that had been me, I think I would have said, "Well, that's nice. So let's go and wait for this wonderful thing that is coming to pass."

But, for the people of God of that day that was not their reaction. Yes, they went to Jerusalem. Yes, they waited but they did a third thing: "They all joined together constantly in prayer." I don't think it is reading too much into the text here to presume that having been promised the power of the Holy Spirit by Jesus Christ, the thing they all joined together constantly in prayer for was the coming of the Holy Spirit.

Poor conditions are ideal revival conditions. Revivals come to the people of God when they are down and out – not when they are in victory and churches are multiplying all over the place. Isaiah 64 sums up this sense of desperation that we begin to feel: "Oh, that you would rend the heavens and come down, that the mountains would tremble before you!" (v 1) Then, like the prophets, we find ourselves praying for the spirit of God to pray through us. Prayers like this: "Oh, that you would rend the heavens and come down." That is a statement of: we are desperate, we have tried just about everything we know. We have formed committees in the church, we have written papers in the church. We have tried human endeavour and human activity and human wisdom in the church and none of it seems to be a solution for the besetting problems that we are facing as a people, as a church, as a nation.

So, we come to the point where we are desperate. I think that is the point at which revivals are born – where we come to the end of our tether and we reach the beginning of the power of God. I would like to go on to consider some of the characteristics of effective corporate intercession.

The first characteristic is **passion**. Speaking through the prophet Joel, the Lord says, "Even now... return to me with all your heart, with fasting and weeping and mourning. Rend your hearts and not your garments." (Joel 2:12) It isn't about models. It isn't about formulas. It is about the cry in the hearts of the people of God, inspired and put there by the Spirit of God.

The second characteristic is **unity**. We are seeking to promote and develop unity. In that verse in Acts, they all joined together constantly in prayer. They united in prayer. They were all crying out to God to send his Holy Spirit. As the people of God seek to unite, looking up at him who is at our head, it seems to draw us closer together on the earth. It brings about a unity. That has been our experience in this activity.

We have had a number of occasions when a number of us have gone away for what we call 'Prayer Weekends'. One of the things that people have said most often after coming back from those weekends is that there was extraordinary unity amongst us as we sought what was on the heart of God together.

The third characteristic is **persistence**. Again in the Acts verse, there is that word 'constantly'. They didn't just pray once or twice. They were at this activity constantly until what they were waiting for had come to pass on the earth. In Luke 18:1 Jesus told his disciples a parable to show them that, "they should always pray and not give up". That speaks of persistence. This is something we are seeking to develop. We wouldn't claim to have arrived, nothing like it!

The fourth and final characteristic is **belief**. Jesus said, "Therefore I tell you, whatever you ask for in prayer, believe that you have received it, and it will be yours." (Mark 11:24) I also come back again and again to what the writer to the Hebrews says: "And without faith it is impossible to please God, because anyone who comes to him must believe that he exists and that he rewards those who earnestly seek him." (Hebrews 11:6)

We have discovered and learned three particular lessons in our limited experience in seeking to establish effective corporate intercessory prayer. The first thing we discovered was the **weekly meeting**. We began from very small beginnings. This current season of prayer in the life of this church [Holy Trinity Brompton] couldn't have begun from smaller beginnings. But we developed here, the 'one hour per week prayer meeting'. We need a regular meeting that calls for commitment. It calls for perseverance, for turning up. If it is at

7 am in the morning, it means getting up quite early. We now have a prayer meeting every weekday morning of the week but it has been a process.

Then we discovered the central role of **worship** in this activity. We see intercession and worship as being instrumental in piercing spiritual darkness. Then we have learnt in the context of corporate prayer meetings, the importance of **leadership**. Corporate prayer meetings need leading. They are all about the people of God uniting and pulling together. It is not about assembling a group of people and saying, "Just pray for anything you like now." There is no point in coming together to do that. We have, therefore, discovered the importance of these meetings being clearly led from the front.

We believe God is calling us to cry out to him for this land. Not just for those in the churches but for those outside the churches, who are on the wide road that leads to destruction. We are to pray for them. We are to pray for change in this land for their sake and for his sake, the author and the perfecter of our faith.

"It is not quite enough to know that we are to pray. What are we to pray?"

Sandy Millar *on finding God's purpose*

In the Apology of Aristides (c. 130 AD) we find the following reference to the prayer life of Christians of that time:

Now the Christians, Oh King, as men who know God, ask from him petitions which are proper for him to give and for them to receive; and thus they accomplish the course of their lives. And because they acknowledge the goodnesses of God towards them lo! on account of them there flows forth the beauty that is in the world.

Let us consider two of the thoughts in that paragraph: "....as men who know God..." and "petitions which are proper for him to give..."

It is very encouraging indeed to see the increased emphasis and excitement that there is today on prayer and intercession. Andrew Murray once wrote that, "the man who mobilises the Christian church to pray will make the greatest contribution in history to world evangelism".

This is even better. This is the Spirit of God himself mobilising the Christian church to pray – in large groups, small groups, in church, at work, as individuals, on our own. The church is stirred from within to want to pray – to be involved with God in bringing into existence plans that are clearly in the mind of God and which he is gradually unfolding as being things that he wants and intends to do in our time just as he did with the early church at the time at which Aristides was writing.

True prayer springs not from duty, guilt, remorse or fear but from love. From within that loving relationship of intimacy, many different people from many different backgrounds and churches today are sensing that **now** is the time to pray. **Now** is the time for concentrated prayer. But it is not quite enough to know that we are to pray. What are we to pray? Here are four things that I believe God is re-emphasising today. They are all "... petitions which are proper for him to give ..."

Firstly, **it is God's will that everyone should know Jesus Christ.** In a light-hearted article in *The Times* recently, Matthew Parris wrote that, "Woolly-minded outlooks are to MPs what wet noses are to dogs – a sign of health." He could equally have been writing about some of us in the church. The gospel is universal and God is not slow in keeping his promise. But he is patient, "not wanting anyone to perish, but everyone to come to repentance." (2 Peter 3:9)

Put another way (this time by St Paul): He "wants all men to be saved and to come to a knowledge of the truth. For there is one God and one mediator between God and men; the man Christ Jesus."(1 Timothy 2:4-5). More significant even than this are the words of Jesus himself: "But I, when I am lifted up from the earth, will draw all men to myself." (John 12:32)

So don't let's waste a moment wondering if God really wants to see our particularly difficult neighbour saved, or his child, or a colleague at work or a cabinet minister or a school teacher etc. – he does! Let's pray imaginatively for every aspect of evangelistic opportunity that comes to our minds; for family, friends, for those involved in Alpha, missionaries, church workers, Earl's Court ministries, schools. The list is endless. Let's pray that the Lord of the harvest will send workers into his harvest field (Matthew 9:38) and bear in mind the very real possibility that we ourselves might turn out to be an answer to our prayers – without even having to move house.

Secondly, **it is God's will that all believers should grow spiritually.** Paul writes to the Christians at Colossae: "We have not stopped praying for you and asking God to fill you with the knowledge of his will through all spiritual wisdom and understanding." (Colossians 1:9) Perhaps you could have a group of friends praying specifically for Christian children, young people, schools, leaders, families, marriages, engagements. You could be praying into existence wise friends for them, people to encourage them – that they may grow into giants for God, pleasing him in every way, bearing fruit in every good work, growing in the knowledge of him, being strengthened with all power according to his glorious might.

St Augustine had the godly Monica (his mother) praying for him throughout his unregenerate youth. No doubt she met with other wives and Christian people, with what wonderful effect. I cannot see how young people, new Christians (or indeed any of us for that matter) can survive if we don't have selfless people pouring themselves out in prayer for us.

Thirdly, **it is God's will that all believers should become involved.** The purpose of God is that all God's people should be prepared for works of service. That is why God provided particular giftings to the church: apostles, prophets, evangelists, pastors and teachers. (Ephesians 4:11) There is thankfully no unemployment in the kingdom of God. There is no sitting around tasting sermons, expressing views like a sort of voyeuristic art critic who looks at things from a safe distance but never gets involved. There is an old poem that you may have heard which goes like this:

> Christ has no hands but our hands
> To do his work today.
> Christ has no feet but our feet
> To lead men in his way.
> Christ has no lips but our lips
> To tell men how he died.
> Christ has no love but our love
> To lead men to his side.
> We are the only Gospel
> The careless world will read.
> We are the sinner's Bible
> We are the scoffer's Creed.
> We are the Lord's last message
> Written in deed and word.
>
> What if the type be crooked?
> What if the print be blurred?
> What if our hands are busy
> With other work than his?
> What if our feet be going
> Where sin's allurement is?
> What if our lips be speaking
> Of things his lips would spurn?

How can we hope to win men
And hasten his return?

Will you start or join in with urgent prayer that every member of Christ's body, the church, today sees this? The only way to testify to the love of God that is in you is to pour it out and spend it on other people.

On the famous occasion just before the Ascension, when Jesus drew from Peter his thrice-repeated expression of love and thereby gave Peter confidence (among other things) to believe it himself, Jesus at the same time showed him how it could be made known in down-to-earth practical terms: "Feed my sheep!" That is, "Don't just talk about it. Do it!" Bedraggled, awkward, angular, difficult some of them may be, but sheep! For Jesus's sake and with his love, we are to love them as the expression of God's nature in us.

Fourthly, **it is God's will for all believers to live in, but not of, the world, in purity and growing holiness.** The writer to the Hebrews puts it more strongly I suspect, than most of us have taken in. "Make every effort to live in peace with all men and to be holy; without holiness no-one will see the Lord." (Hebrews 12:14) Oh, that we might have 150 groups of people – large or small – by the end of this year meeting together to pray for some of these things.

May I appeal to you to pray into existence the extraordinarily wonderful purposes of God for his church today? What could be more exciting than that?

Faith's challenges

"God gave me a song: 'Not the strongest will win, but those who trust in Christ.'"

Paul Negrut *on his life as a Christian in Romania*

I was the third boy in my family. My parents were farmers when the Communists came and took everything – the land, the cattle, the tools and forced my mother and father to work the land for them. A farmer would get a kilo of grain as a wage for a hard working day on a farm.

In that situation, farmers were not looking for more babies. My parents didn't want another one because they already had two and they couldn't feed them – and then I came. This was a big problem for the family because my mum, after she gave birth, was not allowed to stay home and nurse me. She was forced on the field to work the land for the Communists. Otherwise they would not even get that kilo of wheat and they would be prosecuted for sabotage. So when I was two weeks old, my mum had to wake up and go on the field and work. I was left alone all day because there was no-one to look after me.

When I was two months old, I got ill and was in a coma for two weeks. My parents were forced to work every day on the field. They were not allowed to take me to a doctor. The nearest medical office was about 15 miles away, over hills and valleys in another larger village, and my parents were not allowed to take me to that doctor because it would take a whole day.

So after two weeks when my father saw that I did not die, he couldn't bear any more of that situation. He said to my mum, "Even if they kill me, I'm taking this boy to a doctor to see what is the matter with him," but he had no transportation. So with the help of some neighbours, they put together a sort of cart which was almost falling apart. They put some hay on it and put me on it, and my father set off for that village. Half way there, I opened my eyes, maybe because of the bumpy road and my dad was so happy that he turned back home, so I never saw a doctor. But today, I know that this life that I have now is not mine.

The first time I saw butter in my life was when I was 16. I had my first overcoat when I was 16. I saw the wickedness, the injustice, the evils and I grew up with rebellion in my heart. I was determined to go my own way. That created a big problem especially if I tell you that I was good at doing things my own way. I was successful in school at everything I did. When you are rebellious and successful, that moves you away from God and the only thing that I was not willing to acknowledge was that I had to kneel down before God and let him rule my life.

When I was 15, my parents moved from that village to the city of Oradia, where my father got a very poor job. Soon, I identified a group of other rebellious teenagers and I mixed with them and we lived in rebellion. When I was 16, I met a young girl – she was 15. That young girl is now my wife. I do not encourage young people to date that early in life so please do not take my example as an excuse.

She came from a different background. She lost her father when she was nine, and her mum remained without job, social security, or any financial or material support. But she was a godly woman and she lived by prayer. She prayed every day that God would feed her and her nine-year-old daughter. They lived by prayer, and every day God answered their prayers and cared for them.

When my girlfriend saw my rebellious way, she tried to

minister to me but I was determined to resist. She was very kind and waited patiently for the time to come but I was not willing to take the religious way. When I graduated from High School, I decided to go into the military and be an officer – an army secret police officer. Then my girlfriend spoke to me and said, "Paul, I spent a few weeks away in the summer and I met a clinical psychologist." In that moment, there was a light inside my heart. I looked at her and said, "I will study clinical psychology."

So I applied for the University of Bucharest, the only one that had a department of clinical psychology. In order to be registered at a university in Romania for clinical psychology, you need a paper from the Communist party headquarters saying that you are not a Christian. So I went to the Communist party and asked for that paper and since the organisation knew me as a rebel, they were not worried about giving it to me. In 1972 when this happened, there were only 90 places in the clinical psychology department, and there were 2,500 applicants.

I had to pass the entry examination and in Romania, entrance examinations are very difficult. They have two parts – written and oral. For the written test, we were divided into rooms and the professor came and wrote on the blackboard the topics of the essays that we were supposed to write. So I did my best – I wrote whatever I remembered but it was very little and I got a very bad mark. In Romania, marks are from 0-10. 0 is the lowest, 10 is the highest. When the essays were marked, I got 6 which was very low because ahead of me were at least 500 between 7 and 10, and there were only 90 places.

That was the first time in my life that I was confronted with myself and I had failed. I was so discouraged, depressed and ashamed I couldn't face that, so I decided to commit suicide. It seemed the only way to get out of the mess. I packed everything in a small case and wrote a note for my parents telling them what had happened. But before I left the room where I was staying during the exam, I remembered what my girlfriend had told me when I went. She said, "Paul, whenever you come to the end of yourself, remember that then the grace of God will begin for you." I realised that I was at the end of myself and I fell to the ground, agonising and crying out to God. I was not trained in religious matters, but I was there for hours.

When I woke up I was a changed man. There was a deep peace in my heart. My mind was clear and, more than that, God gave me a song with words and music which remained in my mind for two weeks. The words were: "Not the strongest will win, but those who trust in Christ."

With that assurance, I went to the oral examination, although humanly speaking there was no hope. In those days, the oral examination was very crazy in Romania. There was a huge wooden table like in the Kremlin, with five professors behind the table and the table was filled with small pieces of paper like in a lottery. The students picked two pieces of paper, looked at the topics and, out of their heads, had to say whatever they knew about those topics. The professors would stop you, turn you upside down and confuse you because they had to dismiss 2,410 and select only 90.

So I picked two pieces of paper and I looked at my topics, and I thought that the whole world was caving in on me because I had no idea what it was all about. I thought I'd better throw away the papers and run away. In that struggle, there was a voice inside me which said, "Why don't you take a seat?" I turned round and there was a seat there and a small desk; I took that seat and I began to cry out to God again to help me. Then there was an audible voice and that voice dictated my topics. I took up my pen and began to write, very quickly to keep in step with the voice. When the voice stopped, the examiner said, "Negrut, it's your turn, come here and answer."

I began to read my paper because that was all I could do. I read very quickly to give them no time to stop me but as I was reading, they were speechless! I remember looking quickly to see what was happening with those draculas behind the desk; I thought that what I was saying was so stupid, they'd lost their voices. I kept reading.

When I finished reading the first topic, they asked me who my father and mother were, and who trained me for that exam, what kind of books I had and where I got those ideas from. My answer was that I had no professors, no brothers in the Communist party – nothing! Then one examiner asked me what my mark had been in the written test and I told him it was 6. He seemed concerned. Then he said, "Do you know something about your second topic?" I took my notes and I read the second topic. When I'd finished he stood up, shook my hand over that huge desk and said, "Mr Negrut, I am so pleased that you are my student." He gave me the mark 10! It was the only mark 10 that was given in 1972 in the University of Bucharest, Department of Clinical Psychology, at the oral examination. My wife asked me to be sure that whenever I speak about that 10, to remember that it is Jesus's. 10. It's God who gets that 10!

So there I was with a paper that said I wasn't a Christian – and now I was a Christian. Although I had failed my exam I was admitted as a student. I went back home and my girlfriend met me at the railway station and asked me what had happened. I told her and she said, "Paul, we have to tell all our friends what happened." Seventeen of them accepted Jesus when I told them what had happened and were all baptised together in the time of the Communist persecution.

Within a few weeks I started my first academic year. The first course we had was an introduction to atheism. There was a chap telling us that Jesus never existed, that God doesn't exist and that it was myth and not reality. I was boiling inside – how could somebody say that? After a few lectures, I stopped him and said, "Can I suggest to you some books to read about the historical records of Jesus of Nazareth?" He stopped me and called me to the Communist Party office and said, "Shut up! If you open your mouth once again, you are out of this school."

Next time he came to our class, he looked over the classroom and said, "I want to ask you a question. Who believes in God? Please raise your hand." I knew he was after me. If I raised my hand, I would be expelled from school because you are not allowed to study if you are a Christian. By that time I was so confused – I knew that God existed but I was not willing to lose my opportunity to study. I think that in those moments, I understood the apostle Peter when he looked at that servant lady and denied Christ. I was almost ready to deny Christ.

As I was crying out for help not to compromise, I was willing myself to raise my hand. I raised my eyes first to look around and all my colleagues were there with their hands up! They told me later that they knew I was a Christian and that the professor was there to spot me and expel me. They said, "Paul, we felt that we should protect you" and I was the last one to put my hand up! By that time, the professor was so shocked that he looked at one of the best students in our class and said, "Demetrius, are you a Christian?" and Demetrius said, "Mr Professor, Hegel believed in God, Kant believed in God, Heideger believed in God. Mr Professor, who are you that you claim that you do not believe in God compared to those great philosophers?" The professor left!

I graduated from the University of Bucharest as an expert in clinical psychology, and when I was in my last year I married that girl. She is my wife and we have two beautiful daughters.

"I didn't want to become a pastor because I knew what it meant to be a pastor in a Communist country."

Paul Negrut *on life under persecution*

A s soon as I started my job as a clinical psychologist, the secret police were after me. They sent a secret police officer into my office every day. He was in my office eight hours a day watching over me. Whatever I said, whatever I did, he was hunting for something, so he could claim that I used my office for religious purposes. How can you live a Christian life when he is there to identify that you live a Christian life? It is not easy. I will not go into details, but after almost eight years in that office with persecutions and all sorts of threats, God called me into full-time pastoral ministry.

I didn't want to become a pastor because I knew what it meant in a Communist country. I had seen what happened to our pastors before and I was not willing. Again, in a miraculous way, God spoke to me and he forced me into the pastoral ministry. He helped me all the way through.

In 1988, due to the persecution and the pressures that were on us, I had a stroke. I was paralysed, I couldn't move my hand and my left foot, yet three months later I was on my feet again in the pulpit preaching the gospel. Some months later, my wife had a stroke and she too was restored. I then had a second stroke. By that time, the secret police decided to attack us through our children. I will not tell you what they did because I want to protect my family, but it is enough to tell you that one night when I came home, I saw that my family was crushed. My eldest daughter couldn't speak, she was so shocked. She was terrified.

When I saw what they did, I felt that God was unjust with me. I thought God was unfair. I said, "Lord, I know why I am suffering, my wife knows why she's suffering, but this girl doesn't know. She's not yet at an age to make a decision. You aren't fair!" I was angry with God and wanted to leave Romania. Many people crossed the borders of Romania illegally in those days escaping to the western world, so I worked out a plan that I would take my family out and I said, "Lord, I care for this family more than you do."

I went to speak to a friend of mine and told him what happened and what I was going to do. I shared with him all my failures and all my disappointments with God. He said, "Paul, wait here and I will come later to speak to you." He came with an old piece of paper in his hand and said, "Paul, read this letter." It was written by a man who spent 25 years in prison. Tortured every day and after 25 years, because the Communists couldn't break him down, they executed him. Before they murdered him – he knew that this would happen to him – he managed to write a last letter; it was given to his cellmate and somehow, through God's grace, it came out and reached that man's family.

The letter was actually a prayer. It said, "Dear Lord, I know that my time is coming to an end and very soon I am going to see you face to face." Then he developed his idea of the glory of heaven. He described it in his imagination saying, "Lord, I can hardly wait to see all your family together. I can hardly wait to see all your great evangelists and great servants, to see the missionaries, the choirs, singers and all those who serve you. Especially Lord, I can hardly wait to see that moment when the martyrs will come with their crowns and they will lay down their crowns at your feet. Lord, in that day grant me a special favour. Lord, let me come to that heavenly procession in the uniform of a Romanian prisoner because I want to praise you for all eternity as a prisoner for Christ."

That was his last prayer. When I read that letter, I was broken

Sandy Millar

John Wimber

Bishop Lesslie Newbigin

David Parker

Pastor David Yonggi Cho

Richard Foster

Jeremy Jennings

Paul Negrut

Ken Costa

Nick and Jane Oundjian

Jackie Pullinger-To

Chris Woods

Michael Cassidy

Steve Chalke

Gordon Fee

J. John

inside; I knelt down and I prayed saying, "Lord, give me that grace, that I praise you for all eternity as a Romanian for Christ. It would be so easy to praise you today as an American for Christ, as a German for Christ, as an Englishman for Christ but give me the grace to praise you as a Romanian for Christ."

I went home and spoke to my wife and we prayed together. We decided to praise God for all eternity as Romanians. We decided to stay in Romania. Despite more pressures and more persecution, God took care of us and he always gave us enough grace. Now, the gospel is proclaimed on television in Romania and we receive up to 30,000 letters every day from people who have heard the gospel through our ministry on television. When I see the gospel of Christ proclaimed in Romania, I praise him as the Lord of history.

"I was absolutely frightened out of my wits for all 43 treatments..."

John Wimber *on his experiences of radiation treatment for cancer of the throat*

On April 6, 1993 I was diagnosed as having a cancer of the nasal pharynx. Shortly after that, I began radiation treatment – 43 treatments over the next two months. Sometime in mid-July, I finished the treatment and I was told that if this particular type of cancer were going to re-occur, it would probably re-occur within the first two years.

Most people are given a five-year span but evidently this type comes back quicker if it's going to come back. On April 9, 1994 I was examined and told that I had no evidence of any cancer at all in my body. In July 1995, I was through the first year of waiting so now I'm into my second year. [He was speaking in the autumn of 1995.]

I have some limitations. I don't have saliva glands, so it's difficult for me to talk for protracted periods of time. Without saliva, you don't digest food very well, so I get raw food into my stomach and that means I have constant heartburn and stomach aches; I've lost over a hundred pounds – about eight stone – so that's a lot of weight. I'm very weak. When you starve, you don't lose fat, you lose muscle so I've very little muscle on my body. I fall over every now and then. I haven't done it much lately because I've been doing limited exercise in the last two months. I don't sleep well, I've lost a little bit of memory – sometimes radiation does that – and I've lost a major part of my hearing, about 80% in my left ear and about 60% in my right. But they say I may recoup my hearing – it has to do with fluid. In fact, in the last month I have had intermittently better hearing. Some days I can hear better than others. Right now, I feel I'm at the sea shore. I'm 61 and that's not so old but as I have said, it's not the model it's the mileage. I've been very compulsive in my life and I'm a workaholic. I've worked too hard for years.

A question that has often been asked me is, "Did you commune with the Lord through this time?" Commune with the Lord?! I was unconscious, I slept 20/22 hours a day. They had to carry me out of the bed to get the treatment. They put me under this thing and they clamped this other thing over my head. I found out that I was claustrophobic. They took straps and put them over me. You have to be totally immobilised for this treatment because radiation is an exact art and if they miss, they could fry your brain in a few seconds. I was absolutely frightened out of my wits for all 43 treatments, not just one time.

But the Lord was there in the midst of the fear, in the midst of the panic, in the midst of the horror. He was always there. He didn't remove the horror. He didn't remove the panic. I think he could have. He could have healed me of the claustrophobia but he didn't. I've heard of people who fall asleep under that machine. They enjoy the activity but for me they may as well have hung me from a 20-storey building by my heels as far as fright was concerned. But in the midst of that, God met me every time. Radiation is hell. It's the worst thing I've ever experienced in my life. It is utterly devastating. The cancer you're not really aware of. The radiation and the after-effects? You're aware of nothing else.

But God carried me through it and taught me some wonderful things. I realise that much of my life and much of the body of Christ has assumed the avoidance of pain is one of the blessings of being a Christian. I have found just the opposite – that the embracing of pain is one of the blessings of being a Christian. When I have gone through devastating tests and trials like that, all of them have produced great dividends in my life. Most of the growth that's ever occurred in my life has occurred in the midst of great pain: the loss of loved ones, the betrayal of people that have left me, the immorality in the lives of close confidants and colleagues, the devastation of sickness. I'm profoundly proud of God and his willingness to meet us at those deep and dark times of life.

But when I was going through the treatment, it wasn't a time of advancing faith. I couldn't even focus my eyes, so I couldn't read Scripture. Thank God, I had memorised lots of Scripture when I was younger and the few minutes I was awake, I would think about Scripture and I would always wake to the sense of God's presence in the room. There was always that sense of God's immediate presence and I grew a new awareness and appreciation of what it means to be in the presence of the Lord. He went with me through that. He did not abandon me but he also didn't save me from it. So it was obviously his choice, his sovereign will, that I go through that – and I accept his sovereign will.

"You'll have just enough of Jesus to be miserable unless you have all of him and he has all of you."

Ken Costa *on backsliding*

Why did Peter backslide so badly? This is an important question because you and I need to watch it. We need to be careful that we don't go exactly the same way. Peter was so close to Jesus but he denied him. He was a traitor to him. He turned his back on him. Now how did that come about?

This is the history of the collapse: in Matthew 26:31, Jesus gets up at the Last Supper and tells Peter, "This very night you will fall away on account of me." Peter replies, "I never will." Jesus says (v 34), "This very night you will disown me three times." Peter declares (v 35), "I will never disown you." Now what happens when Jesus says one thing and we say another? The point is he disbelieved the word of the Lord. That is the first step. Now when the word of the Lord comes to you, whether in the Scriptures or through a friend or whatever, take care. That isn't the moment to say, "No, it's not." Because this is where Peter's first mistake was: **he disbelieved the word.**

Second, Matthew 26:43 tells us Peter was drowsy in prayer. It's a tragedy. Jesus is sweating blood in Gethsemane and he asks them to pray – and three times they are asleep. The closest friends he has desert him. They are sleeping at Jesus's moment of agony. You ought to ask yourself this question: how do you walk with someone for three years and have him sweat blood and not realise that 'this is the moment that I must be with you'. And Peter was not. He was drowsy in prayer. Jesus wanted them to watch and pray. That's the second step: **they stopped**

praying. Sleep and other things took over, and the backsliding is now beginning to get really quite serious. What is happening is that Jesus is preparing himself at the critical moment of his life for a very important event and when he says in verse 46, "Rise, let us go" he means, "We are now ready and prepared – or at least I am." But Peter was not.

Look at what happens next. He had disbelieved the word; he was drowsy in prayer and now he was distracted by the flesh. Because as soon as Jesus is set upon, Peter (John's gospel tells us) takes the sword out of his scabbard and cuts off the ear of the High Priest's servant. It was a 'magnificent gesture' and 'great attack upon the centres of power'. He takes the sword and what does he do? He *cuts off the ear*... a massively irrelevant act! Because Peter by then is driving on human overdrive. What else can you do when you are not listening to the Lord, when you are not praying? **You are going to be distracted by the flesh** which is strong within us. Here is the old, tempestuous, strong Peter who rushes out and believes that in his own strength he can take the sword and make an act on behalf of Jesus; do something to protect Jesus. It is a complete irrelevance. That's what we do quite often in our own lives. We go into our own strength. We start striving away thinking, "God, I'm really doing you a favour." We don't pray, we don't listen, we don't talk to him and we think we're OK. No doubt Peter thought he was OK too.

Then what happens? He is distracted by the flesh and then in verse 58 it says, "Then Peter followed him... at a distance." **He distances himself from his friend.** He's in trouble. Oh my, he's in trouble.

That is where backsliding starts in our own lives. We start drawing away from Jesus. That intimacy isn't there any more. You are not necessarily going to say he's the greatest man in the world. There is no way in which you or I is going to survive in a world as hostile as the one we have to live in at a distance, I promise you. Don't even try it. You'll just have enough of

Jesus to be miserable. If you can only catch him in passing, don't catch him at all. If you can only just see him come up to you, don't bother. Because the only place to have him is right in your heart and next to you. You'll have just enough of Jesus to be miserable unless you have all of him and he has all of you.

Peter not only distances himself from Jesus, he deserts him. Verse 58 tells us he follows him at a distance, he enters the courtyard and he sits down with the guards to see the outcome. Peter has become a spectator. Do you see that? He comes to watch the outcome. This just cracks me up. It is the same thing that I do: "Please God, move by your Spirit in this place and I'll just watch the outcome. I don't really want to get involved. The homeless are pretty nasty and smelly. I don't really want to be where you are Lord. I want to be in the nicer places." Then verse 69, you know the terrible story. He sits in the courtyard; they are cold and try to warm themselves, but by then there is no amount of human or circumstantial warmth that can warm Peter's heart. His heart has gone cold. His light has gone out. The cock crows and Peter curses by his own name that he has never met or seen this man, and not to the High Priest, but to some servant girl in the outer court of the High Priest's chamber.

I think Peter is so much like us. We just sit out there denying Jesus every day – in our work, our discussions, our talks, our holding back, our commitment, in our lives. Then Peter goes out and weeps; he dissolves as a person. This is the absolute crash – you don't go lower than this – he 'wept bitterly'. Then, you see, he was a broken man. Peter, the strong tempestuous man, was shown to be completely irrelevant to the historical drama that was unfolding. His contribution to this great moment in the life of the Master was to cut the ear off the slave of the High Priest. That was the first leader of the Christian Church.

This comes to all of us in our Christian lives. For some of you it is happening now. You are registering and ticking these things off. But even when Peter went to that lowest point, he wasn't without his God and friend. Because even though he had abandoned his Lord and Master, Jesus Christ had not abandoned him. He'd been called, he'd been commissioned, he collapsed and he received the charge from Jesus at the end of John.

In John 21, here is Jesus at his most gracious reinstating Peter. What does Peter feel? He's sold out. He sits there with Jesus having breakfast and when they have finished eating, Jesus says to Peter, "Simon, son of John, do you truly love me more than these?" And here is the reverse thrust – three times he asks that question, as if by each absolution to wipe the crow of the cock. For every denial, there was an affirmation.

"Feed my lambs"; "Take care of my sheep", says Jesus to him and six weeks later a man gets up on the day of Pentecost convinced by the Spirit. In Acts 2:14 it says, "Then Peter stood up with the Eleven, raised his voice and addressed the crowd..." Where does this new confidence come from? It comes from the work of God the Holy Spirit; it comes from the graciousness of God the Father, who takes hold of Peter and says, "I will reconstruct your life."

Peter in his own strength would have been a disaster to the church. Can you imagine what would have happened? Jesus is gone and it's, "Swords out chaps. Here we go, let's murder a High Priest." Peter had to see the death of Peter the Strong Man in order for a new vision to arise. That is when God says, "This is the vision I give to you" and that vision will be based squarely on the power of the Holy Spirit. Because as he disassembles us, so by his Spirit he reassembles us piece by piece in order that we might be the broken, suffering, but powerful witnesses to Jesus in this world. That's what happened to Peter. You'll have just enough of Jesus to be miserable unless you have all of him and he has all of you.

The first words spoken to Peter and the last words spoken to Peter by Jesus, were the same. In Mark 1:17, Jesus says,

"Come, follow me," and in John 21:19, he said to him, "Follow me." Then the very last words in verse 22, "You must follow me." The start of the life of Jesus and the end of his life – the same words, "Follow me" and never does that change for the life of you and me. Never – from the beginning of our lives as a Christian, to the middle point and to the end point; it will always be the same – follow the person of Jesus.

"Stress substitutes other relationships for the one which is dependent on the living God."

Ken Costa *on combating stress*

The actor John Cleese once wrote a book with his psychiatrist entitled, *Life and how to survive it.* Cleese started his psychoanalysis when he believed he was suffering from a pathological inability to enjoy life. But Dr Anthony Clare, host of the programme *In the Psychiatrist's Chair,* says of him, "He claims to have been freed of inhibition by psychotherapy, yet his three marriages remain largely murky and unexposed areas of private emotion, for all the transatlantic personal honesty."

If you leave this evening with one message, it should be this: that apart from Jesus Christ, I don't believe we have any hope of surviving the tensions that are breaking up our society at the moment. The self-help books may help you to adjust or to accommodate yourself to the prevailing pressures but they cannot help to transcend or to overcome them, which is the heritage of the sons and daughters of Jesus Christ alone.

Stress is universal. Just look at some of the **sociological**

stress around us – death, the loss of a loved one, moving house, family gatherings at Christmas. Then look at **sexual stress**. The pressure to have a relationship whether it works or not is endemic at the moment. Then there is the loneliness of a single person faced with pressure from peers. Thirdly, **secular stress** – am I in the right job? The amount of time that is spent working out whether you are in the right job, is an extraordinary fruitless activity for 80% of the enquiries that go on. We need to discover for ourselves the restfulness of believing that God has brought us into one position and that in due course, if we love and trust him, he will move us on. There is also financial strain. Whether it is that your house is valueless and the debt is high, or whether you're just tossing away the Barclaycard bills when they arrive because you don't dare face them. Fourthly, there is **spiritual stress** – striving in your own strength to accomplish God's purposes on earth. All with the best of intentions. People's hearts are wanting to go along but the striving to achieve it is ahead of God's plan.

What are the consequences of stress? The terrible thing about stress and pressure is that it takes our eyes off the right relationship with God. I've noticed an interesting phenomenon: when stress levels rise, there is a coarseness in personal relationships. Amazingly, selfishness in the most unselfish of people suddenly rises. Stress substitutes other relationships for the one which is dependent on the living God. That is its insidiousness. Stress in the spiritual sense, kills.

But the interesting thing is to look at Jesus because he is our model. There can be no other place to start. Jesus knew what it was like to be hemmed in, to have pressure tightening around him, and yet Jesus had a plan for survival. I am deeply struck by that extraordinary example in Luke 4:28-30, just after Jesus preaches the first sermon in Nazareth. Jesus turned on the people and said that they would not accept him. An extraordinary hue and cry breaks out and they drive Jesus out of the town, and take him to the top of a hill to throw him down from the cliff. The crowd has turned but Jesus (v 30) "walked right through the crowd and went on his way".

It is astonishing sovereignty, isn't it? Here is God in Christ, when all the pressure hems him in. He doesn't duck. He doesn't go for cover. He doesn't out-flank them. He just walks through the midst of that crowd. His sovereign authority is available to us in exactly the same way today. In Christ Jesus, when pressure hems us in we walk through the midst of it. Will it be troublesome? Sure. Will it be difficult? Of course. But will we overcome it? Yes! Why? Because Jesus did it and on the cross, won for us the right to walk in through him.

David the psalmist knew the same feeling. If you look at Psalm 18, you'll find this extraordinary sense that David knows. Verse 6 says, "In my distress I called on the Lord," and then verse 19, which has meant more to me in a hard working environment than almost any on the subject, "He brought me out into a spacious place, he rescued me because he delighted in me." Again in Psalm 31:8, "You have not handed me over to the enemy, but have set my feet in a spacious place." Don't you long for that when pressure is upon you? One of the things I have been studying carefully is that wonderful interchange that Mary had with the servants at the marriage feast in Cana. They came up and said, "There's no wine. What are we to do?" Mary then says these absolutely marvellous words, "Do whatever he tells you." If you had a stress strategy, that would be it.

We need emotionally enriching friendships. Elijah was sent Elisha to be his friend and Paul was sent Titus. David was given Jonathan and Jesus had John, the disciple whom he loved. An emotionally enriching friendship means precisely that. It isn't someone who's going to wag a spiritual finger at you all the time. It's someone you feel comfortable with, who builds you up. We all need it – and particularly in times of stress. We also need to determine those things which are not of God and cut them out of our lives, whether they are in relationships, a work place, or wherever. Cut it out! Recognise that Jesus knew the dependence on the Father and say, "That's what I'm going to do. Whatever I see the Father doing, I will do – no more and no less." Just do the anointed work.

Jesus said, "I know where I came from, and where I am going." (John 8:14) You must believe in your calling. Those who believe in themselves as Christ has modelled them, believe that there is a plan for good and not for evil in their lives. Those are the ones who are able to rest in the Lord, to wait patiently for him. Jesus only did anointed work. Is what you are doing anxious activity or anointed activity? If it's anxious activity, you are going to be stressed out. I am sorry but there are no solutions. We will love you through it but there's nothing we can offer until the relationship is set right. Anointed activity is that activity in which you do whatever he asks you to do. Sometimes you don't hear right. Sure, but at least the heart is right.

Jesus did what he saw the Father doing. No more. Our temptation is to do more than God is doing. It's a very stressful thing to fulfil the calling of someone else. It's an endemic problem to Christians who believe they are called to do what they're doing but really they want to be a worship leader and strum a guitar. "I'd long to do that," they say. If I'm called to children's work, then I want to be with grown ups. If I'm called into the City, then I want to be a clergyman. You can't fulfil the calling of another which is why it's so important to say, as Jesus did, "I can do nothing without the one who shows me. For the Father loves the Son and shows him all he does." That's the answer.

"Idols offer comfort."

David Parker *on how idols provide a false security*

Typically in the modern world, adults are looking for security and significance – the very things that God has called us to in Christ. You can see how so many people get stuck in what they look to for comfort. When we experience pain, fear, anxiety or pressure, opposition or hostility, sorrow, loss, rejection or alienation – or whatever – we need comfort. In the fall, we were born as insecure beings and unless we get healed and changed we will struggle with the issue of idolatry.

What's the connection here? It's this: idols offer comfort. Zechariah 10:2 says, "Idols speak deceit. Diviners see visions that lie. They tell dreams that are false. They give comfort in vain." What idols do is lie. They give apparent comfort but ultimately it's empty, unsatisfying and worthless. What idols provide is a false comfort, a clinging to worthless things that forfeits the grace that could otherwise be ours.

Now what kind of things could be false idols? The amazing thing about the subtlety of the modern world is that many of the things that become idols to us are not idols in themselves but are actually the means of comfort for our lives given by God. It's our looking to them as the principal source of comfort which makes them idols.

What are they? Firstly, **food**. Food is a genuine source of comfort from God but how many people turn to food as the main source of comfort in their life when they are in distress? It's a false comfort when it becomes the source. Secondly, **material security and financial power.** This is much more obvious to me in America than here; your typical middle-class

American person, when they get under stress or pressure goes shopping. "Let's go buy something to make us feel better. Let's go exercise some material acquisition and financial power and get some comfort into our lives." When money becomes the focus of our comfort we are dealing with a very significant idol indeed.

Thirdly, **sexual satisfaction**. This is one of the biggest idols of our time – the belief that if you are not sexually satisfied daily on numerous occasions, then you're going to turn blue and die; if you do not satisfy your sexual cravings you will be completely unhealthy. It is an absolute lie and it comforts in vain. Is sexual intimacy, in the context of marriage, not a given thing of God as a source of comfort? My experience tells me that yes, it is. But outside of that place, there is a serious problem of idolatry with sexual gratification. It has become a main source of comfort in people's lives and it's a completely false idol. There is a tremendous addiction in our culture to pornography and masturbation but I don't believe the seriousness of it lies in its perversion. The seriousness lies in its idolatry.

Fourthly, **entertainment** – fantasy, the movies, television, books, magazines, the escape from reality. The popularity of science fiction and fantasy is because it has become a source of comfort for people and it too comforts in vain. Fifthly, **alcohol and drugs**. Are not drugs a form of comfort given by God for when we are sick? Absolutely, but there is a whole generation that is looking to Ecstasy to provide what only the Holy Spirit can. It is looking to alcohol to give what only the relationship with the Father can provide. Lastly, **praise and approval of friends** and co-workers. Is that not a legitimate comfort? Why else would Hebrews tell us to encourage each other daily? But when we are addicted to the affirmation of others, it becomes an idolatrous relationship which offers nothing to us in the long run.

What's the true source of comfort then? What did Jesus say

in John 14? He said, "I will ask the Father and he will give you another Comforter to be with you for ever – the Spirit of truth which I have told you about." We have got to get in touch as Christian people with the genuine comforting role of the Holy Spirit in our lives. I think the major issue for most Christians is coming into that place of receiving comfort from the Lord. I don't mean to condemn in any way but today I believe, the Lord says, "You got idols? Burn them. Destroy them. Tell yourself they are not going to comfort you any longer." So many times in my ministry people, have said to me, "This thing, it controls me. What do I do? Do I need deliverance?" Sometimes that's true but most times it's not. The first step towards really getting comforted by God is to cut ourselves off from idols.

"...there was a beautiful four- or five-year-old girl ... and I knew she belonged to me."

David Parker *explains how God prepared him for his wife's miscarriage*

Before my wife got pregnant, I had a dream. In this dream I was standing at a fence and there was a beautiful four- or five-year-old girl and I knew she belonged to me. It wasn't one of my two daughters. I looked at her and she looked at me, and I wept because she wasn't with me and I didn't understand why. I knew that our family was going off in one direction and she was staying there.

After I woke up, I told my wife about the dream and I said, "I don't have a clue what this means but maybe the Lord wants to give us another child." We were really happy before that, I mean, four is plenty! But I thought, maybe the Lord is telling us there was one more that belongs with us that we should open our heart to. So we prayed and opened our hearts and lo, and behold, Nancy became pregnant.

Then, we come to this point – the sadness of losing this child, which I held in my hands; that three-inch-long infant with perfectly formed arms and legs and face. I knew that this was the little girl I saw. In the dream, I had that same feeling of, "I don't understand why you're not with me and why you're not going with us but I'll leave you to God." I tell you, the comfort of having the Spirit speak to me about this little child in advance, provided more foundation under me than all the meals and kindness that so many of you have shown me. Not that I don't need all that, but the reality is, this is a role of the Holy Spirit – to comfort our lives. He speaks to us and embraces us. We can feel him and know him, and he's with us always.

"Compassion cannot remain inactive."

Tom Gillum *on the response of a compassionate person to suffering*

Some time later the son of the woman who owned the house became ill. He grew worse and worse, and finally stopped breathing. She said to Elijah, 'What do you have against me, man of God? Did you come to remind me of my sin and kill my son?' 'Give me your son,' Elijah replied. He took him from her arms, carried him to the upper room where he was staying, and laid him on his bed. Then he cried out to the Lord, 'O Lord my God, have you brought tragedy also upon this widow I am staying with, by causing her son to die?' Then he stretched himself out on the boy three times and cried to the Lord, 'O Lord my God, let this boy's life return to him!' The Lord heard Elijah's cry, and the boy's life returned to him, and he lived. Elijah picked up the child and carried him down from the room into the house. He gave him to his mother and said, 'Look, your son is alive!' (1 Kings 17:17-23)

Elijah's compassion on the death of this young child comes out in two particular ways: first with action and secondly, with prayer. Compassion always leads to action. As your heart is pained with the fact it is a person that's suffering, there is a cry from within that says, "I've got to do something to help." There is an urge that simply won't allow you to stay sitting where you are. Also, there are no glib words. That is one thing a compassionate person will avoid.

On 7th April 1983, all five children of a Nigerian hospital chaplain who worked in Bradford died in a fire at his home. In one half hour spell, he lost all his children and his home. He spoke about the ghastliness of what he was going through saying, "It was a disaster. It was untidy. It was illogical, horrible and shocking – an affront to life. My world turned upside down. Reactions? Horror, shock, anger, utter disgust at life's cruelty. There was one lobby which saw the children's death as God's will, to which I could only respond with a certainty that it was not. Then there were those who felt that it was a judgement or some form of holy treat that we'd been selected for."

I know how easy it is to come up with a glib word, because you feel the need to say something and you feel the need to justify on God's behalf. You find yourself saying things which often come out in the most unhelpful and awkward ways. I've learnt the hard way by finding myself saying things and before you know it, they are deeply unhelpful. When I'm in the hospital talking to somebody who's just lost a child, I've got no more than 10 seconds' and probably five seconds' concentration level when they're going to be actually listening to me and probably rather less.

Elijah doesn't try to justify what has happened, which is very significant. He takes the child in his arms, presumably because that was what he felt God was telling him to do. For us, the action that compassion leads to, is precisely the same. It's what we feel with the Spirit of God whispering in our ear, and what we feel with our common sense is the best thing to do in the circumstances. Often the best thing you can do is give a good hug and cry with them. Not to say a word but to hug them – using your discretion – and to express complete solidarity and involvement with that person.

You could take them a meal. They may not want your company but compassion is always saying, "I'm there if you need me and I'm not going to impose myself on you, but I need you to know that I'm here. I'll do anything that is helpful." So it's a hug, it's a meal, possibly a telephone call, a letter. It's including them in whatever you're doing. And it's doing it over a period.

Usually in the case of bereavement, there's a flurry of activity in the first months or so after the death. However it is the period, three months to a year thereafter when the pain is no less and when everything is just the same, that this practical side of things needs to continue. It is relatively easy to do it for a little bit, but we need to keep going with it.

If the first response of compassion is action, the second is prayer. Elijah takes the child in his arms up to the room where he is staying, lays him on his bed and then he cries out to the Lord. I'm sure there are tears rolling down his face because this is deeply painful. "Oh Lord my God, have you brought tragedy also upon this widow I am staying with, by causing her son to die?"

The first thing I note is, there is a recognition of the reality of what's going on – this is a tragedy. As Christians, don't let's anaesthetise ourselves from these ghastly realities of life. The compassionate person will see it very vividly. The Nigerian man who lost his children doesn't want to deny the reality, and the compassionate person, the person praying, will address that to God. That's the place it should be articulated – to God.

The prayer starts off with the reality of the earthly circumstances, not blunting that at all but then going on to the character of God. "Have you brought tragedy also upon this widow I'm staying with, by causing her son to die?" which I read as, "No, you haven't." It's an element of, "You can't have done this, God!" "The God I know doesn't behave like this," is what Elijah is saying. "You're not like that." Elijah knew the character of God and that God could be trusted. He is proclaiming the truth of who God is.

It is important that we speak the reality of who God is – that he's not the God of death. He doesn't bring disasters to make life miserable. But he is the God who can be trusted and the God of love. The fact that these things happen is very much a feature of living in a fallen world, where things are very unfair, very hurtful and very cruel. There is a real power of evil that is around which, if we ignore it, means we don't get the full picture. God is not the originator of any of these things.

"I cried very briefly at the cremation but don't remember crying again for the next 14 years."

Nick and Jane Oundjian *tell the story of the tragic death of their 13-month-old son, 17 years ago*

JANE'S STORY

When my mother died 31 years ago, she had been ill for a long time. I remember she was on morphine and so wasn't conscious much of the time. But we didn't go and sit and talk with her at all. She was simply upstairs in her room and when she died, I remember creeping upstairs and peeping through the door feeling that I was doing something wrong. We didn't touch her, speak to her or hold her hand. When the undertakers came to the house, we shut ourselves in the kitchen and listened to music on the radio while she was taken away. I cried briefly at the cremation but don't remember crying again for the next 14 years.

That is an extraordinary thing and hopefully, something that would not be allowed to happen now. What effectively happened was that I was living with a dormant volcano inside me – I thought it was extinct and I had dealt with it. But of course, the eruption came with the next loss. Nick and I were childless for 10 years before we had Jeremy. He was a completely healthy child, thriving and full of beans.

When Jeremy was 13 months old, Nick went to India and Pakistan on a month's business trip. He suggested that I take Jeremy to stay with my best friend, Jeremy's godmother, in Connecticut, USA. While we were staying there, he caught what we thought was a gastroenteritis bug from a little boy of the same age. The other children in the area all had it and got better. Within a week, Jeremy had died of it. After I had nursed him for two nights, he was taken to hospital and I was persuaded to go home for the night. I did and arrived back at about seven the next morning. It turned out to be about 20 minutes after he had died. Nobody asked if I'd like to see him and I didn't think to ask – I never saw him again. It was appalling. Whilst nobody said to me he would have lived if I had stayed, I've had guilt about that for the last 17 years. I've talked about it endlessly and I don't think it will ever go away.

I also think it's a little easier to accept if you know why someone has died. Either Jeremy was that one in 5,000 who die of gastroenteritis or maybe he picked up some other branch of the virus. The unsatisfying thing for us afterwards was that although tests were done to find out what actually happened, we never got any concrete answers. These two experiences are why I'm so keen on good bereavement care.

For the first weeks after Jeremy died, all I talked about was my mother – my grief had lain buried all those years. People on the outside often want to put a time limit on bereavement. About three months after Jeremy died, a very good family friend came and said that he would like to talk to us. He said that it was the opinion of everybody that enough was enough, and we should be putting all that away now and getting on with life. I think that what he was really saying was that he couldn't cope with any more of it. This I understand. People outside just don't know how to cope. But we shouldn't be saying to bereaved people, "Enough is enough." It may be something that goes on for years and years. The guilt doesn't always disappear. It is quite common that we get left with some of it.

"Grieving is a very painful process. Some people take a very long time and don't do it very well. That was me."

NICK'S STORY

I was in Karachi when I received the news. I phoned up and Jane's best friend said, "There has been an accident." At the time I was an extremely strong and confident guy and I thought I could cope. I knew it would be all right. I'd get on the next plane, be in New York and sort it out. Then she told me that Jeremy was dead. It was 1AM and I went out and ran down the streets of Karachi in the dark. I somehow managed to get to the airport and took the first plane home. I spent nine hours underneath a blanket quietly crying.

Once I got home I felt an incredible amount of guilt that I hadn't been with them. I was absolutely convinced that it wouldn't have happened if I had been there. Stupid, of course! Every time the telephone rang during the next weeks, I was absolutely certain of Jeremy's return. They had found him. He was fine. Or when the door bell rang, I knew that there would be somebody there holding him. Of course there wasn't. As I went out to the shops, I would look in every pushchair. I was sure that he was around. This was in the immediate period after he had died. I was angry for years.

There was also confusion and helplessness. Jane would say, "Could you go to the corner shop and get a box of Bran Flakes." There is nothing easier, but I would spend 40 minutes in there deciding whether I should get ordinary Bran Flakes or Kelloggs Bran Flakes. I still remember that Kelloggs Bran Flakes were 73p and the other one was 58p. It stuck in my mind. It was such a problem for me trying to decide that.

What really made things better for us were simple things. Two or three weeks after his death, I was out walking and saw two people watching television in a shop window. They were watching a running race. I happen to love running and I watched Steve Ovett on his third lap of 1,500m. I was miserable but I was thinking, "Is he going to win it?" and he won. Then suddenly I got miserable again and I thought to myself, "Hello, I've just had 90 seconds of pleasure." That was so amazing and important. A friend of ours turned up at our door every day for six months. She had decided to come every day to our house and prevent us from being miserable the whole time. That was amazing.

The biggest contribution to my healing was going running. From the age of 12, I had gone running each day. Quite soon after losing Jeremy, I went to Battersea Park every morning and I would pound the ground and cry out in anger, tears coming down my cheeks. One day, a friend said, "I might come running with you." He had never run before and hated it. He got better at it and, after about two months, we began to talk and I would get things out. After about four months, things were improving and by the end of the year he was a better runner than me! This whole relationship was incredible because I began to realise that what he needed was to work through and grieve the loss of his father during his early adolescence. Four or five years later, he lost his son so I was able to help him work through that as well. We ran together for 12-14 years. What he did by coming out and giving himself was fantastic and possibly the greatest single contributing factor to my recovery.

Grieving is a very painful process. Some people take a very long time and don't do it very well. That was me.

"They must be allowed to be sad."

Jane Oundjian *on the importance of bereavement care*

It is helpful to remember that bereavement is not just about death. It is to do with loss, deprivation – having to do without something upon which we had been counting. It is also a loss of future hopes. These losses can include: death, divorce, disability – maybe loss of limb, sight or hearing later in life – miscarriage, abortion, redundancy, abuse and the consequent loss of childhood and innocence, rape, or in fact anything which seriously changes our perception of ourselves and our ability to function as we did.

It is absolutely biblical to grieve. There are two sides to the Christian response to bereavement. Both are very important. The first is that we know and believe that we have a bright future and that those we love who are Christians, will have gone on to everlasting life. Death for us is a continuation of our relationship with Jesus. Secondly, Jesus wept at the death of Lazarus. Jesus acknowledged and recognised what death meant for us. It is absolutely biblical to grieve. Throughout the Old and New Testaments, there are people who grieve and mourn and are encouraged to do so. It is very important that our faith isn't used like a sticking plaster to put over an unsightly and uncomfortable wound. Our faith should be used like a bowl of warm salt water and we should be bathing our wound in it. It will sting and it will hurt but it will be cleansed, purified and healed once and for all.

There are, however questions that come up for Christians: "Why me? Why should my child die? Why do I have cancer? Couldn't God have intervened to prevent this?" I think sometimes in Christian circles, a trite answer can be given by someone meaning well, like: "I'm sure God knows what this is going to bring for you." This kind of answer is given in kindness but actually conveys that the person doesn't understand the agony of the question, because it is a question that can't be answered. That doesn't mean that it must not be asked. There is also the question, "Where is God in all that's happened? I gave him everything. I became a Christian. Is he punishing me? What am I meant to be learning?"

Another very big question concerns where the person has gone, particularly if we weren't sure where they stood in relation to faith. That's a difficult one to answer. The first thing I would say is: we don't know for sure the state of anyone else's heart, right up to the last moment. We must never forget the parable of the workers in the vineyard in Matthew 20. The man paying the workers says, "I want to give the man who was hired last the same as I gave you." People really do have until the very last moment to get right with God. I think that is what he wants for them because he is a generous God.

My mother died 31 years ago and I often worried about where she might be. Two years ago, I learnt that three years before she died she went to a Billy Graham meeting in London and she went forward. For 29 years, I never knew that and I might never have found out.

Another example is Ian McCormack, a young man who was swimming somewhere in some exotic islands and was stung five times by poisonous jellyfish. Amazingly, he managed to get to shore. He was not a Christian but when he was in the ambulance he remembered what his mother had said to him: "If ever you are in trouble you must turn to the Lord Jesus and he'll forgive you." He recited the Lord's Prayer in the ambulance and when he got to the line 'Forgive us our trespasses' he remembered two people he had not forgiven. So he forgave them and finished the prayer. He survived. But he might have died and no-one, not even his mother who had prayed for him for all those years, would have known for sure. We think we're sure about people because we've known them for a long time but actually, we don't know their heart. So that's one thing that we must hold on to. Another point is that we do know that God is absolutely fair and we can never be more fair than he is.

Another burden for Christian people is the feeling, "I should be coping better than somebody who's not a Christian." I think that's an unfair burden to carry. In the end there will probably be a wonderful fruit, but it's not going to be like that right from the beginning. That's not realistic. As Christians, we must be prepared to accept unconditionally the way that our bereaved friend or relative is feeling. We must be able to cope with their sadness. They must be allowed to be sad. Often, it is a question of just being with them – sitting with them, crying with them. We must not always feel we must make it better. The bereaved person is probably longing to talk – they can't tell their story enough times. People need to talk. We can also help them by accompanying them to church, meeting them beforehand so it's not intimidating. Pray with them on a regular basis and tell them, "Two or three of us are going to pray for you."

However, the first thing is that they need a lot of practical help – washing, ironing, shopping. Going into places to buy food is daunting if you're in the first stages of grief. Say something like, "Couldn't I come in one day and do a bit of your ironing with you – I love ironing." It's just a huge help. They may want you to do something a few times and then suddenly, the fourth time they say, "No thank you" and you may feel very rejected. You have just got to take a deep breath and realise that it was the wrong moment. Try not to be too timid to go back again a week later and ask how it's going. We've got to try to bury our sensitivity. If people are having a bad day they might be quite abrupt.

When you know someone who has been bereaved, do write them a letter. Often there is an inhibition. "I'd like to write," you think, "but I didn't know them very well," or "I'm not quite sure what I would say." It's worth writing it though. I hear people saying over and over again, "The letters are so wonderful and I've kept them and I read them over again and again." You hear people saying, "I didn't know that so many people thought so much of him." So I would say if anything prompts you to write, to pick up the phone, to cross over the road or to drop in and see someone – do it, risk it!

"Every Christian is a Simon of Cyrene, voluntarily taking up the cross and following Christ."

John Collins *on 'our little crosses'*

> If anyone would come after me, he must deny himself and take up his cross and follow me. (Mark 8:34)

Immediately after scourging, it was the practice of the Romans to lay the cross beam on a condemned man's shoulders, and rope it there. This must have been appallingly painful. Then he would be led a long way round the streets of Jerusalem, for about a mile and a quarter, so that everybody could have a public display of what happened to those who disobeyed Rome. That is what it meant to take up the cross. So it is a very sombre picture when Jesus said, "Take up your cross and follow me."

At the least, it seems to me, it must involve an open following of Christ, in our work or wherever we are, on Monday, Tuesday, Wednesday, just as much as on Sunday – fully recognising that inevitably this will bring us pain. It will bring opposition, misunderstanding, dislike, contempt, and being passed over. It will bring injustice, persecution and in some parts of the world it will bring death. Traditionally, all the apostles apart from Judas and John were martyrs. Today one doesn't have to explain what it means to take up the cross in such countries as China, Ethiopia, Turkey, Malaysia, Bangladesh or the Sudan. In 1993 Bernard Levin wrote an article in The Times in which he described incidents of crucifixion – the real thing – by Islamic soldiers of Christians in Sudan today.

Even in this country, Christians are increasingly facing all sorts of subtle pressures from many factions of society – in schools, industry, the media. Listen to this:

> One of the hardest things for me just now is to accept the strain of the battle and the way it is showing in my face and is telling on my health. I suppose I've aged 10 years in the last three. This is the cross – to realise there is no glamour, no appreciation to be asked or expected; nothing but ridicule, pain and loss. But it is in this that one finds Christ.

Who was this? An ordinary Christian housewife and mother. One day God said to her, "Will you do something about pornography and violence on television?" It was Mary Whitehouse.[1]

When the pain comes, do we sit down and cry? Do we complain? Do we say, "I didn't think the Christian life was going to be like this?" No, in this we find Christ, and enter into the fellowship of his sufferings.

In the Book of Acts, when the disciples were beaten and flogged by the rulers of the synagogue, they rejoiced that they were worthy to suffer with Christ. It has been well said that every Christian is a Barabbas. We look up at the cross and say,

---

[1] Extract from her book, *Who Does She Think She is?*

"I ought to be there, but you have set me free." But also out of love and gratitude for what Christ has done, every Christian is a Simon of Cyrene, voluntarily taking up the cross and following Christ. Jesus asks "a cross for a cross". He invites us to take up our little crosses in response to his great cross. The irony is that those who lose their lives in this way for Christ and the gospel are the people who are fulfilled. They are the people who realise their potential. They are the people who become strong.

"Jesus, as he prayed to God the Father said, 'Father, is there another way?' and God the Father said, 'No. The only way is the cross.'"

Paul Negrut *on how God answered the prayers of Romania*

When we celebrate Christmas in Romania, we have a small Christmas tree with tiny boxes underneath. It is a special time for our children when the whole family stands around the tree and they are allowed to open those boxes. You should see their expectations as night comes. Their whole minds and personalities are under the tree. If Mum and Dad say, "Kids, it's time to go to sleep," and send them to bed, do you think they will go to sleep? They can't unless they open the boxes. They know that Mum and Dad will have something new for them – some new toy or gift, and they are so excited to see what is there.

Do you expect something from God this morning? Do you have expectations? Do you expect God to answer, to speak to you, to do something that is new and unique? Jesus said to his disciples, "Come and stay and watch with me!" Now when you stay and watch, you expect something to happen. But the disciples didn't have expectations.

I grew up in a Communist country and I remember decades of expectation as I saw churches being pulled down, pastors and church leaders arrested and killed, people being humiliated; I saw the Bible, the word of God, being confiscated, burnt or turned into toilet paper; I saw the name of God being denied or openly mocked and despised in those nations. I remember the churches looking up to heaven and expecting God to intervene. They were long decades of darkness and the church was crying out, expecting God to intervene. We met by night. We were not allowed to have prayer groups or Bible study groups. We were not allowed to bring up our children in the fear of the Lord. They were taken from us and trained in atheistic schools. But even then we had expectations.

Whenever we have expectation, God will not fail us. He is going to answer. Peter, John and James thought that the night was just an average night when Jesus said, "Stay and watch and pray!" Sometimes you feel that when you pray there is no answer. In 1974, my church started to pray that God would bring Romania times of revival, that he would open the doors for the gospel. We prayed that the gospel would be preached in Romania in stadiums, on radio and television, in newspapers and that it would be proclaimed in the parliament. People thought that we were crazy. Do you know, in 1990 those prayers were answered. We prayed in 1974 and received the answer in 1990!

Every morning at 5 o'clock, my church meets for prayer. It started in a very interesting way: an old lady about 85 years of age came one day to one of the pastors of the church and said, "Pastor, can we have a little room here in the church to pray every morning at 5 o'clock? I feel that God wants me spend the rest of my life in prayer and I have a small prayer group who want to meet every morning. We are old ladies and we want to give those morning hours to God for prayer." So the pastor said, "Yes, of course you can have a room here." That lady came with five others and they started to pray. Two days later, the pastor was very curious about what was happening there so he went to see. As soon as he stepped into that room, he felt that he should stay there. After the pastor joined that prayer group, other people heard and the group started to grow. The group grew to 20, 30, 40; there was no more room in that office for them so they moved. Now, every morning we have 400 to 500 people meeting for prayer.

In Romania, we all pray with a loud voice, not at the same time, but one at a time. We all pray and each one participates in each prayer. How can we do that? We know that God loves paragraphs but specially he loves short sentences so we pray with short sentences. One starts and says, "We pray Lord this morning that the gospel will be proclaimed on radio." Another prays for television and another for newspaper, another for the army and it builds up a prayer.

Secondly, Jesus encouraged his disciples to understand the time. This is an hour when there are so many forces of darkness marching towards eastern Europe. It is time to pray. Pornography, drugs, prostitution, all kinds of crimes, the filthiness of the Western world is moving towards those countries. It's time to pray that God will spare and save those nations that were in bondage for so many decades. This is the hour God gave to the nations in eastern Europe to hear the gospel. This is the hour to start orphanages, schools, medical centres, universities, to penetrate every single social group with the word of God. On that night when Jesus prayed in the Garden of Gethsemane, he understood that that was the great hour of salvation. It was a great hour but then Jesus, as he prayed to God the Father said, "Father, is there another way?"

and God the Father said, "No. The only way is the cross."

When you respond to God's call, you expect great things but then there is a price to be paid. Is there a way for us to serve God without paying that price? No, there is no way but do you know that we do not pay the price for salvation? We are paying the price for promulgation. Jesus paid the price for salvation. Our price is just to spread the good news.

In Romania in the days of the Communist regime, it could cost you years in jail to spread the gospel. Whenever Jesus calls us, there is a price to be paid. Are you willing to pay the price? To go to the former Soviet Union to proclaim the gospel, there is a price to be paid. To go to Romania, there is a price to be paid. To go to downtown London to spread the gospel to others, there is a price to be paid. To be faithful, there is a price to be paid. But the one who pays the price is the one who will get the crown.

"He saw that I was angry and said, 'Paul, we are not here to complain. We are here to praise our Lord. Let's kneel down and pray.'"

Paul Negrut *on what one persecuted Christian taught him*

I will tell you a story of a man who spent 17 years in Communist prisons for spreading the gospel. He was tortured every day. Sometimes he was put in the sewage of the prison. And then he was placed in the courtyard and all the other prisoners would come in and spit on him and kick him and he was asked to give up Christ. Each time after being tortured he would go into his room and write a poem and a song for Jesus. Those songs came out and now they are in a book that circulates through the churches. There are more than 800 songs he wrote in jail.

When I was in a military concentration camp, I went through times of persecution and one day I was so discouraged I was despairing. That evening the officer in charge called me and I didn't know what he wanted with me. He said to me, "Negrut, are you a Christian?" Of course he knew that I was a Christian. I was there for that reason. I said, "Yes sir, I am a Christian." He pulled me closer and said, "Paul, my parents are Christians but nobody knows. This is the secret of my life. If my bosses find out that I am from a Christian family, they are going to dismiss me or maybe kill me. Then he said, "Paul, I am the only officer in charge tonight. There is nobody around. I am the only one watching over the camp. I can give you two hours of freedom. Go somewhere." Two hours of freedom from a concentration camp! Where was I to go? He said, "If you are not back in two hours and somebody comes to inspect the camp and you are not here, you know that they will shoot me."

I remembered this man who had spent 17 years in jail and overcome torture and hatred, who lived just a few miles away over a hill. So I ran to that man's house expecting to see a shining face, to see a man that would be like an angel who would comfort me, strengthen me. I ran to his house and I opened the door, and it was not a shining face but a bleeding face. There were open scars and blood was coming down his face. I asked him what had happened and he said, "The secret police have just left my house. They searched the house and they smashed me."

I was so angry, and he saw that I was angry and said, "Paul, we are not here to complain. We are here to praise our Lord. Let's kneel down and pray." I remember that I knelt down with him but I didn't have a prayer that night. I said very few words.

Then that man started to pray and he prayed with such fervour, excitement and love. He prayed for his enemies, he prayed for the Communists, for the secret police. He asked God's blessings over them; he asked God's forgiveness; he asked God's love to flow over their families. I opened my eyes to see if that man was normal. I never heard somebody praying for his enemies with such love as that man. After that prayer he spoke to me and said, "Paul, they come twice every week to torture me, and whenever they torture me I look straight into the eyes of the secret policeman and I say to him, "Sir, I love you. I want you to know that I love you." Then he said, "I tell him, 'Sir, if we see each other before the throne of judgement, I want you to know that I love you. But sir, if you will be eternally lost, I want you to know that you will not be there because I hate you. You'll be there because you rejected Jesus's love and my love. Sir, I love you."

One night that officer came to this man's house and the officer said to him, "Sir, I didn't come tonight to beat you. I came tonight to let you know that we will see each other before the throne of judgement." Then he said, "Sir, we will be on the same side." He said, "Brother, your love melted my heart and through your love I saw Jesus's love, and I came to know Jesus." Then he said, "I have only a few more weeks to live. The doctors have discovered that I have cancer. Within a few weeks I am going home but, before I see Jesus, I came to ask your forgiveness. I came to pray with you. I came to be reconciled with you." They prayed together. Can you see the torturer and the one tortured praying together? The officer disappeared and a few weeks later he was gone. This man endured the torture, paid the price and said I love you. Aren't you glad that Jesus paid the price? He went to the cross and gave his life. We are saved and we will see him face to face.

"'Can somebody sing here?' he asked himself. 'Can somebody praise God and say, "What a foretaste of glory divine" in this hell?'"

Paul Negrut *gives an illustration of faith in solitary confinement*

Let me tell you about one man who was sentenced for many decades. He spent years in solitary confinement and he didn't know if it was day or night. He had no understanding of time. Was it winter or summer? He was totally out of time and space, in darkness all alone. One day or night, he felt a prompting of the Holy Spirit to sing a song. Now if you are in a Communist prison, and you sing a song, that's death for sure. But he couldn't resist. There was that kind of prompt, that push of the Spirit. So he began to sing: "Blessed Assurance, Jesus is mine. Oh what a foretaste of glory divine. This is my story, this is my song, praising my Saviour, all the day long!" And he sang and he rejoiced.

In the next room, in darkness, was another prisoner, a non-Christian. That man was in the middle of a psychological breakdown. He had decided he couldn't live any more and would commit suicide. So he had taken his shirt and made a rope and hanged himself from one of the iron bars in the prison. He was hanging there to die when he heard his neighbour singing, "Blessed Assurance, Jesus is mine. Oh what a foretaste of glory divine." He was amazed. "Can somebody sing here?" he asked himself. "Can somebody praise God and say, 'What a foretaste of glory divine' in this hell?" The man said, "I have to live and find out!" So he loosened himself.

Months later, they were both taken out and were given dirty jobs in the prison just to keep the humiliation and persecution going. The Christian was asked to polish all the stones in the courtyard of the prison with his palms until they were shining. So he was polishing them, bleeding and hurting. The other one was asked to do another dirty job some yards away from him. They didn't know each other. As they were there, the Christian again felt the prompting that he should sing this song but now he was a little afraid. You see, in the courtyard even if he was still a prisoner and persecuted, it was a little better than in the solitary confinement. So he was afraid that if he sang the song he would be sent back there. Can you identify that feeling when you know that you have to do something but you are hesitant, and you look for a compromise? You cannot say a definite no but you do not want to say a definite yes.

Finally he came up with a creative alternative – he would whistle the song. As he whistled, the other heard the tune and he recognised it and forgetting about everything – prison, persecution, punishment and terror – he approached this man and said, "Do you know this song?" and the man said, "Yes." The other said, "Tell me, were you in that wing of the solitary confinement?" and the Christian replied, "Yes." The man said, "Did you sing that song there?" and the Christian said, "Yes, I did," and the man said, "Thank you for saving my life. I was hanging there, committing suicide when I heard you singing this song, I decided to leave and find out. Tell me!"

The other one shared Christ with him there and the non-Christian accepted Christ. The new kingdom of God began to grow in prison. There are many stories I can tell you like that.

"Great things start with great decisions."

Paul Negrut *on being ready to die for Christ*

How do you live your life in the world but not as the world? First of all, who is your master? We live in a world where it is popular to do whatever you want. The Bible says no. We are servants. God from eternity took upon himself the image of a servant. When Christ came to teach us how to live in the world, he taught us the lesson of servanthood. Do you know the only right a servant has? The only right is that of perfect obedience.

Does somebody claim total authority over my life? Yes, God does. Jesus says, "Unless you deny everything, take your cross and follow me, you are not worthy." When we speak about Christianity and when you live in a Communist country, Christianity is not, "Let's see. We will decide tomorrow." Christianity is, "I am ready to die for Christ." If you are ready to die for him, you are ready to live for him. If you are not ready to die, you are not ready to live.

Daniel was ready to die. When he said, "I'm not going to defile myself," he put himself in the place of death. He said, "I am ready to die. I belong to God so completely that I am ready to die, I am not going to turn away from God." An army general came from the war and was interviewed by the press. A journalist said, "What was the number one cause of casualties in the war?" The general said, "The number one cause of casualties in our ground war was that our soldiers didn't take decisions once and for all before they entered the war. My greatest problem was to teach my soldiers to take decisions once and for all. They went to war assuming that in every situation they would evaluate the circumstances and they would decide according to those circumstances. As they were trying to figure out the things they might do, the enemy shot them because the enemy had already taken the decision. My soldiers looked at the enemy wondering, "Should I or should I not kill him?" They died. If we'd had soldiers who had taken decisions once and for all before they entered the war, we would have won the war with very few casualties."

Why do the churches lose so many members? Because many Christians do not take decisions once and for all. When you come to Christ, you have to take the one decision from which there is no way back: "I totally belong to him." When the man who spent 14 years in jail took that decision, he was ready. When the interrogation started, his decision was already made. Now do you have decisions to make?

We all dream of doing great things with our lives but great things start with great decisions. I worked in secular society for seven years as a clinical psychologist and in those days, I agonised because I couldn't witness to any of my colleagues because I was so much under interrogation and persecution and many other restrictions on my life. All my colleagues would run away from me because if they had been seen speaking to me, the secret police might assume there was a connection between us and they too would undergo persecution. After seven years, it seemed to me, that time was almost useless, that my life there didn't make any difference.

After the Revolution, so many of my colleagues who had refused to talk to me came to know Christ that, in the Christian University we started, the Department of Theology and Psychology/Social Work is composed of my former colleagues who refused to speak to me in those days. When they were baptised, we asked them how they came to know Jesus Christ and some of them told how they had been watching me closely in those days when we were under persecution, to see if I would compromise. They said, "We were longing that God would bring to our lives the day when we could take decisions and stand for Christ." If you live a godly life where you are, one day in your lifetime or after you have gone into eternity, you will see the difference.

"No, I will not divorce him. He is my husband and I am going to live here and he will see my love and my faith and my faithfulness until the very last day."

Paul Negrut *gives an illustration of one woman's commitment*

One of my brothers was, for a number of years, the pastor of a small village church. He had a godly lady in his church whose husband was a very wicked, ungodly man. That man was a drunkard, a wild fellow and he would beat his wife whenever he came home. Her family told her she should not live her life with this man and that she had a right to divorce him. She said, "No, I will not divorce him. He is my husband and I am going to live here, and he will see my love and my faith and my faithfulness until the very last day." Some years later, that man began to bring prostitutes home and live with prostitutes in the same house as his wife.

About the same time, she got ill with cancer and as she was lying in bed he would bring the prostitutes to the same room under the very eyes of his wife. Now by that time her family was so angry they went to take her out and said, "We want you to die in peace. You cannot die in this hell. This man is a demon." She said, "No, I will not leave this house. I married this man and I am going to live here until God will take me away. He will see that I am going into eternity in love and respect for him." And she died.

My brother led the funeral. There in the cemetery, standing over the grave and the corpse, my brother spoke to the crowd. As he did so, the husband broke in and said, "Can I speak? I killed a saint, I murdered a godly woman. Is there forgiveness for me under the sun?" He fell down near the coffin; my brother stopped the procession and approached this man and witnessed Christ to him. The man accepted Christ there on the graveside and now he is an active member in that church! The whole village is now coming to church to see the miracle of God and you can trace the miracle back to that woman who took a very strong decision.

You say, "Is God fair to me?" Well, let me ask you, "Was God fair to Christ? Was God fair to let him die for us? If you say God was unfair to Christ, you can say God is unfair to you. But my question is, "Was there another way for salvation?" There is a great glory for God when you are in the world but not as the world.

"Whenever you have nothing, that's the greatest starting point. Nothing is raw material for God!"

Paul Negrut *tells the story of an unusual Lord's Supper in prison*

In the early 1950s when the Communists arrested all the religious leaders and imprisoned them to destroy Christianity, initially they scattered them in different parts of the world so they would not be two Christians in one place. They would be isolated and alone. However, several years later, the Communists got together a group of Christian leaders in one prison cell. One Sunday morning, after about seven years of being tortured and persecuted, they saw each other and it was such a joy that they decided to celebrate. It was Easter Day and they asked what should they do to celebrate their gathering together.

One of them said, "Let's celebrate the Lord's Supper." Another of them said, "It's a great idea but we have nothing to celebrate the Lord's Supper with. Why don't we wait until we have something?" Richard Wurmbrand, who was among them said, "No, we cannot postpone it. We never know if we will have another time to celebrate. Let's celebrate the Lord's Supper with nothing." So one of them took nothing, he blessed nothing, he broke nothing and he shared nothing with each one of them. They ate nothing but remembered the body of Christ. Then another one took nothing, blessed nothing, poured to each of them nothing, they drank nothing and they remembered the blood of Jesus. The glory of God came into that room and they were filled with power, and with the assurance that God was there, he was alive and the Spirit was there. They were so joyful.

That afternoon, they were scattered and for seven years none of them saw another Christian. When they came out from prison, Richard told me this story and said, "Paul, we learnt in prison this lesson – whenever you have nothing, that's the greatest starting point. Nothing is raw material for God! He created the whole universe out of nothing."

He said, "Whenever you have nothing, it is a new beginning of creation. If you wait until you have something, you will never start. If you wait until you have a car, you will not be good enough. If you wait for 10 million pounds, there is a recession and you will need 20 million pounds. If you have nothing, give it to God. This is how we work in Romania."

"When you stand before him you'll know it was just and fair, and merciful and loving because that's his nature. It's his character."

John Wimber *reflects on eternal life and a conversation he had with Patrick Pearson Miles, a young man suffering from a severe kidney disease*

I want to talk about eternal life in the context of a couple of exchanges I had. One of them occurred during lunch with a number of Vineyard leaders from England. It was a mixed group and one of the older guys said to me, "How are you feeling these days?" I said, "Well, just full of gratitude. I am so grateful for the blessings of God in my life."

One of the younger, newer people said to me, "What do you mean?"

I said, "All of my children love the Lord and have all married spouses that love the Lord. They're raising their children in the Lord. They love the church. They love the cause of God. Nothing would make a person more devastated than to have children who didn't love the Lord. Frankly, everything else that comes along as a blessing or success, is a bonus."

As we were leaving the place this same person said to me, "How does that match up with your recent stroke and your cancer, and your heart attack a long time ago?" I thought, "Oh no, here we go again." I said, "It matches up perfectly because I am not that focused on this life. I gave it up when I became a Christian. I realise that this is a little different to what is preached by a lot of people but it's the very essence of what I understand to be Christianity. When I came to Jesus I gave up my sin but I also gave up my life. He gave me a new life – eternal life that would extend beyond this carcass."

What we get in this life is a gift from God – and the main purpose of this life is to discover that gift. I spent 29 years not knowing that it existed. Then we encountered somebody who told me all about it. One night I received Jesus. I prayed and he received me because from that day until this – which is over 31 years – it's been good. There have been bumps – you know like speed bumps – every now and then that have happened in life but there is nothing that hasn't been in his hands and in his control. There is nothing that has taken the quality of life away from me.

From time to time, I have talked to brothers and sisters who have had a difficulty. They've lost a husband or wife. They've lost a child. They've had great pain in life. I am not making light of that but I just can't feel all that bad, particularly when they've lost them to Jesus. I recognise that it is hard to live alone – the sheets are cold and no-one else is in the room and you have to make your way with a new kind of focus.

Paul writes: "Paul, a servant of God and an apostle of Jesus Christ for the faith of God's elect and the knowledge of the truth that leads to godliness – a faith and knowledge resting on the hope of eternal life, which God, who does not lie, promised before the beginning of time."(Titus 1:1-2) He is an apostle with a purpose and that purpose is to preach eternal life. I believe that all of the church has been called to this preaching. All of the church is to prophesy the life that's in Christ. We are to do it to anyone that will stand still long enough to hear us. It is, 'a faith and knowledge resting on the hope of eternal life, which God, who does not lie, promised before the beginning of time.' I think it is really important that you have that underlined in your Bible. For God, *who does not lie*. You see one of the principle challenges of the enemy from beginning to end is, "Hath God said?" It brings into question the veracity of

God. Has God said? Can you trust God? Can you trust what God says? When Satan spoke with Jesus, one of the underlining issues was, "If you are the son of God, then do this etc." Again, veracity, truthfulness, integrity – these are always attacked by the enemy. Obliquely, he will do the same things to you.

During the first trip after my recovery from cancer, Sandy Millar asked me to speak at Holy Trinity Brompton and he invited me to lunch afterwards. A handsome young man came in who I could see was quite ill. He sat with me and we talked for about two hours. When he began sharing his story with me, it became apparent to me that he was quite desperate to be healed. He was dying of kidney failure and it had been a long journey of about ten years through various stages of the problem. He was very focused on healing and he had sort of a 'if God does not heal me, I cannot believe there is a God' kind of mentality.

He was aware of my cancer and knew that if I were to get it again, it would occur in the next two months and that unlike a lot of other cancers, the type I had usually re-occurs within the first two years of treatment and I was coming up to the first two years. I had my first examination and they did not find any cancer in my body at this time. I'm glad for that but the truth is, it could still re-occur any time. But I am not laying awake at night worrying about cancer. I believe a song we used to sing, "He has the whole world in his hands," – it's simple but profound. It's all in his hands and we can trust him.

The guy and his wife blinked at me. I said, "Do you save milk cartons?" They said, "Well no, when the milk's gone we discard them," and I said, "How about bread wrappers. Do you save those?" They said, "We throw them away after the bread's used." So I said, "Well, isn't that what you're going to do with this life? Why are you clinging to it so much? The value was never in the carton or the wrapper. It was always in that which it contained."

I am going to touch on some of the highlights of an article about the young man I met at HTB – an article published in that church's newspaper, *Focus*, some months after our talk – because I think it is important you understand the way he viewed things at one time, and the way he viewed them after our meeting.

Here he describes the condition – it's called Nephritic Syndrome – and he said:

> They think I got the disease from a throat infection, literally a sore throat. Apparently, a bug gets in through the throat and perforates the kidneys and the protein in the blood stream then flows out through the holes. When we were initially told about my illness, it was quite a shock and I prayed then and I have prayed nearly every day since then for healing.

As I have said, the day I spoke with him he was very fixed on healing and very desperate. It is one thing if you are 75, 80, 85 or 90 and you are desperate to cling to life. This young man would have been around 30. I have children that age and I felt very compassionate towards him. I also felt the need to instruct him that he had already received the more important gift in life and that was salvation, the gift of life that comes in Jesus. If God chose to give him healing, well the more the blessing, but if he chose not to, God had not failed him nor had he failed God. It was perfectly all right to ask. It was perfectly all right to pursue healing.

I was happy to pray for him that day. He asked me to and I did but I said, "I have no revelation in my heart that God is going to heal you at this point but I am happy to just pray for you and ask God that he will heal you." But the point I was trying to make for the young man – and we laughed together – was, "It's all God. We can ask, but it's all up to him and if he chooses not to give it to you, he'll answer for himself. When you stand before him you'll know it was just and fair, and

merciful and loving because that's his nature. It's his character." The young man was not really conscious of that so we
talked at length that day about this greater gift.

At another point in his story, he said,

> I had always said that if my kidneys packed up, I was not keen to
> go on dialysis. I didn't fancy the idea of that and my mum had
> always said that if she matched, she would give me one of her
> kidneys. So it was decided that we would go for a transplant from
> my mother. This is after about eight or nine years of various kinds
> of treatments all of which were exhausted. The doctors were no
> longer recommending anything else. The only thing they could do
> was a transplant. We had a number of matching tests and one was
> not a good match for some reason, and another was good and the
> last one was borderline. As the testings were uneven, the surgeons
> were hesitating. They wanted for each test to come back strong and
> say, "Yes, this kidney will survive in that body." And so they were
> slightly apprehensive about doing the transplant but kidney
> transplants from live donors have a very good record of working
> and particularly from relatives. So they went ahead and took the
> chance. But as it turned out the kidney failed.

At the time I met him, he had just found that out about six
weeks earlier. He had begun dialysis which was for him the
worst thing that could happen. It was in a sense worse than
dying because he had resisted it for so long. He says:

> In about May 1994, they made the decision to remove the kidney
> because it was killing me. They discovered that it was riddled with
> the original disease which was extremely unusual. The disease
> would normally take at least five years if it did come back. Mine
> had taken two months. The whole period was really difficult and
> the doctor told me afterwards that in his opinion, I nearly died on
> three different occasions. They decided not to tell me and
> afterwards I was glad because, I was having a hard enough time
> with just what I knew.

Partially, this is what I have called 'clinging to the container'. Again, it is not something you would blame anybody for, particularly a young man with a beautiful young wife just beginning life and wanting to succeed. But for me, it is a secondary issue. It is not the primary reason for existence. It's just that if I am going to keep on breathing and functioning, I would rather be doing it in a way that leaves me some flexibility in terms of the quality and the dignity of life. Here, he talks about himself and his wife:

> From then on, it has been a matter of getting used to life on dialysis and we have prayed a lot and nothing has gone according to plan. But at each stage that it has been very dangerous, we have been brought through. I now have a dialysis machine at home. I do just under six hours dialysis three times a week.

I don't know how many of you are familiar with dialysis but it is quite a painful process. Three times a week, he has six hours of treatment – no fun. He goes on to talk about a major change that occurred between the time he realised he was going to have to go on dialysis, and the time he did the interview which resulted in this article. He says:

> A major change in my perspective of God has happened through all of this. My faith has grown enormously. Up till now I have always been very self sufficient.

That is so much in the American ethos – this business of self sufficiency. Self reliance, self sufficiency, doing our own thing. It's so built-in. It's very difficult within our Christian understanding to yield to the power and presence of God. In fact, we have difficulty in understanding anything outside of our self sufficiency in God. But I understand the desperation of the dialysis at the time. He said:

> Although I had given my life to the Lord, I was quite happily doing

things in my own strength because I was able to and I was strong and fit…..

The implication was that he thought it was the proper way to live the Christian life. But I tell you, the Christian life is not about strength. It is about weakness. In a sense, it is weakness in us that gives revelation to his strength. In our weakness, we give ourselves to him. In our sin, in our inability to alter the course of our lives we come to Jesus. We say, "Oh Jesus, take my life. Take my sin. Take me in my weakness."

So often in my own life, I treated my conversion as a jump-start on a cold March morning with the car and then said, "Oh thanks, I'm under way now. Thanks Jesus, I'll see you up in heaven," and I was off and running. But again and again, he had to allow the battery to go down and the vehicle not to function before I got the understanding. He gave it to me in Scripture but he also gave it to me in life. It became apparent to me over the first half a dozen years that it wasn't about me getting strong. It was about the revelation of his strength in me. Though I had become quite skilled in Scripture in those years and I had memorised literally a couple of thousand texts (I had joined a Bible Memory Course) and had witnessed to a lot of friends and seen them saved – still, the truth was that when I was left to my own devices, I would always turn to sin.

Now I am not turning to the same sin – thank God. I am not turning to the same grade and quality of sin that I would have as a younger Christian. Nor am I captured in the ways that I was at different times in my spiritual pilgrimage. There have been some improvements in my record so to speak, in my walk with God. But I don't see anything of self reliance at this point in my life that is worth giving any energy to.

The father of this young man is a vicar in an Anglican Church. He is a man of about my age. He came up behind me one day, handed me a letter and kissed me on the cheek. He had tears running down his face. He said, "I am so grateful for what you did for my son." Well, I'm so grateful for what his son did with what I did. He believed it. You see it takes two to make it work.

God had to do what he did through Jesus and you have to do what you do in life – and that's receive, believe, embrace and draw him to yourself, and rely on him in every circumstance or every situation. Nobody had it any tougher than Paul. Remember when God spoke to Ananias he said, "…go and tell Paul the things he must suffer for my name's sake." (Acts 9:16). Nearly every chapter of the gospel of John deals with eternal life: "Just as Moses lifted up the snake in the desert so the Son of Man must be lifted up so that everyone who believes in him may have eternal life. For God so loved the world that he gave his one and only Son that whoever believes in him shall not perish but have eternal life…" Over and over again – eternal life, eternal life. That's what you got when you came to Jesus – eternal life. So don't cling to the wrapper or container so hard.

The mission of the Church

"Where shall wisdom be found?"

Bishop Lesslie Newbigin *on knowledge of God in public life*

There is a mine for silver and a place where gold is refined. Iron is taken from the earth, and copper is smelted from ore. Man puts an end to the darkness; he searches the farthest recesses for ore in the blackest darkness. Far from where people dwell he cuts a shaft, in places forgotten by the foot of man; far from men he dangles and sways. The earth, from which food comes, is transformed below as by fire; sapphires come from its rocks, and its dust contains nuggets of gold. No bird of prey knows that hidden path, no falcon's eye has seen it. Proud beasts do not set foot on it, and no lion prowls there. Man's hand assaults the flinty rock and lays bare the roots of the mountains. He tunnels through the rock; his eyes see all its treasures. He searches the sources of the rivers and brings hidden things to light. But where can wisdom be found? Where does understanding dwell? Man does not comprehend its worth; it cannot be found in the land of the living. The deep says, "It is not in me," the sea says, "It is not with me." It cannot be bought with the finest gold, nor can its price be weighed in silver. It cannot be bought with the gold of Ophir, with precious onyx or sapphires. Neither gold nor crystal can compare with it, nor can it be had for jewels of gold. Coral and jasper are not worthy of mention; the price of wisdom is beyond rubies. The topaz of Cush cannot compare with it; it cannot be bought with pure gold. Where then does wisdom come from? Where does understanding dwell? It is hidden from the eyes of every living thing, concealed even from the birds of the air. Destruction and Death say, "Only a rumour of it has reached our ears." God understands the way to it and he alone knows where it dwells, for he views the ends of the earth and sees everything under the heavens. When he established the force of the wind and measured out the waters, when he made a decree for the rain and a path for the thunderstorm, then he looked at wisdom and appraised it; he confirmed it and tested it. And he said to man, "The fear of the Lord – that is wisdom, and to shun evil is understanding." (Job 28)

This passage from the book of Job is a wonderful celebration of the powers of human technology. We are given a picture of men burrowing into the very heart of the mountains, opening up shafts deep in the earth, breaking the flinty rocks and smelting out of them gold, silver, copper and precious stones. Here are all the marvellous achievements of human technology beyond anything that the rest of creation can boast. However, at the end comes that haunting question, "But where shall wisdom be found?"

Doesn't that speak to our situation? We are very proud of our technology. Technology is developing at a fantastic speed, faster than ever before. We are discovering ways of doing things that we never dreamed of doing. Yet at the same time, as we celebrate our technology, we are also frightened of it. We don't know where it is leading us. It seems to create for us problems that we simply cannot solve. It's a long time since the days of the 19th and early 20th centuries, when people like H.G. Wells and many other popularisers of science were telling us that science was the real religion for the future; that science and technology would solve all our human problems and enable us to live the kind of life we want to live on earth.

Even as recently as the 1960s, we had the same burst of confidence in our technology, celebrated by John F. Kennedy on his inauguration day when he promised to put a man on the moon within a decade. Our own Harold Wilson talked about the 'white heat of the new technology' which was somehow going to raise the nation to a new level of greatness.

Today, however we are much more inclined to question where our technology is leading us. It seems as if we are not leading our technology but that it is leading us. What are we to do with the new achievements with genetic engineering? Are we really now to be made responsible for the kind of human beings we are going to allow to exist in the world? Who is wise enough to make those decisions? We seem to be led by a power that we cannot control. The former head of the European Commission, Jacques Delors, used a vivid metaphor when he said that it seems as if the world is like a plane on an automatic pilot; nobody knows where the pilot has been programmed to go and nobody knows how to unlock the pilot. We seem to be fixed on a plane headed for a destination that we do not know and cannot control. So we ask the question, "Where shall wisdom be found?"

We know the difference between cleverness and wisdom. We know the difference between the power to do what we want to do and the wisdom to know what is worth doing. I sometimes think that one of the most poignant illustrations of our dilemma is provided by our modern television. If you go and stay in a hotel in the United States, there will be a TV in your bedroom with 30 channels to choose from; if you ever waste your time trying all the channels, you will find that you have a choice of 30 different brands of rubbish. Isn't it strange that the incredible wizardry of satellite television, with all the amazing achievements of technology that make it possible, is used to deliver a cataract of trash into our homes. Where shall wisdom be found?

The same problem faces us in our political and social life. There is a constant conflict in our economic order between human needs and human wants. It often seems that our economic system is geared to satisfy any want, however crazy. Yet it leaves fundamental human needs unmet. How do you decide between needs and wants? If we were rational people, we would want what we need to bring us to our true goal, to the true end of our journey. But we are not allowed to know what the true end of our journey is. Not so long ago, every child in a Scottish school was taught, as one of the first facts to be learned, that man's chief end is to glorify God and enjoy him for ever. That is what we are made for but no education authority would allow you to teach that as a fact in a school today. That's 'just a personal opinion'. We have no public truth about what is the end for which we exist. What is the purpose of human life? Therefore what are the things that are worth desiring? What are the things worth putting our technology to serve? Where is that wisdom to be found?

We are all part of a society that has been shaped by the great change that took place roughly 300 years ago in the public life of Europe. For more than 1000 years, European thinking had been shaped by the Bible which gives us a clear picture of God's purpose for human life, a picture which is known to us by revelation through Jesus Christ. But in those terrible religious wars of the 17th century when Christians were fighting each other over their different understandings of the Bible, things changed. There was a great revulsion against the whole idea of revelation and men like John Lock, in this country, arose to say, "Look, there is a better way. Forget about these divine revelations. Nobody can be sure about them. Use your reason. Study the facts. See what is actually the case and then use your reason to relate the facts to each other so that we understand this world that we live in." That seemed so reasonable and rational that it has been the solution adopted for the last 300 years. "You can have your religious ideas if you keep them to yourself but don't bring them into the public area. Don't bring religion into politics. Don't bring ideas of divine revelation into the world of science."

However, there is one very great snag. There is a great deal that we can learn from observing the facts and using our reason but there is one thing that the use of reason and observation can never tell us. That is the purpose for which things exist. For those 1,000 years before, it had been accepted that the way to understand something was to know its purpose. But our modern world has eliminated that and believes that the way to understand something is to use observation and reason. If for example, you were someone who had never seen a clock and found a clock lying on the ground, you could use your powers of observation and reason to find out completely how it works. You could work out what causes which wheel to move, why and how far. But how would you know what it is for? Is it for decorating the sitting-room or is it for throwing at the cat? What is it for? No one can answer that question except either the designer of the clock, or someone who is accustomed to clocks and knows what they are for. When you move from studying the way it works, to asking the question, "What is it for?" you move on to a different logical level.

We could use another illustration. A neurosurgeon can examine the workings of the brain and learn how the incredibly sensitive nerves and synapses in the brain function but even the most spectacular extension of the powers of neurosurgery would not enable the surgeon to know what the man was thinking at the time. That is a completely different logical level.

That same distinction of levels runs right through all our knowledge. If there was time to do it, I could show you how the different sciences work on different logical levels. Physics deals with the basic atomic structure of things. Chemistry deals with the way the molecules combine in various ways. Chemistry depends upon physics but you cannot replace chemistry by physics. So it is with the boundary between chemistry and mechanics, or between mechanics and biology. Similarly, you cannot replace sociology or psychology, by biology. Each of these levels of learning has a distinct autonomy but not an absolute autonomy.

If that is true, then it must surely be that the highest level of all, is the level where the purpose of things finally resides –

namely, in the mind of God. That must be the highest level. Not that theology would interfere with, or seek to control, the other levels of learning but that none of them would be complete without that final level. If you ask, "How can we know the purpose for which the world exists?" the answer can only be: "If the one whose purpose it is tells us." So to exclude divine revelation from the field of public knowledge as Europe did 300 years ago, is to exclude the possibility of knowing whether our life has any purpose at all.

The second consequence of that is: if you do not know the purpose for which a thing exists, you cannot say whether it is good or bad. You cannot use the words, 'good' or 'bad', of anything unless you know what it is for. When I was a school-boy, there was a big World Boy Scout Jamboree at Anfield Park in Liverpool. Scouts from all over the world gathered. Just about that time, there was a new product unleashed upon the world called Shredded Wheat. One morning during that camp, Shredded Wheat was issued to all the units for breakfast. At 10 o'clock, there was a complaint from the Nigerian Scouts: "These pan-scrubbers are no good." If you don't know what a thing is for, you cannot use the words, 'good' or 'bad'. If there is no public doctrine about what a human being is for, then there is no way by which you can say that some kind of behaviour is 'good' and another is 'bad'. You cannot use those words. So we don't use those words. We don't talk about good and bad. We say, we have 'different values'. That's where we are now.

We here, thank God, are witnesses of the fact that God has made his purpose known. We are witnesses through what God has done for us in Jesus Christ, to the fact that this whole world is not a meaningless mindless machine but that it has its origins in that glorious communion of love and joy which is the holy Trinity – Father, Son and Holy Spirit. This whole created world is an overflow of that love so that there might be a theatre for God's glory. We have been put within this universe to shape it according to God's plan in order that at the end we may share in the joy, the love and the peace of the divine being. We are here as witnesses to that fact and that is our witness to the world. Note two things about what I have said:

Firstly, when we talk about God revealing his purpose, we are not just talking about the communication of some information. As we know, it is by the costly act of the atonement wrought in Jesus Christ, that he has reconciled us from our alienation so that we cannot only know, but also love and serve the purpose for which God has created the world. We are not just talking about information. We are talking about incarnation, invitation, reconciliation, about God drawing us into his own purpose of love.

Secondly, when we speak this way, some of our contemporaries will accuse us by saying that this is just a leap of faith. "You can't show any reasons for it. It's just what you think. It's just an irrational action of faith," they say. What shall we say to that? I think we can say three things. The other day I was trying to communicate the gospel with a young man, who said, "Well, that's just what you think." I said, "Well, of course it's what I think. Can you know anything without thinking?" There is no way of knowing except by using our minds which are limited, creaturely minds. The second is that we can turn upon our questioner and say, "Tell me what you believe," and it will not be difficult to show that it rests upon commitments which cannot be proved in advance. Thirdly, this is not an irrational leap into the dark. It is the response to a personal call. It is the Lord saying to us, "Follow me" and we follow. If we imagine that there is something more reliable, more fundamental upon which we can rest our lives than what God has done for us in Jesus Christ, then one has to say that that is simply an illusion. We believe, because we have been called by the mercy of God in Jesus Christ and by the power of his Holy Spirit in his community, to bear this witness. There are no grounds upon which we can be accused of being irrational.

So here is the answer to the question, "Where shall wisdom be found?" As it is given in this chapter of Job: "The fear of the Lord is the beginning of wisdom." That means – to know the Lord, to love him, to fear him. That is wisdom. That has two consequences, one negative and one positive.

The negative consequence, as I have already hinted, is that we have to unmask, de-mythologise, all the claims to wisdom that rest upon some other foundation. The world is full of claims to knowledge, many of which are simply illusions. We have to be ready to be sceptics. People always think of sceptics as those who doubt the Christian religion. But why should that be so? I am a sceptic because I doubt an enormous amount of what is daily handed over to me on the radio and in the newspapers. I am a sceptic about an enormous amount of what is simply taken for granted in our public life. For example, that 'the main business of a nation is to increase its gross national product'. Or that 'the main purpose of human life is to express oneself and develop oneself'. There are many other things that one could mention that are nonsense but which are simply accepted as truth.

The positive thing is that we accept a calling to 'bring every thought into captivity to Christ'. We read in the letter to the Colossians, a wonderful passage about Christ as the cornerstone of the whole cosmos, the cause and the cornerstone of the world. "Christ the beginning and the end, Christ the one who holds all things together, Christ the one in whom all things shall finally be made one." To acknowledge that, sets us on a tremendous pilgrimage of re-thinking all our thoughts in whatever sphere. We're not talking here about religion. We're talking about the public life of the world – its economics, its politics, its science, its culture, its art, its music, everything. We're talking about bringing every area of human life into captivity to Christ.

Now that is a very big task. It calls for everything that we have to give. It calls for our working together with those in the same sector of public life so that we can pray together about ways in which the Lordship of Christ is to be manifested in this or that sector. It means that we do not withdraw into a private world as the secular world would like us to do, where we keep our religious beliefs to ourselves and do not allow them to get out into the public world. It means that we abandon the sort of timidity which so often makes Christians apologetic in the face of what are supposed to be the assured truths of some secular science.

It is a call to be extremely bold. It is a costly warfare because it exposes us sometimes in very dangerous situations, to the powers of this world. But, as Paul says in the letter to the Romans, "I beseech you, be not conformed to this world, but be transformed by the renewing of your minds that you may know what is the good and perfect will of God." That 'renewing of our minds' is our calling. It demands everything that we have. It demands that we help one another in doing it and it demands that we call upon all the resources of the Holy Spirit to strengthen us in our service. Therefore our whole life in the public sector will be a provisional manifestation of that glory – the glory of the triune God, the glory which is his purpose for the whole cosmos, the glory which he has revealed to us in Jesus Christ and of which he has given us a foretaste in his Holy Spirit. To him, Father, Son and Holy Spirit, be praise and glory for ever.

"He's chosen the weak because they don't have anything except Jesus."

Jackie Pullinger-To *on ministry with the poor*

All they asked was that we should continue to remember the poor, the very thing I was eager to do. (Galatians 2:10)

When, in this passage, the early church was sending Paul and Barnabas out to start a new church, they gave them one piece of advice. I'm very interested in this piece of advice. If you were sending out a team to church plant or to start a new mission somewhere, what would be the piece of advice you would give? I'm very interested to find that the piece of advice here was this: that they continue to remember the poor. Now, this is fascinating because of all the things that they could have added like, "Keep the people tithing," or "Remember prayer is most important," or "Don't forget to break bread," or whatever. The only extra advice for this couple who were going to plant where there had been no previous planting was they should remember the poor. I wonder why. What I hope to share with you is the fact that one of the reasons we are asked to remember the poor is that it is for our benefit.

You see it's a paradox. Many of us, when we think in terms of being involved with poor people or difficult people or delinquent people, imagine that it is going to cost us. Most of us feel threatened because we feel that some demand is going to be made on us which is greater than that which is going to be made on other people – therefore this ministry becomes optional. People say, "Oh, Jackie's got a mercy ministry." I don't like the term 'mercy ministry'. You see, I believe that all of us, as part of loving Jesus should be involved with the poor and that this is not optional. I believe one of the reasons this is so is that it keeps us passionately dependent upon the heart of God and that's a mercy.

I want to suggest that ministry with the poor is not an optional ministry for 'those poor people who are going to have to suffer for the rest of their life'. It's a privilege for those who will accept it and it is the greatest, because it is what Jesus did. Look at I Corinthians 1. This is what I call God's bias:

> Brothers, think of what you were when you were called. Not many of you were wise by human standards; not many were influential; not many were of noble birth. But God chose the foolish things of the world to shame the wise; God chose the weak things of the world to shame the strong. He chose the lowly things of this world and the despised things – and the things that are not – to nullify the things that are, so that no-one may boast before him. (I Corinthians 1:26-29)

He's saying to them: amongst you there are not many who've got good education by human standards, or who come from good families, or who know the right people, or who would get things done. We see from Scripture that it isn't that there won't be any well-educated people in heaven; it isn't that there won't be any who come from good families or there won't be any with influence in the world. It just says that there won't be many. The majority are going to be the others. That's another reason to minister with the poor because they are easily going to be the majority in the Kingdom of God.

In the world, we do it the other way around. We look for those that we think would influence people. We look for those that we think have leadership qualities. We pick those that look good. I see from Scripture that the Lord's done the opposite – always. He's picked the least. He's chosen the weak, the hopeless, those of no account. Why? Because they don't have anything else except Jesus. Many of us look at it like this: we say when we are praying about who might next come to the

Lord, "Wouldn't it be super if so-and-so came to the Lord. He could influence so many people."

It's not necessary. God doesn't need that kind of influence. He needs the poor in spirit because they can be filled with his. He doesn't need those who are influential in this world because they'll use their influence instead of his. He may choose to use some of those people but it will not be because of their influence. It will be despite it which is what Paul, of course, learned. And it is what he says in Philippians 3:

> If anyone ... thinks he has reasons to put confidence in the flesh, I have more: circumcised on the eighth day, of the people of Israel, of the tribe of Benjamin...; as for legalistic righteousness, faultless. But whatever was to my profit I now consider loss for the sake of Christ... I consider them rubbish, that I may gain Christ... (Philippians 3:4-8)

He says, "If anyone has reason to boast in this world I have: I went to the right school, I was in the right family, got the right qualifications, theological school, the whole bit." Then he goes on to say, "But now I consider that which was to my profit, loss for the sake of Christ. I consider them rubbish." And the word in Scripture is much ruder than rubbish. He says, "I consider all that good family, influence, education and training as..." and it's a very rude word, it's ruder than dung. When he chose to lose the importance of all those things, then God may or may not have used them in his ministry. But he didn't need them.

God needs men who are desperate for him and who are desolate without him. That's why, you see, there's a paradox throughout. Satan tried to get Jesus to do it the opposite way around, right at the beginning of his ministry. Satan said, "Now have a look round here. You can rule." And in terms of the world, he could have ruled. He could have had a quick empire which would have looked rather better than three years of work, ending up with $11^1/2$ disciples who ran away. That was the temptation – to take control in the way men take control.

He resisted the temptation and said, "No, I'm going to do it God's way."

Why would we think there is a better way to rule the world than the one which God, in his wisdom, planned before time? It's through dying that men come to life. It's through the giving up of our lives. Mostly it is going to look foolish.

One of the things I encourage our people with is this: I say it is worth your whole life to minister to one old man the love of Jesus. If he swears at you for 20 years and you still go on loving him, that's worth your whole life, even if he doesn't come to Christ. Because that's what Jesus did for us. That's the heart that you minister in and of course, if you minister with a heart like that, the world will be won. He's chosen the weak because they don't have anything except Jesus.

"Jesus says, 'Will you give me your lunch?'"

Jackie Pullinger-To *on how God multiplies what we give*

The mystery of this particular ministry is that it multiplies grossly unfairly. It's like the loaves and the fishes. I often think about that little boy who was on the Mount with Jesus and those 5,000 men. I think about that little boy giving his fishes and his loaves. I think he thought he was giving his lunch to Jesus. He couldn't have known what was going to be done with it. We can see the figures and percentages of the starving in the world today and we feel threatened. We say, "I can't cope with that", and we do our little bit.

But Jesus says, "Will you give me your lunch?" That's all. The whole lunch. And when we share our whole lunch with him, 5,000 people are filled fit to bursting. That's how it works. It is the most illogical ministry I know. The multiplication is grossly out of proportion to the effort and heart that's put in because I think it has an ingredient of Jesus's heart. Personally, I think that the quickest way for world evangelism is through the poor. I'm absolutely convinced of it.

So where do you start? It is not a question of, "How do I help Ethiopia" or "Let's make a collection and send it to Jackie in Hong Kong." We don't want that. I'd be terribly disappointed if that was your response. I'm not saying we don't want your money but I don't want your collection instead of your broken heart for your neighbour. You just start with the one, and then there'll be another and another.

You know that the Lord has told us to heal the sick. We receive the power of the Spirit and we pray for the sick. When they're not healed, we go on praying for some more sick until we understand better spiritually how the Lord will work through us. We believe his promise anyway, whether the results we see are immediate or not. It is the same with ministering to the poor and feeding the hungry. You have to start somewhere. If we don't practise it, we won't get better at understanding how the Lord works it. One of the things I am absolutely certain that we as Christians are going to have to practise for the world to be saved, is multiplying food. I know you've practised casting out demons and healing the sick. Have you practised multiplying food?

Now, I am absolutely serious. Because if we wait until Christians have redistributed their wealth – our wealth – or the world has got a bit fairer in sending food wherever it's needed, still millions will have died. What would you say if you happened to be in a place where there are thousands of people and no food? You have to believe that the Lord has enough. You have to believe that it's perfectly all right to share what you've got by giving Jesus your lunch, and they'll be fed. But maybe he's not going to start you on those things right now.

Maybe he's going to start you on some little practices. That will be possible if we can get free from the fear of sharing what we've got, in case we don't have enough left.

Some years ago, a whole lot of Vietnamese refugees were put on an island in Hong Kong and this particular island had no water and no food. There were 6,000 and we heard from somebody that these people had no food and drink. As soon as I heard that those people were dying, I knew we had to do something. So I said to one of my colleagues, "Would you please ring up the government" – who were looking after the refugees – "and ask them how we can help." She came back and said, "The government were not very impressed by our phone call and said they don't want Christian do-gooders sending a little aid. They said that if you send oranges, you should send 6,000 or there will be a riot. And don't just send oranges once; you need to send them every day. Also, if you are going to send oranges, you must arrange your own transport." It is four hours by sea from Hong Kong.

So my colleague came back and said, "Shall we call a prayer meeting about this to see if we should do it?" I said, "No, we don't need a prayer meeting. They are our neighbours. We'll send 6,000 oranges daily from tomorrow onwards." You are supposed to help your neighbour. I then went and spoke to our accountant. He said, "If we send 6,000 oranges a day according to the money that we have, all of us will be starving within three days." All I can tell you is that we fed them for two months. I don't know how it happened. All I know is that money came in for the oranges; it came in and it went out so quickly. This is what it means when it says the right hand doesn't know what the left is doing. This is how it works.

Months later those refugees wrote to us. They knew what we'd done. We hadn't been allowed to preach the gospel, by the way. We didn't send little tracts with the oranges. We prayed over them, and those Vietnamese knew that they came from Jesus. How it worked, I can't tell you because actually we must be the poorest church in Hong Kong. But that's why we're the richest.

In the end, they moved the refugees to another place and they were OK. There was water and food. We didn't have to do it any more. The embarrassing thing was that we had, by this time, started an account called the 'Orange Account'. We ended up $100,000 over, so we gave it all to Ethiopia because we saw in the paper that there were people dying there. So you see how rich we are.

"Would you mind if I lay down on your bed and slept?"

Jackie Pullinger-To *on recognising our poverty*

I remember one time, there was one particular man, and I was really tired. I was actually exhausted. I said, "I'm really sorry, but I'm terribly tired. Would you mind if I lay down on your bed and slept?" So I lay down on his bed and slept. It was really nice because I was so tired. You know, after lying down on his bed I could do anything with those men because I was one of them. It was not a hard thing to do. It didn't matter that it was dirty cardboard and it smelled. It was his bed and he was awfully pleased to have something to offer me. It was very easy for him to receive prayer and rice because he could give me his bed. That is why I say that if we can recognise our own poverty, then we can minister with the poor.

"The Lord has answers to all this. Otherwise, I would have left years ago."

Chris Woods *on Christian leadership in an urban priority area*

Neither of my churchwardens had a telephone until a year ago. People don't have telephones where I live. To communicate in my parish, you have to go round and see them and if they are not there, you just have to go round again. It's very good for your figure. Now both church wardens have phones but one of their phones only takes incoming calls and you can't dial out on it. That's better than nothing. Those suffering the effects of poverty have no cars, no driving licences, no holidays, no credit, no telephones. One of our churchwardens, Eddie, has been out of work for 15 years. Before doing this job, I had never met Englishmen who didn't have a driving licence. If you have a driving licence, you can borrow a fellow Christian's car but if you haven't even got a licence, you're stuck and you are even more dependent upon somebody else. Some have no bank accounts and therefore no credit so they go to loan sharks for money. They borrow £100 and pay back £180 two months later. That's the nature of the loan shark game and it's very real. Broken limbs are the penalty for not paying up.

I had a woman come to my house with one of her six children. She was a widow whose husband had dropped dead walking out of the betting shop at the age of 43. She had come to Christ and while she was talking to me, her child ate her way through an entire packet of Penguin biscuits, one after the other. Meanwhile, her mother sat in my study, begging me for money to pay her rent. I said, "What's the problem?" and she told me that she gets her money from the social security on the Thursday and the rent man comes the next Tuesday. Of course, she should have put aside the money for the rent but she can't budget for five days ahead. She said she knew it was not a question of shortage of money. "It's just that I can't organise it," she said. Of course, we are all perfectly organised with our money, aren't we?

Then there is the effect upon the physical environment of living in an urban and industrial area. There is poor housing, heavy traffic, industrial pollution, factory chimneys, self-inflicted litter. Local authority decisions are taken by officials who do not live locally. When you are powerless, people take authority over you. This means that decisions are taken which vitally affect people – even about their houses and yet they have no power to overturn those decisions. There is widespread vandalism with wrecked playgrounds and excrement on swings. We had a car burned out in the yard behind the church. Our living room is right on the street and once two drunks fell off the pavement into the room through the window. When you hear running footsteps at 10 o'clock at night, you know something is wrong. On one occasion, a car had been picked up bodily and been tipped right over on its side. You may be feeling angry. It's the devil doing these things which makes us feel angry.

St Helens was identified in the *Daily Mirror* as the sickest town in Britain. There is widespread heavy smoking on top of the industry and traffic pollution. People live on a poor diet of junk foods. I've known a child who at midnight, ate five Mars Bars at one sitting. I've seen many children, including five year olds, with blackened stumps for teeth right to the gums. There are enormous numbers of grossly overweight people. It's desperate. Children start smoking at the age of nine. Other addictions like gambling (betting shops), glue sniffing and drugs are rife. We've been burgled over 20 times in the Vicarage. We've now got iron bars over the dining-room window which is where they get in. They need money to fund their addictions.

Then there are the video nasties. I had to go to a house where the six-year-old boy was suffering from what they called 'behavioural problems' at school. He was hitting people violently with rocks. I went to the house because I knew the mum vaguely – she is a single mum. This child was watching *Child's Play 3*, the video nasty which was linked to the James Bulger murder and to the murder of a 16-year-old girl in Manchester who was tortured for a week, then burned to death with petrol. In *Child's Play 3*, there is a demonic doll called Chucky and this child was watching the video right through, rewinding it back, watching it again and again. At the local school, he's called 'Chucky'. He has behavioural problems!

One of our sons had four bikes stolen in 16 months; then the garage where we kept them was burned down so that was the end of that. We now keep them in the house. There's a pub across the street called the Glass Barrel but the local name is the 'Blood Tub' because there have been three murders in there. I've buried a man who had his brains beaten out outside the 'Blood Tub'. There is a lot of domestic violence and many refuge centres for battered wives. I've buried three children run over in the street: a five-year-old who was run over playing on his own at 10.30 at night; a nine-year-old who was out even later was knocked over by a huge truck and another one during the day. These children run wild in the streets from the age of three upwards. They are completely unsupervised – and there's heavy traffic where we are. We had one 10-year-old who smashed 193 roof tiles on the brand new nursery school wing of the local primary school. He was the one who burned our garage down.

When we first arrived 17 years ago, my wife and I thought we must begin a youth club with snooker and so on. We'd already met one or two local families so we called about 10 or 12 together in an old disused school which we thought we might use as a venue. Within 40 minutes, they'd all fallen out with each other to such an extent that they got up and walked out except for me and one married couple. These were local parents trying to get together to organise a club for their children and they couldn't even have 40 minutes together without getting into such a state that they had to get up and walk out. It's coming from a lack of love and manifestation of love in their lives. Some of the people who have been Christians for ten years or so understand; they will tell you it is the presence of unforgiveness, unresolved hurts, bitterness, rejection, abuse from their childhood. If you tried to be a bit breezy with some of them, they wouldn't speak to you for six months. People are not secure so they can't take a joke at their own expense. I buried a man who had been married for 35 years but his wife, living in the same house as him, had not spoken to him for the previous 18 years before I took his funeral. Not a word. She had taken some vow, 'I'm not going to speak to you again' and didn't.

So we've had to work right through that. We've now seen people who have come to Christ becoming secure in the love of Jesus and the love of their fellow Christians. We have some wonderful times and there are some beautiful changes and healings in those areas. The Lord has answers to all this. Otherwise, I would have left years ago.

"At that stage, I used to say as we passed the plate around for the offering, 'If you haven't any money, take some out!'"

Chris Woods *on some of the principles, values and priorities important to his ministry in the UPA*

*A**ccepting people where they are.** So many churches expect newcomers to behave like Christians as soon as they step across the door of the building. If they are smoking as they walk in, everyone throws up their hands in horror. But what do we expect? We must accept people as they are and then we will gradually seek to see change in various areas. Smoking comes about number 147 in our list of don'ts! One of our top ones is, 'Stop punching your wife.' That's a good one to start with after you've become a Christian!

We have 164 adults on our electoral roll, so it's not a big church. We grew fastest when we moved out of our church building (when the heating broke down) about ten years ago. We had to go into our church hall to worship. It was quite a convenient building and it didn't have that 'churchy' feel about it. They felt much more at home and they came in smoking, eating crisps and drinking Coke through the service. We didn't mind at all. At that stage, I used to say as we passed the plate around for the offering, "If you haven't any money, take some out!" and our giving kept on going up and up. It was amazing really. After I stopped saying that, the giving stopped going up as fast.

Discipling, Healing etc. We encourage people in the church to minister to one another and pray together to develop more maturity in Christ. Any number of one-to-one talks are going on at any given time during the week.

Intimate Relationship with God. It is important to value highly an intimate relationship with God through personal and corporate prayer and worship, walking in his ways and the fear of the Lord.

Experiencing God together. We seek to allow the Holy Spirit to move amongst us in restoration, healing and conviction of sin. John Wimber has helped us to see that the works of the devil are sin, sickness, demons and death, and the works of Jesus are forgiveness of sin, healing of the sick, driving out demons, raising the dead.

Freedom and Openness. We put no value in being legalistic or religious. We value flexibility and the desire to be open to God, to one another and to change. We also value integrity and accountability. One of the marks of brokenness in a Christian is flexibility and willingness to change. People who are totally inflexible are certainly not people who have been crucified with Christ, you'll find.

Servanthood. We have had to discourage those coming in from outside who have tried to run things rather than being prepared to serve. If you mix middle-class and working-class people, the former always dominate the situation. Many of the working class are so used to being told what to do, they sit on the church council and are quite happy to be dominated but I think that God is wanting to empower them to take decisions and be responsible. We have a very clear mutual accountability in recognising how we treat one another. We've had times of repenting of sin and attitudes.

Perseverance, Patience and Commitment. We value expressions of 'long-term faith', as in many areas of life and ministry, results are not quick.

Our first priority is **Worship and Prayer.** We spend more time, energy and money worshipping God than on any other activity. **Discipleship** is our second priority. There is no point in having fellowship together if people are going to fall out with each other. Discipleship comes before fellowship so that we can see some growth in Christian maturity. Then, when fellowship does take place, people are going to have a good time. **Fellowship** comes third.

Then there is **Outreach**: At a recent Alpha course we were electrified when 53 teenagers came in off the streets, straight into the church to see what was going on. We fed them tea and cream buns and we're taking them on! We're wrestling with the implications of how to lead this particular group but we praise God for them. It seems as if they've just come. They're local kids but they've never been near the church before except to throw stones at it.

Our other priorities are: pastoral care, training, counselling, inter-church unity, wider UK outreach and overseas mission. We believe that these priorities are helping us fulfil our purpose for being here, according to our stated values.

"I do not want South Africans ever to be able to say, 'We did it by our own right arms'...but rather that people would know it was the living God who intervened."

Michael Cassidy *on God's miracle in South Africa*

In the year King Uzziah died, I saw the Lord seated on a throne, high and exalted, and the train of his robe filled the temple. Above him were seraphs, each with six wings. With two wings they covered their faces, with two they covered their feet, and with two they were flying. And they were calling to one another: "Holy, holy, holy is the Lord Almighty: the whole earth is full of his glory." At the sound of their voices the doorposts and thresholds shook and the temple was filled with smoke. "Woe to me!" I cried. "I am ruined! For I am a man of unclean lips, and I live among a people of unclean lips, and my eyes have seen the King, the Lord Almighty." Then one of the seraphs flew to me with a live coal in his hand, which he had taken with tongs from the altar. With it he touched my mouth and said, "See, this has touched your lips; your guilt is taken away and your sin atoned for." Then I heard the voice of the Lord saying, "Whom shall I send? And who will go for us?" And I said, "Here am I. Send me!" (Isaiah 6: 1-8)

God gave us a mighty historical miracle during the South African elections. In 1994 we in South Africa lived through one of the most awesome and divine happenings in modern history; we moved overnight from the lip of the canyon of catastrophe into the most peaceful and crime-free five days in our history as our first democratic election took place, bathed in the miraculous love and reconciliation of the living God.

We do want to thank so many British Christians who stood by us, who prayed for us and expressed concern. There were many also who gave financial help. Maybe you would like to continue to pray as we are not out of the woods yet by a long way. There was an editorial in a major Sunday newspaper recently which said, "South Africa's transformation in one short year has been universally hailed as a miracle. It is hard to refute those who believe that events have been guided by a higher power who, still today seeks our harmonious co-operation towards a better future for all." That's from the *Sunday Tribune* in KwaZulu-Natal.

It is that divine involvement in the run-up to the April 1994 elections that I have sought to chronicle in my book (*A Witness For Ever*, Hodder and Stoughton) so that it might indeed stand as a witness for ever. The title is taken from Isaiah 38 where the

Lord speaks to the prophet and says, "Inscribe it on a tablet and write it in a book for the time to come as a witness for ever." I do not want South Africans ever to be able to say, "We did it by our own right arms. We have gotten ourselves this victory" but rather that people would know that it was the living God who intervened. If we start saying 'we' did it, it will be morally, socially and politically perilous.

The hard fact is that we need the Lord as much now or more than ever before. We have escalating and intensifying tensions and confusions that are building up once again, especially evidenced among young people in our country. And in KwaZulu-Natal the tensions between ANC and Inkatha Zulus could plunge us into a Rwanda-type scenario. Actually in the troubles in Rwanda in 1994, our team leader and his family were all lined up and shot. Other members of our team and Board were murdered. Some of our Board members were shot, our offices ransacked, our vehicles dsetroyed, computers taken, typewriters smashed. But our AE team there is again rising out of the ashes, praise God.

But now in South Africa itself the need we all have is for a fresh vision of God himself. We need to see who he is, to see what he does, to see how he does it, to see what he does and doesn't want us to do. We need to see what he expects from us, to discover where he would lead us, to discover what he wants us to say, to be and to do. There is always an interplay between the being and the doing. The doing has to come out from the being. Here especially do we need to grasp the truths of Isaiah 6, where the breakthrough vision of God came "in the year that King Uzziah died" (v 1) – in other words at a critical political moment when one dispensation was giving way to another. Always and everywhere, in times of change, bereavement or loss, marital trauma, financial pressure, social or political upheaval, emotional, psychological or spiritual crisis – when things we have held dear have died or are threatening to die, we need, like Isaiah, to see the Lord.

Our need is not to see Mandela or Clinton, or the House of Commons or the United States; our need is to see the Lord afresh. Our need beyond that is not to focus on Asuza Street or Toronto, Jonathan Edwards or history but on God. In South Africa, it is time for us to turn from our political miracle to the Lord behind the political miracle. Hosea 10:12 says, "It is time to seek the Lord." How then did Isaiah see this Lord? First of all, he saw him sitting on a throne high and lifted up. He lifted up his eyes to the throne and saw one who was a King, one who was Sovereign, one who was in charge and powerful and he had to bow down. It is a very important thing for us to grasp that God is Sovereign; he is in charge. I don't care what the problem is in your life today, God is in charge. He is not about to lose it in any way. He has his ways which are not human ways.

In our situation in South Africa God did something very unusual through a brother from Kenya named Washington Okumu. Few had really heard of Washington Okumu in South Africa. Everybody was looking to Henry Kissinger and Lord Carrington and other household names. Yet it was Washington Okumu, a Christian diplomat, through whom the breakthrough in human terms came in South Africa. It was Washington Okumu, a man of God around whom we had put a tremendous amount of prayer and who had taken time to invest in relationships and who had done things quietly behind the scenes, whom God used. I think that God looked out over South Africa and said, "Where is the weakest and frailest initiative and let's use that in some special way." It was precious how God just broke past all the big ones. We cannot rely just on politicians. We have to look to this living God. Isaiah saw him high and lifted up. He saw a God who was worthy of worship. Whenever I go into a church, I can monitor what's going on by the worship. We need a fresh spirit of worship throughout the world based on a new vision of who God is.

Isaiah saw the Lord as, "Holy, Holy, Holy". It's easy for us to trivialise the holiness of God or to trade on his mercy and forgiveness and to forget that the Holy Spirit is indeed the *Holy* Spirit. He wants to make us holy people. Jesus Christ is not just the baptiser in the Holy Spirit, he is the baptiser with fire. He seeks to burn away and scorch away the dross, impurity, hypocrisy, insincerity, laziness and lack of integrity which is rampantly in all of us. So it is absolutely, fundamentally and critically important that we see God afresh as one who rebukes our sinfulness, our idleness, our willingness to allow our society to go to hell while we just have a wonderful time as Christians. I believe it is so important that we take our faith right out into the societal arena and into the market place.

There were tremendous consequences for Isaiah once he had seen this Lord afresh. First of all, a deep conviction of sin and a need to confess came to him. He said, "Woe is me, I am lost." I believe we are all such lost people. That parable in Luke 15 [the lost sheep, the lost coin, the prodigal son] is not three parables, it is one. One parable in three parts on lostness: the sheep by nature, the coin by circumstances and the son by choice. Isaiah felt lost when he saw the holiness of God and he realised his sinfulness. He said, "I am a man of unclean lips." So often what is destroying us is what we say. It's our bitterness, our cynicism. Maybe it's not just a matter of how we use our lips but how we don't use our lips. We don't use our lips adequately in prayer or praise or testimony. Isaiah was aware that he dwelt in the midst of a people of unclean lips. If you don't think that you live in a people of unclean lips, turn your TV on any night. In South Africa, we are buying the whole garbage of what's coming in from the neo-pagan West. We need to repent of what we allow to be said from our own lips and from public forums in the land.

Then Isaiah, as he saw his lostness, called on God. We need to have a sense of, "Yes I too have sinned, failed, am lost." As soon as we come to that place, we are ready for a fresh experience of forgiveness. God can put away the past, or whatever is in the garbage department of your life or mine, by the precious blood of Jesus.

Then Isaiah had another wonderful consequence; he heard the voice of the Lord (v 8). We need to hear what is being said by God. There may be some of you who have been touched, blessed, had inner healing and all of that. But now you need to be ready to hear the voice of God afresh as he comes to us and he says, "Who will go for us and whom shall I send?" Many people are doing this, that and the next thing and there is no one to send.

But the Lord may be wanting to get our attention and have us hear his voice anew saying to us: "Go evangelise, seek the Spirit of God afresh, take a fresh stand for biblical morality and ethics, go prevent abortion on demand, go and speak to the government, go to the educationalists." "Who will go for us, whom shall I send?" was the divine cry heard by Isaiah. Most wonderfully he replied, "Lord here am I. Send me." When we come to this God and we get a fresh vision of him, we will surely hear his voice afresh and he will be saying, "Whom shall I send? Who will stand in the gap for me in this place?" Will you do it? Will you say today, "Lord here am I. Send me?"

And as you respond, don't forget also to speak prophetically to your nation, to kings, queens and prime ministers. It's not just enough for you to come to the Lord. Your nation must come to the Lord. If you don't bring your nation to the Lord then Britain is going to go down the tubes. South Africa is going to go down the tubes if we don't hold it for Jesus Christ at this time. Jesus said, "When the Holy Spirit comes upon you, you will be witnesses unto me in Jerusalem (where you are), in Judea (the area round about you), in Samaria (ie the people with whom you normally have no dealings) and to the uttermost parts of the world." That's the Holy Spirit's work. As the Holy Spirit comes upon us and is released within us, so then rivers of living water will flow out from our innermost beings to touch people around us. That's what he wants and as we go out we will be saying several things in our testimony.

What sort of things are we going to say? I believe that in this neo-pagan, effectively atheistic age, the first thing we have to do is to say that *God is there*, is alive, is real because we are in an environment that is atheistic. The Bible says, "The fool has said in his heart, there is no God." Atheists can't be consistent with their presuppositions. I heard about a man thundering from his soap box in Hyde Park Corner and he said, "My great-grandfather was an atheist and so was my grandfather. So was my father and thank God, I'm an atheist too." Well, we for our part have to say that God is really there! We have to be a witness to a God who is. Then, we have to say that *God is powerful.* He is in charge and he can do incredible things. He is powerful to change us in our hearts through the new birth as he blesses us, sanctifies us, gives us inner healing, fresh experiences of the Holy Spirit and blessings in the supernatural. God has power. Jesus said, "I have all power on heaven and on earth." There is no problem we can bring that our Lord Jesus cannot deal with.

This God to whom we come is also moral and holy. The ten commandments are not the ten suggestions. We need to make that very clear to our society and seek constantly to re-embrace it ourselves. God's laws are written not only in the Bible but in the fabric of the universe. Then I believe we have to say that this God is the God and Father of our Lord Jesus Christ. 1 Peter 1:3 says, "Blessed be the God and Father of our Lord Jesus Christ." See what Jesus is like and you know what God is like. He is all power in heaven and on earth. "Without him was not anything made that was made." I remember when I saw Niagara Falls that it was a religious experience. When I saw that, I worshipped. When I saw Victoria Falls I said, "Jesus you are marvellous." When I snorkled in the Great Barrier Reef, I tried to praise God mightily underwater and nearly drowned! Before you die, you have got to try and see the Great Barrier Reef and you will never believe what God has put under the sea – the marvels of those coral reefs. Jesus is the creator of all that. Praise his name. He is all powerful. Our creator Lord.

Last year, when we called the huge pre-election prayer meeting in South Africa, people wanted to call it the 'Interfaith Rally'. But we said, "No, it's got to be the *Jesus Peace Rally*." Then some tried to make it an 'Interchurch Rally' but we said there's no power in the word 'interchurch'. The power is in the name of Jesus. Indeed, there is no other name given among men whereby we may be saved. As we come to the cross of Jesus, there is forgiveness no matter what anyone has done. I don't care what you have done. The blood of Jesus cleanses from all sin. Then there is the resurrection to tell us that he is alive. And Pentecost tells us that the Holy Spirit is available to fill, flood and transform, and take us all to a new place. Let this be the year and the moment we all see the Lord afresh. The consequences could be awesome not only in our personal lives, but in our churches and in our nations.

"If God called you into finance and you become a preacher, that isn't the highest calling in the world. It's actually to reject the highest calling."

Steve Chalke *on working in the world*

The essential quality of a leader that marks him or her apart from those they lead is simply this: they know where they are going; they are able to see the future; they have that gift of foresight and direction. A leader by virtue of the name *has* to be going somewhere. What we have been called to do corporately is to lead society. We are 'Jesus' for the UK and for the world.

Everybody has got dreams of where they want to be headed, but a leader isn't someone who just has an idea about what is going to happen in the future – a leader is someone who knows *how* to deal with the future. Without leadership we become victims of what's happening; with leadership we become architects of our own future.

We slowly tend to get out of touch with what is really happening out there. Every time I get in my car, if I listen to a worship or a ministry tape and that is my whole diet, I slowly become isolated from the culture that I am called to reach and understand. Listen to your tapes but also to your radio. Listen to what is going on in the world around you. Be good judges of the times – that is what leadership is all about. Winston Churchill said, "Always listen to your best friends and your worst enemies because they are both telling you the truth about yourself from a slightly different perspective."

We need happy hearts but we need heads that are wise and full. The following passage is called 'The Jesus Manifesto'. Jesus wants to sum up all he is going to be doing in the next three years. This is what he is about: "The Spirit of the Lord is upon me because he has anointed me to preach the Good News to the poor. He has sent me to proclaim freedom to the prisoners. The recovery of sight to the blind. To release the oppressed. To proclaim the year of the Lord's favour for people." (Luke 4:18-19)

If this was Jesus's manifesto, his job description, how he summed up what he was going to spend his life doing, then we've got to take it in and think about it hard. Why? Because now we are Jesus for the world. We are the body of Christ. Jesus's manifesto must be our manifesto. Otherwise we're about something other than what Jesus was about.

All service is Christian service. At Oasis we run a training course for Christian youth ministers. It's a two year course, accredited by a university. Someone came to do the course from a church I know. His cousin at the same time went and did a youth and community degree, basically the same course as we run, but he went to do it with Suffolk College where it is a purely secular course. Throughout the last two years, the entire church has been praying for the guy that's been in our Christian youth and community course. At no point, has anyone even acknowledged that the other guy is on a course. Why? Because we've divided the world neatly into Christian and non-Christian bits.

So we say, "This is to do with 'spiritual' things. It's not about terrible things like housing or homelessness. It's not about issues of economic problems or fair trading." But Jesus comes along and says, "You've got it all wrong because you've tried to divide up my world just like your culture tells you to."

But it isn't that way. These verses are true spiritually and they are also true politically. They are true socially and economically. They are true materially and emotionally. These verses are true at every level and the task of the church, if it is to be like Jesus, is, "That you are anointed by God's Spirit so that you can bring good news to the poor." That's what it means at every level so that you can proclaim freedom, proclaim recovery of sight to the blind.

Biblically, the truth is this: if I am called to preach, I'd better preach and that is the highest calling in the world as far as I am concerned because God called me to be it. But, if God called you to be an engineer, if God called you to be a pilot, a nurse, a doctor, a plumber, a builder, or to work in advertising, in graphics, in law, business, industry; if God called you into finance and you become a preacher, that isn't the highest calling in the world. It's actually to reject the highest calling.

All we get is a little bit more withdrawn from the world, all we get is a little less salt in society and one more useless preacher who is going to bore people stupid for the next 50 years when he or she should be out there in the world.

If God called you to be in the police force, stay in the police force and strive for excellence there because we need people who will understand that God has got something to say about law and order, justice and righteousness. If God called you to be in the world of finance, don't just say, "I'm doing my bit but actually I help out at the Sunday school at HTB. That's where I *really* serve God." Get in that bank, stay in that bank, strive for excellence in what you do and apply Jesus's ethics. Apply all that the Bible has to say to that world in which you work.

You may ask, "Well how do I do it? It's really hard." I know it's really hard. If it was easy we would have cracked it before. I am not a banker, I know nothing about banking; I can't even keep my own bank account in order. But there are some of you in this room who are good at banking. What the Bible is telling you is that you are to be Jesus in that world of finance because we are to be light and salt. We are to bring truth at every level. We are to set free those who are financially oppressed. We are to drive back unrighteousness in every level. Then it will transform what you do from Monday and Friday into something you must strive for excellence in.

What about all the people who are out there, working? Are they serving God or not? Of course they're serving God and they are on the cutting edge. Prayer meetings tend to be to pray for the pastors: "Let's pray for the full time workers of the church, they're on the cutting edge." Everyone prays for them and that is great. Then you pray for the missionaries serving in Africa and places like that. So you pray for the church leaders and you pray for the missionaries. Nobody even knows where everybody else works, let alone prays for them!

We, as pastors, ministers, curates, are *not* on the front line. If you read Ephesians 4:11-12, you discover there that Paul says we are on the back line: "Some evangelists, some prophets, some pastors, some teachers ... all of these people are there to equip the church for the work of ministry." They are there in a back-up role. They are there to equip the church for its service on the front line. Where is the front line? It's in the local school, hospital, bank, – that's where the church is working, where the front line is. The problem is that the whole church has been looking the wrong way for too long. We are utterly confused. We think the back line is the front line and we think the front line hardly exists at all.

Our church leaders have made two errors. Our first is in our assessment of the situation. We have over-estimated the role we play and under-estimated the role that everybody else is supposed to play. The next error is the error of empowerment. Because when you don't notice that the front line actually is the front line, you don't bother to empower the people. You don't pray for them, you don't equip them. So there's a lady sitting in the church, she's got enormous issues at work, hiring and firing people. Nobody even knows what she does. They don't acknowledge this is the front line.

We need TV presenters but the presenter is at the end of a very long chain; we need Christian producers, we need directors, editors, researchers, programme controllers, people in PR, people running agencies. That's where we have to invest our strength. When someone gets into the world of media or the world of arts, it's not, "Oh well, there goes another one..." it means there is another one on the front line. When someone gets involved in the world of finance, education, nursing, medicine, there's another person on the front line.

A boy called John at 14 years of age, heard a sermon on mission work. He said, "God, I don't really want to be a missionary, I want to be a builder. Even though no one has mentioned that building is of any importance to you, and it seems utterly unimportant, I'd really like to be a good builder. If I make it, I promise you Lord that I'll invest everything I've got for you."

His name was John Laing. Laings became the biggest building company in the world. London Bible College was built on John Laing's money. Colleges and churches all over Great Britain and around the world were built because one 14-year-old boy knew that he wasn't a write-off because he didn't want to be a preacher.

The poem, 'The Gas Lamp Lighter' by Robert Louis Stevenson, gives a mental image of this gas lamp lighter wandering the streets, slowly punching hole after hole in the darkness until the whole place is ablaze with light. That's what we're about. That's what Jesus is talking about. You are called to punch holes in the darkness. You are called to serve him, called to give your best to your King.

Jesus said, "The spirit of the Lord is on me and he has anointed me to preach good news, to set free the oppressed, to proclaim liberty to the captives, to announce that this is the year of the Lord's favour." Spiritually, materially, physically, emotionally, economically, politically, we are to bring the good news, to bring justice. That's what we're about. We are all on the front line.

The power of the Spirit

"Paul ... would not have understood a Christian faith in which the experienced life of the Spirit was not the key to every dimension of that life."

Gordon Fee *on the Holy Spirit in Paul's epistles*

Iwas born and raised in a Pentecostal preacher's home. He was a unique pastor in the American Assemblies of God in that he read good books and preached out of the good, hard work that he did on the biblical text. I look back on that and recognise that I had the unique experience of being exposed to good biblical teaching in the context of which the power and the presence of God was welcomed, sought and desired.

Even so, the idea of being an academic was about as far removed from my personal history as one could get. The Pentecostals saw the dangers of young men and women on fire for God going away and getting their heads screwed up somewhere and losing that passion. I knew that, whatever else, I didn't want to lose that passion. On the other hand, when Jesus said, "Love the Lord your God with all your heart and with all your mind." I always felt it was a bit of a shame that we Pentecostals loved God with all our hearts, but cut off our heads and threw them away, as it were.

One day, when I was in my fourth year of pastoring a church, I walked into my church study – it was right after lunch – and picked up the mail. Amongst it was a copy of *Christianity Today* and I was sort of glancing through it when I came across the name of a fellow minister of my own denomination who had written a letter. It was one of these typical Pentecostal letters, excoriating *Christianity Today* for its egg-head Christianity. He concluded his letter with these words: "I would rather be a fool on fire than a scholar on ice!"

In that moment the Holy Spirit spoke into my heart and I dropped my head on my desk and I wept and wept. The Holy Spirit said, "There are two other options." I had seen fools on ice, but I had never seen a scholar on fire. In a deep calling and commitment I said, "Lord, if that is possible, I would be one of those."

So the pilgrimage has been a long one. I received my PhD from an American university in 1966 in New Testament Studies and became the first person from the Pentecostal tradition who had received a university PhD in Biblical Studies.

About eight years ago, in response to an invitation by a group of friends, I sat down to write an article on the Pauline texts with a particular emphasis on the Spirit in those letters. And I discovered two things.

First of all, I discovered that there was no book on this subject anywhere. It didn't exist. That surprised me to no end because you would think that everything in New Testament scholarship had been done by the year 1988. What new rock would you look under for something new? But there was no book on the Holy Spirit and Paul. There were books on Pauline theology that had very small sections on the Spirit. There were books on the Spirit in the New Testament that had their appropriate Pauline sections, but there were no books on the Spirit in Paul. Later I was invited by a publisher to beef up that article. I had no idea this book was going to go as long as it did. I figured a 500 page book. I had no idea a 900 page book was coming out of this.[1] The working on that material changed my life.

The idea that you can talk about Paul and not talk about the experience of the Spirit is a scholarly absurdity. What makes

[1] *God's Empowering Presence*, Paternoster Press

Paul tick is the experience of the Spirit. If that doesn't objectify very well, that is our problem. You can't read Paul very long without recognising that it is the experience of the Spirit that lies right at the heart of things.

That doesn't mean the very heart. Paul does not say, "For me to live is the Spirit." He says, "For me to live is Christ."

But the Spirit has been marginalised both in New Testament scholarship and in Christian theology – particularly when it comes to Paul's theology.

In traditional Christian theology (particularly from the Reformation), we pay perfectly decent lip-service to the Spirit. But we keep the Spirit at a safe distance in our creeds and theology to keep him out of the life of the church.

We want to be in control of the life of the church and the Spirit won't always let us do that. That makes us nervous!

So what developed in the church is the quietest view of the Spirit. To use the imagery of Moses from Exodus: that God was not in the wind, the fire, the earthquake – but in the still small voice.

Now what absolutely intrigues me is that that passage from the Old Testament has become the major theological centre for understanding the Spirit in most Protestant theologies.

That *Old Testament* passage, mind you. And nobody even blinks doing that kind of hermeneutics, but we are comfortable with the still, small voice. And in doing so, we have marginal-ised the Spirit in our understanding of Paul. We just haven't been fair to the apostle.

We have run out of steam by being primarily Binitarian and not Trinitarian. We believe in the Father and the Son, and believe in the Holy Spirit, but do not recognise the central role the Spirit plays in Pauline theology.

I came to the conclusion (and I might be quite wrong) that the key to this generally quiescent attitude towards the Spirit lies in a failure to take seriously the Spirit as person and presence.

The Spirit, after all, is a word to which we don't relate very well. We think of the first two persons of the Trinity who, because of the incarnation we know and image in relational terms as father and son. There is a kind of general fuzziness in the church with regards to the Spirit.

Many years ago when I was first teaching in a denomination school, a Pentecostal student came to one of my colleagues and said, "God the Father I understand. God the Son I can relate to. But the Holy Spirit is a grey oblong blur."

For Paul, the Spirit was none other than God's personal presence. He never thought impersonally of the Spirit. We do, but he didn't.

Some say, "We believe that the real reason for the Spirit is to produce the fruit of the Spirit" and the others are saying, "We need to have the gifts of the Spirit." But we need both. What kind of reading of Paul can you imagine would ever bring about that 'either/or'? Paul wouldn't understand us.

For Paul, the Spirit was an experienced empowering reality. Paul would not have understood most historic Protestantism. I know that is unkind but it is true.

The reason he wouldn't have understood it is because he would not have understood a Christian faith in which the experienced life of the Spirit was not the key to every dimension of that life.

Look at the way Paul argues in Galatians chapter three. He begins with the experienced life of the Spirit. He says in verse two, "This alone I want to learn from you. Did you receive the Spirit by works of the law or by the hearing of faith?"

Do you understand that when he says, "Did you receive the Spirit?" that's where most of us would say, "Did you get saved?" "Did you become a believer?" That is his way of talking about becoming a believer. He doesn't understand Christian faith that doesn't think first in terms of "Did you receive the Spirit?"

This was a visible and experienced reality. It is certain by the way the rest of the argument unfolds. "Having begun in the Spirit are you going to come to completion by the flesh?" (which in this case is a play on circumcision).

Our English translations tend to fail us here. Verse four – Paul does *not* say, "Did you suffer so much in vain?" [as it is translated in the NIV]. There is no evidence of suffering anywhere in Galatians. This is the Greek word for experience. He says, "Have you experienced so many things in vain?" Then, typically, he says, "If indeed it is in vain" – and he knows it isn't.

Now listen to what he has done. He has appealed to the beginning point of their conversion. "Did you receive the Spirit?" Then he says, having begun that way, "Do you become now completed by works of law?"

So he goes back and reminds them of their conversion in-between. "Have you experienced so much in vain?"

Then verse five turns all of this into the present tense. Therefore, based on the appeal to experience in verse four, Paul says, "He who supplies you with the Spirit and works miracles among you, does he do this by adherence to works of law or by the hearing of faith?"

This was so presuppositional for Paul, he doesn't even bat an eye. He simply begins by aiming straight at their experienced life.

Now that is the passage that reminds me of how far we are from them in understanding New Testament Christianity. I am not a Pentecostal who is talking about, "You have got to get baptised in the Spirit or you are not with it."

I am talking about what is absolutely essential, at the heart of Christian faith. That is the experienced empowering reality of the Spirit of the Living God. That is not some addendum, some extra.

"Nothing else can take the place of presence."

Gordon Fee *on the presence of God*

I would like to look at the understanding of the presence of God as a motif in the Old Testament. That begins in Genesis when, because of human fall, the presence is removed. God doesn't walk with them any more.

Presence is a delicious word because it points to one of our truly great gifts. Nothing else can take the place of presence – not gifts, not telephone calls, not pictures, not reminding mementoes, nothing.

Ask the person who has lost a lifelong mate what they have missed the most. The answer invariably is presence.

When we are ill, we don't need soothing words nearly as much as we need loved ones to be present. What makes shared life, games, walks, concerts, outings and the myriad of other things, so pleasurable? Presence. God has made us this way. What we lost in the garden was the most significant expression of presence of all and that is the presence of God.

Can you understand that when you read the Psalmists they do not cry out to go to the Temple and sacrifice? They cry out to go to the Temple because God is there. "My soul longs for the Living God."

They long to come and appear before God. "Oh, a day in your courts is better than a thousand elsewhere." They long to be in the presence of the Living God.

Friends, this is what makes the fall of Jerusalem and the exile such a tragedy. Because with the fall of Jerusalem and the destruction of the Temple, the Jewish people lost the place of the presence.

They were no longer identifiable as a people of the presence. They did become a people of the Book – we can thank God for that. But they were not a people of the presence. They thrust this longing for the presence right out into the future.

The key passage, the one that I want you to note now, is Isaiah 63. Because at the end of the prophesies of Isaiah, we have this incredible thing that has taken place in Old Testament understanding, namely that the presence of God in the Tabernacle and the Temple is none other than the Spirit of God himself.

I pick this oracle up in Isaiah 63:9: "He became their Saviour in all their distress. It was no angel or messenger but his presence that saved them. In his love and mercy he redeemed them. He lifted them up and carried them all the days of old. Yet they rebelled and grieved his Holy Spirit."

That is the language Paul picks up in Ephesians 4:30 "Do not grieve the Holy Spirit of God." That comes right out of that text. They grieved the Holy Spirit.

Then you go down to Isaiah 63:11 and he says, "Where is he who brought them through the sea (This is speaking now of the presence) with the shepherd of his flock (which is Moses)? Where is he who set his Holy Spirit among them?" (That is referring to the presence) Finally in v 14: "Like cattle that go down to the plain, the Spirit of Jahweh gave them rest." (Referring to their entering into the land).

The fulfilment of these Spirit expectations are crucial to Paul's understanding of what it means to be the people of God in the new covenant.

"We get to cooperate with God in what he is trying to do..."

Sandy Millar *on working with God in the ministry of the Holy Spirit*

> Then he took them [the disciples] with him and they withdrew by themselves to a town called Bethsaida, but the crowds learned about it and followed him. He welcomed them and spoke to them about the kingdom of God and healed those who needed healing. Late in the afternoon the Twelve came to him and said, "Send the crowd away so they can go to the surrounding villages and countryside and find food and lodging, because we are in a remote place here!" He replied, "You give them something to eat!" They said, "We have only five loaves and two fish." But he said to his disciples, "Make them sit down in groups of about 50 each." The disciples did so and everyone sat down. Taking the five loaves and two fish and looking up to heaven he gave thanks and broke them. Then he gave them to his disciples to set before the people. They all ate and were satisfied and the disciples picked up twelve baskets full of broken pieces that were left over. (Luke 9:10-17)

This story, amongst many others of course, is a basis for the ministry of the Spirit. It was a foretaste, in a sense, of what Jesus was doing and was going to do, and still does. It is fascinating to consider the agonies the disciples must have gone through. I don't know at what point it dawned on them that there was a link between the 5,000 men – plus women and children – and these five loaves and two little fish. I don't know whether they all came to the same conclusion at the same minute but somewhere along the line, it must have occurred to them, "He's going to ask us to feed them with these five loaves and two fish!" Which is sure enough what he did.

The point I want to make is that at every stage, two things were operating. One was that Jesus – graciously, wonderfully, kindly – was inviting them to cooperate with him if they wanted to. Secondly, he was helping them to see that without him they would fall flat on their faces. You know, I know and everybody knows that you can't feed 5,000 men with five loaves and two fish. What I love to imagine is the moment at which that truth dawned on them.

When we talk about a ministry of the Spirit, we're talking about cooperation with God. Jesus was saying to them, "We have a wonderful opportunity here. Cheer up, smile, we've got 5,000 hungry people, and we've got five loaves and two fish. Why don't we feed them?" They said to him, "You feed them." They each thought it was up to the other to feed them. Jesus was saying, "Why don't we both feed them. We'll do it together." So it's cooperation coupled with an understanding that without him we can do nothing. That's why we are so constantly vulnerable. But it's also why the only thing worth holding out for is the ministry of the Spirit.

On a trip to Poland some time ago, I met a dear lady. I should think she was about 75, dressed in black and with a wrinkled brown face. We were in a conference hall of about 3,500 people. We were praying for anybody who appeared and people kept appearing and asking to be prayed for. It was at one level a frustrating thing and, at another level, an opportunity to rediscover the sort of feeling of the feeding of the 5,000. All we had to do was to pray for them. I can only say that I haven't seen God work in that way for a very long time, if ever. They kept coming and we prayed for them and God did something. Now I didn't do anything except pray for them but I think that was my function because cooperation is the essence of the ministry of the Spirit.

This lady came up and the interpreter said, "She wants you to pray for her left eye," which was twitching. We hadn't much time because there were a lot of people; I looked at her left eye and I asked the Spirit of God to come and do whatever he wanted to do for her. Into my head came the next question, "How long have you had that?" She replied, "About two years." I said, "Did something happen two years ago?" and she said, "My husband died."

So as I prayed the Spirit down on her, it became perfectly clear to me that her twitching left eye was a symptom of a broken heart. Into my head came God's promise, "I will bind up the broken hearted." That is his ministry and we get the privilege of sharing with that ministry. I said, "Lord, would you bind up her broken heart." I can only tell you if you'd seen that woman as I left her, you would have seen that she was with the Lord. There was nothing I had done. I left her in seventh heaven! She was together with God which is what God wanted. He's jealous for her. She's his. She's of formal Roman Catholic background and he loves her and was working in her heart, doing something in her and for her. Her eye stopped twitching when her heart was healed. It was a great blessing to me just to watch and to be able to leave her safely in the hands of the Lord and move onto somebody else.

It was like that in the feeding of the 5,000, if I can put it humbly in that way. We get to cooperate with God in what he is trying to do. It's all the way through the Bible. You remember Moses? Moses was continuously being called to cooperate with God. You remember when he got to the river? God said to him, "Moses, hold out your stick over the water." Why? Doesn't it sound stupid? Why should Moses hold his stick out over the water? I don't know. If I'd been Moses, I'd have said, "Well Lord, why don't you just part the water and get on with it because the Egyptians are coming, and I've got better things to do than stand here." By which he would mean of course, "I don't want to look foolish. There's a big river here and I've got a stick, and I'm just standing. I know that you told me to do this but they don't know you told me, they think I'm just doing it, trying to pretend that this is what you do!"

But somehow there was a dynamic going on that if he did that, God would do the rest. You see it again and again with the saints, the Old Testament prophets, the disciples. They got to cooperate and still get to cooperate with what God is trying to do. At the end of the day, Paul seems to suggest, that is the basis of Christian ministry. The kingdom doesn't consist of words. Paul says it's about power. It isn't that we're power hungry. We believe that God wants to change people and it's immensely frustrating to go on talking and for nothing to change. It's still pretty frustrating from time to time, but that is the basis and the essence of the thing.

I had been ordained for two years when a man who lived nearby, rang up and asked if he could come and see me. I said, "Yes, of course." He said, "I need advice badly. I've just lost my job. My wife has just told me that she can't bear it any longer and I've got two children at schools which I don't know that I'll be able to pay for. I'm very worried." I thought to myself, "And you want to come and see me?" I said, "Lord, you've got about about five minutes because he's coming from number 67." I had nothing to set before him. That is the context for every understanding and receiving of spiritual gifts. I have nothing to set before them. This woman has a twitching left eye. Well, I can't heal twitching left eyes! It is a matter of cooperating with the Lord.

"Do we really believe that what we read in the Bible is true and actually works?"

J. John *on the Word and the Spirit*

Did you know that when Charles Darrow brought the first prototype of the board game Monopoly to Parker Brothers in 1934 they laughed him out of their offices? They said, "That is really a stupid game! It is never going to sell. It is far too complicated. It takes far too long to play. We are experts on games and we have found 52 major flaws in this game."

But Charles Darrow said, "Well, it doesn't matter what you say, because I believe in it. I will market the game by myself." Within one year, one department store sold 5,000 sets. It was such a hit that Parker Brothers confessed, "Well, maybe we were a little too hasty." So they signed a contract with Charles Darrow – who became a multi-millionaire – and they have since sold over 100 million sets of Monopoly in 54 countries and in 26 languages.

What have you got faith in? What have you got confidence in? Do we have confidence in Jesus Christ? Do we actually have confidence in the Word of God? Do we actually have confidence in his Holy Spirit? Do we really believe that what we read in the Bible is true and actually works? Charles Darrow had confidence in a game. Even though he was turned down, it didn't matter. He had confidence and he persevered and he saw all that fruit.

I have been reading recently how we got the Bible. It was so good to be reminded of people like John Wycliffe, the Oxford theologian and 14th-century English religious reformer, who first translated the entire Bible into English in 1382. Wycliffe was not acclaimed by his contemporaries. Three decades after his death, Wycliffe's bones were dragged from their grave and were burned. What had been Wycliffe's crime? He had dared to translate the Bible into a language people could understand. It had been Wycliffe's passionate desire that everyone should be free to read the good news of eternal life through faith in Christ. His hand-copied Bible was circulated widely and eagerly read – all before the days of printing.

William Tyndale began the printing of the New Testament in 1525. It was the first English translation ever to be made directly from the original Greek. Copies of Tyndale's testament were smuggled into England in barrels. They were widely distributed and eagerly studied. But then church leaders ordered that they should all be burned. In May 1535 Tyndale was imprisoned. He was tried for heresy and condemned to death. A decade earlier they had burned the translation. Now they resolved to burn the translator. Tyndale went boldly to the stake still defending his belief that people should have a Bible in their own language. On 6 October 1536 he was tied to a post and strangled, after which his body was burned.

Through the centuries courageous men and women have treasured the scriptures and have struggled to preserve and distribute them amidst great opposition. The Bible is a precious heritage and a priceless gift. The once forbidden book now lies open to each of us to feed from. Isn't that remarkable?

In Psalm 119, verse 105, it says, "Your Word is a lamp to guide me and a light for my path." Many people find the Bible very difficult. But I have been a Christian for 22 years and I have worked something out: if the Bible says 'no', it means no. If the Bible says 'yes', it means yes. If it doesn't say 'yes' or 'no', God doesn't mind. If our Bible is falling apart then we won't be.

In the Bible, it says seven times, "This is the Will of God." One of those occasions is in Ephesians 5:17-18 when it says,

"...Understand what the Lord's will is: do not get drunk on wine; instead be filled with the Holy Spirit." What does it mean to 'get drunk'? It means that you are under the control and influence of alcohol.

What does it mean to 'be filled with the Spirit'? You are under the influence and control of God. Have you noticed that when someone is drunk they have a lot of courage? When you are filled with the Holy Spirit you have a lot of courage. Have you noticed that drunk people love to sing? When you are filled with the Holy Spirit you love to sing.

I went to India a couple of years ago. I had a terrible time. I came back with dysentery. I was so ill that when Killy [his wife] picked me up at the airport I could hardly push the trolley. I vowed that I wouldn't go back to India.

When the Kansas City prophets came to HTB [a conference on prophecy in 1991] I was at the conference. After the first day, I thought, "I really want to meet with God. I am going to get up early and seek you Lord before I go to the conference." The next morning, I got up. I had my Bible. I thought, "Oh Lord, it is so early in the morning and I don't know what to read." So I closed my eyes and opened it at random – something I usually tell people not to do! I opened my eyes and read Isaiah 54:2-3: "Enlarge the place of your tent, stretch your tent curtains wide, do not hold back; lengthen your cords, strengthen your stakes. For you will spread out to the right and to the left."

When I got to the HTB conference, I was asked, "Would you like to meet these prophets?" I said, "Yes." There were about five of them. I sat there. One of them got up and said, "I have got a word from God for you: Isaiah 54:2-3. 'Enlarge the place of your tent, stretch your tent curtains wide, do not hold back; lengthen your cords, strengthen your stakes. For you will spread out to the right and to the left.' Does that mean anything to you?" Hmmmm. Then the next one got up and said, "You are going to go to India. When you go to India it is going to change your life." I said, "He's not a prophet because, if he was, he would know I do not want to go to India."

That was five years ago. I went to India this year. It has radically changed my life. The first conference I went to had 15,000 people. Eight thousand were seriously sick. I went to another conference and there were 200,000 at this conference. The word multitude has taken on a whole new meaning. The sick were healed en masse. The paralytic got up and walked. The eyes of the blind were opened. There was worship, preaching and signs and wonders accompanied the preaching of the Word.

This is the God of the Bible. We can root all of this into the Bible. The Bible brings Jesus to us and makes him alive and real. What Jesus did then, the Holy Spirit continues to do now. He wants to stretch out his hand today and nourish us and inspire us and do things deep within our hearts. And touch us spiritually, emotionally and psychologically and physically.

Recently my son Simeon broke his leg and had it in plaster. We went for a check up with the doctor two weeks after he had the plaster on to see how it was doing. The doctor took two X-rays and said, "I am sorry, but we are going to have to take the cast off and re-set it because the leg has moved. We are going to have to do it today, otherwise the leg will set and we will have to break it." He said, "I just need to pop out, but I will be back in five minutes."

I said, "Simeon, we've got five minutes." We laid hands on his legs and this was no 'messing about' prayer. It was "Lord Jesus, fix this leg. Lord, sort his leg out now." Then the doctor walked in and said, "Let me just take one more X-ray." He took another X-ray, put it up on the screen and said, "W... Well, ... We don't have to take the cast off after all." I said, "While you were out I consulted another physician." He asked, "Who was that?" I said, "In the Bible he is known as the Great Physician." What an encouragement to Simeon and to me. That is our Jesus.

The great church elder, Tertullian, said in the third century AD: "The two hands of God the Father are the Word and the Spirit". The Word tells us that our Jesus did all this and the Spirit continues to do it today – in different ways. The will of God is that we be filled – intoxicated – with his Holy Spirit and that we be released to love and serve him in the world through word and deed.

"I don't think I've been to any real living, believing church where there were not prophetic people in the midst, placed there by the Lord Jesus."

Steve Nicholson *on prophecy*

Therefore, my brothers be eager to prophesy – 1 Corinthians 14:39

To me, prophetic ministry is nothing more than one more tool in the tool box of bringing God's kingdom and God's mercy to people. It's not the most important thing necessarily. It's not the thing we should focus on. In fact, its prime function is really to point us towards Jesus and to give us a greater revelation of who he is.

It was he [Jesus] who gave some to be apostles, some to be prophets, some to be evangelists, and some to be pastors and teachers, to prepare God's people for works of service, so that the body of Christ may be built up until we all reach unity in the faith and in the knowledge of the Son of God and become mature, attaining to the whole measure of the fulness of Christ. (Ephesians 4:11)

Jesus gives these gifts – and wherever there is a living, believing church, he does not cheat or short change us. I don't think I've been to any real living, believing church where there were not prophetic people in the midst, placed there by the Lord Jesus because he loves his church. He loves us. He cares about us. He wants to help us. He never intended that our lives should be bereft of that sense of the presence of God, and his working and acting among us.

The point of all this is of course, so that the body of Christ will be built up. He wants us to be stronger. He wants us to be more encouraged, to be more full of faith, to be healed. Even more important, it is to help us grow up in the knowledge of the Son of God. It's to help reveal Jesus himself – who he really is.

Paul says: In the church, "pursue love and desire spiritual gifts, especially that you may prophesy." (1 Corinthians 14:1) "Especially that you may prophesy?" Why? Because it is so beneficial. And in 1 Corinthians 14:3, he says, "But everyone who prophesies speaks to men for their strengthening, encouragement and comfort." It's important to keep in mind here in the New Testament, that the function of the prophetic gift is not entirely the same as the function in the Old Testament. New Testament prophets are not necessarily bringing judgement on the nations. Their main function is to do these three things: (i) to bring a strengthening, encouragement and comfort to the body of Christ; (ii) to build us up, to make us stronger in faith; (iii) to draw us closer to Jesus, to bring comfort and healing and restoration to us.

I've known something of prophecy all my life but it was fairly intermittent and not very strong. I'd heard stories about some of those folks down in Kansas City [where a strong prophetic ministry had grown] and my first reaction was like a lot of people, "Well, I'm never going to have anything to do with that!" So one day, God spoke to me and said, "Why are you judging people you have never even met?" So I started repenting of my judgements on people and then I began to find that somewhere inside, I was really frustrated being a leader of a church and always feeling like I was stumbling around in the dark in terms of what was really going, what was happening spiritually. Everything was always catching me like I was a blind man. I said, "Lord, you know, what is this?" and he said, "Well, you know you're blind. You don't have the bodily equivalent of eyes which is the prophetic ministry." So I started praying. I said, "Well Lord, then start releasing that."

A few months later, I started hearing about some of the things that started to happen. During that same period of time, I was asking God about the book of Acts. I was reading through Acts 2 and one of the things I tend to do when I'm reading the Scriptures is I'm always looking to find out: "What's in there that we're supposed to be doing or supposed to be experiencing that we aren't doing yet?" Peter says on the day of Pentecost that when the Holy Spirit comes, "Your sons and your daughters are going to prophesy and they're going to dream dreams and see visions." "Well," I said, "we believe the Holy Spirit has been poured out on us, so why don't you release the dreams and visions?"

A month later, I was saying, "Lord, that's enough now. Do you think you could hold it back a little bit? I've got more dreams and visions than I know what to do with." They started to come. The giftings, the dreams, the prophetic ministry was already there – already given by the Lord – but until I opened my heart to it we weren't receiving it. Boom! Then it came. It started to be released. It's very interesting all the many different kinds of ways it has helped us in the last few years. Sometimes, God uses prophetic ministry to equip the people of God to do ministry. A lot of times, what prophetic people will do is call out the different things that God has already given us confirming our ministries so that we have the courage and the strength to press through to do those things.

We visited a church here in England and I had a prophetic guy with me. We were in a meeting and a young man came in late and our friend looked up at the young man and said, "There's Philip the Evangelist." The guy's name was Philip and he had an evangelistic call on his life. Needless to say, it got his attention instantly. Here's this person he's never met, calling him by name and telling him his ministry. Then he went on about how his evangelism was supposed to happen in the political arena, that God was calling him to go into politics to be an advocate for the poor. It devastated him because that had been his lifelong dream. He had begun to think that it wasn't godly enough and was going to walk away from it. Just at that moment, through the prophetic ministry, God intervened and said, "Hold on, you're about to throw away something valuable."

It also helps people to understand how much the Lord loves them, how much mercy he has for them. That's probably the thing we see the most often. It is also, I should add, something that can be used to reveal sins. We have a very quiet, little Asian lady in our church. She gets dreams, and one time she came to us and she had a list of about 12 people. God had revealed to her the secret sins of these 12 people. She said, "What am I supposed to do with this?" We looked at each other and we said, "Well, if there is anyone from whom they would want to hear their secret sins, it would probably be from her because she's the least intimidating person on the face of the earth." So we told her, "We want you to go to all 12 people and just share it with them and then ask them if that's right and then pray with them." So she did and every single one was right. Every single person responded, repented and prayed with her. So those are some of the things that are the benefits of prophetic ministry.

Let me just add one more important thing. Scripture is pretty clear; if you read in 1 Corinthians 13, the prophetic ministry that we have is imperfect. In some ways, it's not that much different from any of the other manifestations of God's presence and power. We live in this time of conflict between the kingdom of heaven and the kingdom of darkness and there is inconsistency. We pray for people. We see people healed. But we also pray for other people and they're not healed. We see people respond to the gospel and other people harden their hearts. The same thing is true of prophetic ministry. We see breakthroughs, powerful things happen and yet, there are mistakes that happen along the way and problems. How do you deal with it? The answer is in 1 Thessalonians 5:9.

It says, "Do not put out the Spirit's fire. Do not treat prophecies with contempt." Why would he even have to write that? Because obviously sometimes, they didn't turn out right or they caused difficulty. So he had to tell them, "Don't throw it all away just because there's a problem. Don't treat prophecies with contempt. Instead, he says in verse 21, "Test everything and hold on to the good." So one of the things we've had to do is develop a certain set of testing rules. You allow for people to test the prophecy so that it's not used to control, manipulate people or hurt people. One of the things we always encourage over again is that we do not have secret prophecies, where a prophetic person takes somebody off in a corner and gives them some word. It should be open where the body can test the validity – where, particularly, pastoral leadership can help people sort them out and deal with them. If this part is good and this part is not good, keep this part, throw this away: 'Well, we're not sure about this one, let's just put that on the shelf for a while' and so forth.

"She just said over and over again, 'I had no idea there was so much love.'"

Steve Nicholson *gives an illustration of prophecy*

A few years ago, I was in another city and a woman came up to me – she was obviously just new in the faith and she'd had a rough life. I was praying for her nose or some physical thing and she felt a little better. She said, "Thank you" and as she was walking away, this thought came into my mind. The Lord said to me, "Tell her that the baby she lost is with me and everything is OK." My first reaction was, "You've got to be kidding! I'm going to tell her that? What if it's wrong? I'm not going to say something like that." But then the Lord pressed me. "You're going to say it." Then I thought, "Well, I'm leaving town."

I just said, "Well, there is just one other thing." She came back and I said, "I just had this sense that there is a message God wanted to give to you and it was this – the baby you lost is with him and everything's OK." At first, she just stood there in stunned silence and said nothing. Finally, she broke down and began to pour out the story of how ten years previously, she'd had an abortion. When she had come to faith, the one thing she hadn't been able to feel forgiven for, and she was carrying this crushing weight of guilt about, was that baby. She just said over and over again, "I had no idea there was so much love. I had no idea there was so much power." It just broke through all those things in one fell swoop and cracked her heart wide open to how much Jesus really loved her. He loved her enough to give her that message just when she needed it. That's part of the point of the gift of prophecy.

"Jesus wants a bride who is absolutely in love with him."

John Arnott *on receiving the Holy Spirit*

It took me years to fully discover that a relationship with God wasn't merely about discovering truth but more about romance. Have you heard that God is love? We are called into intimacy with him. That's what he is after. Jesus doesn't simply want a group of people that will serve him. He could have made robots to do that. He wants a group of people that will be absolutely in love with him. He wants a bride that truly loves him. Do you blame him for that? How many young men want a bride that will love them? I sure do. What's the purpose of being married if there is no love in the marriage? That is what renewal is all about. But I didn't understand it at first.

I would say to Carol my wife, "Why can't I receive like you do?" and she would say, "I think it is because you are controlling." She meant that I would look at someone on the floor laughing and say, "I don't want to do that." A controlling person is always negotiating, always setting the terms of what the Holy Spirit can, or should or should not do. How many of you know that God wants to be God? The Lord wants to be the Lord. The boss. So we need to come to him like a little child and say, "Lord, whatever you want to do, I trust you enough. If you want to humble me; if you want to take me out of my comfort zone; if you want to fill me with joy or peace, or make me cry or whatever – I trust you and know that you'll turn it to good. Do whatever you want to do in my heart." That is really quite a statement. It is really risky.

I would always analyse everything. Analysis is a form of control. "I won't go along with it unless I understand." How many of you have said things like that? What we're doing is putting our own ability to analyse and understand as number one. Yet we read clearly that the natural mind does not understand the things of the Spirit of God. God is saying his ways are not our ways. We need to come into the place of intimacy. Revelation 2 says a lot about intimacy. For instance, God says to the church at Ephesus, "You do not love me as at first." People will, on the other hand, do all kinds of things that they don't understand because it feels good. What about kissing? There's only one reason for it – it feels good. Don't let people accuse you of being experience-oriented. There's more to marriage than experience and loving, however. You get up and go to work whether you feel like it or not. There's a whole practical side. Jesus has called us to love the Lord with all our hearts, soul, mind and strength, to enter into that place of intimacy. When the Holy Spirit comes and touches people powerfully and they fall down and cry or laugh or shake, perhaps they're just having a wonderful time with him. It doesn't need to make sense. You can check the fruit of the life afterwards.

"If you are going to be in love with someone you can love them without holding their hand – but it is nice to hold hands."

John Arnott *on the importance of focusing on God*

Let me talk about receiving the Spirit's power. In my experience, my wife Carol, would always receive the Holy Spirit very easily. She would fall down on the floor and would not be able to get up sometimes. Yet her heart was so yielded to the Lord that when he came on her the last thing she would ever say was, "No Lord." On the other hand, I was very unreceptive and would say, "I'm just not given to that sort of thing." I had been in the charismatic movement for 30 years and I know what it is to be pushed over by zealous ministry team people and evangelists. I would be braced on the inside thinking two things: (i) "This guy had better not push me," (ii) "Lord, I want the real thing. If this is not you God then I'm not going anywhere." I found out much later that my focus was totally in the wrong place. If you are going to receive from God, your focus needs to be on him.

Carol was so able to give her heart and love to the Lord that he would come and touch her every time. Meanwhile, I'm there analysing and evaluating myself and taking a reading on my balance. I would be saying, "Is this you Lord?" On the one hand, we don't really care about the manifestations but on the other, they are most precious and wonderful and sensitive. It is a way of your heart being touched by the Lord so that you know that you are dealing with something real. In other words, if you are going to be in love with someone, you can love them without holding their hand – but it is nice to hold hands. It is nice to experience the intimacy of that other person.

There are two dynamics – fear and pride. Fear will put control in place to ensure that you protect your heart. The way out of that is through repentance and moving into faith in a loving heavenly Father who would not give you a stone when you ask him for bread. The other is a pride that would put control in place. The way out of that is through humility and vulnerability which will lead to intimacy. I found these two things have been very important to my own understanding, and in helping many other people break through into having an experience with God that was very real and precious.

When the ministry team come and lay hands upon you and you receive a 'blessing' through the laying on of hands, it is like a jump start. It will get you going when you need help from your brothers and sisters. But the ideal place to experience the Lord, is you and him alone with the door shut where you just pour out your heart to him in secret. The bottom line of receiving from God is that there is something that calls out to him from the depth of your being that says, "Father I need you. I need to know your love. I want you. I'll seek you. I'll fast. I'll pray. I'll look for you in the secret place." I've noticed it's so dependent on hunger.

"It had never occurred to me that God was vulnerable..."

John Arnott *on intimacy with God*

The Lord said, "I will cause all my goodness to pass in front of you, and I will proclaim my name, the Lord in your presence. I will have mercy on whom I will have mercy, and I will have compassion on whom I will have compassion. But you cannot see my face, for no one may see me and live." Then the Lord said, "There is a place near me where you may stand on a rock. When my glory passes by, I will put you in a cleft in the rock and cover you with my hand until I have passed by. Then I will remove my hand and you will see my back but my face must not be seen." It's a wonderful picture of Jesus here. If you want to see the glory of God, if you want a revelation of who he is, you must hide in the cleft of the rock. The rock, Christ Jesus, has been split open for you and if you'll hide in him then the Father's presence will pass by and he'll show his glory.

Before this move of the Spirit started, the Lord told us he wanted our mornings, so we put those aside and we would pray and seek him. We were reading this same passage one morning and my heart cried out, "Oh God, why are you so hard to find? I want to see your glory. I'm hiding in Jesus," and just like that, he spoke back and said, "Because when I reveal my heart to people, I become very vulnerable." That hit me like a ton of bricks. It had never occurred to me that God was vulnerable at all. As I meditated on what he said, I realised that when someone comes close to you in intimacy, they extend their heart and it becomes very easy to hurt that person by responding in inappropriate ways. I began to realise that every time I felt God drawing near to me, I'd get my shopping list out and say, "Lord, I'm glad you're here. We need a new car and we need money for this… etc." I'd realise how I had hurt him whenever he desired me to come near to him in intimacy.

We wept and repented and cried together that day. Then the Lord spoke again and said, "Many of my people have married me for my money." I broke down again and said, "Lord I don't want you for your money. I don't want you for your power, your blessings or your gifts. I just want you for you. I want to have an intimate relationship with you." If that's what you want, that's what the Holy Spirit is offering. It's going to cost you your sophistication, your pride, your controlling fears.

"It is truly a 'time of refreshing come from the Lord.'"

Sandy Millar *answers the questions posed by the recent move of the Spirit*

We are in a very exciting time at the moment. Many people are being wonderfully touched by God. It is truly a 'time of refreshing come from the Lord.' (Acts 3:19) People are finding Christ – Christians are discovering a new love and fresh intimacy in their walk with God, new boldness and sense of direction in their lives, forgiveness, freedom, a new love for the Bible, a new concern for those whom God loves, those on the fringe of society, the poor, etc. and in many other ways experiencing closer communication with God. So who can complain about that and what are some of the principal things that are said to be wrong with it?

Firstly: **I don't like some of the manifestations.** It is not always put like that. The objections are usually couched in more apparently objective theological terms e.g. God wouldn't cause someone to do this or that – moo, roar, roll, etc. God wouldn't cause it and it is happening – it can't have been caused by God and must therefore (so the argument runs) be being caused by the devil.

In the first place, we need to emphasise again that it is not principally the manifestations on which we rely to authenticate a work of God. Prima facie, we believe that this current move is of the Spirit of God because he is now responding to the same prayer that we have always prayed. For many years now we have prayed, "Come, Holy Spirit" along the lines that Ezekiel was commanded to do in Ezekiel 37:9. He has come and we have been able to watch the fruit of that over the years. Use whatever biblical test you want to use – the generosity of the church members; their love for one another and 'the brethren'; their collective desire to serve God through ordination and more locally; their zeal in evangelism. I speak as a fool (2 Corinthians 11:21) but thousands of mainly unchurched people are going on an Alpha course somewhere around the country and the world each week, and most (it is worth repeating, *most*) come to Christ before the course is out. Alpha is a work of the Spirit and like most other works of the Spirit, it takes time for the fruit to grow. Of course, some of the manifestations may be of the flesh. Occasionally (but in our experience, it is much rarer than people might think) some may be of the devil. But just as you wouldn't feel safe in founding a biblical doctrine based only on one verse, so it is equally unsafe to express very settled views about manifestations based on only one visit to the church – and some of our more confident critics haven't even done that. The manifestations vary from time to time. I think it was John Wimber who was quoted as saying that if the price we pay for all this increase in the fruit of the Spirit is an occasional 'moo', it is a price worth paying.

Secondly: **These things all ended with Jesus, or the Apostles, or at the end of the Acts**, and therefore they can't be of God. This argument is one of those I described earlier as following a well-known path. There have always been those who think that signs and wonders (spiritual gifts, as we know them) are not for today. What I would say though, is it is important for us to see that a great deal of the criticism that is levelled at this current move of God's Spirit is in fact no more than a repetition of old and well-rehearsed arguments against a ministry of the Holy Spirit as we have always understood it.

The issues remain the same – nothing has changed since so-called 'Toronto' arrived. We are convinced that all the gifts, ministries and fruit of the Holy Spirit that we see in the New Testament remain a priority for the recovery of the church today. They did not, and were not intended to end with Jesus.

Thirdly: **This recent move of 'God' originated with X or Y; they were connected with Z. X, Y and/or Z hold heretical views in other areas, ergo this recent move of 'God' is based on heresy and can't be of God.** I am calling them X, Y and Z because it isn't always clear that the names are the same. The fallacy of the argument lies in the fact that the blessing of which we are speaking, comes direct from God and not from X, Y or Z. In our case, we learnt of what God is doing in other parts of the world from Eleanor Mumford. She simply taught us. How is anyone to hear about something (e.g. the gospel) if no one tells them? That doesn't mean that what we received was an 'Eleanor blessing'. She told us what God is doing elsewhere; she raised our faith and expectation and then prayed for us that GOD would pour out his Spirit and bless us in the same way. This is not a movement of God's Spirit associated with any one or group of teachers – that is one of its noticeable strengths. It is part of something God is doing all over the world. We are naturally interested in what others are teaching or saying elsewhere, but we shall continue to judge this move of God's Spirit along recognized New Testament principles in the light of what we see here and by what people here are experiencing.

Fourthly: **When the Holy Spirit really comes, there will be repentance, not laughter.** Our difficulty with this is that we cannot be sure what the laughter is caused by. What if it is an expression of the joy experienced in heaven over a sinner who has repented? Certainly, it is undeniable that we have seen a great deal of repentance as part of the more obvious and immediate fruit of this movement of God's Spirit – reconciliations, apologies, repentance as seen perhaps, most obviously in the remarkable number of conversions in the Alpha courses. I suspect this question is really expressing an underlying uneasiness with laughter in church or possibly with laughter in the kingdom of God at all. It is perfectly true that laughter in the Bible often has negative connotations e.g. God laughing at his enemies.

So the question we have to ask is: is it so far-fetched to include laughter as an element in what is described in the Bible as, "an inexpressible and glorious joy" (1 Peter 1:8)? A banquet, a party with music and dancing ... (Luke 15:25)

I think not. Indeed, it is difficult to imagine an occasion of such a joyful celebration in a Christian setting which wouldn't feature a great deal of innocent laughter. So I think we come round full circle. Those who have experienced this touch of God's Spirit that inspires great and spontaneous laughter (including myself) have found it an immensely refreshing thing. It might not be the be-all and end-all of our Christian experience but it certainly is a wonderful antidote to some of what the Bishop of London called (in a different context) our 'po-faced' so-called spirituality. So let's keep laughing and let's keep crying but above all, let's keep close to Jesus Christ and to one another; let's make every allowance for our brethren who find these things difficult but yield to none in our gratitude for being alive in these times to see the beginning, as we hope and pray this is, of the answer to the prayers of so many Christians over so many years, who have cried out – "Oh God – revive your church."

"I had to tell him to see because I saw that in the Bible!"

John Wimber *on healing*

I remember I was in Johannesburg, South Africa, and a man came up to me that had been born blind. He couldn't speak English – he was an Afrikaner and his wife was interpreting – and he said, "I understand that you heal blind people." I was out of resources at that moment and I remembered this text and thought, "Well, I've got a little bit of faith," and so we started praying for him. We didn't know when to stop. We didn't have any rules and so we kept saying to him, "Do you see anything? Do you see anything?" and he said, "No, no, no." He kept saying, "no" over and over again.

Now, "no" for an hour is a drag but we just kept asking, "Oh God, please heal this man. Give him his sight." Then all of a sudden, it popped into my head that I had to tell him to see because I saw that in the Bible! So I just said, "See," and all of a sudden he blinked up towards the lights above. I said, "What do you see?" and his wife said, "He doesn't know. He doesn't know what 'see' is." I said, "Why is his head tilted up?" and he said, "Something's up there." I said through her, "What is up there?" and he said, "I don't know but I counted and there's eight of them." Well, there were eight lights, four on each side hanging up there. "What do they look like?" Wrong words – how would he know?

So I realised that there had to be not only language translation but imaging translation. The brain had to learn to see.

But his eyes began rolling and we kept praying for him and pretty soon, he started reaching out, touching cheeks and foreheads and bodies and you knew that he was beginning to see. All of a sudden, I got images of little babies reaching out, touching their toes and finding their fingers – all the things that little babies do and I realised this guy in front of us who was about 60 years old, was learning to see. I almost fainted it was so incredible. I started saying, "He's learning to see," and he was crying, "Yes I know, I know."

When you see something like that, you have one part of your mind saying, "This ain't happening. It can't happen," and another part of your mind saying, "It's happening, it's happening alright, but I don't know why." You don't feel good enough. You don't feel Godly enough, but God will use his people to do his work.

"We've equated knowledge of God with having God."

John Wimber *on the importance of expecting God to intervene*

One of the difficulties we have today in the contemporary church is that we're so loaded up with information and ideas about God that we think we have God. Do you understand? We've equated knowledge of God with having God.

Let me put it in another context. If I were teaching you about sky-diving and I had a big board, and drew diagrams, talked about aerodynamics and how to get your suit on, what to do when you're jumping and what altitude you need to be at, what the best kind of plane is and what the best kind of clothing to wear is, and everybody got all their notebooks full – then I say, "Well, now you're sky-divers."

Somebody might raise their hand and say, "But don't we do it? Don't we have to get up in a plane and put on a uniform and test this theory out?" and I say, "No, it's enough that you just know that you can." You'd say, "Wait a minute. I didn't come to take this course just to learn about sky-diving. I came to take this course to be a sky-diver."

That is the problem today. We have Christians who know about Christ. We have Christians who have a great deal of information. They can make all the diagrams and fill in all the blanks at the appropriate place but they haven't ever jumped out of an aeroplane. They haven't allowed God to touch them. They don't walk in a daily way in which there's communication and flow and reality and relationship.

You could say to me, "Haven't you been saying that to us for a long time?" Yes. That's really the only message I have. Anything we talk about comes to that. Because I believe that what we have in the church today are people who have a theology that's based in theism but a practice that based in deism. By and large, most Christians today are deists – we don't really expect God to intervene or interact, especially when we're in a high-rise place with the air-conditioning on. How could God get around in those places and accommodate that kind of situation? We think God's confused by the advance in technology that we've brought about but, honestly he isn't. He's just as available now as he was in the time of his incarnational visit and we Christians need to know that.

"I don't make it look easy.
God makes it look easy."

John Wimber *on being natural in ministry*

At the root of most pastoral problems that I have dealt with
– and we have a big church – is the basic assumption that,
'In my case God couldn't love me'. Someone came up to me
once and said; "Will you pray for me for a blessing or for
empowerment so that I can go and minister?" So I questioned
them and out it came: "Well, I feel so powerless," and I laughed
and said, "Well, that's the anointing. You don't understand.
That's the way you are supposed to feel when you do God's
stuff." Just how much of God's stuff can you do? Can you
change one hair on your head? Can you add a cubit to your
height? You can't even lose five pounds very readily!

I remember at one point David Watson [the English evangelist who died in 1984] was following me around, watching
people getting healed and he said to me, "How do you do that?"
I said, "Oh easy. Give me your hand," and I put his hand on a
woman's eye that was blind and she saw. David walked around
for the next hour staring at his hand and saying, "I did that, I
did that. I participated in that."

I said, "Sure. What are they for if they are not for laying on
people." He said, "But you make it look so easy." I replied, "I
don't make it look easy. God makes it look easy. What do you
want me to do – try to pretend it is hard? It's not hard. It's
impossible."

My fat little freckled hands can't make something well.
Think about it. How much can you add to God? What can you
do in addition? Are you going to fall on your knees and pray

THE POWER OF THE SPIRIT

harder? "Oh God, I've been such a sinner." He knows that. He's the one who saved you, remember? What are you going to add? I worked all that through a few years back and decided I don't have anything to add but what I can do is obey.

I don't have to float around like a butterfly and sting like a bee. I don't have to do something pretentious or stagey or theatrical. I don't have to raise my voice or act like I just came off from a mountain with a cloak over my shoulder. I decided a long time ago I wanted to multiply 'supernaturally natural' people. That meant I had to be natural.

"What I'm focused on is the major benefit: the church is being revitalised."

John Wimber *on the manifestations which sometimes accompany the move of the Spirit*

A young woman in our church came to me very lovingly, and said, "I'm about to have our baby." She had been married a couple of years and was pregnant and about to deliver. She said, "We would like you to come." I said, "To the delivery?" and she said, "Yes." I replied, "Honey, maybe I'm an old man but I don't want to know you that well. I don't want to participate in the birth of your child. I'll be happy to affirm you, love you, 'ooh' and 'aah' over the baby after it's born, but while it's being born I'd like to leave you to yourselves." She was quite puzzled by that and I realised that she was operating from a different set of assumptions about life than I am. I think we're all delighted with babies but I don't think many of us want to attend the birthing process.

I believe what we have in the church is a birthing process. I believe that the Holy Spirit has chosen to visit and revitalise the church and with it there are all kinds of noises and activities that would be best done behind closed doors. But church is an open activity and God has chosen to visit the church. I'm a little puzzled myself by some of the things that God chooses to reveal publicly but it happens that way, and so therefore I'm just one of those spectators too. I don't have any more explanation or idea of what it means than anybody else but I love the after-effect. Just as I love babies but am confused by the birthing process, I love what happens afterwards.

I talk to hundreds of young people in my own church as well as visitors. They tell me they love the Lord more and they read the Bible more. They're giving more and praying for the sick more, and they're operating in new gifts. Frankly, I don't care what the means is if it produces that benefit. What I'm focused on is the major benefit: the church is being revitalised. I was talking to two vicars and they've now had to open their church three additional times a week. Well, I think that's good news. I like that. That thrills me. It blesses me. So if somebody's got to make an animal noise to do that, I don't care. But I don't think it's anything we ought to legitimise and theologise, and emulate and try to get other people to do.

"It's like you've been cast in a role of Clark Kent."

John Wimber *on finding the 'phone booth' of faith*

You will be weak all your life in Christ for you can do nothing without him. On the other hand, you can do everything in him. We are always weak but appearing to be supermen and women. I was telling the young people in our church about this and I said, "It's like you've been cast in a role of Clark Kent. You're all Clark Kents but every now and then, you find the 'phone booth' of faith; you step into it and you emerge with your uniform on and do a mighty deed for Jesus." The kids took that literally in 1981 when we came to Chorleywood. We came a day or two early and were in Hyde Park when two of the young girls found a phone booth – one of those big cast-iron phone booths – went inside, 'found faith' and came out and started talking to people in the park.

The first person they talked to was a young Japanese student who couldn't speak much English. So they tried to explain salvation. They couldn't get much across but he liked the attention of two attractive young girls so he stayed there and listened. Finally, they asked him if they could pray for him and he didn't know what they meant but he said, "Yes." So they laid hands on him and he immediately fell down and began shaking violently. A crowd gathered because they were sure he was having an epileptic fit. They stood him back up and said, "Do you feel that?" and he said, "Ye-Ye-Ye-Ye-Yes." "Well, that's Jesus," they said.

So they led him to Christ in front of this group of 30 or 40 people. We have been called to a life of weakness and power. Isn't that an interesting paradox? We are asked to do such incredible things – heal the sick, cast out devils, feed the hungry, witness to the lost. Find the 'phone booth' of faith. It doesn't always look like a phone booth but find that spot of belief and say, "Lord, cause me to do in power what I can only do in weakness," and watch what happens.

Also edited by Mark Elsdon-Dew:

The God Who Changes Lives

"I went up to my bedroom with this terrible pain... I screamed, 'Oh God if you are there, do something...'"

"I had decided that my marriage was not recoverable and had left home..."

"I thought that if God was alive then he must be extraordinarily boring and certainly not worth getting to know..."

Does God act in people's lives today?

In this book, a variety of people describe how their lives have been transformed – often in dramatic circumstances – through an encounter with God. Some have been healed, some powerfully changed and others given the strength to face troubled times.

This is a book for anyone interested in whether God is there – and what he can do.

"There are some very beautiful stories in here, and they all serve to remind us that if the church is anything, it is about real people."

Methodist Recorder

"One of the great strengths of such a large number of testimonies is the variety. Drink, drugs, heavy metal music, Tarot, marriage breakdown, cot death and illness figure, together with the Lord's solution... It should prove a valuable addition to church bookstalls, and for giving to enquiring friends."

The Church of England Newspaper

Alpha Resources

The *Alpha* Course is a practical introduction to the Christian faith developed by Holy Trinity Brompton Church in London, England. *Alpha* Courses are now being run worldwide.

Alpha books by Nicky Gumbel:

- *Why Jesus?* A booklet recommended for all participants at the start of *Alpha*.

- *Why Christmas?* The Christmas version of *Why Jesus?*

- *Questions of Life* The *Alpha* Course in book form. In fifteen compelling chapters the author points the way to an authentic Christianity which is exciting and relevant to today's world.

- *Searching Issues* The seven issues most often raised by participants of *Alpha*: suffering, other religions, sex before marriage, the New Age, homosexuality, science and Christianity, and the Trinity.

- *A Life Worth Living* What happens after *Alpha*? Based on the book of Philippians, this is an invaluable next step for those who have just completed *Alpha*, and for anyone eager to put their faith on a firm biblical footing.

- *Challenging Lifestyle* An in-depth look at the Sermon on the Mount (Matthew 5-7). The author shows that Jesus' teaching flies in the face of modern lifestyle and presents us with a radical alternative.

- *Telling Others* This book includes the principles and practicalities of setting up and running *Alpha*. It also includes personal accounts of lives changed while attending *Alpha*.

Alpha **Resources**

Other resources available for setting up an *Alpha* Course:

- *Alpha* Introductory Video
- How to run an *Alpha* Course on Tape and How to run an *Alpha* Course on Video
- *Alpha* Team Training Tapes or Videos
- *Alpha* Team Training Manual (one for each small-group leader and helper)

Other resources available for running *Alpha*:

- The *Alpha* Course Tapes
- The *Alpha* Course Videos (5-video set including 15 talks)
- *Alpha* Manual (one for each small-group participant and leader)

Visit your local Christian bookshop or call the *Alpha* Hotline at STL for telephone orders: 0345 581278
(all calls at local rate – Please allow three working days for delivery)

In North America, all *Alpha* resources are published by Cook Ministry Resources, a division of Cook Communications Ministries.

In the USA, call or write:

Cook Ministry Resources
4050 Lee Vance View
Colorado Springs, CO 80918-7100
I -800-426-6596
1-800-36-ALPHA (1-800-263-2664)

In Canada, call or write:

Beacon Distributing
P.O. Box 98
55 Woodslee Ave.
Paris Ontario N3L 3E5
1-800-263-2664

For more information about *Alpha* please contact:

The *Alpha* Office, Holy Trinity Brompton,
Brompton Road, London SW7 IJA
Telephone: 0171 581 8255
Fax: 0171 584 8536
E-mail: HTB.LONDON@DIAL.PIPEX.COM

TIM MOORE

Tim Moore's writing has appeared in the *Daily Telegraph*, the *Observer*, the *Sunday Times* and *Esquire*. He is the author of *Gironimo!*, *French Revolutions*, *Do Not Pass Go*, *Spanish Steps*, *Nul Points*, *I Believe In Yesterday* and *You Are Awful (But I Like You)*. He lives in London.

ALSO BY TIM MOORE

TIM MOORE

Vuelta Skelter

Riding the Remarkable
1941 Tour of Spain

VINTAGE

1 3 5 7 9 10 8 6 4 2

Vintage is part of the Penguin Random House group of companies
whose addresses can be found at global.penguinrandomhouse.com

Penguin
Random House
UK

First published in Vintage in 2022
First published in hardback by Jonathan Cape in 2021

penguin.co.uk/vintage

A CIP catalogue record for this book is
available from the British Library

ISBN 9781529113792 (B format)

Printed and bound in Great Britain by Clays Ltd, Elcograf S.p.A.

The authorised representative in the EEA is Penguin Random House Ireland,
Morrison Chambers, 32 Nassau Street, Dublin D02 YH68

Penguin Random House is committed to a sustainable future
for our business, our readers and our planet. This book is made
from Forest Stewardship Council® certified paper.

To José Luis Navares González

PROLOGUE

'We will live in your journey. You do this for all of us. We are in your heart and in your mind.'

It was 4 July 2020, and there we were outside Biketown, a shop in Madrid's northern suburbs. Three fortysomething Spaniards and me, all in shorts and facemasks, sunglasses steaming up in the monstrous midday heat. And a fortysomething road bicycle, thin and silver, leaning against the sun-scorched wall behind us.

Two months had passed since I'd chanced upon a photo of this graceful old machine, in a blog post composed by Gerardo, the stubbled one. I had made contact, asking if it might be for sale. Gerardo gently replied that it wasn't, on account of a deep sentimental attachment: he had inherited the bike from an elderly cycling companion who had passed away the previous year. He said he would confer with Javier, the tall one, Biketown's manager and the silver bike's co-owner. Gerardo's next email, composed like all of our correspondence via Google Translate, had pricked my eyes with tears of emotion and gratitude. 'Our friend José Luis was a great lover of cycling and would have much love for your project. I have spoken to Javier and we are happy to lend you José Luis' bike free of charge.'

Antonio, the one who spoke English, flicked a finger towards Gerardo, who had taken off his sunglasses and was drawing a bare forearm across his eyes. 'See? Now he cries. He has thoughts of envy for you.' Throwing Covid caution to the winds, Gerardo strode over and gave me a great big unprotected hug, along with several slaps on my hot, woolly back. It was probably now that I first regretted my choice of facemask: a florid Liberty-print affair that made an awkward contrast with Gerardo's dourly masculine black number.

I pulled down the peak of my little white cap, then went over and straddled the bike. This wasn't a graceful procedure with a big saddlebag in the way. Looking from face to covered face, I tried hard to convey appropriate emotions with the small visible parts of my own visage. No thoughts of envy for myself, it's fair to say, but a welter of sadness, pride and affection for the late and mystical José Luis, for these three masked benefactors, above all for the extraordinary cyclist whose name was plastered all over the bike beneath me. Then I hoisted a string-backed glove, yanked off my poncy mask and freewheeled waywardly down the empty, sloping street, bullying feet into toe clips and doing ugly, crunching battle with the gear levers on my down tube.

CHAPTER 1

skreek
skreek
skreek...

Before I hold down the rewind button and spool way back into monochrome history, let's just give it a brief prod, returning to those balmy, barmy dog days of that first Covid lockdown, when the sun burned bright in a cloudless sky and time went all wrong. Afternoons that seemed to stretch out for a whole week; whole weeks that shot by in a flash. It's not exactly a hard sell, but this would be an adventure born of stir-crazy, weapons-grade boredom.

My first task under house arrest was to settle down and watch a career in travel journalism die before my eyes. That took care of half an hour. Then I drank cider in the garden. Three days in, my wife came down with a fairly apparent dose of what my daughters called rona – headache, leaden fatigue and a total loss of smell. It dragged on and on, but got no worse than that. I took my son's bedroom window out of its frame, carried it out on to the patio and somehow spent five whole days doing stuff to it with brushes and spatulas. I drank more cider; I drank stronger cider. I eradicated every last rhizome of every last buttercup from my flower beds. Just after my wife started feeling better, I started feeling worse. But I was lucky, too: a couple of days in bed, another week mired in a kind of jetlagged hangover, all the while with that same unsettling vacancy in my nostrils. Still, what a towering relief it was when I recovered, and could at last re-string our rotary washing line, pickle seven kilograms of carrots, and devote an entire fortnight to restoring the old traffic lights I'd left in my parents' garage thirty years before.

Towards the end of April, I had scraped the bottom of my barrel of projects and pastimes. Then it came to me. With juggling, topiary or transvestism just hours away, I braved the horrid, spidery depths of my shed and effortfully extracted the bike I had ridden round France two decades previously. What a terrible state it was in, poor old ZR3000. Cracked and airless tyres, great coils of detached handlebar tape that spooled down to the floor. The front derailleur had broken off and everything was covered with rust, dust or both.

Resurrecting this forlorn machine to its proud, factory-fresh glory was more than a project – it was a duty of care, a moral obligation I had been postponing for at least fifteen shameful years. Make that sixteen and counting. I flicked off the biggest insects, pumped up the tyres, slashed away all the bar tape and gaffer-taped the redundant front derailleur cable round the seat tube. Then I went for a ride.

The sky was blue and the roads of London were weirdly, wonderfully empty. I went into town and had Oxford Street and its shuttered shops all to myself, in broad, bright daylight. I went out of town, south-west to Chertsey, up the Thames Path to Staines, back home down the Great West Road. A 30-mile circuit right under the Heathrow flight path, yet the loudest noise was bird-song. Well, that and ZR's unlubricated shrieking. But I could live with that. The greatest legacy of my previous two cycling endeav-ours, in which I covered more than 15,000 kilometres on bikes with 140 years and three gears between them, is that everything I've ridden since seems like the finest, fastest, human-powered two-wheeler ever conceived. It's just such a shame that I haven't ridden anything since, not really. Those 30 miles were a good 27 more than I had cycled on any single day over the previous five years. But sometimes it doesn't take much to rekindle the flame. Turns out, all I needed was the gentle nudge of living through a global pandemic with my front door welded shut.

I did the Chertsey loop an awful lot after that, getting my head down, pushing the speed up, loving the footloose freedom and successfully blotting out the plague's ratcheting horrors. In previous years I'd have been watching the Giro d'Italia about this time, but along with the Tour it had been postponed. My Chertsey rides were filling a grand-tour-shaped hole in my life. One espe-cially sweltering afternoon I even contrived an adverse reaction to a surfeit of performance-enhancing substances, chugging a giant flagon of Pepsi Max outside a petrol station because it was cheaper than a can, then throwing it up next to a taped-off playground down the road.

I felt myself being drawn ever deeper into this one-man, half-speed, groundhog grand tour. Lockdown seemed to lend itself to the endeavour: the soothing routines; that unkempt, fuck-it grub-biness; the sense of living in a bubble, a parallel world where everything seemed both tediously familiar yet utterly alien. By night I began to work through my pile of cycling books. Having written three of these it's not entirely surprising that I get given a lot, but I always dread opening them. Why upset myself? When you read a book about cycling, the very least you deserve is an author who knows a lot about it, and ideally does a lot of it. Because I tick neither box, by the end of the first page I feel guilty and ashamed, laid bare as the total fraud I so clearly am.

It may have been thoughts like these that put *Viva la Vuelta* on top of my bedside pile. Spain's national bike race is comfortably the least grand grand tour. It didn't get going until 1935, twenty-six years after the Giro joined the Tour de France on the cycling calendar, and since then has been shunted all around the season – April, June, August, October – trying to find its niche. And failing, because the race has perennially struggled to attract the world's best riders: Eddy Merckx only bothered with it once, casually destroying the field in 1973.

When the Vuelta does make history, it's usually the wrong kind. After winning the 1974 edition by eleven seconds – then the closest ever margin in a grand tour – José Manuel Fuente astounded the foreign press by revealing that he'd calmed his last-stage nerves by chain-smoking through the night. In the 2013 edition, forty-one-year-old American rider Chris Horner became the oldest grand tour winner of all time, and by a margin of five years. It was only his second European race victory of any sort. And whereas the other grand tours have only ever been cancelled due to global conflict, Spain went five years without a Vuelta in the 1950s because nobody could be arsed.

Given all this, it's probably no surprise that the English-language *Viva la Vuelta* appears to be the only published history of the race. Not even the Spanish have bothered with one. And yet I only got as far as page 25 before dropping it on the floor. To be clear, *Viva la Vuelta* is a most engaging read, and some weeks later I picked it up again and finished the whole book in a single sitting. I didn't drop it in despair or indifference, but in the very frankest astonishment. By page 25 I had absorbed a potted account of the 1941 Vuelta a España, focused on the man who won it, and on how he had spent the previous five years of his life. By page 25 I knew how I would be spending the next few months of mine.

CHAPTER 2

The story of the 1941 Vuelta a España actually begins in 1936, on a train carrying two Spanish cyclists to Paris for the start of that year's Tour de France. At twenty-four, the younger man has left his homeland only once before, competing in an Alpine hill climb that had brutally introduced him to the ferocious chicanery of the continental racing scene. The older is a veteran of two Tours, but as they rattle through the countryside he doesn't offer the debutant any comforting advice. In part because he had spent the first night of his own first Tour crying himself to sleep, in a hotel room full of similarly traumatised Spanish teammates. And in part because the two riders, courtesy of a number of professional run-ins, absolutely despise each other. 'The harmony between Federico Ezquerra and me was like the harmony in modern dance music,' wrote Julián Berrendero in his autobiography, recalling this journey. 'Which is to say – there was no harmony.'

In accordance with a format that prevailed until the 1960s, the 1936 Tour was organised in national teams of ten riders. Spain, where professional cycling was too poorly remunerated to support more than a handful of full-timers, could only muster five, who were imaginatively merged with a quintet of Luxembourgers by Henri Desgrange, the Tour's tyrannical race director. The start-line photos are quite something: five strapping, lofty rouleurs looming over Spain's beetle-browed, diminutive climbers.

Desgrange had great affection for the Spanish riders, but because these were the 1930s and he was a bit of a wanker, he expressed it through the medium of the offensive nickname. Vicente Trueba, a Spaniard of especially modest stature who won the inaugural King of the Mountains prize in 1933, found himself unhappily immortalised as The Flea of Torrelavega. Running with this theme, and adding a dollop of stereotype, Henri dubbed all future Spanish competitors 'our little fishermen'. But he pulled out the stops for the rider who would emulate his countryman Trueba's feat in 1936. Julián Berrendero had unusually dark skin, and, for a Spaniard, unusually pale peepers. And so, for the long balance of his career, Berrendero would read through race reports and magazine profiles – in both France and Spain – hoping in vain that this time he wouldn't encounter any reference to The Black Man with the Blue Eyes.

In Paris, Berrendero was overwhelmed before the race even started. The street outside the team's hotel was crowded day and night with autograph hunters, well-wishers and pretty girls, puckered-up and ready. 'Our shoulders hurt from all those claps on the back, and our lips from all that kissing,' he remembered in said autobiography, *Mis Glorias y Memorias*. The Spaniards were driven about the city in a complimentary taxi, and ate for free at fancy restaurants, entertaining waiters by miming their orders. (Up to a point, at least: Berrendero caused rather a scene when he asked for eggs with physical reference to a Spanish euphemism – by cupping his bollocks.)

The starting pistol had been handed to black film star and jazz dancer Josephine Baker, who batted for both teams and routinely posed topless. There weren't many Josephine Bakers to the dozen back in hidebound, Catholic Spain. 'She gave a carnation to every rider, and a kiss to those who wanted one,' recalled Berrendero. 'I got two.'

What followed, though, was as appalling as Ezquerra could have told him it would be. Shattered by the relentless pace ('Who were these crazy supermen, riding close to 40kmh for hours on end?'), some very North European weather and a catastrophic mechanical, Berrendero finished the first stage plum last, an hour and seven minutes down. This was outside the time limit; only a rare moment of sympathetic weakness from Henri Desgrange saved him from disqualification. As he struggled through these bewildering highs and lows, perhaps it isn't so surprising that in his account of these early stages, Berrendero makes absolutely no reference to the worrisome situation developing back home.

The Spanish riders had left a homeland in turmoil. The leftist Popular Front coalition – narrowly elected at the start of the year in what would be the country's last free vote for forty years – was starting to unravel, and with radical elements holding the upper hand, Spain's Nationalist opposition and its conservative supporters were convinced that a full-scale revolution was both inevitable and imminent. Mobs were storming prisons to free incarcerated anarchists and communists, and Falangist death squads ran amok, planting bombs, shooting suspect judges and left-wing MPs, gunning down workers in the centre of Madrid.

On the day the Tour started, socialist leader Francisco Largo Caballero – who had survived an assassination attempt three months earlier – warned of a looming military takeover: 'There is a conspiracy afoot, one which hopes to implant a dictatorial regime equal to those that prevail in Italy and Germany.' Spain had plenty of form in this field. Between 1814 and 1874 there had been thirty-seven attempted coups in the country, twelve of them successful. Another had been on the cards since 1934, when a revolutionary strike centred in the industrialised northern province of Asturias was brutally repressed. Nearly 2,000 people were killed, most of them miners, on the orders of the man sent to crush the uprising: General Francisco Franco.

The race wound south towards the Alps; en route, Ezquerra and Berrendero came to prominence after leading the field over the Ballon d'Alsace, this edition's first categorised climb. The press photos show the Spanish team having a ball, delighted that they've survived a first week that saw eighteen riders abandon, and with their favoured territory now in sight. There they all are, grinning away in a fairground dodgem, around a bar piano, or in one notable instance while carrying a teammate in full drag across a hotel threshold. No trace of the latent enmities that flared up when Berrendero began to attack Ezquerra on the climbs, or of fear for their homeland's welfare. The Tour's relentless, all-encompassing clamour blotted out everything else. But thereafter, as the race got better and better for the Spanish, at home everything went horribly, murderously wrong.

13 July: Ezquerra and Berrendero are first over the Col des Aravis, the inaugural Alpine challenge. Spanish newspapers report the assassination of an anti-fascist police lieutenant by Falangist gunmen; the leader of the right-wing monarchist party is killed in retaliation.

14 July: Ezquerra takes the points atop a snowbound Galibier, remarkably setting a new record time, with Berrendero second. In Madrid, four people are shot dead when somebody has the bright idea of burying both sets of victims of the previous day's murders in the same cemetery.

17 July: After a strong showing over the previous forty-eight hours, Berrendero enjoys the rest day in Digne; he now holds a narrow lead over Ezquerra in the 'Challenge Martini-Rossi', as that year's mountains competition is officially titled. None of the riders are yet aware that Franco has launched a military rising from Spanish Morocco, and declared a state of war across Spain: by nightfall, carefully coordinated manoeuvres see his rebel troops in command of Cadiz, Salamanca and half a dozen other Spanish cities.

18 July: At the end of an inconsequential day in the Alps, the Spanish riders – Republicans to a man – are told the news from back home. By now rebel troops control a third of the country. Ezquerra takes it hardest, suffering 'a grave moral crisis'. Then he defiantly vows to the gathered journalists that he will win the next stage.

19 July: After a heroic comeback on the last of the day's three climbs, Ezquerra is first over the line in Cannes. It is only the second time a Spaniard has won a stage at the Tour. But on the podium, a grim-faced Ezquerra refuses to open the traditional bottle of champagne that is handed to him. Seville has fallen to Franco; vicious street-fighting between workers' militias and rebel troops in Barcelona stains the pavements red.

20 July: At the rest day in Cannes, the Spanish team is relentlessly questioned by journalists. The riders restrict themselves to expressing concern for their families; Berrendero's parents and his fiancée Pilar live in Madrid, where that night over a thousand

people will die in a battle between rebel troops and civilian militias. Another Spanish rider, Mariano Cañardo, a personal friend of Catalonia's Republican president Lluís Companys, goes a little further, expressing his team's solidarity 'with the children of the Spanish Republic'.

But as the race headed into the Pyrenees, the Spanish riders were abruptly disconnected from events on the other side of the mountains. France's socialist government, wary of a copy-cat coup and perhaps ashamed of their reluctance to send aid or arms to a 'sister republic', imposed full censorship on all news from Spain. The last reports that got through would have cruelly deceived the riders: the pro-Republican press was already seeking solace in wishful thinking and straight-up fake news. 'Fascism defeated by the Republic: the final defeat of the rebels is imminent!' crowed *La Libertad*, above a cartoon of a swastika-bearing tree being felled by an axe labelled 'Popular Front'. Madrid's *ABC* spelled it out, and spelled it really badly wrong: 'Message to our Tour team: Cañardo, Berrendero, Ezquerra, Molina, Álvarez, ride easy; the Republic is saved.'

And so, in time-honoured sporting fashion, they let their bikes do the talking. Berrendero's, for one, was yelling its wheels off. On the first Pyrenean stage, a horrendous 325-kilometre ordeal encompassing four cols, the man I shall henceforth be routinely referring to by his initials and sundry over-familiar nicknames impressively extended his lead in the mountains competition. While doing so, he initiated what would become a signature move: with the points in the bag, he dismounted atop the day's final climb and took leisurely refreshment at the summit café. It was a habit that might conceivably have cost him a podium finish. By his own subsequent admission, it definitely cost him a couple of stage wins. The beneficiary that day was Sauveur Ducazeaux, an amateur rocking a three-speed derailleur, who gleefully took the first and only victory of his career.*

Since those sombre rest-day interviews in Cannes, the Spaniards seem to have lightened up no end. The knockabout photocalls are back, JB and his teammates pushing each other around in prams and bouncing about on huge beach balls. They sign autographs and pose with fans. Journalists are treated to breezy predictions of the riches the team hopes to earn: a target of 100,000 francs in Tour winnings is mentioned, roughly 100 times the size of the biggest prize pots then on offer in Spain. The riders' blithe ignorance of what has by now descended into a full-scale civil war – aerial bombardments, heavy shelling, summary executions – is betrayed when they express hope that 'Spanish fans will come over the border to cheer us on these tough stages, despite the unpleasant weather'.

Luchon–Pau was this year's queen stage, taking in the mighty cols of Peyresourde, Aspin, the Tourmalet and the Aubisque. Jools led the field over the first and scored bigly on the other three. Ezquerra finally cracked, and with nothing but rolling vineyards and sunflower plains until Paris, the Challenge Martini-Rossi was over. On his Tour debut – and in only the second proper stage race of his career – Julián Berrendero would be crowned King of the Mountains.

Back in Spain, troops were already digging in for the long haul. Franco controlled much of central and western Spain; the

---

* Derailleurs had been around for some time, but naturally enough Henri Desgrange despised the 'artifice of variable gears' and banned them from the Tour. Curiously, however, amateur touriste routiers who entered the 1936 race were permitted derailleurs, in consequence humiliating several professionals when the Tour hit the steep stuff. This tour would be Henri's last: his successor put an end to all the nonsense, and every bike on the 1937 start line had multiple sprockets on its back wheel.

Republicans still held Madrid and Barcelona. Death squads from both sides were executing suspected enemy sympathisers by the hundred. An air raid on 22 July killed forty-five children in a small Basque village. In the space of a single grand tour, the conflict had exploded from scattered street-fights to nationwide fratricidal slaughter – and a full-blown proxy war, with Hitler and Mussolini sending Franco planes and weaponry, and Stalin's Soviet Union reciprocating for the other side.

Still largely in the dark about this awful turn of events, Berrendero rode back into Paris in defiant triumph. 'Those who had said I would suffer for my inexperience, what did they think now?' he wrote in *Mis Glorias y Memorias*. 'So much for those birdbrained gossips who flattered veteran riders and belittled the new generation.' As the *coup de grâce*, and in a spirit of chest-beating egomania, he went third-person on their birdbrained asses. 'Julián Berrendero is King of the Mountains!'

But the people of Paris knew more than he did about the fate of their sister republic. Riding into the Parc des Princes and up to the finish line, Berrendero was astonished to receive louder acclaim than the overall winner, Sylvère Maes. 'The crowd showered me with cheers and bouquets of flowers, a real hero's welcome such as I had never received.' Suddenly it all sank in, the good, the bad and the ugly. *El Tour de 1936*, a recently published account of the race, paints a poignant picture: 'Sitting on the ground with his bike laid down beside him, Berrendero cried like a child.'

JB recalled this extraordinary moment in his autobiography, using words that seem pretty bold for a book published in 1949, when Franco's regime stood at the height of its censorious powers. 'These tears came from something more profound than simple excitement, or even the absence of my loved ones: a deep nostalgia for my homeland, which was suffering the most cruel and tragic of all evils.'

It was a theme he had expanded on before, during one of those infamous summit stops. When a journalist wandered over to Berrendero atop an unnamed col, he didn't expect to get much out of this ever reluctant interviewee. But for whatever reason – perhaps he just wanted to distract himself from the terrifying descent ahead – Berrendero shot his mouth off. When the chat turned to events back in Spain, JB blurted out words that would change the course of his life.

The original of this interview – its setting, its writer, its publication – has proved maddeningly elusive. All I've found are detailed, but indirect, references. *El Tour de 1936* says Berrendero delivered an 'impetuous declaration of republicanism'. A host of post-Franco newspaper profiles have him condemning 'the fascist aggression in my homeland'. Berrendero himself never confirmed or denied the fateful quotes, though years later he hinted at a bit of a stitch-up: 'The French press exaggerated what we said.'

But in spite of everything, it had been an extraordinary Tour for the Spanish. Cañardo, a dogged, beefy hardman, finished sixth overall; Ezquerra, notwithstanding his collapse in the mountains competition, ended as the team's top money winner courtesy of that stage victory. Remarkably, despite the Spaniards' best efforts to destroy one another – Berrendero and Cañardo also had some very unhelpful history – the Luxo-Hispanic squad even came second behind Belgium in the team category, spanking France into third by an hour and a half.

The lucrative post-Tour race contracts duly rolled in, along with all manner of commercial endorsements. *Mis Glorias y Memorias* is often alarmingly light on detail and accuracy – JB forgets riders' names with a blithe shrug, admits to conflating memories from multiple races and inexplicably makes no reference whatsoever to his start-to-finish victory in the 1942 Vuelta – but the author displays photographic recall of every penny he was ever paid, for what and by whom. The caption below a snap of him being poured a drink in front of a promotional brandy-mobile: 'For this pose I was paid 1,000 francs.' There is a painstaking audit of his Tour winnings: 57,700 francs in total, several times more than his accumulated career earnings to date.

Jools hit criteriums – big-money local show races – all over France and Belgium. When he was spotted in the crowd at a Paris velodrome, the track boss begged him to ride a lap of honour: 'As he makes this request, he puts a thousand-franc bill in my hand.' A whirlwind of cash and flattery: he was living the dream, and loving it. Until he went to bed, and found his thoughts 'flying to Spain'. Back in Madrid, his parents and fiancée were facing nightly raids by German and Italian bombers, the first sustained aerial assault in history. In the two-year siege that lay ahead, Madrileños would end up fighting off hungry dogs as they stripped flesh from horses and mules killed by shellfire. But Berrendero couldn't go home. The Francoists were hardly about to overlook his fateful sermon on the mount, and the Republicans had turned against the self-exiled riders: *El Mundo Deportivo* – the Barcelona-based sports daily – slated Berrendero and his teammates for 'avoiding their responsibilities to the Republic'.

All the other Spanish riders also stayed on after the Tour to earn the big French bucks, minus *domestique* Salvador Molina, who'd abandoned on Stage 7 and was currently back in Barcelona. With the race season nearing its end and the Civil War entrenched, what could they do? Cañardo, in particular, had given an awful lot of feisty interviews. And in the final analysis, they were all money-minded working-class professionals, who rode to support their families. Why leave the road-race Eldorado of France? They wouldn't earn a peseta back home with a war on.

Emiliano Álvarez, the team's other *domestique*, ran a bike shop in Pau, and lived above it with his French wife. And so Cañardo, Ezquerra and Berrendero – those very best of enemies – all moved in. The three of them raced again at the 1937 Tour, co-signing a letter that swore solidarity with the brothers in arms who fought for Spanish independence, along with a pledge to donate half the team's winnings to Republican war orphans. Cañardo and Berrendero won a stage each; Berrendero went first over five cols and came fourth in the mountains prize. But when the pair of them turned up on the 1938 start line, there were no such stirring pronouncements; by then, Franco had the war all but won.

A few months later, Ezquerra and Cañardo slipped home over the border. JB stayed on in Pau, winning a lot of regional races and still earning a decent wedge off the back of his Tour successes. But there was no place for him in the 1939 edition, what with Republican Spain having ceased to exist three months before its start. A month after it ended, Hitler invaded Poland. 'The international situation promised an imminent and new catastrophe,' wrote Berrendero. He had swerved a civil war by staying in France; to swerve a world war, he now left it.

In September 1939, three and a bit years after leaving Spain, Julián Berrendero headed home, changing trains at the French border town of Hendaye. Clanking over the railway bridge that linked the two nations, he must surely have recalled that cringingly uncomfortable outward journey, twelve hours cooped up with a man he couldn't stand, and who couldn't stand him.

After his own return, Federico Ezquerra had found himself with some explaining to do: Spain was now ruled by *il Movimiento*, Franco's Falangist governing authority. Questioned about his refusal to pop the stage-winners' champagne in apparent protest at Franco's coup, he imaginatively claimed self-defence: a full, uncorked bottle was, he insisted, his only weapon against disgruntled French fans who were threatening to turn nasty. Anyway, it did the job. After a short period in *il Movimiento*'s sporting sin-bin, Ezquerra's racing licence was returned. More remarkably, so too was Mariano Cañardo's, despite a much longer list of anti-Nationalist transgressions. By the summer of 1939, both riders were back on the road and winning races. (Salvador Molina, who'd spent the last year of the war organising benefit races for Barcelona's anti-fascist militia, wisely fled to Mexico.)

So when Berrendero's train hissed to a stop at Irun, just inside Spain, he would have felt more anticipation than concern. Soon he'd be reunited with Pilar, 'my dear, faithful Pili', his sweetheart since they'd met outside the school gates, aged thirteen. They'd get married and buy a house. Yes, he might have to do some official apologising, eat some shit, serve out a short ban. Or maybe not even that. So many Madrid friends had written to him in France, promising it was now safe to return. Guess what? It wasn't. Berrendero stepped on to the platform and was promptly arrested. 'From that moment and time, in my life and my career a parenthesis opened, a silence. A silence that lasted eighteen months.'

Employing the euphemism demanded by circumstance, in his autobiography Berrendero glosses over this year-and-a-half hiatus as 'the period when my licence was suspended'. On balance, I guess that was less likely to alert Franco's censors than 'the period when I was imprisoned in three concentration camps'.

After his arrest at Irun station, Berrendero became one of the estimated 900,000 Spaniards and foreign Republican volunteers who would disappear into Franco's network of 296 internment facilities by the end of 1939. By grim and simple definition, most would qualify as concentration camps: too many inmates in not enough space. The preponderance of political prisoners, widespread forced labour and appalling conditions further justify this emotive nomenclature – as indeed did the title of Franco's own departmental authority, the Inspección de Campos de Concentración.

'You should know that every prisoner is a ten millionth part of shit,' the commander of one Barcelona camp told his inmates. Water was generally rationed to a small tin every three days. Food was so scarce that any trees inside the camp compound would be quickly stripped of their bark. Dysentery and tuberculosis were rampant; a typhus epidemic that spread across Spain two months before the 1941 Vuelta accounted for 502 prisoners in a single camp in Córdoba. Those like Berrendero who had been taken prisoner after the end of the Civil War – *posteriores* in the official terminology – were by default suspected of involvement in guerrilla resistance, and often tortured horribly with electric shocks and near-drownings.

The official purpose of these camps was *depuración* – the process of cleansing, or reprogramming, or otherwise re-educating enemies of the state. Berrendero uses this precise phrase in *Mis Glorias y Memorias*. But there weren't any classroom lectures. Camp life more typically involved camp death. At least 10,000 prisoners perished, from hunger, disease or a bullet in the head. One inmate called the camps 'cemeteries for the living'. Any Republican deemed 'irrecoverable' by the authorities faced summary execution, with all the other prisoners lined up to watch. Franco himself passed cold-hearted final judgement, leafing through death sentences over his afternoon coffee. The names he wrote an 'E' beside would be executed; a 'C' commuted the sentence. Anyone he felt worthy of making an example of had *'garrote y prensa'* scribbled next to their name – garrotting and press coverage. 'No honourable Spaniard should shrink from the painful duty of punishment,' he told the nation in his end-of-year message on 31 December 1939.

Berrendero was taken first to a holding camp in a repurposed timber warehouse in Torrelavega, just along the Atlantic coast. From there he was sent by train to Espinosa de los Monteros, a lonely town in the northern mountains, and imprisoned at another temporary camp for two months. By the end of 1939, he had been transported down to Rota, near Cadiz, on the southern coast. Housed in a burned-out tuna cannery hidden away in the sand dunes, the Almadraba concentration camp at Rota was a permanent facility that would process 9,000 prisoners before its closure in June 1941. Their principal ordained task, conducted in brutal heat, was laying pavements in Rota town centre.

'You – come with me!'

Berrendero, for obvious reasons, never once mentioned his camp experiences while Franco was alive. 'A small misunderstanding' was his stock answer when anyone asked about those missing years. After Franco's death, most former prisoners still found it difficult to open up: a Spanish historian who interviewed several camp survivors in the 1990s noted that they would abruptly change the subject whenever one of their children walked in. 'Fear remains in the blood,' he said. Even when it was safe to do so, Berrendero seems to have made only two public references to this period, in magazine interviews that came out shortly before his death in 1995. But the tale he told was worth waiting for, and its extraordinary denouement begins with an officer's barked order as the malnourished, flea-bitten Rota prisoners lined up on the sand for roll-call one morning in early 1941.

What did the captain want? Berrendero swallowed hard: when prisoners were summoned in this manner they were generally never seen again. Shaking with fear and foreboding, he followed the captain into his office. In his own incredible words, this is what happened after the door was closed.

'The captain rushed up and embraced me. "Don't you recognise me?" he asked, with tears in his eyes. He said he was José Llona, an amateur cyclist from Bilbao who had raced with me before the war. Then he led me to his desk and offered me the plate of breakfast that lay on it: two fried eggs and potato.' This was the first proper meal that had been put in front of Berrendero for over a year. 'It tasted like heaven, like glory.'

The remarkable Captain Llona, one assumes at no small personal risk, told Berrendero he would take care of him, and do what he could to procure his release. He found Berrendero work around the camp that would help rebuild his fitness, and kept bringing him food. From here on the details become ever sketchier, but soon after Llona seems to have engineered Berrendero's transfer to his home city of Madrid. Here he blagged the rider some kind of community-service placement: a driving job that allowed him ample time off for training rides. By the start of March, Berrendero's rehabilitation was officially declared complete, and at the age of twenty-nine, he had his racing licence returned.

After eighteen months in concentration camps he could hardly have expected much from his 9 March comeback event: a short, sharp 10-kilometre race up a Basque mountain in the company of Spain's top climbers. 'I decided to give everything from the beginning, full gas,' he recalls. Nobody could stay with him, and Berrendero won by more than two minutes. Three months later, he lined up in Madrid for the start of the first Vuelta a España since 1936, and the first under Franco. Organised under the creepily Orwellian auspices of *il Movimiento*'s Department of Education and Leisure, the 1941 Vuelta was billed by the Falangist press as 'The Tour of a Nation Reborn'.

In his autobiography, Berrendero freely admits that he never expected to ride professionally again: 'I thought I had hung up my bike for good.' But when he retired in 1949, he did so as his country's most celebrated cyclist, and its most successful. Conforming to the post-professional tradition, in 1950 he opened an eponymous bike shop in the outskirts of Madrid, relocating a few years later to more central premises in the capital's Chamberí district.

Bicicletas Berrendero was a studiously unpretentious community business. From dawn to well beyond dusk JB was ever present behind the counter or in the workshop at the back, fixing old ladies' punctures and adjusting kids' brakes or gears. Come summer he'd be ready with a gruff quote when a sports journo popped in to ask for his Tour or Vuelta predictions, which invariably descended into a diatribe against the pampered milksops in the modern peloton. A few representative samples from the Sixties and Seventies: 'In my day we fought more, we suffered more. We were much more resistant to everything: cold, heat, rain. Only the *domestiques* suffer like we used to. They're the ones who leave their bones on the road ... I won the King of the Mountains without any gears. Now they have ten-gear bikes lighter than the wind, you can get 70kmh out of them ... We rode on country tracks. You just hoped someone had been out and cut the grass the day before ... Cyclists get big salaries now, so they never really push hard in races. We only got paid in prize money, we had to win to eat, to ride ourselves into the ground for a bowl of lentils. We had no support crew. We raced as if we had been abandoned by everybody. If I suffered today half of what I had to put up with in my best years, I would be a millionaire.'

Most of these interviews appeared in print below a portrait snapped outside his shop window: ever more jowly as the decades passed, but consistently black-browed and sombre. In one or two he looks straight-up menacing, heavy set with his receding dark hair slicked back, like an old Mafia hood on his rounds. 'So, uh, what do you call that bike of yours in the window there, the one with the two seats? A tandem, huh? Ain't that something. I would hate to see that beautiful machine all bust up and, you know, kinda melted and stuff.'

Ever the commercial opportunist, in these photos Jools would generally pose beside one of the Berrendero-branded machines he sold at his shop from the 1960s onwards, cheap-to-mid-range tourers, road bikes and kids' bikes, mostly rebadged Spanish-built Orbeas and BHs. You can occasionally find one of these for sale on Madrid's online second-hand marketplaces. I know this because I found five. An idea had suggested itself almost the minute I read the bare bones of his story, and it was one that now possessed me: I was going to ride the route of that 1941 Vuelta, and I was going to do it on a Berrendero.

The bad news, which sunk in as classified advertiser after classified advertiser failed to respond to my urgent enquiries, was that I wouldn't be riding the route on one of these Berrenderos. Covid-19 had hit Madrid harder than any other city in Europe, but by May, London was hot on its heels. The Seventies and Eighties Berrenderos I'd located were all pretty shonky, and thus extremely cheap; no Madrileño in his or her right mind was going to risk a face-to-face transaction with some rona-riddled Londoner for the sake of €60.

The much better news came via my email exchanges with Gerardo, whose vintage-bike blog I had come across in my wide-ranging online quest for information on Julián Berrendero. Because the bicycle bequeathed to him by his late friend José Luis, as detailed in the many photographs of it on his site, was a very different kind of Berrendero: a really, really good one. The machine that Gerardo and Javier had so very generously agreed to loan me was no careworn, mass-market clunker, but a bespoke, race-ready, mid-Seventies beauty with Campagnolo stamped all over the gleaming bits that made it move and stop. And with its vendor's name proudly emblazoned in decals that ran up and down every single tube on the frame. From our first contact, Gerardo had expressed deep reverence for this legendary rider, and for the bicycle that must have ranked among the finest he ever sold. To Gerardo this was no mere bike. In his words, and now by inheritance in mine, this was La Berrendero.

With Gerardo's extraordinary offer in hand, I just had to bide my time. An antibody test confirmed that I'd had Covid, which made me feel an awful lot better about even considering this trip: at least I could now travel round Spain confident that I wouldn't be getting it, or spreading it. But Spain had imposed a tit-for-tat ban on British travellers, and wouldn't remove it until UK deaths and cases declined to acceptable levels; Madrid remained on a red-alert lockdown that forbade all travel out of the city. It was a pretty disgraceful waiting game I played, willing the Covid figures downwards to expedite my departure. Timmy's Summer Bike Adventure: tragically on hold while this selfish, boring plague burned itself out. I'd already got in trouble with my wife for expressing relief when the UK's death toll eased past Spain's, thereby removing a moral impediment. My planned tour seemed moderately less inappropriate now that I wouldn't be riding around the most grimly ravaged country in Europe.

On 21 June, the UK travel ban was lifted. A week and a bit later, the province of Madrid was downgraded to an alert level that permitted free movement in and out. I struck. On 3 July I got on a plane, and just before 1 p.m. the next day, eased La Berrendero to a halt outside a parade of stucco-fronted old mansions on Calle de Alfonso XII in downtown Madrid.

A quick selfie: there I am crouched beside a shiny silver bike, its slender frame weighed down by the fat holdall slung laterally beneath its saddle, the toolbag cable-tied to the rear of its top tube, and the battered bar-bag filling the gap between its brake levers. On my head, a white peaked cap of vintage design. On my feet, tan-coloured retro cycling shoes over white ankle socks. And in between, a short-sleeved, flappy-collared, blue-and-white woollen jersey with an elaborate crest embroidered on one of its two front pockets, plus – because I'm not that bloody stupid – a pair of spanking new, high-end Lycra shorts. All in all, a reasonable tribute to the outfit worn by Julián Berrendero throughout the 1941 Vuelta a España, modelled on the pavement outside its official starting point: the former headquarters of the Ministry of Education and Leisure.

CHAPTER 3

To give a flavour of Spain's politico-sporting vibe in 1941, here's the end of a newspaper football-match report that popped up alongside the first archived Vuelta stage communiqué I scrolled through: 'The game finished without further change in the score-line, and shortly afterwards Capella, captain of the Azul team, came forward to receive the magnificent Catalan Cup, leading the crowd in a chant of "Franco, Franco, Franco!"'

Two years into his dictatorship, el Caudillo – Spanish for Führer – was moving out of his murderous-repression phase and considering how he might unite the country he had broken in half. A bike race that circumnavigated Spain seemed an obvious means of fostering national togetherness, with the bonus of showcasing fascist-friendly physical and spiritual virtues. 'All of Spain will discover that cycling is a healthy and cleansing sport,' declared race referee Manuel Serdan, in an interview with *El Mundo*

Deportivo. It was a theme Serdan had warmed to a couple of months earlier, when asked by a journalist if Julián Berrendero would be competing in the Vuelta. 'He has completed his military service,' replied Serdan, smoothly mastering the regime's odious doublespeak. 'Of course he dreams of being reintegrated. He is in good physical shape; now let us see what has resulted from his purification.'

Franco had little personal interest in sport, so the Vuelta's relaunch was overseen by General Moscardó, first boss of *il Movimiento*'s newly established National Sports Delegation. The general was a sports nut who fully exploited the career opportunities of a venal one-party state by later bagging himself the role of Spain's Olympic football coach, despite a total lack of relevant experience. Under his leadership, the Spanish would mystifyingly fail to qualify for the 1948 and 1952 Games.

But in 1941, General Moscardó was a very familiar name in Spain on account of a rather darker tragedy. During the early months of the Civil War, he had been Nationalist commanding officer at the Siege of the Alcázar, in Toledo. When the Republican forces surrounding the Nationalist-held fortress captured Moscardó's son Luis, they telephoned the general to advise him that unless he surrendered, the boy would be killed. 'Let me talk to him!' demanded Moscardó. When the phone was handed to Luis, his father shouted: 'Boy, commend your soul to God and die like a patriot! Long live Spain!' He was shot on the spot. Two months later, after Nationalist reinforcements broke the siege, Moscardó swiftly directed their attention to his Republican hostages. All 130 patients in the fortress's hospital had their throats slit, including twenty pregnant women. A further 180 Republican militiamen were locked in the seminary and burned alive. As the indiscretions of a sports administrator, these rather put Sepp Blatter's in the shade.

Putting a European grand tour together in 1941 would have been an unusually large ask. Despite its nominal neutrality in the world war, Spain remained effectively bankrupt and half starving. The devastation left by a three-year civil conflict that had introduced the world to the horrors of blitzkrieg and carpet bombing lay in scorched, rubbled heaps right across the country. After Spain's absence from the previous World Cup and Olympics, Franco had hoped to pitch the race as his country's reintroduction on to the international sporting stage, but in the rather trying geopolitical circs that wasn't going to be easy. Even before all this war business, Spain had struggled to attract foreign riders: the money was awful, and the roads and facilities routinely failed to belie the snotty French jibe that 'Africa begins at the Pyrenees'. In the event, the only foreigners Moscardó could procure were a fairly undistinguished quartet from fellow war-neutrals Switzerland.

With commercial backing inevitably in short supply, the Ministry of Education and Leisure stood in as effective race sponsors. In a curious bid to foster some sense of team rivalry – and, one imagines, to get the Franco-hating Catalans on board – the Ministry split the top riders into two squads representing Barcelona's dominant football clubs. Berrendero would race in the blue and white colours of RCD Espanyol, along with Fermín Trueba, younger brother of The Flea and a friend of JB's, plus – light the blue and white touch paper! – Federico Ezquerra, that most hated of adversaries. Preeminent among those given the blue and maroon jersey of FC Barcelona was another old foe: Mariano Cañardo. With just thirty-two starters, the '41 Vuelta still ranks as the smallest ever grand tour. The race organisers hoped to atone through sheer immensity of distance: at 4,442 kilometres it was, and remains, the longest bicycle race in Spanish history.

And so on the morning of 12 June 1941, a modest peloton gathered in front of officials and spectators outside the Ministry offices on Calle de Alfonso XII. On dutiful cue, every right arm was raised in fascist salute, and every voice joined a rendition of 'Cara al Sol', 'Face to the Sun', the Falangist anthem. Berrendero would have known the words better than anyone, having been obliged to sing it twice a day in the camps, where any mistake with the lyrics earned an automatic beating. At 8 a.m. sharp, the start flag was lowered by the Spanish Cycling Federation's new president, General Uzquiano – a natural career progression for Franco's erstwhile deputy chief of staff.

Seventy-nine years and three weeks later, pedalling through the welcome shade of the plane trees that lined the Calle de Alfonso XII, I set off in their ghostly wheel tracks. In the total absence of tourists, and with the Saturday traffic dramatically thinned by lockdown, it wasn't too hard to imagine the scene. As I rolled down the six-lane avenues, the loudest noise was the buzz of crickets getting busy in the formal gardens alongside.

Back home I'd spent a great deal of time inputting the 1941 route into Komoot, my phone's bike-focused navigation app, harvesting stage details from Berrendero's autobiography, and from contemporary sports reports in Spain's impressively comprehensive online newspaper archives. What a shame that my hopelessly stunted grasp of Spanish had obliged me to consult these splendid resources through the wayward auto-translation miracle of Google Lens. Ever tried it? You fire up the app, aim your phone camera at whatever you want translated, and the software's best effort appears on the screen. Sometimes I'd point my phone at a yellowed page or PC monitor and see fully formed, cogent revelations take shape before my widened eyes. But sometimes runners were thrown into trumpets, and champion wood delivered by walnut conference.

The 1941 race kicked off with a forty-five-minute neutralised parade through the centre; I followed it down the wide and graceful Gran Via. During the Civil War this had been known as Howitzer Alley, aligned as it was with the Nationalist artillery emplacements that looked down on Madrid from those mighty western hills. From the end of the war until 1981, Gran Via was renamed Avenida de José Antonio, in honour of the founding father of Falangism and composer of the lyrics to 'Cara al Sol', José Antonio Primo de Rivera. Spain has taken an awfully long time to retitle the countless streets and squares named after Franco and friends. The town of Guadiana del Caudillo is still holding out down near the Portuguese border.

Then it was out around Franco's Victory Arch, a pound-shop Arc de Triomphe finished in 1956. Marooned on a vast traffic island, it looked rather feeble and forlorn, an impression compounded by the graffiti daubed over its lower reaches, and by the skateboarders slaloming through the beer bottles and chunks of displaced marble cladding strewn beneath it. The arch must be the most blatant surviving symbol of Franco's regime, but the civic authorities appear to have felt that knocking it down would be a statement too far. Instead, they've gone for a kind of managed decline, crowbarring out the Falangist yoke-and-arrow motifs and removing all identifying signage. I freewheeled around the arch next to a bus, wondering if the driver or his passengers ever thought about what it represented; whether indeed they even noticed it. As I would find out, the Spanish are very good at letting uncomfortable history hide in plain sight.

The arch wasn't built when the 1941 peloton filed through, but the aftermath of the victory it originally commemorated would have lain all around. An extraordinary photo accompanied *El Mundo Deportivo*'s Stage 1 race report, showing the riders pedalling by shattered hulks of institutional-grade structures, carefully captioned: 'the Vuelta passes the glorious ruins of University City'. In November 1936, with the Nationalists just 300 metres from the centre of Madrid, a fierce and surreal battle raged across this sprawling campus. At times the front line ran through laboratories and libraries; machine-gun nests were built out of encyclopaedias, and bombs sent up in lifts. Almost every building would be shelled to oblivion: Antony Beevor, who ought to know, called it 'a foretaste of Stalingrad'. After the fighting hit a stalemate, both sides dug in for two years, leaving trenches and bunkers that are still visible at the northern end of University City. For the first time, but by no means the last, I realised that although the overarching intention of the race was to bring Spain together, on a micro level, its route was carefully plotted in order to remind the country who had won the war, by rubbing the losers' noses right in it. This first stage ran up the Coruña Road, route of Franco's first assault on the capital, a highway whose final suburban stretch is still named Victory Avenue. And the stage would end at Salamanca, Franco's military headquarters throughout the war.

Actually, I didn't realise any of that, at least not in any coherent manner. In these early stages, I was rather more focused on getting to grips with the absurd heat, the mind-melting scale of my

---

* In truth, Franco could have taken the capital and won the Civil War long before he eventually did. Ever the calculating pragmatist, he drew the conflict out to ensure a suffocating defeat that would drain every last drop of his opponents' morale and defiance. It worked: there would be almost no internal resistance throughout his forty-year dictatorship.

undertaking and, most immediately, this new-old bike of mine. La Berrendero, which Gerardo reckoned had been wheeled out of JB's shop in 1975, was a dream machine in its day, a bike my youthful self would have lusted after. It had a full Campagnolo Nuovo Gran Sport group set: gears, brakes, pedals, hubs, seat post, the lot. Not quite the range-topping Nuovo Record that took Eddy Merckx to five Tour wins, but near enough. It had slender Mavic rims, upon which Javier had fitted a pair of narrow, retro-profile Mavic tyres. And, perhaps most thrillingly for someone whose teenage years were spent hankering in vain for a bike with that coveted green and gold sticker on its down tube, it had a slender frame fashioned from Reynolds 531 steel tubing.

Yet here's the tragic thing: no matter what my breathtakingly fresh-faced good looks might suggest, forty years had passed since I experienced those vain hankerings. Yes, La Berrendero represented an intergalactic upgrade on the wooden-wheeled centenarian I'd ridden round Italy, and on the East German shopper that took me down the Iron Curtain. But it was still an extremely old bicycle. Bikes had got an awful lot better over the last forty years, whereas I hadn't. Before setting off down the Calle de Alfonso XII I was already slick with the sweat of effort and terror: the undulating ride from Biketown had demonstrated that a 1970s road bike with lots of bags and an old man on it didn't like going up hills or down them.

The gearing seemed cruelly inadequate for a fifty-six-year-old whose training rides had taken in nothing more vertical than a humpbacked railway bridge. There were six sprockets at the rear, and two at the front. This pair, to my untrained eye, seemed rather too big. Their hindward counterparts, as well as being far too few in number, were also far too small. Shifting between them, for what good it did, involved applying great manual forces to the dainty little Campagnolo levers on the down tube. I've only ever ridden one bike that required me to take my hands off the bars to change gear. That was a ten-speed Puch, a well-intentioned parental attempt to make my sixteenth birthday one to remember. I've certainly never forgotten it. By the time I blew my candles out that evening both gear cables had snapped.

And La Berrendero's brakes, despite similar inputs of brute strength, had already seen me judder to a wayward halt several feet beyond two red lights. My extended unfamiliarity with toe clips was the olive in this oh-shit cocktail. At one junction I had to use a bloke on an e-scooter to break my fall. He was pretty good about it, at least until he noticed my uncovered face. *'Mascarilla! Mascarilla!'* I'd been assured that cyclists didn't have to wear masks in Spain; a belated look around informed me this exemption did not apply in an urban setting.

Blinking sweat out of my eyes, I did my best to follow the Stage 1 directions, as displayed on the phone mounted rather perilously to the handlebar stem. The race proper began at the Puerta de Hierro, a fancy baroque arch, but I never did find it. After I got home I found out why: 'The monument occupies a landscaped traffic island, defined by several branches of the highway A-6 and M-30, an enclave which is difficult to access.' Komoot led me a merry dance around and over many such alluring interchanges, then into a gravel-tracked, pine-lined park full of weekend cyclists. La Berrendero's back wheel slipped and scrabbled, dispatching dusty plumes that enveloped the family pelotons behind.

I laboured across a hinterland of railway marshalling yards, then through the broiled and silent commuter suburbs. One introduced itself as Majadahonda, fuzzily familiar from my research both as a dreadful battleground in the war's first winter and as a landmark location in a cyclist's fledgling career. Thirty hours later, in a slightly more capable state of mind, I refreshed myself with the details.

In December 1936, 30,000 men died at Majadahonda in a chaotic, fog-bound free-for-all, with the International Brigade – that volunteer army of foreign anti-fascists – bearing the brunt. One IB commander, setting a template for the heroic but tragically self-destructive defiance that would define Republican battle tactics, ordered his men not to cede an inch of territory under any circumstances. In consequence, a battalion that had been formed two months earlier with 1,500 men was reduced to just thirty-five. And four years before, Julián Berrendero had fought his own battle at the 1932 Tour of Majadahonda. Leading the field in a two-man break, Berrendero received a hefty punch from his fellow escapee that knocked him over at speed. He picked himself out of the gutter, and in a rage set off in pursuit. Despite a jammed pedal, he caught his assailant, swung a payback right-hander, then powered away to take his first big win. Only after crossing the line did he notice the gaping wound in his arm, which would put him out of action for the rest of the 1932 season.

I suppose that could have been an inspiration, had I remembered it out on the road. I would have been very glad of it, because with Madrid's city limits barely behind me I was already in all sorts of bother. The digital readouts outside every pharmacy said it was over 40°C and, at 4 p.m., still rising. Desperate, raging thirst regrettably shouted down the smaller voice of hunger, and soon the dizzy sweats of hypoglycaemia came served with a side order of ominous leg tremors. How ghastly are those preludial cramp collywobbles. It's as if your legs have been possessed, as if some horrible, thrashing alien is about to burst straight out through your flesh. The first high-voltage bolt of agony harpooned my left calf on a gently rising bike path by a dual carriageway, almost throwing me off into the crispy dead grass. Almost in tears of pain and shame, I raggedly dismounted and pushed uphill for a good kilometre, the great man's name glaring reproachfully at me from all over La Berrendero's frame.

It's ridiculous, but every time I set off on these rides, I do so secretly wondering if I'll find myself bursting into some late-onset physical pomp. For this one, I had even entertained a theory that my brush with Covid might prove beneficial, in a kind of what-doesn't-kill-you-makes-you-stronger fashion. A bit like Armstrong coming back from cancer to win seven straight Tours, only without the enormous drugs programme. 'The doctors aren't quite sure how to explain it, but at fifty-six, Moore is riding like a man half his age. This is a slow-burn talent that the national selectors can hardly continue to ignore, particularly when it comes in such a sexy package.' It seemed a bit rude that I wasn't even granted a day – one single day – to sustain this fantasy before it was put to the sword so brutally, and so very painfully. Oh well. There's always next time.

I threw in the towel at Alpedrete, a small town in the rolling brown foothills that led up to the Alto de los Leones – the pass across the Guadarrama mountains that I had confidently expected to conquer that day. Sixty-four kilometres of utter humiliation, shorts pulled down and pallid buttocks spanked red.

'Too hot to make exercise!' trilled a masked woman behind the guesthouse-reception Plexiglas when I dropped my passport on her desk. Pulling my own mask on in stifling heat and a state of utter exhaustion had felt like having a hot hand pressed over my mouth. I managed a nod, which sank into a head-drop when she invited me to ferry La Berrendero to its overnight quarters: a basement at the bottom of two narrow, twisting flights of stairs.

I've only retained flash frames of that shattered debut evening, getting down and dirty with all those ugly, half-remembered rituals of life on the road. There I am slumped in the shower mumbling a semi-conscious stream of profanity. Giving my kit a half-arsed sluice in the bidet. And struggling into my après-cycling outfit, whose dominant feature was a pair of crimplene golf trousers I had seen recommended on some cyclo-touring forum for their light weight and crease resistance. Even my impaired critical faculties could sense they were laughably awful, shiny and shapeless, not so much Rory McIlroy striding down the eighteenth as Angela Merkel approaching a lectern.

I weaved out into the hot evening, in no fit state to appreciate or even really notice my surroundings. A lot of widows and whitewash, a lot of tattooed youths on scooters. More by accident than design, I wound up in Alpedrete's compact, bar-lined town square, and half-sat, half-fell into a chair at the nearest empty table.

'*Para comer?*'

The waiter responded to my request with a look of frank bemusement, as if instead of asking him what there was to eat I'd just invited him to draw on my face. I only had three Spanish phrases in my arsenal, and one of them had just crashed and burned before my reddened eyes. With much watch-pointing, the waiter explained himself: the kitchen didn't open until 8.30 p.m., giving me ninety minutes to keep ravening delirium at bay with beer and the saucer of crisps it came served with. So began the ordeals that would make a malnourished, alcoholic mess of so many evenings ahead.

CHAPTER 4

Given all those poisonous rivalries and that heavyweight ideological baggage, the 1941 Vuelta a España came with controversy baked in. Things duly kicked off on the start line, when FC Barcelona's Mariano Cañardo – the pre-race favourite – abruptly abandoned, claiming a swollen leg. The truth, as revealed by *El Mundo Deportivo*'s breezy race correspondent Ramón Torres, was rather murkier. 'It seems Cañardo had been told that the organisers would be supplying all teams with the same tubular tyres,' he wrote, 'but at the start he saw that the official spares were of inferior quality, and that all the other riders had brought along their own.' On the awful, unpaved roads of this era – and there were none more awful than Spain's – most races were decided by punctures. Berrendero's autobiography rails endlessly against *Doña Fatalidad*, Lady Luck, and all the victories she cost him with a prick of her phantom pin. A day without a puncture was almost

unheard of; a day with six was not. 'An unequal contest,' deduced
Ramón Torres, after learning that the RCD Espanyol squad had
been tipped off about the dodgy tubulars. 'That is the word in the
peloton.'

As a Barcelona paper, *El Mundo Deportivo* took the abandonment of Catalunya's top rider very badly. 'We are all dismayed by
Cañardo's decision,' wrote Ramón. You have to say this start-line
retirement, feeble pretext notwithstanding, seems a pretty ballsy
move given Cañardo's history of pro-Republican utterances. Just
eight months had passed since his friend Lluís Companys, erstwhile Catalan president, had been executed at Montjuïc Castle
in Barcelona, refusing a blindfold, kicking his shoes off to feel
the home soil under his bare feet, and shouting *'Per Catalunya!'*
as Franco's firing squad pulled their triggers. (In accordance
with the grotesque euphemisms that *il Movimiento* got a kick
out of putting on their victims' death certificates, Companys officially died of 'traumatic internal haemorrhage'. Those shot in the
head were generally said to have suffered 'organic destruction of
the brain'.)

Nobody dared say it out loud, but saddling the FC Barcelona
riders with dodgy spare tyres looked very much like official sabotage. Splitting the race into Catalan club teams might have been
pitched as a conciliatory gesture, but Cañardo and the rest knew
that *il Movimiento* would never have let an FCB rider win. There
was simply too much history. That age-old rivalry with Real Madrid
had been seriously inflamed by the Civil War: Royal Madrid was
now el Caudillo's team, a monarchist institution firmly aligned
with the Nationalist cause. Barcelona was the progressive, separatist people's club; Real represented wealthy conservatism, the
power of the capital city and stolid Castilian values – all of Franco's core beliefs.

Two years later, in 1943, FC Barcelona made the mistake of beating Real 3–0 in the first leg of a cup semi-final. Before the second leg, Franco's Director of State Security popped into the Barcelona dressing room, where he politely reminded them of el Caudillo's generosity in allowing any team from Catalonia to play professionally. As threats go this wasn't too thickly veiled, and it did the job. Real were 8–0 up by half-time and went on to win 11–1 – comfortably the most ridiculous, lopsided scoreline in El Clásico history.* And no Barcelona fan would ever forget one of the most shocking tragedies of the Civil War's early weeks. On 6 August 1936, four days after Julián Berrendero stood on that Paris podium, FC Barcelona's young president, Josep Suñol, visited Madrid to pay tribute to the Catalan volunteers who were helping defend the capital. After hearing that the Nationalists had been pushed back from the Guadarrama mountains, he asked to be driven up the Alto de los Leones pass to see for himself. He was; they hadn't. Suñol's bullet-riddled body was found a few days later in a roadside ditch, along with three of his travelling companions. As a final courtesy, when the war was over one of Franco's tribunals put Suñol on posthumous trial for being a communist; after he failed to appear in court to answer the charges, his bereaved father was fined five million pesetas. (It's worth noting that back then, the pass was simply known as Alto del Leon after the statue of a lion that still marks its summit; the small but significant 1939 rebrand honoured the 'lions' who fought Franco's good fight on its slopes.)

---

* Ten years afterwards, Franco's cronies would hijack Barcelona's attempt to buy Alfredo Di Stéfano: under very shady circumstances the legendary Argentinian striker went to Real instead, where he would average almost a goal a game over eleven seasons. (During the negotiations, General Moscardó himself proposed an extraordinary compromise: Di Stéfano would play for both clubs, in alternating seasons. Barcelona turned it down.)

RCD Espanyol, however, was a very different sort of Barcelona club. In footballing terms: a massively more shit one. We might as well get all that out in the open. The team my jersey so stridently identified me with was enduring yet another disappointing season in 2020. In fact, this one was properly abysmal: four different managers and only five league wins. Four days into my ride they were relegated, beaten at the last by Barcelona – a team they have only ever finished above three times in a record eighty-one title-free seasons. In this particular one they wound up bottom of La Liga by eight points.

But in terms of political symbolism, during the Franco years RCD Espanyol held all the right cards. Those initials denoted Royal Sporting Club, and that 'Espanyol' spoke for itself. It was the Real Madrid of Barcelona: conservative, traditional, pro-Spanish Nationalism. In the war, an awful lot of Espanyol supporters had joined up on Franco's side. I was very familiar with the club's crown-topped crest, having spent an entire lockdown afternoon stitching a large Espanyol patch on to my retro woollen jersey, over the left-hand front pocket as portrayed in photos of Berrendero and his 1941 teammates. In light of his recent experiences, JB must surely have been more than a little surprised to find himself in Franco's favoured team. Perhaps this was to be a final, crowning test of his reformed character, his *depuración*.

Mind you, as we have already noted, team identity hardly meant much to a Spanish cyclist back then. The prospect of JB and Ezquerra working together on behalf of some rubbish football club who wasn't even paying them would have raised a few wry smiles. In any case, half the starting peloton were given no affiliation, and rode in grey jerseys embellished with the emblem of the Ministry of Education and Leisure.

*

Arse – meet Savlon. I'm sure you two have plenty of catching up to do.

Morning delivered reacquaintance with some grim routines, along with another dose of calorific dismay: just as I wouldn't be eating supper much before 9 p.m. in Spain, so I'd be waiting until 9 a.m. for breakfast. My woollen jersey, still cringingly damp when I pulled it off the bathroom clothes line and over my head, was very nearly dry by the time I'd been served a toasted baguette smeared with tomato pulp, and a glass full of milky coffee. It's always the way on these trips that whatever food I first success-fully order becomes my default meal for the duration. It could have been a lot worse: most of the old blokes sharing my bar terrace were sat before large breakfast brandies.

It was a Sunday and the serious cyclists were out in force: mountain bikers, club pelotons, wiry old geezers on shiny new road bikes. After the previous day's humiliation, I could frankly have done without an audience, though it was pleasing nonethe-less to receive some nods of approval, even the occasional aston-ished stare. The heat built; the towns thinned. Every half-hour I rolled through some sleepy village: old men gathered under a San Miguel parasol, old women fanning themselves with squares of battered cardboard. Madrid seemed a long way behind, even though it rather annoyingly wasn't.

Cresting a low brow, I spotted a monumental stone crucifix atop a distant hill. The Valle de los Caidos, Franco's creepiest, most totalitarian legacy. Below that 150-metre cross – by some margin the tallest on earth – a yawning, pale granite esplanade is laid out before one of the world's largest basilicas. Beneath it lies an under-ground crypt so vast its volume exceeds that of St Peter's in Rome. Over 20,000 Republican prisoners were put to work on this gargantuan project, which began a few months before the 1941

Vuelta. By the time it was finished eighteen years later, several hundred of them are thought to have died.

Franco pitched Valle de los Caidos – the Valley of the Fallen – as 'a national act of atonement and reconciliation', a resting place for Civil War victims of both stripes. But not even his mates believed him. This was to be his monumental, dictator-grade mausoleum, built to inspire awe and fear for all eternity. Some 34,000 people were buried at Valle de los Caidos, but only two had named graves. After Franco died in 1975, he was interred in the crypt, given pride of place before its circular altar. Opposite him, under an identical granite slab, lay the remains of José Antonio Primo de Rivera – dug up in Alicante after the war and delivered to Madrid on the shoulders of Falangist volunteers, like some 300-kilometre rotting-corpse Olympic relay.

Franco's tomb inevitably became a bit of a fascist magnet, and after decades of protests and appeals, in October 2019 – just nine months before I rode by – his body was exhumed and reburied in a small cemetery north of Madrid. But Primo de Rivera, quite astonishingly, is still down there. I'd planned a detour to visit this extraordinary, abominable site. But I can't say I was too distressed to learn it was closed.

The Alto de los Leones was the 1941 Vuelta's first point-scoring climb – in the winning words of Google Lens, its first puntable crest – and would be the last for almost 1,000 kilometres. It seemed important to give it a proper go, but Komoot had other plans. After crossing a tall dam I was led away into a rearing pine forest, past the mossy concrete foundations of Nationalist bunkers and gun emplacements. Beneath my wobbling wheels the tarmac narrowed and broke up, soon devolving into loose rock and red earth. Even in the resiny shade, the heat was smothering. My front tyre bounced off a fir cone the size of a baby's head and in the slo-mo battle for control I failed to yank a shoe out of a clip, keeling over into the dust. As I hauled myself up, a bloke about my own age hummed and crunched by on an electric mountain bike, giving me a wink that in a just world would have seen him bundled into a Roman catapult and propelled high over the treetops and down to the distant plain below.

For the next hour, doleful and defeated, I half-pushed, half-dragged La Berrendero up a steep, vague trail that was sometimes lost under drifts of pine needles. How galling to remember that Berrendero, along with everything else, was also twice the national cyclo-cross champion. As a master of carry-up-hillo, he'd have been skipping daintily through this tilted forest, bike on his back and a tune on his lips.

I remounted when I reached the red-and-white striped TV masts, those traditional summit harbingers. Ow. A shrieking, raw blister on my left heel: my first injury, and caused by bloody walking. A moment later I re-established contact with the road I should have been on all the time, by that old stone lion and a sign giving the pass's height as 1,511 metres. This would have made me feel pretty smug under normal circumstances: ones that didn't involve pushing my bike for an hour, or starting from 760 metres, because Madrid is the highest capital city in Europe. On the descent, I wanly digested the enduring legacy of this sorry misadventure. The first full day of my tour, and my overall average speed had already been taken round the back and kneecapped.

My breakfast had long since been burned off and at San Rafael, bottom of the helter-skelter ride down, I pulled into a street-side café. I was doing battle with a *bocadillo de tortilla* – a forearm of bread crammed with egg and potato – when a police car pulled in beside me, the same one I'd barrelled past on the way into town.

'*Casco?*' A female officer had her head out of the window, and was tapping it with a finger as she spoke.

The decision not to bring a helmet had been based on (a) my half-arsed quest for historical authenticity; (b) a belief that it wasn't a legal requirement; and (c) the fact that I had ridden a wooden-wheeled death trap all the way round Italy without one, and was therefore immortal.

'*No habla Español*,' I explained.

'*Casco* you must have in Spain,' she said flatly. 'Is ... *obligatario*. Tomorrow you buy.'

Belatedly I understood all those looks of astonishment I'd been receiving, most recently while shooting down los Leones past the cyclists who were labouring up it. They weren't impressed by my period get-up, just appalled at the illegal irresponsibility of its cloth-capped topping. I nodded soberly as she buzzed up her window, thinking, Well, that's (b) down the pan, so just forget all about (a) and (c). But five miles up the road, I'd already forgotten to forget.

The route westwards took me over a buff-coloured rolling plateau, on lonely, sun-softened tarmac. The empty brown vastness of Spain, so compelling through my aeroplane window, was overwhelming down here at eye level. Not for the last time I was reminded of a recent journey across the US: scattered herds of black cattle, the roofless hulk of a dead farmhouse, a towering, scabby grain elevator. And my word it was hot. Praise be for the miracle of free, cascading sweat: even with a good five litres of ingested fluid in me, I rode all afternoon without needing a comfort stop. Just as well, because there wasn't a single tree to hide behind.

In fact, the only scrap of shade I passed in three hours was that afforded by a moribund bulldozer, creaking in the sun beside a taped-off hole in the road. I pulled in to refuel, extracting a day-old packet of chocolate-filled pastries from my bar-bag without enthusiasm. Even fresh off the shelf, these little beige tubes had exerted a powerful suppressant effect on my appetite: each neatly puckered fundament, oozing a glob of filling, unavoidably recalled the bottom of an unwell cat. Peeling open the cellophane I understood that a long spell in that black-canvas slow cooker on my handlebars had intensified this distressing malaise. I forced one into my mouth, then immediately spat it out into the bulldozer's bucket and rode away. Forty-five minutes later I was back, retrieving the gloves I'd left behind.

Sweary, bellowed dismay was becoming my default in-saddle mode, and I'd barely started. The day wasn't done yet, either. At around half four, not long after leaving the rather lovely walled town of Avila, I checked Komoot and saw that the next settlement that might realistically offer me a bed lay 58 kilometres up the road. That was very nearly as far as I'd managed – with immense difficulty – in the whole of the previous day. And now I'd be riding into a hot headwind, and out across a lonely, broiled prairie.

Once again the heat kept rising as the afternoon grew older. At 6 p.m. the sun seemed directly overhead, bearing down from a cobalt sky. On occasion the road corkscrewed into a valley full of blustery heat, demanding awareness and reflexes that were by now almost beyond me. I didn't dare go down into the handlebar drops, because it felt as if I'd never get back up again. The bidon was nearly empty but felt heavy as a house brick when I hauled it out from its cage; I had to rest it on the bars between clumsy swigs. Vicious convulsions of cramp seized both calves, but when at tearful length they subsided, a jostle of rival agonies let me know they'd been there all along. Oh, right, my arse *does* hurt, I *have* lost all sensation in my special area, my shoulder blades *are* on fire, and the balls of my feet *did* just explode.

Cometh the hour, cometh the man. The other man: my redoubt-
able guiding hero, whose deep well of motivation I had hoped to
drink from in times of crisis. It certainly helped that Julián Berrendero looked a bit like me. Big forehead, glowering monobrow,
deep-set eyes and slightly too much hair: aside from the piercing
blue irises, we could almost have shared a photofit. And in
his prime he was a similarly unremarkable physical specimen,
average height, average build. There were even insinuations of a
personality overlap in the rest-day conferences the French press
conducted with cycling's new star during the latter stages of the
1936 Tour. JB comes across as a bit TM: sullen, awkward, snarky.
Interviewing the Spanish team in the hotel room they all shared,
Paris-soir's reporter notes that Berrendero stays quietly in the
background, keeping a watch on events with his deep, close-set
eyes. When he finally wrings a quote out of him, it comes across
as bluntly withering: 'I thought your cols were going to be harder
than that.' Maybe he meant it. But it's just the sort of thing I
would blurt out in misconstrued jest.

It's fair to say, though, that this is as far as JB and I went. A
fundamental divergence in temperament emerged as I read
through the French cycling writers' rather freaked-out descriptions of the young Madrileño's furious, raw determination. 'I spend
much time assessing this angry little dark character,' wrote the
man from *L'Independent*. 'Berrendero cuts a hollow, ascetic figure,
the tarred dust giving him the mask of an old owl. He clenches his
teeth and glares a few metres in front of his wheel, at a point, at
space. Sometimes he puts a hand on his hip, and freewheels, then
his head plunges down and he crushes the pedals once more.' *Le
Petit Dauphinois* paints a truly grim portrait: 'Berrendero twists his
emaciated and jaundiced body about on the bike. Behind the
mask, he is in agony and anguish, like Christ going to Calvary.'

You sense that he annoyed the French by failing to adhere to their patronising narrative. JB was no happy-go-lucky 'little fisherman'. Instead, they were confronted with an especially hard-nosed sporting mercenary who always followed the money. 'In the Tour de France, only a few riders, maybe 14 or 15, are made public idols each year,' he wrote, 'and only they get signed up for those well-paid box-office events in the weeks that follow. I had carefully considered where my greatest chance lay: the King of the Mountains was second only in admiration and popularity to the overall winner, and I would be guaranteed many lucrative contracts with the big promoters.'

And so it went on. The more I learned about Berrendero, the trickier it became to imagine him as a kindred spirit. In all honesty, he slightly scared me. This was a man who once whipped a Spanish police motorcyclist with an inner tube for veering across his path on a finishing straight, and reduced a Madrid grandstand to shocked silence by repeatedly dashing his winner's bouquet into the ground when a group of children came up to ask for a few carnations. In a sport that so often depends on cooperation, JB was a ruthless, hard-boiled loner. 'I never had any mentor or trainer,' he said in one of his last interviews. 'I forged myself, and always rode for myself.'

He made no effort to socialise or engage with other riders on the road; rather, he gleefully wound them up. Leading the 1936 Tour up the col d'Allos in a two-man break with Antonin Magne, Berrendero feigned bemusement when the double Tour winner asked him to share the work – a plainly obvious request, no doubt accompanied by that universal flick of the elbow. 'He told me something in his language that I did not comprehend,' he disingenuously suggests in *Mis Glorias y Memorias*. 'My interpretation was that he wanted me to pull harder.' So he did, much harder. 'By the time I looked back, my companion was far behind me – about three hundred metres down the road. Frankly, it did not go through my mind even for a moment to wait for him.' His account of the next act is a masterpiece of pithy understatement. 'On the descent, the Frenchman caught up and spoke to me again, although his tone seemed less friendly.' If winning big meant playing dirty, bring it on.

JB was a recidivist wheel-sucker – in the appealing native term, a *chuparrueda* – and an entirely unapologetic one. 'In pursuits or escapes I took no turns at the front,' he merrily confesses, 'even though I knew this would count against my reputation.' Related altercations with Sylvère Maes and Felicien Vervaecke – respectively first and third in the 1936 Tour's final standings, separated by Antonin Magne – ensured that Berrendero would be cold-shouldered by every rider who stood beside him on the Paris podium. Here was a debutant with absolutely no respect for the Tour's patrons, or for its code of honour. You can only admire the great big balls of the man. I suggest we all take a moment to do so right now.

Berrendero collected enemies with relish, even if he rode with them. In fact, especially if he did. Because whatever all those toothy beams in all those cheesy squad photocalls during the 1936 Tour might suggest, Jools was anything but an eager team player. 'Our team raced under no orders but God's,' he wrote later. 'I never had any help from my colleagues. Nobody looked after anyone else.' His account of the Tour is strewn with asides about 'the tension that unites the other components of the team against me', referencing 'disputes and constant quarrels'. Battle lines were deepened by commercial conflict. In Spain Berrendero rode for BH, one of the two dominant native bike manufacturers of the day; Cañardo and Ezquerra represented Orbea, the other. 'My teammates never even told me that the bike makers had offered a big bonus to the highest-placed Spaniard in the final classification,' he said afterwards, having belatedly realised why Cañardo bust a gut to overhaul him in the last few stages.

Rival national teams were astonished by what *El Tour de 1936* calls 'the total absence of group strategy', watching with open mouths as the Spanish riders attacked each other up every climb. One memorable occasion, they were seen pulling teammates back by their jerseys, and even trying to ride them off the road. 'To call it a team is a joke,' wrote one reporter. Things grew so ugly between Berrendero and Cañardo, his de facto team leader, that the big Catalan was overheard 'making threats'; the Spanish Cycling Federation felt obliged to ask their French counterparts to keep a watchful eye on the situation. For the author of *El Tour de 1936*, Berrendero was 'a wild, impetuous toreador', always goading the team's veteran bulls.

Berrendero's beef with Cañardo dated from that year's Vuelta, which had ended just a few weeks previously. Cañardo, second overall in the previous edition and his nation's dominant rider, had assumed charge of Team Spain's tactics; Jools felt he was being deliberately and persistently reined in. And so with two stages left he went rogue, recruiting Fermín Trueba as co-conspirator. 'We declared war on those around us,' he remembers, with evident glee. Riding outraged teammates off their wheels, they set off on a mammoth escape that would see Berrendero rise from eighth to fourth in the overall standings. Despite being relentlessly attacked by the rest of his own team all the way back to Madrid, he held on to his place and finished the race as the highest-placed Spaniard. 'What a furore,' he writes, with a conspicuous lack of contrition. 'This was a real *coup d'état*, a revolution!'

But still Berrendero wasn't done. After the race, when the team gathered in the organisers' office to receive and divide their winnings, he brazenly refused to honour the traditional arrangement. 'Fermín and I had earned more money in these two last stages than the rest of the team combined had won up to then; they expected us to split this income, but I had no intention of serving cash on a plate to those who didn't deserve it.' This was fighting talk, and Cañardo responded in kind. 'Things degenerated. Cañardo and I exchanged blows, and because of that I had to leave the room, escorted by guards.' Yet incredibly, this Punchy McPunchface rivalry only made it on to JB's grudge-match undercard. As a friendly-fire fight to the death, Berrendero's duel with Federico Ezquerra makes Hinault–LeMond look like a Chinese burn.

In his account of the 1936 Tour, Berrendero is winningly frank about this open in-team warfare. 'Ezquerra never trusted my purposes: he fought against me as hard as against any other, in fact harder, because in the mountains only I could keep up with him … I set off in pursuit of the rider who was much more my opponent than my partner … Ezquerra and I broke away, but as ever in confrontation not harmony … we reached the top side by side, and the struggle was once more resolved in my favour.' The triumphant relish rings out in those last words, as does the disdainful superiority in these: 'Ezquerra always seemed to attack with imprudence; if you ask me, he had a recurring nightmare that I would steal his position.'

So desperate was their battle up the rearing col du Laffrey that on one especially brutal ramp, both riders shouldered their bikes and scrambled side by side up the mountain on foot. When Ezquerra finally blew up in the Pyrenees, he blamed stomach cramps. But Jools wasn't buying that. 'He attributed his collapse to colic, but I think he was just exhausted, having pushed himself too hard in his obsessive fight against me.' It's impossible to imagine Berrendero composing the next sentence with a straight face. 'The most unfortunate thing was that he also lost second place in the Mountain Prize.' What a totally brilliant bastard. No one liked him; he didn't care. He was the Millwall Madrileño.

Anyway, the lesson of this protracted excursion into the psyche of Julián Berrendero is clear: hate conquers everything. Seeing out his sporting prime in a concentration camp would have filled his reservoir of bitter resentment to the brim, but he was running on spite long before that. Throughout his career, when JB was up against it, he found someone to despise: Ezquerra, *Doña Fatalidad*, the bloke who just punched him into the gutter. Hate put fire in his belly. But out on that lonely road in the dog-day sun there was nobody to hate but myself, and doing that just put lead in my wheels. By the time I creaked to a halt outside a huge old hotel in Peñaranda de Bracamonte I'd long since blown up, like a break-away rider reeled in and spat out the back, shaking my head flatly at a TV camera that wasn't there. It was gone seven and I'd done 140 kilometres since morning. When my head came back to life I realised I'd just ridden further than I had in any single day over the previous twenty years.

I was the only diner in the hotel's palatial restaurant, slumped before a table full of starched linen amid the native hospitality industry's typically jarring audio-visuals: a jazz-lounge instrumental interpretation of 'Karma Chameleon' burbling out of the speakers, and some inconsequential, crowdless football match being sound-lessly played out on an enormous telly mounted high on the wall. The hotel's stately matriarch, trailed by a retinue of facemasked daughters and granddaughters, swept through on her regal rounds as I was checking my reflection in the back of a gleaming spoon: what a freak show, deep white grimace lines etched into a rust-coloured face. She paused before me and issued some strained-sounding acknowledgement.

This gaff was clearly the fanciest in town, somewhere you'd go to propose marriage or celebrate a big promotion, yet in these desperate plague days they were reduced to rolling out the red carpet for a solitary flash-fried foreigner in crimplene slacks. It was beyond awkward. But food and booze eroded my self-conscious unworthiness, before drop-kicking it right over the chandelier after a granddaughter shyly placed an enormous brandy in front of me with the four most beautiful words in the Spanish language: '*Cortesía de la casa.*'

CHAPTER 5

Peñaranda de Bracamonte was a quiet and unpretentious town that had clearly seen better days, to judge by all the derelict old factories I'd weaved past on the way in. But it had also seen some very much worse ones, as I learned from what would become a sombre morning ritual: sitting down with a *tostada* and a *café con leche*, then typing the name of whatever town I was in plus '*guerra civil*' into my phone. The internecine ordeals here stretched back to well before the war even started, and lingered on after it ended: from the four townspeople shot dead by the Guardia Civil in 1931 for celebrating a successful strike, to the mysterious explosion that destroyed a weapons depot in September 1939, flattening half the town and killing over 100. In between, local Falangists took dozens of local Republicans 'for a walk' – the standard euphemism for an enforced outing you didn't come home from.

Sat amongst tables full of placid, genial citizens outside a bar in the town's little colonnaded square, I had to suppress gawps of horrified revulsion as I read what their grandparents had done to each other. A schoolteacher murdered for wearing a red tie. Old men taken for a walk because they read the wrong newspaper. One elderly citizen, then a nine-year-old girl, recently recollected running out to give her father his cap when armed men took him away on a sunny August morning in 1936. 'I said it was hot and he should wear it. They told me that where he was going he wouldn't need a cap.' Her eldest brother, the socialist mayor of a nearby village, was also taken away the same day. Neither would be seen again. Of the half million Spaniards who lost their lives in the Civil War years, an estimated 240,000 were civilian victims of official or extrajudicial repression. Most were buried out in the wilderness, or in mass unmarked graves at the local cemetery; unknown thousands were thrown down wells, or off bridges. Only a tiny proportion have been exhumed and identified; the vast majority will never be found. It was so, so difficult to read this kind of stuff and square it with the low-key, communal good cheer playing out around me. God alone knows how the 1941 Vuelta riders kept their focus, passing through shattered towns bathed in so much bad blood. Ramón Torres, quite understandably, never once dared mention the war or its terrible aftermath – not even when, as at Peñaranda, the race passed right through a recent scene of apocalyptic devastation.

After a tentative start, the 1941 race kicked off on the Alto de los Leones. JB topped it in fifth place, and put the hammer down on the descent. Fermín Trueba punctured and had to toil his way back to the bunch alone; in contrast, when the Swiss rider Weber suffered a '*pinchazo*' his entire team waited while he changed tubulars. *El Mundo Deportivo*'s report lays bare the hardcore, heavy-metal mechanicals pros had to deal with back then: a pair of broken front forks, a fractured crank. One of the FC Barcelona riders, saddled with those substandard tubulars, endured four punctures. Three other competitors succumbed to 'physical indispositions' that ended their participation. A baptism of fire, under a fierce sun.

The run-in to the finish in Salamanca was flat and fast, and I did my best to pay tribute, head down through the cornfields with a modest tailwind. I passed my first Osborne-brandy bull, those black-silhouette billboards that stand guard on so many roadside hilltops, my first church-tower stork's nest, and my first *club de alterne*, the tawdry edge-of-town brothels with pink neon signs on the roof that were everywhere from here on. I suppose it's a reaction to the ultra-Catholic Franco era, when divorce, bikinis and kissing in public were illegal – in the regime's early years, newspapers had to draw a vest on any photograph of a topless boxer they intended to print. But just as in Italy, the pendulum has swung back rather too far.* For good measure, this first club was right next door to a facility where a rather different and much older sort of local sat out front in plastic chairs: the *residencia de majors*.

---

* A survey quoted by Giles Tremlett in *Ghosts of Spain*, published in 2006, suggests that more than one in four Spanish men under forty-nine have had sex with a prostitute – comfortably the highest proportion in Europe. The flabbergasting extent to which *clubs* have inveigled themselves into daily Spanish life is made plain in Tremlett's book. He writes of the minor-league football team who secured shirt sponsorship from their local club de alterne, which came with a bonus clause: a night at the club if they avoided relegation. Interviewing the owner of a club near Valencia, Tremlett learned that it is quite normal for young men to be dropped off by their girlfriends on Saturday nights, with an arrangement to meet up later at a nightclub down the road.

At Salamanca, Jools dusted off his Tour-honed racecraft, powering away from a fifteen-man peloton as it toiled up the steepish, crowd-thronged Avenida de Mirat. The first stage would be his, fourteen seconds ahead of teammate Delio Rodríguez. Ramón Torres dutifully hailed the scene, urging the riders to draw inspiration from the '30 or 40,000 patriotic spectators who lined up on the pavements to salute them, having waited for hours in blazing heat'. The presence of this huge crowd, and Ramón's desperation to eulogise it, was no mystery: Salamanca was Franco Central.

It was here, in September 1936, that Nationalist generals held the meeting that would end with Francisco Franco being declared 'Generalísimo' and dictator-elect. Here, too, where he established his wartime general headquarters, and broadcast his propaganda. What little opposition the 1936 Nationalist coup faced in Salamanca was extinguished with merciless efficiency. On the morning of 19 July, while Federico Ezquerra was defiantly spurning the stage winner's champagne in Cannes, a rebel captain led his troops into Salamanca's Plaza Mayor and began reading out the edict of martial law. A lone cry rang out from the crowd: '*Viva la revolución social!*' In a few seconds, four men and a young girl lay dead.

The subsequent repression was especially horrendous. The city's Republican mayor and a schools inspector met their deaths at a mock bullfight held out in the fields. The Count de Alba de Yeltes, Franco's senior press officer, boasted to an American journalist that he'd shot dead six labourers on his Salamanca estate, 'to set an example'. And indeed to make a start: he told an English reporter that a third of Spain's male population would probably need 'eliminating'. (In 1964, the increasingly deranged count shot and killed both of his adult sons in the family mansion, a crime for which he never stood trial.) Thirty Salamanca freemasons were murdered to satisfy a uniquely Francoist phobia, and the local paper's much-loved bullfighting correspondent was executed for having once been friends with a socialist minister.

And Salamanca was where the Nazis hung out. Hitler saw Spain's Civil War as an ideal sandbox to test out his new weaponry and battle strategies – but Nazi Germany's involvement went much deeper than that, developing and trialling the bureaucratic machinery required to sustain a totalitarian terror state. SS Sturm-bannführer Paul Winzer, Gestapo attaché at the German Embassy in Salamanca, trained Franco's political police, as well as laying out and briefly commanding the concentration camp at Miranda de Ebro, a model for the Nazis' own camps. In 1937, SS Colonel Heinz Jost – later sentenced to death at Nuremburg for atrocities committed on the Eastern Front – was seconded to Franco's Ministry of Public Order, heading up a four-man team in Sala-manca that collated a vast archive of political information. 'We have on file more than two million names, along with proof of their crimes,' boasted Franco to an American journalist in 1938. 'There will be no mediation with these people, because criminals and their victims cannot live together.' This was as close as he ever came to admitting responsibility for the repression that put so many of his countrymen in unmarked mass graves.

I hope you'll forgive this digression, but in case you don't want to, let me explain. These Nazi-curated Salamanca archives were maintained right through the Franco era, and despite a frenzied effort at destruction in the months after his death, some have survived to the present day. Following a tip from Stefan Padberg, a German cycling friend of mine who spent some years in Spain, a few weeks earlier I had sent an information request to the Centro Documental de la Memoria Histórica in Salamanca. Shortly after-wards, the CDMH sent me an email with an embedded link; I clicked on it and was presented with a scan of a wonkily type-written record card:

BERRENDERO Julián

Deja la mitad de sus honorarios en la vuelta ciclista a Francia para ayudar a los huerfanos de la guerra. "MUNDO OBRERO". No. 485 Pag. 3 dia 7 de Julio de 1937. I stared at it for an extremely long time, excited and horrified in equal measure. How innocuous this little card looked, blandly factual and index ready. But there, in three dozen words, Berrendero's fate was spelled out before me. I already knew what most of those words meant – this was a reference to the written pledge the Spanish team had signed at the start of the 1937 Tour, promising to donate half their winnings to war orphans. But there was one I had to look up, and it was probably the most significant. 'Obrero' was 'worker'; the information was culled from a story in the Spanish Communist Party's *Workers' World*. The Nazis who curated the Salamanca archive would clearly have paid very close interest in this Soviet-funded publication: it's a fair bet that anyone whose name appeared in its pages would have been given their own index card. I read it again, realising this was as close as I'd ever get to an answer. Berrendero wasn't incarcerated for anything he said or did, because all his teammates had said and done the same; indeed, in most cases they had gone further. No, he was made an example of because his name alone had once appeared in a Communist newspaper, and it had done so because in 1937 Julián Berrendero was the best-known cyclist in Spain.

---

* 'BERRENDERO Julián. Donated half his winnings in the Tour de France to help war orphans. Workers' World, No. 485, page 3, 7 July 1937.'

As I did my best to force the pace up the Avenida de Mirat – not easy given its incline and all the bendy buses – I tried to imagine how JB would have felt, sprinting away from the field through a thick crowd of Falangists, here in the city where his effective arrest warrant was written. Squeaking to a halt at the Stage 1 finish line, and trying to forget it had taken me three days to reach it, I pulled on my flowery mouth-mask and took stock. Filter out the universal face coverings, and Salamanca was agelessly appealing, still dominated by a dome-towered, golden-stoned cathedral, a city whose yawning, parade-ready old squares remained the principal public spaces. But an enduring anti-Republican conservatism proclaimed itself all around: Queen Square, the Hotel of the Catholic Kings, the Imperial car park. It seemed important to tarry a while and put all this history into context, but after the rolling shambles of my progress to date it seemed more important to crack the fuck on. I stood outside a bar, pressed another epic *bocadillo* inch by inch into my sweaty maw, saddled up and turned south.

Silent and largely dead straight, the N630 would be my home for the next 500 kilometres. The road that followed the old Ruta de la Plata – the Silver Way pilgrim trail to Santiago de Compostela – was a cyclist's dream, its smooth carriageway bordered with a generous bike-friendly hard shoulder. The downside of this zone, as with all hard shoulders, was a scattering of stones, gravel and glass, along with a uniquely Spanish ingredient: bits of burned car. Half an hour out of Salamanca my front wheel passed through yet another carbonised stain on the tarmac, and sent something stout and metallic pinging into the roadside crash barrier. Then my back wheel attempted to repeat the trick, and – ping, hiss, blat-blat-blatblatblatblatblat – instantly and explosively punctured. Ah, *Doña Fatalidad*. I've been expecting you.

Feeling a sense of hard-bitten comradeship, I pulled over on to the shadeless verge and leaned the bike against a roadside marker post. I never really noticed the heat until I stopped, and my self-generated breeze died a death. That morning the TV weatherman had waved his hand over a great crimson blot that spread across west and south-west Spain, a zone of *calor extremo* covering every inch of my route for a good thousand kilometres. In search of a second opinion I'd brought up a long-term forecast on my phone: seventeen straight days of blazing yellow orbs, above a helpful warning, 'LOOKING AHEAD – possible danger of dehydration and heatstroke while doing strenuous activities.'

Anyway, it was now well over 40, and tragically so was I. My heat-softened plastic tyre levers proved useless in those frail and aged hands: every time I forced one into the rim and pushed, La Berrendero spat it out. My bare thumbs fared no better when I endeavoured to employ them in the manner recommended by a breezy YouTube tutorial I squinted at, pulling my jersey up around my phone to shield the screen from the fierce sun. In emulation of the smug young YouTuber, I settled into a half-squat with the wheel between my splayed knees, gripped the tyre in both palms and transmitted all my strength and the full weight of my body through my thumbs. In smug young YouTuber-land, at this point the tyre meekly surrendered and just sort of dropped off the rim. A rather different story played out on that Salamancan roadside. I gurned horribly, limbs trembling, sweat bursting forth from every hole in my body. The tyre implacably held firm. I tried again, and again, and again.

After half an hour, spent, red and just a little tearful, I stooped down to the toolbag and with a whimper retrieved the big screw-driver. 'I'm so, so sorry,' I said, addressing La Berrendero and her absent owners in a cracked whisper. In an ugly minute it was done: a flaccid inner tube in my hands, and an angry gouge in the rim of a Mavic G40. The unmarked original wheels, cherished over four decades by José Luis, spoiled after three days in my hopeless old hands. At least there was no one around to witness this shameful tragedy. No one but a trio of vultures, circling high in the cloudless heavens, and a deafening mass of unseen crickets. These tireless chirpers had been providing the rural muzak since I'd set off, but only now did I get what their game was. One cricket plays a simple, silly tune. But one million is a baying hyena chorus: nature's drunken football crowd, blowing their stupid vuvuzelas and jeering the opposition keeper as he runs up to take a goal kick – YOU'RE SHIT, AAAAAAAAAHHHH. They'd been taking the piss out of me all along, and I would never forget it.

CHAPTER 6

Ramón Torres, *El Mundo Deportivo*'s race reporter, seems to have been a bit of a card. He started out as the paper's billiard and bull-fighting correspondent, never married, and lived with his sister in Barcelona. A photo in his obituary – he died in 1983 – suggests a *Guys and Dolls*-era ducker and diver, short and squat, trilby pulled down over one eye. Despite this unhelpful build, and the fact that he didn't cover cycling until he was pushing forty, when he reported on a race he would endeavour to borrow a bike and tackle its most brutal climb, 'so he could understand what the riders went through'. Torres never used a typewriter, dictating copy down the phone from one of the notebooks he kept in his bulging jacket pockets – 'there were dozens of them, his archive'. But this esoteric approach produced such compelling journalism that during a big race, the police were routinely called to keep order outside EMD's Barcelona offices: the public wanted to hear what Ramón Torres had written, and couldn't wait until the paper hit the streets. 'When you read his reports,' remembered one fan, 'you really felt you were on a bike and taking part. He was such a human writer. He described the mountain stages from back to front, beginning with the agony of those who'd been dropped and ending with the joy of the winner.'

Anyway, old Ramón really went to town in his retelling of Stage 2. Its protagonist was Antonio Montes, a Sevillian rider who had endured a torrid first stage. After snapping a crank he took a wrong turn in Avila that added 20 kilometres to his day's work, eventually rolling into Salamanca an hour behind everyone else. But at dinner that night, the Sevillian captivated the journalists and officials with his jaunty self-deprecation: 'Montes wittily made light of his misfortune,' wrote Ramón, 'making the hotel dining room resonate with laughter.' The next morning, Antonio went off right from the gun and wasn't caught, covering the 214 kilometres to Cáceres at a pretty remarkable average speed of 31.7kmh – comfortably the fastest stage of the race.

Torres would have been well aware that Montes was only permitted to embark on his epic escape because he was already miles behind in the general classification, and thus posed no threat. But he preferred to overlook this, framing Montes's achievement in the most gloriously overblown manner. 'Today the great Sevillian Antonio Montes displayed every gift that God wanted to bestow upon mankind … he had the courage to escape alone, invincible to physical suffering for seven long hours, miraculously impervious to thirst, heat and exhaustion. I say we proclaim this man the King of Masculinity.'

Ramón was driven around the Vuelta in 'Number 4', an aged Fiat piloted with wayward elan by Corporal Pastor of the transport corps. His fellow passengers, cooped up in the hot little car for nine hours a day, were Nivardo Pina, *il Movimiento*'s press officer, and a photographer for *Gol* magazine who went by the enigmatic single-word sobriquet Firmas. I don't wish to cast any shade on this trio's professionalism, but as the race progresses Ramón becomes increasingly open about their relaxed working practices. Number 4's passengers appear to have spent their long days in one of two conditions: drunk or asleep. You don't have to read between the lines, when the lines themselves celebrate 'fresh, sparkling cider', 'White Horse vermouth' and 'the generosity of Don Luis Montero's wineries'. 'From there we left with such euphoria that some, in their contentment, weaved and zigzagged along the road.'

Ramón's colourful, rambling celebration of Montes's escape seems fully compatible with this conduct. His report is suspiciously light on race detail, devoting more space to the haircuts the occupants of Number 4 stopped off for at Guijuelo than events on the road. And to my own considerable detriment, he appears to have slept right through the Puerto de Vallejera, making zero mention of this 1,202-metre pocket bastard, which thus took me by ghastly surprise. How very grateful I was for the roadside fountain halfway up – the first such installation I'd passed that hadn't been shut off for Covid-control purposes.

Bejar, the first settlement on the other side of the Puerto, was a rather bland town in a dramatic setting, hemmed in on all sides by mighty treeless eminences. At 7 p.m. it was a great bowl of soupy heat, yet the main square was thronged with masked strollers. Being so relentlessly gregarious and communal, the Spanish weren't about to be denied their evening perambulation by bone-softening temperatures and a pandemic. Lockdown must have been so much harder here. As a self-contained North European misanthrope I'd coped very well, to the point of secretly enjoying large parts of it. And it was so sad to see such expressive people trying to emote with half their faces hidden. Eyebrows were doing an awful lot of exaggerated work to step into the breach, always either cranked up to the max in parody of gleeful astonishment or furrowed right down in utter, crumpling despair. If you didn't know better you'd think everyone in Bejar had either just found a tenner or had their dog put down.

On the upside, Covid offered a great opportunity for the house-proud, antiseptic Spanish to showcase their germicidal super-powers. Even before the pandemic you wouldn't have found cleaner lavatories south of the Alps. Now whole towns were infused with the alcoholic reek of antiviral fluid: at the Bejar supermarket I went into, shoppers gelled up their hands before donning disposable gloves, then with much squidgy rustling, gelled again. Inside I walked down multiple aisles stacked with bleaches and soaps, all trumpeting their antimicrobial cleansing might in apocalyptic terms. My favourite was a laundry whitener named Blanco Nuclear.

The guesthouse I checked into was the heavily chlorinated encapsulation of this national trait, though my bedroom also paid tribute to an older Spanish tradition: being really short. Men of Berrendero's under-nourished era reached an average adult height of 5ft 4in – almost half a foot shorter than Spanish males born in the 1980s. The consequence, as it would be in so many old family-run hotels, was a tiny room with a doll's-house bed. I'm not even 5ft 11 and my blistered heel rubbed painfully on the bottom ridge of the mattress all night.

I was well placed to assess this as I didn't sleep. At all. First it was the nocturnal soundtrack wafting up from the street: spirited civic nattering until about 11 p.m., then the dogs, then the bells. Oh my word, the bells. Even the tiniest Spanish town has a church that stridently chimes out quarter-hours round the clock. Except it's not a chime, just the irregular clonk of a toneless bronze bucket, the sound of a drunkard wearily belting a bollard with a saucepan. I could, of course, have closed the window, and certainly would have if it had been less than 98,000 degrees Celsius and I'd had air conditioning. I'd lie there, knees up, with my sweaty eyelids slowly dropping, then just as they closed: KLUNG! BRANG! DONK! And so it went on, until 4.49 a.m., when my door – my locked door – flew open and the ceiling light clicked blindingly on. My eyes barely had time to adjust and focus before this process was loudly reversed, but before the room went black and the door slammed I got a clear snapshot of the polite young man who'd calmly checked me in, now frantic, dishevelled and muttering urgently into a phone.

I was left wide-eyed in the dark, my hot head full of fear and questions. Was this some Covid census, a small-hours tally of suspect foreign plague-bringers? Or had he just popped in to check if I'd melted yet? Only two things were certain: I wouldn't be getting back to sleep, and when I checked out the bloke would be hiding and I'd never get to find out what the fuck he'd been playing at. Still, as I blearily concluded while retrieving La Berren-dero from a cupboard under the stairs, you just don't get this sort of excitement in chain hotels. I couldn't imagine it happening in an Ibis. Mind you, if it did, I'd have sued them for everything they had and wouldn't need to finish writing this book.

Spain has more law enforcement officials per capita than any other European nation: over 250,000, getting on for double the UK total, and we have twenty million more citizens. So that rearward whoop of siren, even out on those lonely hot plains, was only a matter of time.

'You speaker Spanish?'

I suppose my variegated skin tones gave me away as a foreigner: rosy nose, crimson knees, ears like shrivelled rashers of well-done bacon, pink and brown with a crispy rind. In the scorching sun, even those lockdown-burnished forearms had begun to peel and bubble. My string-backed gloves had created the silliest tan lines of all time: removing them revealed a neat grid of red stipples across the back of my hands, as if someone had just slammed them in a waffle iron. And my desert-island lips were getting ever crustier, as the Vaseline I kept in one of my front pockets was now almost impossible to apply. In these monstrous conditions, one did not speak of petroleum jelly. One spoke of petroleum.

The older of the two motorbike cops who'd pulled me over rapped a finger hard against his crash helmet, then jabbed it at my head.

'*Casco – casco!* In Spain you must have!'

This probably wasn't the moment to wheel out a Spanish phrase I'd been rehearsing for days, but I went for it anyway. I told him that I was making again the Vuelta of one thousand, nine hundred forty-one, to pay honour this great champion Julián Berrendero.

He made a face that said: Schmerrendero. 'Because no *casco*, I can make you pay one hundred euros.'

I nodded sombrely.

'And I can make you pay more, because I see you like this,' he said, holding an imaginary phone to his ear. I remembered that just before the siren-whoop I'd been recording one of the 1,814 voice messages that have helped imbue this narrative with such compelling immediacy.

'Oh, yeah, right, but I mean no, you didn't, because that was my GPS.'

He smiled joylessly, gave me an unflinching glare then flicked a finger at my second phone, the one prominently affixed to my handlebars with a big map on its screen. 'And this?'

'That's for your mother to send me special pictures,' I might have replied.

'Plasencia, next town, you buy *casco*. If I see you again with no *casco* I make you pay. I will see you again today!' He did, actually. Twice.

There was a bike shop in Plasencia, happily run by a young man who spoke excellent English and nurtured a great passion for old bicycles. Abel had a couple of pristine Seventies road bikes up on his wall and was very taken with La Berrendero. It had by now become apparent that in order to make my guiding hero's name understood in his native land, I needed to pronounce it like someone doing a preposterously over-the-top Manuel impersonation, with much throat-clearing and the spray-and-pray rolling of rs. But tragically, the name plastered all over my bike meant nothing to Abel, and nor did Cchhgghhgghoooolián Berrrrrrren-derrrrro. This would keep happening, in bike shops and elsewhere, and when it did I always felt let down. I really shouldn't have. Why on earth would anyone of working age be familiar with a cyclist who had retired more than seventy years previously? It would be like going into PC World and getting the hump because the girl at the till hadn't heard of Alan Turing.

Abel made me put on a rona-repellent disposable shower cap before trying on the only helmet he sold that cost less than €100 – I couldn't bring myself to pay more than the fine for not having one. I buckled the strap under my chin and turned towards Abel's mirror with deep foreboding. Here I must confess a supplementary rationale for rarely wearing a helmet: on account of cranial irregularities that cause them to perch high on my head, then slide sharply backwards in use, they always make me look stupid. Whenever I wear a helmet I'm always asked why I've got it on the wrong way round. Abel's squinting bemusement as he assessed my profile suggested he was restraining the urge to ask this question, or perhaps a more general one: what the hell's up with your head, you big freak? Instead, he came up and slapped me four or five times on the shoulder, praising my adventure in the warmest terms as he did so. I've just realised that the only people who ever touched me in Spain were men in bicycle shops.

CHAPTER 7

I was in Extremadura now, which if it's famous for anything is famous for nothing: vast unpopulated sweeps of frazzled brown flatness, with dead-straight roads that sometimes ploughed their lonely furrow for 50 kilometres between settlements. The province is also noted – hooray! – for its brutal and relentless summers, perennially the hottest place in Europe, with temperatures that often top 45. That's not sunbathing, it's being staked out in the desert.

The Coke cans in the ditch beside the N630 were all silver, every flake of paint long since scorched away. Cows hid under olive trees; topless, walnut-skinned farmers stumbled about in golden fields. A sort of shimmering, fuzzy heat halo girdled every farmhouse roof, and the wheelless cars dumped outside. When the wind turned and came in at me off the scorching plains, it felt like I'd got too close to a bonfire. All afternoon I flew blind: my phone screen was a glinting white void with the sun overhead, as it always seemed to be. But with my next turning three days away, that hardly seemed to matter.

These were, without question, the hottest days of my cycling life. Every so often the N630's distant parallel motorway would veer up and cross over me, creating a hallowed patch of shade to enjoy what passed for refreshment. In the absence of petrol stations, let alone actual shops, I had to eke out my piping-hot bidon water, and force down the awful, claggy remains of those chocolate-filled pastries.

'Could I interest sir in another leaking-bum cake?'

No, I really couldn't.

'But it's three days old, sir.'

So sweet of you to offer.

'Bar-bag cured, sir. Got to be over 50 degrees in there.'

Oh, go on then. Just the one.

I overnighted at a tiny village in an upscale Via de la Plata pilgrim hostel, shared with the first fellow foreigner I'd met, a middle-aged Dutchwoman en route to Santiago. We didn't get to exchange more than brief pleasantries: the handsome young Spaniard she'd picked up at a bar in Seville seemed terribly keen on receiving his after-hours reward for carrying her rucksack all day, and went on to do so with audible enthusiasm long into the night.

I slept fitfully in a room dedicated – via a sign on the door and a shelf-full of books – to Federico García Lorca, most beloved of poets in a country that really gets off on poetry. Lorca disappeared in August 1936; no body was ever found, but as a gay socialist, his fate is hardly a mystery. Handing my keys back in the morning, I got chatting with the English-speaking proprietor about poetry, and the challenges of its translation. The conversation spooled pleasantly on until I asked what he thought had happened to

Lorca. His cheery, fortysomething face glazed over; he took my key from the table and looked at me with a distant, helpless half-smile. An extremely strange silence ensued, which I eventually filled with a jarring gear-shift statement about the weather.

It was less than twenty-four hours since I had seen this exact expression pass over Abel's young face, when I started talking about Berrendero's time in the concentration camps. The Civil War was clearly beyond the conversational pale, even today, even for those born after Franco died. It was as if the whole nation had been programmed to steer clear of this awful moment in its history, to switch themselves off when it came up. Berrendero was in good company in swerving all mention of it. *El pacto del olvido*, they call it: the pact of forgetting. When Tremlett asked a Spanish academic how he should go about researching Francoism and the Civil War, he was told: on your own, at home. It's a wasps' nest you just don't poke. I read later that Lorca's own family have never made any attempt to find his body.

It was only a short ride to Cáceres, where Stage 2 had ended, with Antonio Montes crossing the line sixteen minutes clear. A tough stage for Jools: he dropped to eleventh after being plagued by a slow puncture, which in Google Lens's appealing take on Ramón's report repeatedly required him to 'descend and swell'. I'd set out from Salamanca with a fair wind on a flat road, daring to dream of a creditable tribute to Antonio Montes's epic breakaway. But that dream had died with my hour-long tube change, then decomposed horribly over three long, hot, stop-start days. Not so much the King of Masculinity as his court jester's wet nurse.

But though we can agree I was hardly ripping up the tarmac, every morning I still couldn't wait to get back out on it. When London lockdown eventually got too much even for me, going out for a ride felt like a break for freedom, a glorious release from all the oppressive, dystopian weirdness. It seemed even more oppressive in Spain, and so much sadder: all those dutiful mask wearers forced to restrain that hardwired native impulse to gather and hug and raucously spray each other with aerosol breath droplets. It was always a relief to hit the open road and leave all that behind, to carry on as if the whole world hadn't spun out of control, as if riding a really old bike for hours and hours in an open-air oven was reassuringly mundane rather than completely fucking nuts.

It helped that every dawn seemed like a reboot, a fresh slate, an opportunity to start all over again, and on the right foot. Whither yesterday's broiled and broken wretch, mumbling swears with his head under a roadside tap? Why, here he comes now – flying across the sun-washed morning plains with the wind in his wheels and a song on his lips. And look: here he is again, half an hour up the road, mumbling swears with his head under a roadside tap. What a tiny interval there was, in these conditions, from 'well, isn't this lovely?' to 'Fugginfugthiggchhtthh'.

Whenever I felt sorry for myself, all I had to do was imagine how much worse it would have been cooped up in the back of a bumpy old Fiat with squat Ramón and his vermouth snoring. The deeper I headed into Extremadura, the easier it became to feel an affinity with the 1941 race. This had been, and remains, the poorest region of Spain, the most traditional, the least changed. It was no effort to picture JB barrelling down this very hill, descending to swell by those gnarled olive trees, flashing by that farmhouse, though maybe back then it would have had a roof and some inhabitants. How I savoured the slow-burn thrill unique to retracing a bike race, that of following in the actual footsteps and wheel-tracks of its heroic sporting protagonists, no matter how dead they might be, seeing what they saw, suffering where they suffered.

I mean, up to a point. On the one hand, the 1941 racers were half my age, and arguably better at cycling. But on the other, they were riding three times as far as I was each day, and doing it much faster: I completed Stage 2 at an average speed of 22.4kmh, more than 10kmh slower than the King of Masculinity. When, in retirement, JB was asked by a journalist to name his proudest achievement, he unhesitatingly detailed his victory at the 1942 national road-race championships: '150 kilometres against the clock with tyres that weighed 750g, at an average of 37.925kmh.' I loved all the decimal places, but who can blame him for such total recall? That is some going in those circumstances.

And let's not forget Berrendero and his peers rode on terrible unpaved roads, on terrible bikes that punctured all the time and kept breaking. Properly breaking, not just some annoying noise or a slight wobble, but full-on I'm-gonna-die structural calamities: forks snapped, frames shattered, handlebars fell off. They had to carry all their own spare parts and tubes and do all their own repairs. They had to share rooms and wash their own kit. Though thinking about that last one – would they have even bothered? It was easier to imagine all that filthy, sweaty wool festering on the bed-board night after night. You might even establish a competitive advantage over your roommates, cowing them with your dominant manly essence, like spraying tiger piss on your flower beds to scare off cats. Wouldn't it be great if that was all I needed to do: just soil my shorts and not wash, then let the potent odours intimidate me into trying to ride away from myself?

And of course, the 1941 boys would have had a rather tougher time than I did in sourcing the 7,000 calories required to ride a bike all day. Post-war Spain wasn't exactly a ride-through all-you-can-eat buffet: the Forties and early Fifties were the *años del hambre*, the Years of Hunger, when half the country starved. The war had decimated agricultural output, and what little was harvested largely went abroad to help pay off the vast debts owed to Hitler for his military assistance. Reimbursing Stalin had already all but drained the national coffers: by the end of 1936, the Republican government had sent an extraordinary 510 tons of gold to Moscow, the bulk of the country's total reserves.

This was an era when cats and dogs were a rare sight on Spanish streets: they'd either died of hunger or gone into a casserole. The poor ate boiled weeds, lizards and acorns; bread was padded out with sawdust and straw. Even middle-class families could only manage one meal a day. The cost of living was five times higher than it had been before the Civil War, and wages sank to nineteenth-century levels. The infant mortality rate touched 50 per cent in the poorest regions. In the four years leading up to 1943, 159,000 Spaniards starved to death or died of a disease linked to malnutrition.

In the 1941 Vuelta, any half-decent food was reserved for the Swiss, who as foreigners had to be impressed. The other riders made do with an insufficiency of whatever crap came to hand: when they got meat it was almost black, and so tough it had to be soaked in water to render it digestible. The cupboard was especially bare in Extremadura: the riders had to start Stage 3 on empty stomachs. 'One kilometre before Merida,' reported Ramón, 'the organisers improvised a control in the middle of the road, with eggs, bananas and coffee, because at Cáceres, the hotels had not been able to fill the riders' food bags.'

This was clearly no one-off: Berrendero told an interviewer in 1972 that 'when we finished a stage in those Vueltas, we didn't know if there'd be another the next day – simply because there might not be any bread'. But beyond that one aside about the empty hotel kitchens at Cáceres, Ramón inevitably avoids any mention of famine or food shortages in his race reports. Instead, he dutifully lauds – and doubtlessly exaggerates – the Ministry of Education and Leisure's feed-zone munificence, and namechecks the local businessmen and benefactors who laid on booze and *bocadillo*s as the race passed through their town. Berrendero, who had endured full-on malnutrition in the camps, paints a more convincing picture of the Vuelta's nutritional reality: he was haunted throughout the race by torturous visions of the groaning tables he had laid waste to at the 1936 Tour. 'At the end of the queen stage in the Pyrenees I remembered eating three whole chickens, one after the other.'

It would be a while before Vuelta riders fared much better. During the 1945 Vuelta, the Basque rider Maximo Dermit found even the most fundamental necessity in short supply: 'Water – that was an expensive liquid! In some places, when we asked for it they preferred to give us wine. There was no water to waste on the likes of us.' Luis Otaño, who rode eight editions in the Fifties and Sixties, recalled eating the greaseproof paper that his inadequate dinners came wrapped in. It was common practice to break into a house, mid stage, and steal food. A Dutch cyclist who retired halfway through the 1946 Vuelta was so famished when he got on the plane home that after devouring his in-flight meal, he wolfed down everyone else's leftovers. The American next to him laid a sympathetic hand on his arm and asked if he'd just been released from a concentration camp. A state-produced documentary of that 1946 race tries hard to conceal the grisly deprivation, but there's simply too much of it. The cycling author Alasdair Fotheringham, who evidently accessed a much better copy of this film than the grainy blur-fest I found online, notes that most roadside spectators are barefoot and cadaverous. There's a tall man wearing only a blanket – he would have bartered his clothes for food – and crowds of black-clad widows, many compellingly young.* Driving around the Córdoba countryside later that year, a horrified *Daily Telegraph* correspondent wrote of 'children with swollen stomachs and fragile limbs, women like human scarecrows with enormous eyes'.

But Spanish cyclists who came of age in this desperate era always felt it gave them an edge: road-race cycling is all about knowing how to suffer. 'They had to fight for food, and that was what made them such tough cyclists,' said Carlos Sastre, the Spaniard who won the 2008 Tour de France. 'Now we have all we want to eat, and just think about stupid things like buying cars.' Almost every interview the big names of mid-century Spanish cycling gave in later life goes full Four Yorkshiremen right from the off, and quite forgivably so. 'If you didn't finish first or second in a one-day race, the organisers wouldn't give you any dinner,' recalled Bernardo Ruiz, winner of the 1948 Vuelta. 'But I'd make damn sure I won, too, because if you didn't they wouldn't give you a hotel to sleep in that night. You certainly never abandoned, because then you had to pay your own way home.'

Federico Bahamontes, who in 1959 became the first Spaniard to win the Tour de France, spent most of the Civil War in a refugee camp in the grounds of Madrid's University City. But, as he told Alasdair Fotheringham and anyone else who asked, things only got grimmer after his family moved back to Toledo. Bahamontes remembers 1941 as the worst year of his life: 'If I caught a cat, I'd cut off its paws and head, and skin it. Then my mother would gut it, stuff it with vegetables and pop it in the oven. We called them "baby goats".' He was then thirteen, and already a veteran

---

* In the absence of a death certificate, a woman whose husband 'disappeared' was not allowed to remarry, inherit his property or receive a widow's pension. The Civil War left a whole generation of desperately impoverished unofficial widows.

breadwinner: digging up live ammunition for scrap, selling rotten fruit gathered from market spoil heaps, stealing beetroot from trucks. To encourage young Federico's work ethic, his father took away the boy's only recreational accessory, a football, and cut it into shreds.

When Bahamontes bought a second-hand bike with his own savings, it was simply an investment: with a trailer hitched to the back, he toured surrounding villages hawking market-reject produce. A move into black-market trafficking earned him a bout of typhoid – he caught it after hiding from police in stagnant water under a bridge – but also instilled speed and stamina. His first racing bike, acquired soon after, was in essence a getaway vehicle.

Julián Berrendero, born sixteen years before Bahamontes, never endured quite this level of hard-bitten deprivation. But in early twentieth-century Spain few had it easy, and no one who did wound up riding bikes for a living. Mariano Cañardo, orphaned at fourteen, spent the balance of his teenage years working as a shepherd. Federico Ezquerra's dad was a road digger. JB was raised in a tiny 'service box', a block-built cabin that came with his father's job as a canal keeper for the Madrid water board.

Berrendero's first months were spent in a 'box' up in San Agustín del Guadalix, a small town 30 kilometres north of Madrid. The water board then relocated his father Martín to another service box in Fuencarral, now a Madrid suburb that is home to Biketown, but at the time fairly rural. JB was always curiously reticent about his family. His autobiography mentions that the Fuencarral cabin was home to nine Berrenderos, but he never explains who they were. The only reference he ever made to any sibling was a single runic aside in one of his last interviews: 'I had a brother, Juan, who rode in two bike races.' Julián and Pilar never had children of their own; maybe he couldn't face detailing all this familial fecundity. 'I can't pretend I don't wish we had kids,' he poignantly told the same reporter. 'It gives me great sadness.'

Or perhaps he was just impatient to get into the gruelling travails of his youthful working life, which, à la Bahamontes, he recounted at length and with some relish. At nine Julián got an after-school and weekend job at a local pigeon shoot, retrieving dead birds and escapees for paltry sums that he inevitably recalls in forensic detail. He then balanced education with stints as a dairy labourer, a weaver and a building-site water-carrier, before leaving school to work as an apprentice electrician, engaged in the construction of a new hospital. Wearied by the 14-kilometre walk to the hospital site and back, at the age of eighteen he acquired his first bike, 'a Pulpí brand machine weighing over 15kg, with mudguards, steel clincher wheels and a huge saddle'.

After trouncing work colleagues in lunch-break five-peseta prize sprints round the block, he rode the Pulpí in a local 'turkey race', a Christmas tradition across Spain. When he won the prize bird and took it back to the cabin, he was expecting a delighted reception: 'With nine of us at home, we had to eat.' Instead, Julián's furious father threatened to sell his Pulpí, telling him that bike racing was an indulgent distraction from the business of proper, remunerative work.

But JB couldn't cut the cord. He was too excited by his own potential. So, for two whole years, he trained and raced in secret. After dinner he'd tell his parents he was going to the cinema, then take the Pulpí far out into the dark countryside. Once a week he rode right through the night, up to Buitrago del Lozoya and back, a 160-kilometre round trip. 'I never went home after those trips, just rode straight into work. I used to catch up on sleep in the cinema.' I have no idea how he got away with it.

On Sundays, his day off, he competed in local races, an object of ridicule on his clunking Pulpí, even with its mudguards removed. Punctures and tactical ignorance initially kept him down among the also-rans. He lost his second race after stopping to retrieve four lemons that bounced out of his jersey pockets: some joker had convinced him these were the superfood secret of success. His third race, in the summer of 1931, was a 60-kilometre run up to his birthplace and back, 'an anarchic stampede full of pushing and tugging'. He escaped with two riders on a climb; one punctured, and, just a kilometre from the line in Fuencarral, the other bloke's chain fell off. 'My prize was a set of tubular wheels; I grabbed them and left, in case anyone I knew saw me.' His thrill at seeing the result printed in the local paper evaporated when his parents read it. 'They took my bicycle, and though I was soon allowed to ride it to work, they never let me have it at weekends or in the evenings.' Pilar, perpetually fearful of serious injury, supported the ban.

It would be more than a year until he rode another race, but by then he was pushing twenty. 'The next summer my parents seemed to accept my determination, and that I was old enough to make my own choices. At first they turned a blind eye when I went off at the weekends, but then my father started to appear at the finish line.' But Julián Berrendero's career was never far from a hiatus,

---

* As one of the few widely available foods, lemons were, in fact, a routine part of every professional's in-saddle diet: Berrendero and Bahamontes both recalled eating plenty, skin and all. Citrus fruit would be the ravenous Vuelta cyclist's last resort for years to come: in the 1968 edition, race leader Ralf Altig was fined 100 pesetas after grabbing three oranges from a roadside tree near Valencia. Rather more severe sanctions had previously been threatened for similar offences. Brian Robinson, the British rider who finished eighth in the 1956 Vuelta, recalls that armed soldiers stood at every crossroads: 'If you stopped to pinch some grapes they would raise their rifles to stop you.' Robinson came home from that race with dysentery.

and just as it looked like taking off he was called up to do his national service.

I plodded southwards, heading deeper into the almost extraterrestrial emptiness of the mesa. Gone now were all those club-strip riders on sleek machines: my only fellow cyclists across these ochre plains were tubby farmhands wobbling home on heavy old mountain bikes, grubby flapping hi-vis tabards over bare torsos. But even these characters taunted me with their superior machinery, idly clicking through a plethora of gears as the road gently rose and fell. I was still only using three of mine. For any incline at all: absolute bottom, low front, lowest rear. For anything even slightly downhill: absolute top, high front, high rear. For everything else: low front, highest rear. The incremental differences in between were almost imperceptible, though there was an exciting moment about a week up the road when a headwind and a false flat introduced a new gear combo.

In the summer of 1936, these lonely hot flatlands were the Civil War's bloodiest killing fields. For years beforehand, a sort of peasants' revolt had been rumbling on across Badajoz, the region of Extremadura I was now passing through. Fuelled by the medieval injustices of their lot, and inspired by the strikes up north, agricultural labourers periodically seized land from their aristocratic and ecclesiastical overlords, and burned down the odd church. So when, in August 1936, Franco's African Legion marched north from Seville to Cáceres – heading through Badajoz up the very road I was now heading down – its brutal commander, Lieutenant-General Castejón gave them free rein to extract vengeance. The enthusiasm with which these Moroccan mercenaries complied saw Castejón's corps swiftly dubbed the Column of Death.

Some truly terrible scenes played out all along the southern half of the long, straight N630. The wholesale decapitation of farm labourers was jokingly referred to as 'agrarian reform', their bodies left piled up at every crossroads as an example. Castejón's men set up roadside stalls selling looted booty and some horrific curios, pitched largely at the foreign press corps: just south of Cáceres, the *Daily Express* correspondent was offered several pairs of ears. One American journalist walking up the N630 found 'four old peasant women heaped in a ditch', and '30 or 40 militiamen with their hands roped behind them, shot down at a junction'. His most traumatic memory: 'I remember a bundle in a town square. Two young Republican assault guards had been tied back to back with wire, covered with gasoline and burned alive.'

In Almendralejo's siesta-emptied main square, I freewheeled under the palm trees wondering yet again how all these dozy little towns could have witnessed such dreadfulness. Over 1,000 citizens were killed here in the days after the Column of Death marched in; some were crucified, others burned alive. Entire families were shot dead, with the children killed first to maximise their parents' suffering. A Portuguese correspondent was so haunted by what he witnessed that he wound up in a Lisbon mental asylum.

How on earth could Ramón and the riders have blotted out horrors that were then still so fresh? The slaughter and savagery had started while the Spanish team were racing in the Tour, and had barely ended when they rode down this road. Even eighty years on it was all too easy to imagine, in this ageless landscape dotted with ancient buildings. Just before Merida I passed a couple of picture-perfect little fairy-tale castles; that night I Googled them out of curiosity, and discovered they had been requisitioned by Hitler's Condor Legion as the Panzer tank corps' training base.

In my first few afternoons, the street-vacating double whammy of siestas and Covid restriction had imparted an appealing tranquillity. Now it made these little towns feel desolate and haunted. Sometimes it seemed as if something dreadful was about to happen, rather than having distantly taken place. There was an ominous, *High Noon* vibe, all those flaky whitewashed storefronts and shuttered houses staring at each other across the dusty, deserted tarmac, all those walls plastered in peeling, faded bull-fight posters. And this was pig-farming *jamón* country: the air hung heavy with the stench of death.

But even a ghost town is better than no town at all. When you ride a bike out of any settlement in Badajoz, you take a bit of a gulp: ahead lies a lot of hot nothing to conquer, an immensity of russet-red soil studded with squat, gnarled vines and ancient olive groves. The only shade on offer is worse than no shade at all: when I pulled over against a tall bamboo fence, the taunting sound of splash and frolic came from an unseen swimming pool behind it. Every well-to-do Spanish family runs a *finca* – an old family home-stead out in the sticks, many of them now lavishly upgraded.

I stopped at Zafra. It was a sweet little town, full of wonky cobbled squares bordered by palm trees and old brick church towers with storks' nests stuck on top. But all the same, I couldn't warm to the place. It started to go wrong at the cemetery, which I rode past on the way in. I'd read there was a memorial here for victims of local repression, but the gates were closed. As I remounted, however, my eye was drawn to a cluster of small, circular hollows in the cemetery's lofty white wall, at about waist height, just to the left of the iron gates. I knew it was common practice for death squads to 'walk' their victims to the cemetery and gun them down against the wall; with a heavy heart I got out my phone and Googled those now familiar key words. Sure enough, one morning in September 1936, twenty-one men were 'walked' down the long, straight avenue that led to the cemetery, shot against the wall and left there. One elderly local who lost his great-grandfather that day had recently shared his story on a local internet forum: 'He didn't even have any political beliefs, he was arrested at the union office where he'd gone to ask about finding work. When my great-aunt Lucía, who was 12 at the time, went to the jail to take her father his food, as she did every day, they just told her that he was dead, that they'd killed him.'

A couple of hours later, sat outside my delightful hotel at the corner of the prettiest square, I extended my research into Zafra's blackest summer. Much of what happened was no more than typically horrendous. After taking control of the town with barely a shot fired, Castejón gave his Africanistas the usual reward: two hours to do their worst. Women were raped, homes looted and torched, and forty men were slaughtered. The mayor was ordered to provide Castejón with the names of sixty citizens to be shot, and in an especially sadistic mind-fuck, townspeople were allowed to remove three people from this list as long as they added three replacements. When the executions took place, forty-eight of the sixty victims were substitutes.

Before Castejón's men left, they recruited an enthusiastic volunteer whose exploits in the weeks ahead would set him apart, and guarantee that I would struggle to retain fond memories of this appealing town. Juan Bermejo was priest of the church whose tower peeped over the colonnaded townhouses opposite me. By the end of the summer, tagging along with the Column of Death with a pistol under his cassock, the tall, glossy-haired Bermejo had been nicknamed the Killer Priest of Zafra.

In the interests of context, the summer of 1936 was a deadly and terrifying ordeal for the Spanish Catholic Church. Anti-clerical hostility had been running high for decades in a country that was still mired in the ecclesiastical Dark Ages, where no fewer than 115,000 clerics – far more than any other European nation – colluded with the wealthy and powerful to keep the poor in their place via feudal land practices, and what Antony Beevor calls 'the age-old trick': promising heaven to the biddable, dutiful meek. By the 1930s, even left-leaning moderates had become violently anti-clerical. Manuel Azaña, the Republic's last president, said he would rather have every church in Spain burned down than see a single Republican harmed.

The Civil War brought these grievances to a murderous head: within four months, more than 4,000 priests and 280 nuns had been killed, many in the most appalling circumstances. Nuns were raped before being murdered; castrated priests were burned to death in their churches. When reports of these atrocities reached Britain, distraught eminent Catholics sent huge donations to Franco, who had set himself up as the Church's valiant defender. The Earl of Bute is alleged to have contributed £3 million. The Irish went further still: 7,000 Irishmen had volunteered to fight Franco's fight by the end of 1936, and a 700-strong Irish Brigade later arrived at a Nazi-run training camp in Cáceres. For many Catholics, this was a bona fide holy war: a fight against Soviet-inspired Godlessness in which no quarter could be given. It was a narrative that ran deep in traditionalist Spain, still haunted by five centuries of Moorish rule, and still glorifying the *cruzados* that had finally secured their nation's Reconquista.

All of this doubtless explains why Bermejo decided to join Castejón's division. But nothing can begin to justify the psychopathic sadism that would earn him his nickname. When the priest found five Republicans taking refuge in a cave – one a wounded woman – he forced them to dig their own graves, then shot them in the legs, kicked them into the pit and buried them alive. A man he discovered hiding on his knees in a church confessional was shot dead on the spot. By the end of 1936, Zafra's Killer Priest would boast of having killed over 100 people. 'These rats deserve extermination by any means,' he remarked. 'And God, in his immense power and wisdom, will applaud those who exterminate them.' In Franco's Spain, this stuff looked great on a CV. After the war, Bermejo was given a cosy little sinecure as chaplain to the Corps of Wounded Veterans, and later taught the children of railway workers. He saw out his career as a parish priest, and died peacefully in 1973.

With a bowl of stew and three beers in me, I headed sombrely off into the warm, narrow streets. Ambling among the chatty, masked minglers in Zafra's well-shaded municipal gardens – couples, groups of teenagers, multi-generational families – I was struck once more by Spain's love for public congregation. Whenever there's a national outcry, vast numbers gather on the streets in protest. Million-strong marches are commonplace in Madrid; after the terrible train bombings in 2004, an estimated eleven million Spaniards – a quarter of the entire population – expressed their horror in mass demonstrations. The Spanish love a big household: half of all men in their twenties still live with their parents, albeit in many cases through economic necessity. And over half a billion quid is spent annually on local fiestas that reliably fill every town square in the land. When Covid hit, the Spanish government didn't need to remind its citizens that they were all in this together.

But how – *how?* – did the people of Zafra, of all of Spain, progress from fratricidal massacre to this place of happy coexistence? Did they just get all the murderous hatred out of their systems in the Civil War? I had to hope so: how terrible to imagine this was all a façade, a brittle veneer over murderous, hot-blooded resentments that still bubbled furiously just under the surface. That fondness for mass gathering had also found expression after

Franco's death, when half a million Spaniards queued up to pay their respects. (In the 2019 general election, 3.6 million people voted for the neo-Francoist Vox party, securing it fifty-two seats.)

And though my head kept telling me it was all a long time ago, my heart was in a different time zone. When you're reliving 1941, the Civil War doesn't seem like ancient history. Perhaps, too, Covid played its part in making 1936 seem so very close to home. It had struck me back in London that this pandemic was the nearest I'd ever come – thank fuck – to living through a war. The curfews and shortages, the stirring sense of common purpose as people kept calm and carried on, and those awful moments when the mighty undercurrents of fear and mistrust broke through and everyone fought over bog rolls and tore each other's masks off on the bus and shopped their neighbours for having a few friends round. In fact, if this pandemic was a war, then it had most in common with a specific type of conflict. 'A civil war is not a war but a sickness,' wrote Antoine de Saint-Exupéry. 'The enemy is within. One fights almost against oneself.'

CHAPTER 8

SEVILLA 137

On a bike, with your undigested breakfast still sloshing about, it's never much fun to see the day-end destination followed by a huge number. Of late I was even being denied the traditional free morning kilometres – that quick 20 or 30 you can sneak in before your body has a chance to realise what's going on. In this heat, the sun always blew my cover within a couple of miles, when the day's debut rivulet of sweat burst forth from the base of my spine and worked its way down: a moment I'm afraid I came to enshrine as First Cleft Trickle.

And with the onward march of that miserable wanker Old Father Time, pain seemed to clock on ever earlier. I changed my riding position a dozen times in the first half-hour but still my palms hurt, my elbows hurt, and every single bodily extremity had shed any vestige of sensation. Fearsome beings flew in at me off the plain, locust-sized crickets and clumsy beetle things that unerringly homed in and smacked into my helmet, or the areas just beneath it where people with normal heads would have enjoyed protection. Soon after that ceremonial FCT, my brow started leaking painfully into my red eyes, sweat mingled with suncream; the hot crosswind got in on this act by flicking those enormous flappy collar tips into my peepers. In a sport so fixated on weight reduction, these substantial and entirely superfluous accoutrements seemed bewildering. I wondered if they prevented chafing from all the spare tyres the riders had to carry round their necks. I dunno. Maybe they blew their noses in them. Such were the thoughts that sustained and diverted me across the last, vast plains of Extremadura.

Trees had now beaten a full retreat from the sandy tussocks that spread out to every horizon, clotted here and there with prickly pears and sage grass. The whole scene might have been painted with the desert-camouflage Humbrol enamels that were such a fixture of my early adolescence. Presently the road pitched up the drawn-out Cuesta de la Media Fanega. It wasn't hideously steep, but it was hideously hot. My bidons, decontaminated overnight in hotel shower gel, were now as squidgy and flaccid as Dali's floppy clocks: the merest squeeze dispatched a mighty jet of warm, soapy bathwater down my gullet. For the first time I confronted the enormous dead-weight, sweat-soaked wooliness of my jersey. Sunburned blisters were popping out on my pink ankles where my socks had slipped down, the elastic stretched to death by the heat. Somewhere deep inside, a small voice urged me to man up and get my tribulations in perspective. 'Hold the back page, Ramón – we're hearing the elastic may have gone in Berrendero's socks.'

Ramón had once more gone to sleep in the back of Number 4, and only woke up when the road plunged down the other side of the cuesta. Its modern successor hugged the hillside, but I could make out fragments of old, brown tarmac winding through abandoned olive groves at the bottom of the gorge below. Then I topped another brow and dropped down into a tweaked landscape, more rolling, less bleak, cluttered with eucalyptus trees and droopy brown sunflowers. Adios, Extremadura; hola, Andalucía.

ATENCIÓN – *GLORIETA*!

That's the rather wonderful Spanish word for a roundabout, and the outskirts of Seville were littered with them. The fact that each came introduced with a strident warning sign suggested a certain native unfamiliarity with rotary traffic management, as my experience had already confirmed. Spanish drivers are overall pretty capable and very cyclo-tolerant, but it was always just a bit terrifying to see how often they needed reminding not to do unbelievably stupid and dangerous things, like driving the wrong way down a motorway slip road or around a *glorieta*. The preferred *glorieta* gambit was just to get the whole awkward business out of the way as quickly as possible, shooting in, round and out without troubling your brake pedal or indicator stalk. Indicating was in general a bit of a national weakness, along with a phobic reluctance to put even half a wheel over chevrons painted across the tarmac. 'Well, now here's a dilemma, Miguel – there's a cyclist on our right and some diagonal white lines on our left … here goes … Oh *puta madre*, would you look at that, how am I going to get all those bits of elbow off my wing mirror?'

I rode past a smoking patch of wasteland where a dozen firemen were lethargically stamping out a small brush fire, then veered into

the cobbled, narrow streets of Triana. This Sevillian neighbour-
hood – named after its most famous son, Trajan, the first Roman
emperor born outside Italy – witnessed the Civil War's inaugural
horror: a massacre that gave the Column of Death its name. On 18
July 1936, 4,000 of Franco's Africanistas marched into Triana, a
heavily Republican working-class area, lobbing grenades through
windows and rounding up children to walk in front of them as human
shields. Seventy men were randomly hauled out of their homes and
shot; their wives were given ten minutes to clean off all the anti-
Falangist graffiti in the streets or face the same fate, scrubbing away
in desperation as their husbands bled to death at their feet. By the
end of the year, Triana's entire male population had been taken away,
and effectively eradicated: 9,000 Sevillians were murdered in five
months. No wonder that when the first Nazi 'military advisers' arrived
in Seville, they found themselves hysterically cheered in the street
by terrified citizens, fearful that any shortfall of enthusiasm might
earn them a 'walk'. German diplomats did their best to shut them
up: they'd been trying to keep Hitler's involvement a secret.

Once again I had cause to question the 1941 route-planners.
You could just about make a case that, given the limited alternatives, they had little choice but to direct the race right up Franco's
Victory Avenue in Madrid and right down the Column of Death's
murder march. But as I meandered through twisty, claustrophobic
Triana – now a regenerated, hipsterish collation of bistros and
craft galleries – it was blaringly apparent that this was very far
from an obvious route into Seville. Suspicions of another nose-
rubbing propaganda detour multiplied when I crossed the River
Guadalquivir and at once joined a broad ceremonial avenue that
made a much more convincing finishing straight.

Or so it would have seemed to the likes of Delio Rodríguez, JB's
sprint-meister teammate who wound up the pace and eased to

victory down these avenues. For me, every stage that ended in a city-centre sprint – which is to say all of them – was a maddening, stop-start anticlimax. Just as I was working up to a grandstand finish I'd find myself funnelled into a segregated bike lane and imprisoned there while it criss-crossed the bordering boulevard, waiting long minutes for little red bikes to turn green. In Spanish cities, cyclists who spurn bike lanes receive very short shrift: such transgressions earned me the only angry horn-honks I received on my entire ride, with taxi and bus drivers taking an especially dim view. By the time I rolled past the botanical gardens and up to the equestrian statue of El Cid, standing proud at the centre of a busy *glorieta*, enforced urban pootling and red-light vigils had scrubbed 1.2kmh off my daily average speed. Writing this now, I'm thinking: So what? But out there on those hot paving stones, I set up a selfie by El Cid's plinth with tears of fatigue and frustration brimming in my red eyes. A neutralised start is one thing. But there is no place in the world for a neutralised finish.

Seville was the first place on this trip that I'd been to before, so I knew what to expect: expansive architectural loveliness, largely dating from the time when New World colonial treasure made it one of the richest cities on earth. My plan was to overnight at the Hotel Simon, where the 1941 riders had stayed and which I was stupidly thrilled to learn still existed. But when I creaked to a halt before the smart old townhouse in question, the shutters were down, with a multilingual note stuck to them: 'Temporarily Closed Because C-19'.

I found an alternative just off the regal, tree-bordered and arrestingly deserted Plaza Nueva. When I rode round the Tour de France route all those years ago, the hospitality industry nurtured a brazen disgust for the cyclo-tourist that saw me turned away from obviously un-full hotels, and metaphorically spat on and beaten by those who reluctantly let me in. Things have progressed an awful lot since then, but I'm still routinely welcomed with a very fixed smile, then dispatched to a tiny, weirdly proportioned attic bedroom down the end of some forgotten, wandering corridor, with mismatched furniture and curtains, a broken air conditioner and at least one properly imaginative pitfall: a flip-flop under the pillow, perhaps, or a bloodstained face flannel in the minibar. I thought I'd lucked in at this place until I went for a small-hours pee and saw that a polystyrene ceiling panel had fallen into the bath. In the morning I had a closer look and noticed two of its corners had been nibbled off.

The Vuelta enjoyed its first rest-day in Seville, and Ramón and the riders spent it at the Hotel Simon. The night before – possibly still under the influence of a vermouth and cider feed-zone free-for-all at Almendralejo – he'd phoned in an extraordinary report that showered praise on Seville in terms that progressed from sarcasm to open sedition. 'All of the city's esteemed First Authority were present at the finish ... the organisation was absolutely formidable, and how very pretty were the *falangistas* who handed the bouquets to stage winner Delio Rodríguez.' Even the tram system came in for some weirdly glowing acclaim (though Google Lens's triumphant 'I had a great ride for a fat bitch' proved no more than a reference to the national nickname for the 10-cent coin, which featured a tubby lion of canine aspect). Then the line-crossing finale: 'And how kind the authorities were to provide the sergeant who, as I dictate this article by telephone, has been listening in via the headset, very close beside me, for a full half-hour.'

Franco's authorities nurtured a reflexive suspicion of all Cata-lans, and coming from a Barcelona-based journalist, this would surely have gone down like an especially leaden balloon. I was faintly surprised to see Ramón's byline surviving above *El Mundo Deportivo*'s coverage the next day. Perhaps to create a diversionary controversy, his rest-day report sensationally blew the lid off the Vuelta's 'secret factions', in the process making a mockery of the teams they officially represented. Who were the principal protagonists in this intrigue? You will simply never guess.

'It is us four against the rest,' says Berrendero when we journalists meet him in his room with Delio Rodríguez, Trueba and Antonio Martín.

But, we ask, isn't Ezquerra an Espanyol rider like you?

'Yes, but he has never been on our side.'

And as Delio Rodríguez is aware how strange this must sound, he interrupts to say: 'Look and you'll see that it's not only Ezquerra who's against us, but everyone.'

By way of background explanation, Ramón tells his readers how since the start, most of the FCB riders have been aiding and abetting their nominal rival Ezquerra, and vice versa, and how Berrendero's 'gang of four', his nominal teammates, absolutely haven't. During the previous stage, the occupants of Number 4 saw Ezquerra giving one of his superior spare tyres to an FCB rider in distress – then attempting to mount an escape in order to distance Delio Rodríguez, who'd suffered consecutive punctures. Berrendero had eagerly chased him down.

'Why on earth would we ever let that man Ezquerra escape?' says Berrendero. 'He is not one of us.'

When Ramón and his fellow journalists went into Ezquerra's room up the corridor, they found him resting on one bed while

Antonio Escuriet – an FCB rider – lay stretched out on another, having his legs massaged by the Barcelona team's soigneur. Ramón cut to the chase:

'I didn't know you were an enemy of your club teammates,' I say. Federico jumps up from the bed and answers in a booming voice: 'They're the ones who have declared themselves my enemies!' Ezquerra is no fool. He talks to us enthusiastically about various FCB riders, and doesn't hide the service they could offer to help him win the Tour of Spain and beat the quartet that has declared themselves his opponents.

But JB was no fool either. That carefully curated foursome covered all bases: his old mate Trueba was perhaps the strongest climber in the field, Delio without question the leading sprinter and rouleur, and Berrendero himself the dominant all-rounder. Antonio Martín, runner-up to JB in that year's national road-race championship, would make a more than capable *domestique*. (Quite wonderfully, at the time of writing, Martín is still with us, aged 102.) Ezquerra had been comprehensively outmanoeuvred by his old enemy.

Escuriet, face down on the pillow, makes a muffled contribution. 'In all honesty, I've never seen anything like it. But of course I also have an account to settle from the 1936 Vuelta.'

Ah, yes. Antonio Escuriet had been the leading Spanish rider – and thus the biggest loser – when Jools and Trueba rode away from their furious teammates in that race. Berrendero really did make an awful lot of rods for his own back. I found myself wondering if his Millwall defiance, the nonchalance with which he accumulated and cultivated grudges and resentments, was another reason why this comparatively apolitical sportsman wound up in a concentration camp, while his more outspoken teammates walked free.

Ramón, who'd been dabbling in his own dangerous game, was well placed to assess the peril of these subversive factions. This Vuelta was a coordinated propaganda exercise, and going so defiantly off piste would have laid down a gauntlet to the organising authorities. 'There is a contempt for the colours of both club teams that these riders must surely be aware of,' wrote Ramón, 'but to which they are blinded by personal rivalries.' In his autobiographical account of the 1941 Vuelta, Jools conspicuously makes no reference whatsoever to the teams that were officially contesting the race. In some ways I was quite heartened to see the determination with which these ancient, dysfunctional grudges were still being pursued, regardless of the high political and personal stakes. Perhaps, after all those intervening years of internecine horror, the riders took solace in banal sporting enmity. At the same time, two words kept recurring to me as I pondered these internal rifts, and the first was 'civil'.

Ramón painted an appealing picture of the Vuelta's departure from Seville, and I followed his downtown route up Las Sierpes, a compact showpiece street whose ambience could barely have changed since 1941, possibly even 1841: 'The awnings high above us are open, stretching across from roof to roof, so that the elegant Sevillians who sit in rows of chairs, drinking coffee and reading newspapers, are saved from the sun.'

Then it was out through the quiet Saturday suburbs and into a scrappy hinterland of old quarries and ruined factories, where defunct railway tracks lay half buried in sand. Under a vast old bridge that spanned a canal, I passed the impressively durable young survivors of an all-nighter, dozens of them swaying vacantly about to the Euro-techno thumping out of a colossal speaker wedged in an open car boot. Only after I'd bumped on to the towpath did I process the fact that none of them had been wearing masks – the first al fresco Spaniards I'd seen without them – and that this was a *botellón*, one of the youthful outdoor gatherings that the TV news were blaming for a recent upturn in Covid case numbers. The second wave was building across Spain, and before the week was out it would be breaking all over the land.

For Ramón, this was a time-travel stage. Extremadura might have been arrestingly impoverished, but the ageless rusticity of Andalucia simply blew him away. As a Barcelona city-boy he's astonished when Number 4 'stops at a farmhouse where milk is served to us straight from the cow', and entranced by 'the frequent caravans of donkeys and mules that haul ploughs and saddlebags towards the fields'. With open mouths, the occupants of Number 4 return the salutes of rural horse guards who stand by the road in their wide-brimmed cordovan hats.

I paid unanticipated tribute to Ramón's adventure through bygone backwaters, courtesy of Komoot's purportedly bike-friendly interpretation of the Stage 4 route, most of which now lay beneath the A92 motorway. For a long while I juddered and slid along the sandy, rocky canal-side path, overtaken by weekend mountain bikers who exhibited open hilarity at my choice of ride for this terrain. Presently I was steered past an isolated women's prison and on to an actual goat trail, full of actual goats. One panicky herd stampeded by in a narrow, rock-sided section, leaving me lost in a cloud of ancient orange dust. This was the off-est of off-roading, all sand and boulders, my wrists jarred by a million staccato impacts, my calves slashed by crispy thistles. It began to feel like some James Bond pursuit in the slapstick Roger Moore era, from which I'd emerge festooned in twigs and dead grass, with a bleating baby goat on my handlebars.

Then it was on to a gravelly tractor path that ran alongside the A92 for hours, rising and falling relentlessly, up atop the cuttings the motorway passed through far below, down at the foot of embankments it was raised on. Seeing all that velvety tarmac so close and yet so far, with nary a car upon it, was as tantalising as the giggling pool splashes that had tortured me from behind all those *finca* fences. Even on the flat bits, my trail repeatedly plunged into drainage culverts whose every dusted fundament was a mess of loose rock and deep sand. Each dramatic loss of stability in these exciting sections came accompanied with a compound juddery shriek from my trusty random swear generator: bollocking shit flaps, perchance, or maybe a fuck almighty crapping horse cock, the whole ensemble topped off with a simple, strident FAT FANNY!

Some farmer in an old Land Cruiser bounced past trailing lorry tyres on a chain, pretending to grade the trail surface while intently peppering my soft tissue with bullets of gravel. An explosive thrumming thwack drew my attention to a dust devil crashing through a field of sunflowers, a column of spiralling vegetation that soared a hundred feet or more into the cloudless sky. Once again the sun interrupted its progress between the horizons in order to pause directly over my head for three straight hours. The bleached white gravel did its bit, bouncing heat and light straight into my desperate face. I dabbed a glove against my tender, crevassed lips, and saw it smeared in blood. How I missed the N630.

As the day wore on, a weary, cack-handed fatalism set in, and I skittered recklessly down every descent. This was a game of *pinchazo* roulette, and sure enough a developing under-bottom rumble soon alerted me to a slow puncture. Moore descends and swells. And swells and swells: each lusty stroke of my hopeless micro-pump delivered no more than a kitten's yawn into the rear tube, and it took ten red-faced minutes to make any tangible difference. Even then I knew I was wasting my time, because slow punctures always get quicker, fast. A couple of miles up the road – sorry, 'road' – I made the inevitable tube change under an olive tree. Why did it have to be the rear again? It always takes me a filthy-fingered forever to get the chain back on round all the pulleys and sprockets, and even when I do it seems like a fluke. And that was only the filling in a pain sandwich, bookended by a deep new screwdriver gouge in the rim and a Sisyphean ordeal with the micro-pump. The crickets were out in force. They fucking loved it.

The now-traditional late-afternoon mistral bent the dead thistles in half and hurled dust in my face. Rabbits shot madly out from the fields right in front of me, giving my vacant eyes yet another hazard to neglect. Some very obscure muscle groups began to protest, done in by the stress and strain of wrestling La Berrendero up and down these trails, now gripping on for dear life, now braced for a cataclysmic fall. And that was before *Doña Fatalidad* sneaked up and once more stuck her yellowy fangs in my rear tyre. I processed the under-buttock rumble like a footballer watching an extra-time back pass roll slowly through his keeper's legs and over the goal line. By the time I'd fitted and inflated my penultimate spare tube, I didn't feel exhausted so much as battered, as if I'd been shaken and slapped all day by some tireless bully.

Osuna wobbled into view on a heat-hazed grey hillside ahead, those tightly packed white houses giving it the appearance of a giant rock slathered in guano. In fading sun I scaled its rearing, narrow cobbled streets, fatefully draining my last reserves: the ones that allow me to enter a hotel without dropping my bike straight on to the reception floor, bags and all, and just staring at it. When at length I slowly raised my gaze to the desk, I saw those now-familiar emotions battling it out on the small visible parts of a masked face: Thank you, Lord, for delivering us a paying guest in this time of crisis, but next time, could we have a nicer one?

In the morning, I stared at my frankly terrifying reflection in the bathroom mirror and made a decision. This was a face that had had enough, those crow's-feet grimace lines like pale beige star-bursts cut into burned ochre, a bit Pablo Picasso on his death bed, a bit Trump on gas mark 10. It looked as if a toddler had tried face-painting me as a tiger. In fact, everything from top to bottom had had enough: the glassy wrists that struggled to unclamp the clothes pegs on my bathroom laundry line; the little toe that screamed in pure, neat agony where my left-hand pedal clip had been compressing it for almost a thousand kilometres.

And the bike had had enough, issuing creaks and shrieks that spoke of distorted metal and the ingress of dust and gravel. It was ever easier to understand why the 1941 riders, hammering down tracks like this for twelve hours a day, suffered all those devas-tating structural calamities, and all those soul-sapping *pinchazos*.

La Berrendero and I had paid tough, true tribute on those unmade trails, but now we were spent. Henceforth we would stay on piste, on tarmac, on the straight and narrow and off those bendy, bouncy, gravelly shit-paths, even if it meant taking small liberties with the 1941 route. I told myself this wasn't an admis-sion of defeat, just a recalibration of priorities, like a pre-race favourite who loses half an hour on the first day and gamely insists that he's still looking forward to bagging the odd stage win. My new target: completing each 1941 stage in no more than two days, Moore-maths parity for someone who was twice the riders' ages.

Here's that headwind you ordered, sir, straight off the Sahara, hot and strong, just how you like it. When I filled my bidons that morning the hotel taps hadn't run cold – from hereon they rarely would – but in these conditions it hardly mattered. After an hour in the saddle, even iced water would be room temperature; after two, it was womb temperature. I laboured into the blood-warm gusts on a forsaken road through red hillsides speckled with olive groves, laid in neat geometric grids like orchards on a Victorian map. God's own fan heater blasted *pinchazo*-grade crap across the tarmac: sticks and stones and shards of beer bottle, even the tattered husk of a dead yellow snake. For once I was glad of my baggage, dead-weight ballast that just about kept me upright.

The far-flung towns had a flyblown, frontier feel, where mobs of dusty sheep roamed the streets, and farmers piled huge heaps of wheat on the forecourts of defunct petrol stations. Ahead of me, mountains took shape in the hazy, crazy heat. You lot can sod off, I thought. But you know what? They never did. Straight after Antequera, where I ate a squid-ink paella that stained my teeth black and left a parallel digestive legacy, I passed a sign that said CARRETERA DE MONTANA. Vertical geography had been wonderfully absent from my route since the first day. That right was about to be wronged. And with beastly injustice, because the 1941 race outflanked these towering crags on a distant valley road that was now another motorway.

Delio Rodríguez had put on the leader's jersey – a plain white number – after his win at Seville. JB would never have let his secret teammate keep it, but as it was, the 57 kilometres that separated Antequera from the Stage 4 finish at Malaga did the job for him. 'The road is heavily sown with gravel,' reported Ramón, 'which makes for frequent punctures. Yet when our driver puts his foot down, it takes an age for us to catch the lead group of 12 riders. Their pace is strong.' Too strong for Delio, who drops off the back as the road exits a tunnel and the sparkling Mediterranean appears far below. 'When we lean out of the car to shout motivation, the signs of Delio's despair are obvious. "I'm done," he tells us, simply.'

Ahead lay a mad, 30-kilometre swoop down to Malaga – Ramón talks of 'endless curves and dangers' – and in no small part it would decide the race. In quick succession, seven of the eleven riders suffered punctures, Berrendero among them. On a light-speed descent there seemed no chance of regaining lost ground, and six of those seven would duly roll into the finish miles behind. Further back still, Delio Rodríguez was on his disconsolate way to losing eleven minutes and any hope of overall victory. But further up, 'with a supreme and sustained effort', one rider reeled in the leaders just as they wound up the sprint on Malaga's palm-lined promenade. JB crossed the line second, and held fourth overall, behind Trueba, Escuriet and Ezquerra. Only twenty-three seconds separated the top five. For the first time in the race, in those 30 kilometres it had been every man for himself – just the way Berrendero liked it.

Just the way I liked it, too, though for rather different reasons. You don't want company when you're really old and slow, and riding up a 9 per cent gradient into a massive headwind. The first hairpins of my ride wound up a broad, brown pasture between the fiendish peaks, dotted with derelict shepherd shacks whose rusty iron roofs clattered and sang in the wind. By now I should have grown accustomed to La Berrendero's inhumane gearing, but still I glared down at the sprockets with something close to outrage.

Small ring up front, biggest at the back: this was as good as it was going to get, and it was shit.* My speed dropped to single digits, but I hadn't got off to push since the Altos de los Leones and had sworn never to do so again. Yeah, OK, a low bar and all that, but at my stage of the game there really should be a special jersey for it.

Behind and far below sprawled a misty beige patchwork of fields. Ahead and above towered some leering crags, which received the extremely loud home truths they so richly deserved. Pretty sure they won't be giving cyclists any more bother. My heartbeat was filling my head and my bidons were down to the hot, flobby dregs. And what in the name of all that is fat and naked did that heat-seeking, me-seeking wind think it was playing at? No matter which way the switchbacks steered, it always blasted right in my face, sending dented cans clattering up the tarmac and more than once bringing me to a dead halt. I did my very best to hate this wind to death, as Berrendero would surely have managed to, but only made it angrier.

I topped the first col with fiery tears streaming down my face, as if instead of a prize bonus and some valuable mountain points I'd been rewarded with a squirt of battery acid. But the road didn't go down for very long, and soon I was squinting up at a smooth line that ascended a sheer flank of rock, before squiggling precariously around its top edge. Was that … a road? Please don't be my road. But it was my road, it is always my road, just like every other worst-case conundrum the long-distance cyclist wastes his time agonising

---

* I feel the need to point out here that my gearing was brutal even by professional standards. The easiest, most hill-friendly combo available to Luis Otaño when he rode the 1958 Tour de France was 42x22. 'Try getting a bike like that over the Alps,' he complained recently, cocking a snook at modern pros who can call upon a 38x30 in the steep stuff. At 42x21, my equivalent was even tougher than Otaño's. But you won't hear me moaning about it.

over: of *course* you have a slow puncture, of *course* it's going to rain, of *course* you're completely lost and your wife has left you and Donald Trump has just been crowned World King for all eternity.

The road was a single tracker that gingerly hugged the steep rock; between me and a plunging eternity stood an Armco barrier that creaked loudly in the heat, pierced here and there by a car-sized gap bridged with fading police tape. I passed through a desolate village, wincing as the sun bounced at me off windows and whitewash. Then something appeared on the narrow tarmac just ahead, which as I toiled forwards revealed itself as crudely painted, weathered words, and those words were VAMOS JULIÁN. I rolled over them and felt all fear and pain melt from my hot, wet face, replaced by awe and joy. This was the first painted name I had seen on any road, and what a name to see.

I can report that my progress to Malaga took on a rather different character thereafter. It probably helped that almost at once I topped a brow and saw the sea: it was all downhill from here. VAMOS HOOOOOOLIÁN! I threw La Berrendero down the crazy, steepling descent, gripping the levers with slippy, sweaty palms and pulling them towards me like a man milking a concrete cow. Old rubber shrieked painfully against old metal as I swept round the switchbacks, clipping apexes and flirting with the sandy gravel scattered perilously along the tarmac's extremities. I was channelling JB's full-gas, balls-out pursuit down these slopes, and carried on channelling it into Malaga's steeply pitched peripheries, barrelling along its six-lane boulevards, straight through its red lights and right up to the doors of its very cheapest downtown hotel. I dismounted, hyped and happy, then thought: If this wasn't Sunday afternoon in a pandemic, I'd probably just have died.

CHAPTER 9

Anyone who'd been tracking my progress with creepy close-focus – I'm looking at you, Mr Google Maps Timeline – might have wondered what the freaking flip I was up to on the morning of 13 July 2020. After days of painful, anticlockwise progress around Spain, there I am shooting west out of Malaga, heading the wrong way at immense speed for 259 kilometres. Aren't cars great? Small vans might be even greater: I didn't have to dismantle La Berrendero in any way before laying her to rest in the dark warmth of my rented Citroën Berlingo's cargo bay.

I could have left the bike in Malaga, but we were in this together. Never more so than now. I pulled off the motorway just past Cadiz, bypassed an enormous US naval base, and found myself crawling down narrow streets full of leathery native holidaymakers. This was Rota, where Julián Berrendero served his longest stretch in a concentration camp, and where Captain Llona picked him out from the roll-call one morning and thereby resurrected the career of Spain's greatest cyclist. Malaga wasn't exactly close at hand, but it was as near as my route would come to this hallowed site. La Berrendero and I were here on a pilgrimage.

I'd booked into a guesthouse just behind the beachfront. It was run by a little old man in a grubby facemask, who spoke passable English with a heavy American accent and matching idioms: a legacy, I presumed, of the naval base that opened in 1953, earning Franco $3 billion and pulling Spain out of its Years of Hunger. When I asked him where the Arroyo Hondo tuna cannery had been, he answered with confidence: 'Is now a *parque*, buddy. You wanna walk on de *playa* for such maybe kinda couple kilometre.' But my follow-up question about the cannery's penal afterlife just drew shrugs and mumbles, as that *guerra civil* omertà brought the shutters down once more. However pathetic and offensive, my only relevant frame of reference was Brexit – a subject we have all learned to swerve when conversing with strangers, in order to avoid a heated and pointless argument.*

This was the first time I'd worn my Merkels by day, and what a shiny, humid liability they were. Driving down the motorway I kept sliding forwards off my seat; in any vehicle livelier than a diesel van, every dab of accelerator would have pitched me straight into the footwell. My shoes were better at least. To all Spaniards of a certain age, *alpargatas* – more familiar to us as espadrilles – are imbued with deep socio-historic symbolism. They were the rope-soled peasant sandals your grandparents wore if they couldn't afford proper shoes, and JB's autobiography is strewn with poor-but-proud references to them. The grey *alpargatas* he had to walk miles and miles to work in as a boy, even after they wore through;

---

* Being right, I find this terribly frustrating.

the white *alpargatas* he put on for his first proper bike race, memorably teamed with a billowing nightshirt and a pair of underpants ('Don't worry,' he writes, 'I stitched up the opening'); the red *alpargatas* he wore in the Wham! tribute act I just made up. My own pair was black: I had come here to put myself in JB's *alpargatas*, while wearing mine.

The revelation that my quest would involve a long walk across sand caused me to reconsider La Berrendero's participation. As it turned out, motor vehicles weren't nearly as good as I may just have suggested: instead of parking my holiday wheels in a cupboard under the hotel stairs, the nearest place I'd found to leave the van was a good fifteen minutes' walk from the guesthouse. That made the decision even easier. At a stroke, the florid sentimentality that had inspired me to load La Berrendero into the van melted into callous indifference. In fact, quite preposterously, I didn't lay a finger on the bike until I was unloading it back in Malaga the following day.

I flopped westwards along the beach, a broad arc of sand that started out from the fuzzy grey masts and funnels of the naval base behind me, and carried on past the holiday apartment blocks as far as the eye could see. There were a fair few sunbathers, most older than I was, and all much more Spanish. I'd been told that many were Madrileños, escaping their city's pitiless summer: although there wasn't much spangled Med between here and the Sahara, the sea breeze took the edge right off the heat. Perhaps, too, some of these seniors had come to flee the ravages of Covid: Madrid, a metropolis with one of the EU's oldest urban populations, had suffered the worst death toll of any European city. Every place I'd been through so far had been in a state of hyper vigilance – having left London at a time when barely anyone wore a mask as a matter of course, I was still getting used to seeing them cover every single face. But here in Rota, they had taken it to the next level. Even drivers alone in their cars had one on. Wandering into a grocery en route to the guesthouse, I'd been shrieked at in outraged disbelief for failing to notice the gel dispenser inside the door, and as I gazed down the beach I saw several pairs of Covid wardens strolling about in hi-vis tabards.

The sand began to empty and the apartment blocks gave way to pine-studded dunes. I walked across to them and spotted a small gate, with a sign beside it warning me that I was about to enter a chameleon protection zone. Just inside the gate stood another sign, welcoming visitors to the Parque La Almadraba. It had been an early start and a long day, and I suddenly realised I wasn't emotionally prepared for this. Dry of mouth and feeling rather overwhelmed, I walked in.

Some months before, I'd found some photos of the Rota camp being offered for sale on an online Spanish collector's site. A jack-booted officer engaged in pistol practice by a barbed-wire fence; three more grinning on a veranda; some lowlier soldiers standing guard on a lofty dune, with a blur of prisoners trooping through the spindly tree trunks below. Shuffling along a plank walkway laid through the pines, I tried to place these images in context. It wasn't easy, especially after the portent-puncturing discovery that one corner of the site was now occupied by the Chill-Out Beach Club. I was about to give up when I spotted some aged concrete foundations sticking out of a long drift of pine needles, behind a line of brick stumps. Trees would have grown a lot in eighty years, and dunes would have shifted. But by orientation and proportion, these did look very much like the remains of that veranda-fronted building. Without any evidence at all, I'd long since decided that one of those grinning officers was Captain Llona, and that the building behind was his office, which Berrendero had gone into expecting a bullet, and emerged from full of breakfast.

I stood there for quite a long time. Wind brushed through the pine tops, mingling with the gentle swash of wavelet on sand. Down in the breezeless dunes, the heat was fierce. The chronology of JB's incarceration remained stubbornly vague, but he would have endured at least one summer here. And he would have spent it laying pavements. How heartbreaking it was to imagine this great champion sitting out his prime being re-educated under these trees, or, even worse, dragging stone blocks along the shadeless streets behind. Every day, for eighteen horrible months, he must have wondered, with ratcheting bitterness and bewilderment, why he alone, amongst all his sporting peers, had to suffer this. 'Even today I don't understand why my licence was suspended,' he writes in *Mis Glorias y Memorias*, leaning back on that trusty euphemism. 'I have never understood why riders who were also absent from the homeland, who always competed next to me outside of it, and who like me were strictly sportsmen, did not experience my bad luck on their return. But I should draw a veil over this; it apparently had to be that way.'

Perhaps that was why I'd also convinced myself, on the basis of his extraordinary kindness to Berrendero, that Captain Llona was a bit of a Mr Barraclough, doing his mild-mannered best to make the prisoners' ordeal bearable. 'Now, chaps, I'd much rather you didn't think of this as a concentration camp, but more of a chill-out beach club.'

I shuffled out through the gate at the far end, past a sign that urged me to call 112 if I saw a young chameleon in danger, and hit the beach by Rota's *corrales*, manmade fish-catching pens built way out into the sea that have been in use since Roman times. Then, still deeply lost in melancholy, I looked up and saw two pairs of hairy brown buttocks almost directly in front of me. As I passed, their owners turned full face, hands on hips, chorizo and eggs on proud display. Why are naturists always so bloody pleased with themselves? One of them definitely shouldn't have been. Is that a young chameleon in danger, or are you just not terribly happy to see me?

I walked back up the beach, accompanied by the crunch of shell under *alpargata*. Everything seemed a little different. I hadn't previously noticed the Spanish flags draped over half the holiday-block balconies. Those lifeguard huts on stilts now had the look of a different type of watchtower. The Covid wardens seemed rather less benign, as if they weren't reminding sunbathers to maintain a safe distance but surreptitiously scrutinising their reading matter. But then I turned my head and gazed back at the dunes and pine trees, and considered the deliciously perfect fate of Franco's fear factory. A male nudist beach and a chameleon sanctuary. Take that, el Caudillo.

CHAPTER 10

A day off is always a risk. It doesn't help to be reminded of the other ways you could be going about life, all demonstrably preferable to exceeding your sweatiest physical limits up some forsaken mountain trail. Rolling down the Malaga seafront the following afternoon, I gazed flatly at the sunloungers and frosted beer glasses on show between me and the Med, pretending to hate all that prone indulgence, while really hating myself for having spent the second half of my day in Rota doing it.

I don't imagine Jools ever had this problem after a rest day, or the heavy nights that the Ministry of Education and Leisure appeared to encourage: following his punishing ride into Malaga, he reports being taken out 'to savour the famous anchovies of this city, and of course its many delicious wines'. He was just way too focused, eyes on the road immediately ahead, and – in most races – the riders distantly behind. Sprinting for the finish with six others at the 1935 Malaga Grand Prix, Berrendero had his eyes fixed so firmly on the prize that he didn't notice the spectator's car veering over towards them until it was too late. All seven were knocked down like skittles just as they crossed the line, and rushed to hospital: a photo in his autobiography shows Berrendero with a big white dressing on his knee, flanked by a rider with his left arm in a plaster cast, and another with a fully bandaged skull. But JB had only one concern: who won? There was some consternation when the official who snapped the photo-finish demanded 1,000 pesetas for the dramatic, conclusive print. 'But it was paid, because we found out we had all smashed into him just as he pressed the shutter, and that as a result he had lost an eye.' (Jools never does reveal who crossed the line first, from which we can deduce that it wasn't him.)

I hadn't got started until noon, but the loop-tape endlessness of this promenade, and its cast of half-cut idlers, engendered a sense of lethargy. How happy I was to take my lead from the pictographic signage that ordered cyclists to take it easy: a big red cross through the silhouette of a hunched racer with speed lines flying off his back, a big green tick beside an erect pootler. Malaga seamlessly gave way to ranks of high-rise hotels, some suggesting a colossal stack of egg boxes, others like cruise liners stood on end. But Torre del Mar and its neighbours were pitched squarely at North Europeans, and therefore stood eerily moribund: padlocked water-parks, roped-off play areas, darkened cafés with 'FULL ENGLISH €5' signs in their dusty windows. An awful lot of my ride up the Med felt more like November than July. Apart from the blistering heat, which lent itself pretty well to erect pootling.

In 1941, nobody came on holiday down here. Back then, and for centuries before and decades after, this whole coast was nothing but fishing settlements and rocky, barren peace and quiet.

Except in February 1937, when the road out of Malaga witnessed a hundred-mile civilian massacre that shocked the world. Malaga had resisted Franco's 1936 coup, and for eight months after, the city was a haven for those who'd fled from the Column of Death as it marched north. When it finally fell to the Nationalists, bolstered for the first time by Mussolini's troops, ships and aircraft, 100,000 refugees fled east up the coast road: 107 miles of exposed nothingness from Malaga to Almería. What happened in the days ahead has been described as 'one of the most horrendous atrocities perpetrated against Republican civilians'. And by Paul Preston, who as the author of *The Spanish Holocaust* would appear bleakly well qualified to pass judgement.

Most of the civilian massacres I have hitherto related were justified in the eyes of their Nationalist perpetrators as reprisals, or at least reprisals for reprisals. Before being captured by Franco's troops, most towns and cities were softened up by air raids and artillery assaults; the typical local response for the death and destruction these caused was to drag a few imprisoned rightists out of jail and shoot them, then maybe burn a church down. But in Malaga, this 'red terror' went horribly out of hand, courtesy of the anarchists who had seized effective control after the coup was repulsed. In retaliation for a deadly bombing raid on Malaga's main market, they first shot all the jailed right-wingers, then took to rounding up and killing anyone who looked rich; by the end of September 1936, 1,100 people had been executed. In the Spanish Civil War, the revenge ratio always seemed to hover around fifty eyes for an eye.

So when Franco's men took Malaga, comeuppance went off the scale. The defenceless refugees were slaughtered without mercy, shelled from the sea and strafed from the air. Horrified foreign journalists and medical aid workers wrote of corpses strewn across the road all the way to Almería, of babies suckling from dead mothers, of exhausted pensioners giving up and lying down to die. There was no food or water, and most refugees were barefoot, hobbling desperately away from the Italian troops who marched in pursuit, machine-gunning stragglers. When the survivors eventually staggered into Almería and gathered in the main square, they were welcomed by a carefully targeted bombing raid. By then, it is estimated that more than 3,000 of them had been killed.

Yet in terrible truth, they were the lucky ones. By 1944 – according to the Nationalists' own estimates – some 20,000 of the Malagans who stayed behind had been executed, a toll unsurpassed across all of Spain. Most were sentenced by chief prosecutor Arias Navarro, the Butcher of Malaga, who went on to become Franco's last prime minister – and the first under King Juan Carlos, a truly shocking continuity.

And so on I pedalled. That habitual contrast between Spain's cheery, community-spirited present and its not-so-distant fratricidal past would never be so haunting, here on this road of death that now threaded its way through the pleasure playgrounds of the Costa del Sol. The resort of Torremolinos is still struggling to throw off its Brits-on-the-piss package-tour infamy, enshrined by a Monty Python sketch I used to know off by heart, though I'm glad I don't any more as I just watched it on YouTube and found it alarmingly xenophobic. But consider that against the town's previous notoriety, as home to one of this region's largest Francoist concentration camps.

First laid out by the Romans, the N340 – formerly the Via Augusta – is one of the world's oldest roads, and it would be my companion all the way up the Med. At least most of the way: no matter how carefully I re-programmed my route, Komoot still did me over at least four times a day. I'd think I was just cleverly outflanking a stretch of dual carriageway, then find myself crunching slowly and unsteadily across gravel motorhome parks or sliding about down the sanded trail of a defunct coastal railway. One morning, straight after breakfast, I dopily followed the digital directions up a perpendicular footpath that would result in both bidons being drained by the time I rejoined the cliff-topping N340, less than a mile from my start point.

The seafront esplanade detours had a similarly deleterious effect on my average speed, but were otherwise the most welcome. Here there would be food and liquid, the latter ingested in awesome quantity. Everything I consumed, from a *bocadillo* the size of a canoe to a *café con leche*, was washed down with an *agua grande*, typically a 1.5 litre mega bottle. Some days I drank four, along with the contents of both bidons. With temperatures now down in the mid-30s, my body was once again offloading fluid through the traditional exit point rather than just boiling it all out through my pores with an audible hiss: all hail the regular beach-side facilities, each one overseen by a facemasked Covid matron in a hi-vis jacket, sat before a camping table full of hand gel.

Even without Komoot's sabotage, the N340 proved a temperamental mistress, fond of weaving miles inland, into and up the barren coastal foothills of the Sierra Nevada. Nearly all its traffic had been sucked away on to the motorway that on occasion passed high above me on towering concrete stilts, so up I toiled in muggy silence, just me and my humid panting, the blue sea twinkling far below beside a crescent of sand neatly gridded with tiny sunloungers. On occasion a rearward droning buzz would alert me to an approaching oboe: old bloke on e-bike. There were a fair few in the hills round here, most in smart strips on fancy-looking mountain machines.

The Spanish like to abbreviate greetings, and these gentlemen simply loved to. '*Luego,*' they would murmur, or sometimes '*Buenas*', raising a few fingers very slightly from their right-hand bar in muted accompaniment as they eased smoothly by, eyes straight ahead. I would watch them disappear round the next brown bend and think: What a wonderful new lease of cycling life for someone who through age or infirmity would otherwise have had to hang up his cleated shoes. Then I would grip the bars, lower my head and empurple myself with reckless sustained intensity, knowing that I had a fighting chance of catching up on the descent if only it came soon enough, and that if it did and I reeled him in I would coast alongside and scream 'LUEGO!' right into a terrified old face, then reach down and yank his battery out and hurl it into the sea. But it never did come soon enough.

Steep and hot, up and down. My first tunnels granted reacquaintance with the acoustic perversity that amplifies the subterranean approach of a Fiat 500 into a pant-wetting apocalyptic roar. They also brought me up to speed with my latest geriatric deficiency: for several exciting seconds after entering a tunnel or leaving one, I rode entirely blind. As I'd forgotten to bring my lights, the bits in between were barely less memorable.

The fuzzy silhouettes far over to my left soon came topped with snow, and I wondered which one of them was Mulhacén, the highest mountain in Spain, referenced by Ramón in a Stage 5 report that came lavishly garnished with descriptions of 'white mountain villages that seem to float in the air', and so forth. Ramón's front-page story was headlined '220 PANORAMIC KILOMETRES', which must have seen a fair few *El Mundo Deportivo*s tossed unread into the bin. But what could he do? The relentless heat had brought about an effective truce in the peloton, so there was nothing relevant to write about. Nothing except the relentless heat: two Swiss riders didn't make the start in Malaga, too sunburned to move, and Ramón reveals that the team's two survivors would ride that day with their arms and legs smeared in petroleum jelly and wrapped in bandages – a *Curse of the Mummy* look that must have caused rather a stir in the more remote villages, where the simple excitement of seeing a man on a bicycle was in itself almost too much to bear.

This seems a good moment to reacquaint ourselves with race referee Manuel Serdan, last seen pondering the effectiveness of Berrendero's *depuración*. Serdan, an erstwhile amateur racer and cycling reporter, was a brutal old loon who was always threatening to punish the riders for going too slowly: a week up the road, he started withholding the stage-finish prize money. He also nurtured a number of eccentric fixations on the secret of cycling success, writing that 'the great cyclist is not muscular or even unusually fit, just clean-living and healthy, a man who knows his sport has only two secrets: breathing properly and finding the right position on his saddle'. Above all, Serdan railed against 'water drunkenness', decrying riders who quenched their thirst as unmanly and unprofessional, even in a race that he himself accepted was being run 'in terrible, extraordinary heat'. He laid out his absurd, sadistic theory in a long article for *Gol* magazine: 'Thirst has become an obsession for our riders, but drinking litres and litres of water will only result in a copious sweating that weakens them. For an athlete, riding for 10 hours in such heat should not be an effort, but merely an exercise. The true aces will drink only four sips of water in 10 hours. It is not acceptable to drink more.'

To this end, the referee's car weaved through the Vuelta peloton snatching bottles away, much to Ramón's bemusement and the riders' cotton-mouthed dismay. 'The only way we can get water is to beg for it,' croaked the FCB rider Izquierdo, doing just that as he wheeled up to the open window of Number 4. 'The energetic referee seems determined to put an end to "water drunkenness",' wrote Ramón, 'and when he sees the riders smuggling bidons to each other, he intervenes with the gestures of a traffic policeman.' Now That's What I Call Fascism. You may not be surprised to learn that Manuel Serdan wound up as head of the Spanish Cycling Federation.

My first stray dogs and ruined windmills; my 14,000th scuttling lizard. The resorts thinned out and were periodically interrupted by agro-industry; as my route bent north and headed for the Costa Blanca, whole valleys and hillsides came sheathed in tattered beige greenhouse plastic. A hemp-like miasma of basil and tomatoes hung in the air, now soured by a skip full of unsold rotten melons, now sweetened by the tang of citrus from the orderly orange plantations that marched down to the sea. Tourism might overshadow agriculture as a GDP player, but Spain remains an agrarian superpower: it has more vineyards than any other country on earth, tops the world olive table, and is Europe's dominant supplier of everything from citrus fruit to onions. It just seems rather a shame that this garden of plenty has to look so desperately unappealing. Nobody wants to imagine a sweat-bathed Jolly Green Giant commando-crawling under a grubby mile-long tarp, or the man from Del Monte's frail, parched 'yes' being drowned out by synthetic rustles.

The more ramshackle hothouse plantations looked more like refugee camps than farms. Perhaps appropriately so. My principal two-wheeled companions were now African migrant workers riding shonky old mountain bikes in their flip-flops; I would very occasionally see one of them duck in or out of a plantation's opaque entrance flaps, though they always did so with haste and stealth, denying me even a snatched peep inside. How unutterably hellish it must be in those places, at this time of year. On top of everything else, they had to be super-spreading Covid factories. A grim parallel existence was hiding in plain sight, lives being led in conditions that would surely have challenged those in Berrendero's camps. I pedalled on and considered my daily travails placed very firmly in perspective.

The towns degenerated, careworn settlements that smelled of sewage and phosphates, each one of them engaged in some furious campaign whose slogans were daubed on every other scabby wall. 'SUBSTATION – NO!', 'EUCALYPTUS – NO!', 'FEWER PROMISES – MORE WATER!', or the catch-all 'LESS TALKING, MORE SHOOTING!'. Lorries bounced past and dropped shrink-wrapped cucumbers into my path; the wind sent used facemasks and plastic gloves tumbling across it. Finding places to eat was becoming a bit of an issue out in these lonelier areas: inadequate breakfasts and late dinners, with sometimes nothing in between. I soon learned to load up in my hotel room before starting out, with a stash of supermarket comestibles bought the night before. Two packets of sliced chorizo, three bread rolls, a few muesli bars, and perhaps a couple of the week-old pastries I still kept finding in the recesses of my bar-bag. What a story they'd have to tell my stomach acids! Then the fluids, horrific both in volume and queasily incompatible variety: a litre of drinking yogurt, another of gazpacho and a big can of *bebida energética*. Every time I piled it all up on the bed it looked monstrous, less like one man's breakfast than a food bank.

Gazpacho was also the new cornerstone of my efforts to tackle the menace of Spain's 9 p.m. dinner starts. A litre of the red stuff, consumed in full and ugly public display as I walked round the town square and waited for the outside tables to be laid. There was a downside to this brilliant tactic: putting on my flowery mask, as I did perhaps twenty-five times a day, brought unsavoury reacquaintance with whatever I had last belched through its threads. As a product containing around 4,000 per cent of your recommended daily allowance of raw garlic and onion, gazpacho has a distressingly long afterlife.

The wind really got going as I rode along the steepling coastal highway into Almería, ferrying flecks of wave right up at me from the shore far below. The Stage 5 finish straight was another palm-lined avenue, then named after Primo de Rivera, and it brought Delio Rodríguez another victory. He had to fight for it, though: 30 kilometres from the end he bonked horribly, and weaved over to Ramón's car pleading for jam – the 1940s energy gel. They had a jar and handed it over. Lord alone knows how he consumed it – I'm thinking Winnie the Pooh with his paw in a pot of honey – but it evidently did the job.

I reread El Mundo Deportivo's stage summary on my phone as I sat down to dinner: fried eggs and chips, Captain Llona's fabled breakfast offering, albeit served in micro proportions on a tiny roofing slate outside a hipster tapas bar. As ever, the newspaper's blithe route rundown left me cold with fury. 'Malaga, Cala del Moral, Rincón, Victoria, Torre del Mar, La Caleta, Salobreña, Motril, Calahonda, Adra and Almería.' To see these towns separated by nothing but bland little commas was an outrageous insult to the hours and hours of sunburned, gale-faced suffering I had endured while bridging them. But at least I had bridged them all within my two-day target.

Little slates kept arriving with bijou arrangements of food on them; I ordered a third beer and a second litre of water. When it arrived I found myself thinking of Manuel Serdan, and what a terrible shame it was that nobody, not even the King of Masculinity, ever got round to lashing him by his ankles to the back of a bike and dragging him down a mountain. If only Manuel were here with me now. 'No, my friend won't be eating. I'm afraid he suffers terribly from food drunkenness.'

CHAPTER 11

'We have entered an uninhabited new planet.'

I rode inland out of Almería wondering when, or if, Ramón's bleak assessment of Stage 6's backdrop would kick in. It didn't take long. Spanish cities rarely peter out; you ride round a corner full of cafés and commotion and – whoa! – you're out in the arse-end of beyond. Ahead and all around yawned a scrubland of craggy canyons and sagebrush, stretching desolately up to the feet of the Sierra Nevada. On cue, a little ball of tumbleweed bounced across the hot tarmac.

The Tabernas Desert is Europe's own cowboy landscape, which explains why I was soon pedalling by the first of many 'visitor experience' parks clustered around the old Hollywood film sets that lay out in the sand. Most of Sergio Leone's spaghetti westerns were shot here, as were *Cleopatra*, *Lawrence of Arabia* and large chunks of the Indiana Jones series. But that was then, and with all the visitor experiences mothballed by Covid, there was nothing and nobody out here in these deserty badlands. Nothing but me and the invisible budgie who had set up home in my bottom bracket, and was down there chirping his dusty little heart out.

I was soon glad of the company. After reeling in a shirtless farmer on a shopping bike, I turned off the N340 – the last chance, Komoot assured me, to swerve its distant merger with the A7 motorway – and at once the badlands got worse. An hour went by without a single car passing. To think that just a couple of days before, pedalling through the Costa del Sol's endless beach resorts, I concluded my lonely days were behind me. But as I should have remembered from flying over it, loneliness is Spain's default mode.

I dismounted atop a dusty brow, gazed out at a huge and hostile sweep of hot, brown nothing, and drained the igneous dregs of my bike-mounted bottle. Popping open the bar-bag to swap it for the full bidon I always kept there, I saw a bad thing: I had forgotten to fill it. The convulsion of panic that knotted my innards segued into a drawn-out fart of raw terror when I additionally realised that all I had to eat were three tubes of energy gel, acquired at a bike shop in Almería along with a new pump. Of late I had become reliant on those in-room enormo-breakfasts, topping them up at petrol stations along the way. But the parade of chorizo-stuffed rolls I'd forced into my protesting gob that morning was now almost spent, and the desiccated wilderness ahead could only have looked less promising as a source of purchasable calories had it been completely ablaze.

I was still waiting in vain for a petrol station or any evidence of rival lifeforms when Komoot directed me down a freshly tarmacked side road. This took me deeper still into the dune-like ochre hills, the sun-baked solitude now turned up way past 11. Here I did battle with the full family-pack of cycling's cruellest deceptions: the false flat, the false summit, the false café-bar with its false help-yourself Coke fridge out front.

Ever since riding away from Biketown, the toolbag cable tied to my crossbar had lightly brushed the inside of both thighs with every single turn of the pedals. This had been a maddening companion for almost a thousand miles, but as I laboured forth into no man's land I found myself drawing pathetic solace from every contact. It began to feel like the comforting nuzzle of a faithful horse, though even as I formulated this curious thought another part of my brain – a distant and diminishing part – warned me I might be lapsing into delusion.

The Spanish have a number of words to describe a profound nutritional crisis, and they're all much less jaunty than our own 'bonk'. *Pájara* – which also means a cunning, unscrupulous woman – has a mystical, dark drama to it, and *el hombre del mazo* – the man with the hammer – speaks for himself (at least he did once I'd realised Google Lens wasn't having another funny turn). These words hark back to the Years of Hunger, when even professional cyclists struggled to source calories, and reflect the townless, foodless wide-open spaces that still dominate the country's interior. I was about to be given a lesson, while in no fit state to learn it.

Light of head and dry of throat, I pulled over and squeezed an energy gel between my blistered lips. Every swallow was a wincing ordeal; it felt as though the back of my throat had somehow caught the sun. Maybe it had. I now recognised that I'd just spent a very long time – perhaps as long as half an hour – yelling some Robbie Williams song that had unhappily snagged itself in my ear as it wafted out of a beach bar a few days earlier. This seemed pretty good going as I literally didn't know a single one of the words. Then I went past a derelict cement works, rounded a corner and saw the tarmac give way to dust and rock. I'd gone much too far to consider turning back. To consider anything.

For the following two hours I pushed, pulled and carried the bike up and down a disintegrating trail, one long forgotten by all except flies, crickets and Komoot's perverted algorithm. At times the trail vanished entirely, leaving me to pick my way across the Martian emptiness with only the vaguest on-screen suggestions. Heat-stroked monologues now began to sidle unbidden into my head, rudely barging more practical solutions to this ever-more petrifying predicament straight out through my steaming ears. 'How remarkable,' I told myself, 'that the hostile emptiness we call the Tabernas Desert should have hosted so many treasured land-mark moments in the history of popular entertainment.'

Presently I arrived at the rim of a deep ravine, into which the trail tumbled like a sand and boulder waterfall. I looked down it and thought: It was here, of course, that Charlton Heston famously shared the first on-screen kiss with a mule, as well as the third, fifth and twelfth. Then I clamped both sweaty, trembling hands to La Berrendero's dusty crossbar and held the bike sideways in front of me like a Zimmer frame, digging the wheels into the crumbly rock for purchase, shuffling downwards inch by inch, inch by inch, then inch by 30 skittery mad yards as the bike and I lost our purchase and bumped crazily down through clouds of dust and whimpered profanity. A flailing foot jammed itself into a cleft, which brought me to a miraculous if messy halt about 50 feet from the bottom, at the cost of a shrieking klaxon of agony.

With my ankle pulsing and swelling like a cartoon malady, I skated and slipped to the ravine's fundament, running on adren-alin and some kind of animal instinct – perhaps that of a really stupid duck. Breathing raggedly, I propped the bike against a rock and rested on its crossbar until the flies drove me onwards, hobbling away down the canyon floor. 'Yet who now remembers that the first *EastEnders* Christmas special was set in this lonely gorge,' said my head, thoughtfully adding a tone of cracked desperation to its own internal blatherings, 'or that Roger Hargreaves created his much-loved Mr Men after wandering lost through the Tabernas Desert for two weeks in the company of Mr Shitbeak, a story-telling seagull?' And so it went on.

'Is that a car? I think I can hear a car.'

I had turned my voice recorder on a long while ago, figuring posterity might thank me, much as it has thanked Scott of the Antarctic for live-scribbling his own death in that forsaken Antarctic hut. It was a car, and it was on a road. Half an hour later I was sat outside a truck-stop café with four empty cans of Fanta in front of me, my limbs and no doubt my entire head smeared in a henna-like paste of dust and sweat.

At the end of some days I fancied myself as the suave, wryly detached chronicler of appealing small-town night scenes. But this was the end of one of the others, when I stumbled blankly and blindly about the main square like a lobotomised gazpacho addict, swigging messily from a soggy carton. Huércal-Overa seemed like a nice enough place; certainly too nice to deserve this. When I went into a bar toilet, the mirror showed me a man who had just been pulled from an open boat after two months adrift. This was a face beyond suncream; I didn't bother with it again.

'Pay attention!' At Puerto Lumbreras, the photographer Firmas issues the following proclamation to the locals, his voice and gestures endowed with a Madrileño's typical grace. 'Soon a great many men on bicycles, wearing shorts and colourful shirts, will pass down this street. Do not be alarmed: they are professional cyclists, competing in the third Vuelta a España.'

Ramón's account of this address, delivered from the running-board of Number 4 as it drove ahead of the peloton through the Stage 6 scrubland, held several fascinations. On the most basic level, its manner and content is once more suggestive of sustained back-seat vermouth action. That reference to Madrileño grace drips with sarcasm, given what I'd been severally told about the capital's long-standing reputation for pushy, flash brashness. But the main takeaway is its insight into just how incredibly rustic this country still remained in 1941. Puerto Lumbreras was a proper town, and not even an especially remote one by the lethally lonesome regional standards I now knew all about, yet its population was evidently unfamiliar with bicycles in general, and might be driven to panic or rage by a gaudy peloton in full flight. Just a few years earlier, villages across Castile had been scarred by this very experience when the GP de la República – the Vuelta's effective precursor – passed through. It was the bare legs as much as anything. 'They're coming!' shouted one small boy, running down the village street to forewarn his neighbours. 'They're coming and they're all naked!'

As I rolled through the light-industrial peripheries of Puerto Lumbreras, it was much harder to imagine such scenes than it had been the day before. Beyond the trading estates lay an outer ring of half-built *urbanizaciones*: satellite settlements knocked up in the deranged and shady construction frenzy that powered Spain's 1990s economic boom, and its subsequent drawn-out bust. Half the towns I passed through were girdled with these ghost suburbs: *glorieta*s and playgrounds being reclaimed by the deserty scrub, streetlights sticking up out of dead weeds, the hulks of a few unfinished townhouses and a lot of very overgrown spaces where many more were never started. Had we now reached peak town? Would this pandemic be a turning point for the way we live? I thought long and hard about this and came to a conclusion: Fuck knows. But what a pleasant novelty to think long and hard about anything, instead of having all that parched gibberish spool help-lessly through the heat-shrivelled husk of my brain.

For the post-traumatic cyclist, there can be no better therapy than an endless, slightly declining plateau between two hefty mountain ranges. From Lorca to Murcia, the N340 follows one of Europe's greatest sustained descents: downhill for 70 straight kilo-metres. The cycling bookshelves are now crammed with hairy-chested celebrations of climbing: *100 Mountains You Must Ride Up While You Die*, *Perverts v Gravity*, that sort of thing. It's about time someone wrote a mirror-image downhill companion series for normal people who enjoy life, and that someone should be me.

Yesterday I had hated everything and everyone; now I loved Spain, and Spaniards, and bicycles. Until, while working my way through three Snickers bars outside a petrol station, I made the mistake of checking up on Ramón's Stage 6 report and reac-quainted myself with his account of JB's strength and power in its final hour. 'We have proved that Berrendero is the dominant force, because when the Madrileño takes command at the front, the speedometer of our Fiat always moves to 44 or 45kmh, whereas Delio, Fermín, Antonio and the rest could manage no more than 40. And in addition to taking the most turns, Berrendero was also the one who spent most time with the wind in his face.' Dammit all to hell, JB. Even on this endless descent with a following breeze I struggled to keep it much above 30 for long.

Yet somehow, Ramón's recognition of Berrendero's supremacy always comes across as slightly begrudging. His cold praise for JB's 'tactical intelligence' is distantly removed from those romantic paeans composed in honour of Antonio Montes. Ramón's reports rarely even mention him by name, and when they do it's never as

'Julián', not once, in stark contrast to the first-name chumminess Ramón routinely accords his rivals. You sense that he knows JB is going to win, and that he'd much rather someone else did. There's a conspicuous lack of affection, just as there was from the French journalists at the 1936 Tour. Once again Jools refused to play the PR game, the team game, or any other game that didn't have a big cash prize he could keep all to himself. And once again I loved him for it. As someone who through a cruel twist of nature was born without a killer instinct, I've always had a soft spot for hard bastards. Berrendero wasn't just any old ruthless, selfish, miserable git – he was mine.

Arrival in Murcia meant another anticlimactic anti-sprint down a park boulevard under heavy and invasive reconstruction. I plumped for a nice big hotel right in the centre, where for the first time in my entire life I managed to wangle an upgrade – no mean feat, as I noted in the lift mirror, for a man with actual steam coiling off his head. 'Come on, I know you've got some balconies. Saw pictures on your website.' It's the way I tell 'em. Being the solitary apparent guest may have been a factor, I'm guessing, and I was somehow unsurprised to find my balcony dominated by an enormous funnel that would infuse my drying laundry with powerful gusts of sewer.

Stripped of tourists and clustered with palm trees, Murcia was rather winsome on a Friday night. The locals were dining out in force: sufficient force to lure back the rose sellers and violinists, whose presence held no fear for a scary, sun-grilled loner. I dined in the grandest square, beneath the mighty but endearingly care-worn cathedral, big clumps of dead weeds spilling out from the upper reaches of its monumental baroque façade.

Here I made two arresting discoveries. The first arrived as I was dutifully reprogramming my Stage 7 route, a nightly ritual that now required both phones: the one I used to navigate displaying the following day's directions as agreed between Komoot and me back at home, and the one I used for everything else open on the Google Maps satellite view, closely examining suspect sections of this itinerary for their potential to incite punctures or lead me to a lonely death.

Being a man, I am biologically obliged to ignore or gloss over operating manuals and all other tedious impediments to instant action, which may explain why Komoot's opening menu had never previously detained me. For some reason it did so now, immediately displaying a prominent option-box that revealed I had selected my Stage 7 'sport' as 'Bike Touring'. I had no memory of ever selecting a 'sport' at all, but when I now tapped the options several alternatives appeared. One was 'Road Cycling'; I pressed it, and when I returned to the navigation screen, Stage 7 had been magically redrafted to follow nothing but paved surfaces. Well – that was easy! I tutted indulgently, shook my head with a smile and wondered how this irksome misunderstanding had come to pass, soon ascribing it to ham-fisted screen blindness in all those hours spent squinting and prodding at Komoot in my sunny back garden.

Scrolling back through the digital archive of Stages 1 to 6 confirmed that Komoot and I had never previously done any Road Cycling. Nor indeed had we done much Bike Touring. Stage 2, it transpired, was a joint exercise in Mountain Biking. But the other stages, all the other stages, had been undertaken via a navigational remit that caused my brow to furrow, my jaw to clench and my fist to curl tightly around the handle of my fork, with a view to plunging it into the flesh of my right thigh, deep and often. 'Sport – Hiking.' The accompanying pictogram of a jaunty stick-man with a rucksack on his back helpfully illustrated the intended beneficiary of all those fol-de-ree tractor trails and goat tracks. I stared coldly at this hateful, prancing imbecile for some time, then slammed the phone face down on the table. There had been a clue all along, I now realised, and it was far from cryptic. Six times I'd stopped the Komoot clock to mark the end of a stage, a moment of some ceremony. Five times I had been presented with the same congratulatory message: 'What a hike!' *What a twat*. I released my grip on the fork and sat stiffly back in my chair, a stance that my friction-free Merkels soon readjusted.

I was still chuntering darkly to myself when, en route back to the hotel, I made the night's second grim discovery. Passing through a smaller square that backed on to the cathedral's towering left-hand flank, my eye was drawn to a large side entrance with an inscription prominently engraved beside it, just above head height. I veered over.

JOSE ANTONIO PRIMO DE RIVERA. ¡PRESENTE!

Sorry, what? I gazed at these neatly chiselled words with an open mouth, then looked around at all the well-dressed strollers ambling beneath it, waiting for them to slap their collective foreheads, put up a few stepladders and erase this inscription with a frenzy of hammer blows. To see the founder of Falangism's name on public display was shocking enough, but having it hewn so proudly into the walls of a cathedral … I couldn't – and still can't – get my head around it. Almost fifty years had passed since Franco died. How had this inscription survived?

The next morning, Googling away over a buffet-blitzing three-tray breakfast, I got the whole story. Primo de Rivera, who turned Franco on to anti-Semitism and provided the ideological justification for the coup and his dictatorship, was arrested and imprisoned by Republicans at the start of the Civil War, and executed at Alicante in November 1936. Franco, the definitive opportunist, was secretly delighted to see a dangerous potential rival shoved permanently out of the frame, but as a good totalitarian he knew the value of a fallen martyr: his propagandists swiftly created a personality cult around the man they reinvented as *El Ausente* – The Absent One. The inscription I'd seen was once commonplace on Spanish churches, that '*¡Presente!*' included as the reply to a Godly roll-call that invoked Primo de Rivera's enduring spectral attendance.

I could understand why the Church might have gone along with this at the time, when memories of murdered priests and nuns were still raw. The Killer Priest of Zafra's horrific rampage told you all you needed to know about the strength of ecclesiastical feelings back then. But now? Still? Really? It didn't help to learn of the repeated petitions that have been submitted to Murcia's Catholic authorities over the last decade, pleading for the inscription's removal. At the time of writing, they had not troubled themselves to respond to a single one.

CHAPTER 12

CRACK...

The Vuelta would leave Murcia with only twenty-two riders, following the retirements of the penultimate Swiss rider and Antonio Montes, the King of Masculinity himself. Ramón didn't seem especially keen on revealing the details of his hero's withdrawal. 'This Vuelta has been deprived of its great entertainer,' he reports sadly, but simply. 'The race's medical officer, Dr Riobo, tells us that Antonio Montes has suffered an injury that will prevent him from starting tomorrow's stage.' I understood his reluctance after finding the full story in a rival press report. 'Upon arrival at the hotel in Murcia, Antonio Montes suffered an accident in the bathroom. After he climbed on to the sink, it broke, and when he fell to the floor a shard of porcelain punctured his thigh. He is now being treated at the city hospital.'

Well – where to begin? As to what the King of Masculinity was up to in that sink, we can only speculate. So let's do just that.

Best-case scenario: washing his crown jewels. Worst: some complex auto-erotic ritual involving tap heads and a bar of soap. At any rate, I had to share his pain, as this is always my greatest fear on these undertakings: that I won't be undone by heroic over-exertion or lonely dehydration or even a wayward 32-tonner, but by some off-bike misadventure so daft or shameful that not even my own family could pity me.

'They're still trying to work out the precise sequence of events, but it seems to have started when he got the back of his shorts jammed in the lift door.'

'That's what I thought, but apparently you can overdose on gazpacho.'

'We've never seen crickets behave in this way. Your husband must have done something to really upset them."

I sped out of Murcia on deserted Saturday-morning streets, and was soon riding under the belly of an EasyJet plane as it made its deafening final approach into Alicante, an orange-and-white beacon of hospitality hope. Then there was the Med once more, fronted by palms and high-rise hotels, weekend yachts and speedboats carving white arcs far out in the blue. You have to say that Alicante hardly seems an obvious location for a massive seaside resort, dominated as it is by enormous cliffs that vault up right behind the sand. But as I squeaked along the gaily tiled promenade, the beach beside me

---

* Much as I might like to pretend otherwise, my statistical risk of coming home in a box was extremely modest. Those who take a creepy and obsessive interest in these matters – let's call them life insurers – assess dangerous activities in terms of 'micromorts', each unit corresponding to a one-in-a-million probability of death. It has been calculated that cycling 20 miles is worth one micromort: by riding 3,000 miles I therefore accrued 150 micromorts, which in terms of risk apparently equates to giving birth by Caesarean, taking ecstasy every day for a year or doing one third of a base-jump.

was fairly well stocked with sunbathers whose pallor betrayed their North European origins: aside from a party of boorishly drunk Dutchmen in Malaga, the first tourists I'd seen. I later learned that Spain, a country so heavily dependent on foreign holidaymakers, endured an 80 per cent drop in visitors across the whole of 2020.

Ramón conspicuously had nothing to say about Alicante. In his report, it didn't even get a namecheck. Perhaps, with a uniformed *Movimiento* press attaché always listening in, silence seemed the prudent option. This, as noted, was the site of Primo de Rivera's execution. And when Franco made his final push towards the Med, the Republic made its last stand here: as the Nationalists marched in, hundreds of refugees and soldiers killed themselves, many by jumping off the cliffs. Or perhaps I'm just getting ahead of myself, and he was merely saving his column inches for La Carrasqueta: the Vuelta's heftiest mountain challenge to date.

Tawny, jagged and treeless, Spanish mountains look more New World than Old. If the Alps are Julie Andrews, the Sierra Nevada is Charles Bronson. All morning its bald brown peaks had been glaring down at me from the west in flinty silence; after Alicante, the N340 turned inland and suddenly my view was filled with walls of savage bare rock that tore into the cloudless sky. I'd got myself into a bit of a state about La Carrasqueta, because nobody gives a name to a small, gentle mountain climb, particularly not a name that sounds like a psychotic Mexican wrestler.

Komoot's undercover hiker didn't go down without a fight, the little shit: the Carrasqueta-climbing old N340 had been rebranded the CV-800, and finding it somehow required me to traverse a colossal sandy canyon, on a track hemmed in by towering fronds of bamboo. Then I hit empty hot tarmac, swapped helmet for cap, and did my best to get into a groove.

Shortly beyond the last outposts of agriculture, the road began to tilt properly upwards. The sign that warned me of a 7 per cent incline and the first hairpin was one of the last I could make out: most of its successors had been bleached white by umpteen brutal summers, and the first one that wasn't had a big snowflake on it. I did my best not to look up at the overwhelming zigzags above, bordered with wandering battlements of concrete blocks that imparted the look of an enormous impregnable fortress. Looking down wasn't much better, with the buff plains now dizzily far below. There were a lot of very excitable weekend motorcyclists up here with me, though not as many as there might have been: with sombre regularity, I laboured past roadside shrines adorned with faded plastic flowers and photos of tragic, foolhardy young idiots astride their superbikes.

La Berrendero's bottom-bracket budgie was in a bad way, chirruping madly at the top of each pedal stroke, hacking up ground glass at the bottom, the painful chorus amplified as it bounced back at me off those scabby concrete blocks. The pre-cramp tremors returned, opening up a new front on the back of my left thigh. Whenever something good happened, it had to be counterbalanced by something bad. Apparently I couldn't have a nice breeze without my back starting to really hurt. Need an energy gel? No problem, but I'm afraid that will mean riding through a big pothole and squeezing most of it all down your front. In fact, it had been this way since Alicante. Three petrol stations had wobbled up out of the heat-haze in drawn-out succession, each tantalising me with the promise of life-giving chilled refreshments: the first two had closed down, and the last was a nougat factory.

The gradient picked up a bit but I didn't panic, settled now into my natural rhythm: somewhere between Coldplay and the passing of the seasons. There were still 10 kilometres to go. Or so I had obscurely come to believe when a brown sign appeared right in front of me, with digits and a name on it. I knew what this meant: that I had topped the col and was a great man. This achievement could not be measured in numbers, or so I quickly decided after seeing the rather unimpressive one on the sign: 1,020 was several hundred metres short of expectations. Let us turn instead to the sprawling, steepling prospect laid out beneath us, to the contours and clefts of the mighty but inferior eminences around, to the vast battlefield diorama laid out between them, above all to the blocks and spires of Alicante fading so distantly into the misted Med. Let us consider the young cyclist now labouring past the sign, and convince ourselves he has been struggling to keep up since the first hairpin. And let us place this achievement in its 1941 context, when Julián Berrendero did what he did best: pissing on chips.

Antonio Escuriet was the local favourite, and his cheering fans stood in force along the Carrasqueta. Ramón reported that an unofficial 'Club Escuriet' had sponsored a prize for the first rider over the top. In the last kilometre, JB and Escuriet broke clear from the other leaders, 'standing upright and pedalling hard'; but of course the Madrileño proved impervious to sentiment and etiquette, muscling his front wheel over the line just in front to break Escuriet's heart and dismay his massed supporters. Berrendero didn't care about the mountain points, and even he wouldn't have bust a gut for the prize: 100 pesetas and a packet of Alicante nougat. But Escuriet was on his grudge list, and that was reason enough.

Alcoi, the first town on the other side, was a rather remarkable place. Hemmed in on all sides by great leering hunks of geography, it sat astride a deep ravine that was spanned here and there by spindly old bridges. At the bottom lay Alcoi's gurgling raisons d'être: the trio of rivers that its bold nineteenth-century fore-fathers had tapped for propulsive power. In a few decades, this isolated and inaccessible mountain settlement would explode into a thriving centre of industry. Rather fantastically, Alcoi's boom years were underpinned by its invention of fag papers: in the early years of the twentieth century, this town dominated global production of an industry that then accounted for a remark-able 2 per cent of Spain's entire GDP. Better still, the inventor of the cigarette-paper booklet was a Benedictine monk who lived just over the mountain. What is it with these guys? Everyone is familiar with their eponymous liqueur, but it's less well known that Benedictine monks also bequeathed us the crack pipe and the butt plug.

The grand old red-brick water-company headquarters had been repurposed as an upscale hotel; I got a room, cleansed flesh and fabric, then hit the steep streets. Alcoi's challenging situation made this a dramatic experience: I went into a supermarket's back entrance, and emerged out of its front after climbing three flights of stairs. Whenever I looked down a side road I saw it end in a forbidding wall of granite and greenery. It didn't take me long to note that the average age was conspicuously low by Spanish small-town standards; perhaps the young people were all desperate to leave but couldn't find the exit.

The new-infection numbers that scrolled across the bottom of every TV screen had been inching up for days, but the second wave was now crashing in at full force. Smaller towns always seemed a little more fearful than big cities, and Alcoi was on the highest alert. My hotel room had been festooned with more hazard tape than the scene of some terrible crime: everything from the hairdryer to the Nespresso machine was identified as an 'AREA DESINFECTADA', with the same message draped across every door along the corridors. When I went into a JD Sports in search of new socks, an appalled young sales assistant rushed over: 'Caballero! Caballero, por favor!' he cried beseechingly, both hands pointed at a gel dispenser I'd once again failed to notice. (*Caballero*, meaning cavalier, must be the best word for 'sir' in widespread contemporary usage.)

Later, as I ordered insufficient calories at a table outside a sushi restaurant, the waitress recoiled with great drama when my accent betrayed me as a filthy, free-roaming foreigner; after she departed, I glanced around and noticed that my elderly neighbours were all pulling their masks up from under-chin standby. It wasn't a rational reaction, but then what good had reason done them? Small-town Spaniards were the most disciplined, responsible, rona-ready people I had encountered – the London I left behind seemed shamefully lackadaisical in comparison – yet the virus was once more on the march in their neighbourhoods. It seemed so horribly unfair. Not for the first time I recognised what an outrageous fluke my presence here was, how I'd blithely and unwittingly pitched up in Spain in a tiny episode of calm between the Covid storms.

I didn't sleep much: it never pays to underestimate the caffeine content of energy gels, or the nocturnal decibel output of Spanish youth in a town crammed between echoing walls of rock. My morning mission in Alcoi was thus conducted in a state of some bleariness, compounded by the monstrous downtown gradients I had to conquer while completing it.

Just as Alcoi's business leaders made the town an unlikely trailblazer in industrial mechanisation, so their workforce led Spain as the stroppy vanguards of radical insurrection. In 1821, when Alcoi's fortunes rested on its wool-spinning industry, workers who spun and carded yarn at home ran amok through the new factories that were taking away their livelihoods: dozens of water-propelled machines were destroyed in what were Spain's first Luddite riots. Fifty years later, during a general strike, Alcoi's urban guard opened fire on workers gathered outside the town hall; the survivors stormed the building, killed the mayor with their bare hands and dragged his mutilated body through the streets. Ahead of the curve or what? You could quite plausibly argue that the divide into which Spain would tumble in 1936 first opened up in Alcoi; equally, there was a case to be made that this terrible rift began to heal here.

Because by the time of the Civil War, the people of Alcoi seem to have got a lot of death-dealing class hatred out of their systems. Almost uniquely, there wasn't a single local reprisal when Mussolini's bombers dropped 629 bombs on the town and killed sixty-four citizens. Nor, despite the fact that Alcoi had long since been taken over and run by anarchists, was there any significant repression after the town fell to the Nationalists. OK, the anarchists did kill a priest, and the Nationalists did kill the mayor. But Alcoi nonetheless harboured a rare spirit of only lightly murderous reconciliation, and here I was, up in the saddle and blowing hard, ascending its perpendicular outskirts towards the edifice that embodied it.

In most towns across Spain, when anarchists took charge the first thing they did was burn the church to the ground. But in Alcoi, reverse-engineering the ingenuity required to design and construct this drastically pitched town, the Revolutionary Committee carefully dismantled the Church of Santa Maria – then recycled it. The tower and its clock were taken down and rebuilt beside the town hall; the rest was carted up a hill and used to build an Olympic-sized municipal swimming pool that still stands today. Its highlight, in the photos I'd seen, was a lofty diving board whose elliptically arched legs were a homage to the art nouveau bridge that vaulted so gracefully across Alcoi beyond my hotel window.

So you may imagine my panting, red-faced dismay when I dismounted in the car park of the Piscina Municipal and stared at a set of very green, very closed doors, and the mighty walls that encircled the compound behind them. In the pandemical circumstances I'd never really expected the pool to be open, but a decent over-the-fence inspection didn't seem too much to hope for. But it was, and I'm sorry to have wasted your time and mine.

If the news was all about Covid, the TV weather was *calor, calor, mucho calor*. As I toiled up the desolate mountains that imprisoned Alcoi, I realised it was no accident that *el tiempo* meant both time and weather: the seasons here were set in stone, married faithfully to the calendar, with none of the meteorological caprice that powers 73 per cent of British conversations. At the start of the Spanish summer, the dial was set to *mucho calor*, and there it stayed. Blinking sweat out of my eyes as the nougat tarmac passed beneath me with agonising sloth, it was hard to imagine that I'd ever get anywhere going this slowly in this heat. My redrafted mission statement demanded that I make Valencia by nightfall, and that meant riding 150 kilometres, which, when you're traversing a mountain range with all the pace and grace of a blind tramp, seems frankly preposterous. But then almost every day kicked off with a festival of suspended disbelief, and it was only through repeated, weary triumphs of experience over logical expectation that I came to accept that I might indeed make it to my intended destination, and that at some stage on my way there the repulsive, soggy *bocadillo* I had just assembled in my hotel room from gazpacho dregs and slimy chorizo might indeed prove moreishly irresistible.

At weary length I crested the Sierra Nevada's last line of defence, and there was the spangled sea, and here was the ex-N340 motorway service road I would be tracking all the way down to it. It was a Sunday, and when at length I branched off through the coastal towns, the local youth were out and about being really Spanish, sharing joints under railway bridges or carrying massive paella pans down the street. I hit the seafront esplanade, slaloming through heaps of tiles and street furniture ripped up and shattered by a huge storm back in January, then veered back inland through endless groves of squat little orange trees, cheerily flicking the Vs at the left-hand mountains with the sea breeze at my back. I rounded an enormous lagoon and suddenly the view ahead was clustered with dockyard cranes and, more distantly, spires and apartment blocks. I laughed out loud. I hadn't just made it to Valencia – I was here hours ahead of schedule. Even better, the 1941 riders came in ninety minutes late.

'CHAFER WINS STAGE 7.' So read the sports-page headline in *Azul*, the official Falangist daily, affording victory to Diego Chafer: quite the comeback for a rider who had abandoned the race three stages earlier. I'd long wondered about the rationale for this full-fat fake news, and as I built speed along the finishing straight concluded it was a double punishment: the stage had in fact been won by Antonio Sancho, a Catalan, and completed at an average speed of 24.466kmh – which, as Ramón reminded his readers, was 'below the minimum average of 25kmh set down in the regulations'. *Azul* had already expressed a dim view of this 'tranquillity in pedalling', damning riders for 'laziness that deprives the race of interest', and was soon to demand punishments that Manuel Serdan would eagerly mete out.

For Sancho, Stage 7 was a compendium of chaos. He lost an FCB teammate early on: Martín Abadia was 'another victim of iced drinks', which must have delighted the race referee no end. (The severe stomach cramps that put Martín Abadia and at least four other riders out of the race were very probably caused by dehydration – good work, Manuel.) Near the finish, breaking away from the bunch at Silla, near that lagoon, Sancho found himself joined by another erstwhile team colleague, Fernando Murcia. Murcia had thrown in the towel several stages previously, but had been given permission to follow the race as an FCB mechanic; quite hilariously, he was also allowed to keep his bike, which, in Ramón's words, 'allowed him to pedal along with his teammates and encourage them with his enthusiasm'. It was clearly infectious. As the pair hammered towards Valencia, they found themselves joined by 'an abundance of local cyclists, who do nothing but hinder their progress'. Then – and it had been coming – Sancho found his path blocked by a level-crossing barrier, with an endless goods train trundling past. 'We see him stamping his foot on the ground in furious impatience,' writes Ramón, 'and as the last wagon passes he shoulders his bike like a cyclo-cross rider, vaults the barrier and resumes his frenzied attack.'

For once I was able to put in a decent tribute sprint. In 1941, the stage ended on the banks of the River Turia, but I finished on its bed: following a series of devastating floods, in the 1960s the Turia was diverted around the city, and its former downtown course is now a meandering urban park, surreally spanned at regular intervals by many-arched old bridges. No traffic lights; no traffic – just a few ambling families to scatter and terrify as I barrelled head-down between the flower beds.

Valencia had a lot of hexagonal church towers, a lot of blue-tiled domes and a lot of tourists. This latter presence was evidently a mixed blessing, its downside eloquently expressed by the message

I saw sprayed in enormous letters opposite a crowded restaurant terrace: TOURIST WHERE IS YOUR MASK. I cringed reading it. Covering my face was not yet second nature; at least once a day I would find myself in a petrol station or bar and wonder what everyone's problem was, until I went for a pee and caught myself in the mirror. It now seemed inevitable that I would only fully conform to this nation's deep sense of civic duty just after I got home.

Covid was such a stifling presence in these tourist-dependent cities. Whenever I entered any outpost of the hospitality industry, the tension expressed in that graffiti always bubbled away under the surface. Barkeepers and receptionists would welcome me with brittle smiles, their relief at the return of foreign custom tempered by an urge to propel this grubby, rona-sweating alien back out through the doors with a bleach-filled pressure washer. Just before leaving I'd read that Spanish Flu was thus named not because the 1918 pandemic started here, but because Spain was the first country to identify the deadly strain, openly report it, chart it, and put control measures into practice. They are serious about this sort of shit, and always have been.

At the same time, I was in awe of the tourists who were braving such a deeply uncomfortable anti-holiday vibe, at least the ones who weren't Covid-denying mask-spurners. I was required to wipe my feet on two disinfectant-steeped mats before entering my Valencian hotel, where the receptionist sat behind a giant Perspex screen flanked by no less than three foot-mounted gel pumps. She bid me take my key card from a tray of surgical spirit, and in gloved hands passed over a TV remote sheathed in cling film. Waiting for the lift, I noted a five-point diktat to avoid elevator infection displayed by the doors. Number 3 ordered lift users not to lean against the walls. Number 5 was a plea to press the buttons with a 'hygiene stick' – small metal prodders I'd seen offered with every fill-up at petrol stations.

Before I'd left home, this pandemic had already established itself as the most unsettling and disruptive experience of my life. But here in Spain, where economic necessity had opened the doors to a million strangers, things seemed way more weird and scary.

CHAPTER 13

It had been easy to forget, focused as intently as I was on the Civil War, about the somewhat broader conflict playing out as the riders circumnavigated Spain. Twenty-four hours up the fast, flat coast road, squinting at contemporary digitised newspaper cuttings over a seaside pizza at Vinaròs, this oversight dissolved with some drama. The back pages carried reports on Fermín Trueba's unlikely stage win in Tarragona; the front pages, and indeed all the other pages, were devoted to a single story. 'HITLER MAKES HISTORY!' cheered the front page of *El Adelanto*. 'FOUR MILLION TROOPS SWEEP INTO SOVIET TERRITORY.'

The early days of Operation Barbarossa would be Hitler's high-water mark. By the end of its first day, Nazi aircraft had shot down 3,922 Soviet planes for the loss of 78; by the end of the Vuelta, his troops were halfway to Leningrad and had made enormous inroads along a 3,000-kilometre front. Franco was cock-a-hoop: having fought Stalin for three bloody years, albeit by proxy, his enmity towards Soviets and their ideology ran far deeper than Hitler's. As late as 1963, he would still be sentencing Spanish communists to death.

Spain had hitherto adhered to neutrality, but with his old military benefactor on a roll and slaughtering commies, el Caudillo couldn't contain himself. As the Vuelta continued, recruitment adverts began to appear alongside the newspaper race reports, requesting volunteers for the División Azul – a Spanish fighting force that would join Hitler's troops in their anti-Soviet crusade. 'Let us not forget who stood with us when we saw our beliefs, our very way of life, threatened by the Soviet enemy,' declaimed an editorial in the *Pensamiento Alaves*. 'Germany, in taking the fight to the Soviets, is continuing the glorious struggle that began in our homeland. It is our time to come to their aid.'

Backing Hitler in the summer of 1941 must have seemed a pretty safe bet. Indeed, Franco's regime had been buttering up the Nazi top brass for a while: in October 1940, the streets of several Spanish cities were swathed in swastikas as Heinrich Himmler toured the country. During a visit to the Montserrat monastery near Barcelona – four days after the execution of Lluís Companys – the SS Reichsführer went full Indiana Jones Nazi: he had convinced himself that the Holy Grail was kept there, and demanded to see the archives that would reveal its hiding place. When told he was mistaken, he set off on a furious rant, loudly informing the monks that their monastery was built on a Germanic pagan site and that Jesus was an Aryan.

By the time the race finished, over 18,000 Spaniards had signed up for the División Azul, mostly Falangists and ex soldiers, a total that in time would swell to almost 50,000. Hitler privately thought

Franco was a squeaky-voiced irritant ('I'd rather have four teeth pulled out than meet that man again,' he told Mussolini), but he would be deeply impressed with the División Azul's conduct on the Eastern Front. 'These Spaniards have never yielded an inch of ground,' he told his inner circle in 1944. 'One can't imagine more fearless fellows. They scarcely take cover. They flout death. I know, in any case, that our men are always glad to have Spaniards as neighbours in their sector.' The Civil War didn't instil bravery, but insane, suicidal bravado. Later that year, the División Azul would become the only component of the German Army ever awarded its own medal.[*]

But in 1944, of course, the mood was much less Springtime for Hitler. By then the Nazis were in full retreat, and the División Azul had suffered 27,000 casualties. In truth, the tide had begun to turn just a few weeks after the 1941 Vuelta ended, when the German advance stalled, undone by the sheer size of the Soviet Union and its inexhaustible war machine, and Hitler's generals realised he had bitten off much more than they could chew.

I'd come to Vinaròs on account of its own significance in the annals of European conflict. Or rather, on account of my failure to find a bed at the previous resort, which I'd been extremely keen to stay at, because it was called Peniscola. Most of the hotels in Vinaròs were padlocked and dusty; I went into the first one that wasn't, wiping my feet on a succession of disinfectant-soaked doormats on the way in.

---

[*] In 1981, 200 armed Guardia Civil officers burst into the Spanish parliament, the vanguard of a well-planned coup attempt by Franco's surviving old guard. Shots were fired and MPs held hostage for eighteen hours, but the coup folded after King Juan Carlos – who the ringleaders were certain would support them – vehemently denounced it in a television address. It subsequently emerged that several of the leading plotters were División Azul veterans.

'I'm sorry,' said the receptionist as I rooted around for my passport by her desk, 'I must do this now.'

I looked up and saw her pointing a gun in my face. 'Is for temperature,' she explained, replacing one concern with another as she pulled the trigger.

'Listen,' I said quickly, watching the receptionist and a colleague peer doubtfully at the reading, 'I've just ridden 149 kilometres on a bicycle and it's still 31 degrees outside.' It felt like being breathalysed after twelve pints.

'Please – you go outside.'

For ten minutes I waited with La Berrendero by the glass doors. A trickle of elderly guests emerged and gave me a theatrically wide berth. Finally the two women came out; the taller one was holding the temperature gun in outstretched arms, like a TV detective entering a suspect's hideout. She waved it at me, motioning towards the wall. I put my back to the bricks and watched her slowly raise the barrel to my forehead, one eye shut and legs braced. *Per Catalunya!* I yelled, or should have. A squeeze of trigger; an urgent, whispered consultation over a tiny screen; a shrug and a reluctant nod and I was in. An hour later I was back out, scrubbed, splendid and smug, my kit enjoying a long overdue deep clean in my great big room's great big Jacuzzi.

It was at Vinaròs that the advancing Nationalist troops cut what was left of the Republic in half: when Franco's men hit the Med here, on Good Friday 1938, they waded into the sea and crossed themselves. 'The end of our crusade is near,' proclaimed a sympathetic newspaper editorial, 'now that the victorious sword of Franco has sliced in two the Spain occupied by the Reds.' I folded a floppy triangle of *capricciosa* into my mouth and gazed out across the broad promenade, staring past the concrete benches and palm trees at the beach where this impromptu baptism had taken place, marking the start of the Civil War's end. Small children were playing chase on the sand; a few masts swayed above the marina just beyond, lights twinkling cheerily from their pinnacles. For once it all seemed a very long time ago. But what a fearful, fascist future had threatened the whole world on the day the riders passed through Vinaròs and heard the news from Germany. El Caudillo won; das Führer lost. With all respect and the deepest sympathy for those who suffered under Franco, thank Christ it wasn't the other way round.

It was a night for sober reflection, until I accidentally discovered *tinto de verano*. I'd ordered a glass of red wine, but the beverage the waitress came back with seemed a little too pale and much too fizzy. I took a tentative sip and restrained a reflexive urge to return it to the glass with Merkel-soiling, pizza-spattering violence. Lemonade and red wine: an ungodly mixture that should never have been allowed into the world, except perhaps as a tonic for convalescing tramps. *Tinto de verano* replaces lost energy, and just about gets you there in the end, you grubby old soak. But as I reached for my litre of water to sluice the clinging awfulness out of my mouth, I realised I was licking my lips. I liked wine; I craved glucose. I took a second sip, then a swig, then an extended throat-bobbing gulp, and a nightly addiction was born.

And just in time, as the sight that greeted me when I swayed into my bathroom several TDVs later was not one for the abstinent. I flicked the light on to behold a quivering pyramid of froth that rose halfway to the ceiling, presiding over a knee-high sea of bubbles that spilled right across the tiled floor. My eyes did their best to make sense of this apocalypse, and having failed to do so alighted on a multilingual notice that had escaped their weary previous attention, despite being prominently displayed beside the towel rack. 'PLEASE DO NOT RUN THE ENGINE OF THE SPA BATH WITHOUT PROXIMITY,' it screamed. 'Sssh,' I told it, backing out of the bathroom and gently closing the door.

Why on earth isn't the Mediterranean a filthy, dead cesspool? It's a conundrum I have often dwelt on over the years, when driving or cycling by yet another effluent-belching, sewage-spilling seaside industry, and I did so again as I passed my fourth beachfront cement factory of the morning. And with unusual intensity, desperate as I was to find something to think about that wasn't the sodden, soapy kit I had dredged out of the Jacuzzi's residual froth-scum a couple of hours earlier, now getting damper and stickier with every humid pedal stroke.

We're talking about a glorified lake with eighty-six million people living around its shores, a great many of them doing bad things by it or in it. It's the most over-fished sea on the planet, with two-thirds of its marine stock now at serious risk, and comfortably the most polluted in Europe. A third of the world's shipping passes through the Med annually, accidentally or deliberately discharging 150,000 tons of crude oil en route: a litre of Mediterranean seawater will contain on average 10 grams of petrochemicals, a full tablespoon. Two hundred thousand tons of plastic are dumped in it every year, along with untold volumes of untreated sewage, heavy metals and phosphates from all those agro-industrial hothouses. Yet somehow, almost the entire Mediterranean coast remains gorgeously appealing, the water a brochure-ready turquoise and the seafood a perennial temptation, with the correct number of heads and legs and everything. No less incredibly, even here – in the world's beach-holiday hotspot – there were still long, undeveloped stretches of wild, free-range costa. Perhaps Covid had come along just in time to save them.

Tarragona sat atop an enormous cliff, which Komoot decided that La Berrendero and I should conquer most of inside a glass lift: a whole new level of sprint-finish anticlimax. Stage 8 had taken the race into Catalonia, and after Delio Rodríguez punctured twice, the FCB riders pushed hard for a home-soil win. But Escuriet fell dramatically 15 kilometres from the end, 'performing a great somersault down the road', and Vicente Carretero – one of Barcelona's 'secret allies' – was denied victory after the judges decided he'd blocked Trueba in the sprint for the line.

Plum last, coming in almost an hour behind, was the sole surviving Swiss rider: Emile Vaucher, who through the combined misapprehensions of Ramón Torres and Google Lens typically appears in my stage notes as The Swiss Watch. His team had been a selfless source of comic relief right from the start, bemused by the weather, the food, the roads, 'the whole atmosphere of Spain'. Manuel Serdan chided their especially reprehensible water drunkenness; Ramón sniggered at their fateful thirst for cider – bit rich coming from him – and described the Swiss team's desperate bandage-limbed sun protection with a conspicuous absence of sympathy. Their jerseys were funny: bright red with a big white cross on the front. Their names were funny: one of them was called Saladin, for goodness' sake, which must have led to all kinds of merriment in a country still tormented by those centuries of Moorish rule. Tellingly, their disciplined team loyalty was funny: Ramón is tickled pink when he watches them all wait while a teammate repairs his puncture.

The other riders openly and very rudely derided the race's 'international contingent', bemoaning the absence of proper rivals from France or Belgium. They were patronised to the point of persecution: whenever a Swiss rider rode to the front and tried to mount an escape, a Spaniard would wearily lean over and pull him back by the jersey. Ramón sometimes saw this happen a dozen times a day. All this seems especially tough on The Swiss Watch, who though hardly a household name even in his home country was no mug on a bike: most notably, he'd won the 1936 Mont Faron–Mont Agel mountain climb, the savage cheat-fest that had so freaked out Berrendero in what had been his first race on foreign soil. OK, he doesn't appear to have won anything else at all, before or after, but you didn't get a victory like that without being a ballsy character, and with all his teammates back at home TSW now set about making his mark on the 1941 Vuelta. There was only one available option: if you're going to fail in grand-tour cycling, fail big.

Rolling in half an hour behind the winners at Valencia the previous day, TSW grabbed the podium microphone and let loose a charm offensive in broken Spanish. 'The Swiss Watch saluted the people of Valencia for their warm welcome,' reported Ramón. 'Once again, he lamented his bad luck and expressed confidence that he would not arrive in Madrid at the end of the Tour in last place.' This was doubtless rounded off with a wink, because even in these early years of grand tour racing, an upside-down contest had developed down the wrong end of the general classification: finish last as the *lanterne rouge* and you bagged yourself some modestly lucrative publicity and lashings of underdog sympathy, providing you came home last with a self-deprecating smile on your face.

The Swiss Watch played his hand to perfection, aware that as a funny foreigner he always had a trump card. On the Tarragona podium, after Trueba had gone up to take his bow as stage winner and GC leader, there was a special presentation: a bouquet for Emile Vaucher, Spain's newest and foreignest pet loser. It had only been a matter of time before I pinned my colours to the mast of a fellow failure, and that mast was on TSW's merrily sinking ship.

Tarragona gave me an unusually challenging round of War and Peace Disconnect, my habitual civic pastime. I bagged a fourth-floor hotel room on the Plaça de la Font, a most becoming little square bordered with slender, colourful townhouses, then went out to eat and wander, trying in vain to reconcile the delightful people around me with their hate-blinded forebears. Tarragona's Civil War anarchists were a showy bunch: their self-styled Death Brigade went on the prowl in a bus painted black and decorated with skulls, rounding up and murdering 300 right-wingers and 86 priests in the first four months of the war. The post-defeat reprisals in 1939 were almost muted by the Nationalists' usual standards – they satisfied themselves by executing 703 suspected reds and anarchists.

It was especially difficult to get my head around all the horrible history, because Tarragona was so especially appealing. In fact, I wanted to live there. I stood at the clifftop conclusion of las Ramblas, the Vuelta's majestic finishing straight, then looked down and around and wanted it all: that amphitheatre, that beach, those palm trees and the bars beneath them. Even the container port seemed pretty sexy at sunset. I wanted to shop in all these funny little family-run stores, places that sold nothing but men's pants or corkscrews, and eat that *jamón* and those peaches, and sit for ever up on a fourth-floor balcony above the Plaça de la Font, gazing fondly down at the cheery, spirited scenes being played out below. A toddler speeding madly through the densely packed strollers on an electric go-kart, attended by indulgent laughter. A group of teenage boys playing cards round a bar table, as if in training for retirement. A little girl chasing her big brother's friends in and out of every door and under the odd bench. I looked at my watch: it was gone eleven.

Watching this happy world go by, it occurred to me that Spain was like Italy turned down to 7. Spaniards are chatty; Italians are shouty. They're enthusiastic but not histrionic; confident not cocky. The Spanish absolutely adore children, but unlike the Italians don't feel the need to express this through overbearing cheek-grabs and rib-pokes. Spanish men are generally rather unreconstructed, but they don't wolf-whistle on street corners while grabbing their own bollocks. There's none of the slight undercurrent of snideness and aggression that accompanies any gathering of Italian males. A Spaniard would never laugh at another's failings, which is an Italian national sport. Nor do they dump old toilets in lay-bys, which is another. That morning I'd been riding way too fast up the pavement of a one-way street and almost flattened a young guy who walked out of a doorway right in front of me. 'Eh, amigo!' he said, in a tone of mild disappointment; in Italy I would have been swept halfway home by a torrent of hysterical abuse and frenzied gesticulation. Furthermore, every Spanish male under sixty spends the entire summer in shorts. An Italian would rather die. Too cool for school, no matter how hot it is.

And consider driving. Like their Italian counterparts, most Spanish motorists live in old towns with tiny streets, and drive much too fast through them; yet compare the condition of their respective vehicles and you will conclude that the Spanish driver has mastered this tricky art, whereas the Italian has been stubbornly attempting to part walls and shrink oncoming traffic through the sheer force of his motoring personality. As in Italy, urban parking in Spain is an advanced challenge – indeed more so, as

Spaniards prefer not to park by feel. Riding through any city I would find myself regularly startled by a vehicle hurtling out from an underground car park right in front of me, generally up a 45-degree ramp the width of a playground slide.

Every time this happened I was revisited by the trauma of my solitary previous visit to Madrid, in which a miserable defeat for Tottenham Hotspur FC combined with a subterranean parking nightmare to leave me in tears. I thought the worst was over after I successfully manoeuvred my hire car from an alleyway into a tiny lift with about half an inch to spare in every dimension, including height. But beneath the street, the doors clanked open to reveal a small cellar crammed with vehicles that could only have been arranged as they were via the careful use of a crane, having first removed the building above. It took me half an hour, and I had to climb out through the sunroof.

The Spanish nurture a slavish respect for pedestrian crossings that borders on the pathological: they will screech to a halt if you even vaguely break stride anywhere near one. To an Italian motorist, a zebra crossing is a go-faster stripe. The Spanish rarely use their horns and never lean out of their windows to clear a traffic jam through the miracle of aimless shouting. There are big signs on most roads reminding motorists to afford cyclists a 1.5-metre berth when passing, except they don't need reminding. Many of these signs were illustrated with a pictogram of two cyclists riding abreast, a formation that would get you driven into most European hedgerows.

It actually began to feel a bit unsettling, all this courtesy and tolerance. In the absence of those bracing motorist showdowns that are the cyclist's typical daily due, I found myself rehearsing a few just to sort of keep my eye in, role-playing confrontations that ended with me shouting ridiculous Spanglish swears. I was almost relieved when some old bloke in a Seat threw open his car door straight in front of me as I rode out through the outskirts of Tarragona the next day. I had 2,000 kilometres of thwarted, pent-up carrage in me, and he took the whole lot right in his craven little face.

CHAPTER 14

Stage 9 was the shortest to date, 112 kilometres straight along the coast to Barcelona, and I was up early to get it done in a day. In my hurry, you will be appalled to learn that I swept right through the town of Cunit without pausing to take a carefully staged selfie in front of its welcoming road sign. What with this and the related oversight at Peniscola, I wondered if I was losing my touch; happily, I found it two weeks later at the turn-off to Cuntis.

Swallows swooped low over the beachfront esplanades, thoughtfully eating small flying things I might otherwise have involuntarily ingested. Most of the resorts I swept through that morning seemed to be full of retirees, though the music drifting out of the bars and car windows was the same as it always was. I really wanted Spaniards to listen to flamenco or rousing political folk anthems, but neither played any part in the street symphony as I experienced it. The Spanish play nothing but 'Despacito' until they're twenty-five, at which point they all switch to Phil Collins and Dire Straits. A couple of days later I rode past a small electricity substation on the side of which, most endearingly, someone had quite recently sprayed 'RINGO STARR'.

Then the road roller-coastered up and down the cliffs, and I trailed a long line of admirably patient vehicles along it. There was no mistaking the descent where FCB's Claudio Leturiaga came to grief in 1941: a wriggling snake of a road that slithered down to the sea at Garraf. It was an incident that spawned the single most compelling sentence in my collation of Ramón's race reports. 'Despite his cranial haemorrhage, Leturiaga asked for a bicycle to continue the race, losing consciousness shortly after.' A couple of days later, *El Mundo Deportivo* added a postscript to Leturiaga's grisly retirement. 'DOCTOR'S REPORT: Injury incision of 8cm in length contuses the media line of the occipital region.' Yikes on toast. A week afterwards, Leturiaga spoke to reporters from his hospital bed, apologising for his frail voice: 'I lost a lot of blood, but I'm lucky to be alive. I skidded on grit into the stone blocks beside the road, though it's just as well I hit one, even with my head, because it was a long way down.' After that he disappears from the archives: at twenty-six, Claudio Leturiaga's racing days were over.

I'd almost completely forgotten the footballing significance of my jersey, but as I rode into the suburbs of Barcelona it was repeatedly brought to my attention. A few smirking jeers, a few heart-patting gestures of hard-bitten comradeship, a lot of jocular thumbs-ups that seemed to cover both bases. Only now did it strike me that my lethargic, wobbly progress was entirely in keeping with Espanyol's recent history.

How different it had been in 1941, when the RCD Espanyol riders led the Vuelta's nineteen survivors into Barcelona, and then – before an enormous crowd and a full set of Falangist dignitaries – around eight laps of the rearing Montjuïc circuit overlooking the city. The eventual winner was Berrendero's de facto *domestique*, Antonio Martín; JB himself picked up sufficient points on the Montjuïc peak to take the lead in the mountain competition; and with Trueba still leading the GC, it would be a clean sweep for Espanyol on that afternoon's podium. Fixed smiles all round as the bouquets were presented by Antonio Correa, Barcelona's civil governor and a passionate Hitlerphile, and General Mugica, military governor and founder of the SIM, Franco's secret police. Nobody in the crowd or the peloton would have needed reminding that 250 Republicans had been executed in the moat of Montjuïc castle during the Civil War.

Ramón's excitement at returning to his home city had been seeping out through his prose all day – as well as the Leturiaga drama there were absolute scenes at the resort of Castelldefels, where 'male and female bathers ran out of the sea in skimpy costumes to applaud the riders from the edge of the road' – and his infectiously lively account of the breathless Montjuïc laps had lured me into a full-gas tribute. I had spent an age back at home inputting the Montjuïc cycling circuit into Komoot, using a newspaper map dating from Eddy Merckx's sixth win at the criterium that was once an annual fixture, but if I'd seen a 3D projection of it I probably wouldn't have bothered. Only when a cable car glided silently over my head did I realise what I'd let myself in for.

I'd planned on doing all eight laps as fast as I could; after one I was a big red mess. The gradients were savage and relentless, and the descent, when at last it came, was a stop-start travesty marred by mini-roundabouts and the dawdling, wayward learner drivers who were my only companions in this tilted park of nightmares. God knows what the Formula 1 authorities were thinking of when they decided to hold the 1975 Spanish Grand Prix up here, though

I'm guessing it wasn't the ghastly accident that left five spectators dead after a car flew into the crowd on a downhill straight.

After creaking to a halt outside the old Olympic stadium – now named in honour of Lluís Companys, the Montjuïc execution squad's most notable victim – I filmed a post-traumatic video selfie. There's a big white ring of dried sweat and spittle round my mouth, and halfway through my sunglasses fall off my face. I utter only three intelligible words: 'Crapping fuck flakes.'

It was a 7-kilometre ride to Sarrià, in Barcelona's innermost suburbs, and I was very happy to cover half of them freewheeling behind a forklift truck. Then I effortfully wedged La Berrendero into a ridiculous, child-sized apartment-block lift – vertically, with my head twisted through the frame diamond – and emerged at the fourth floor, wearing a bike round my neck. A door opened along the corridor and a familiar face appeared. 'Hello,' I said, meaning, 'I am about to put every single item of clothing I currently possess into your washing machine, then spend the rest of the day wrapped in one of your towels, which on account of ongoing fungal issues you may later wish to take out on to your balcony and incinerate. Please stand aside.'

Adam and I have been friends for more than forty years, so he probably knows me better than I know myself. On this basis, you could argue that he only has himself to blame for relocating to a city on my Vuelta route, and for owning a spare bed, a fridge full of gin, and the aforementioned laundry equipment. It was a fair exchange: he got to laugh at my tan lines.

During the four days I spent with Adam, we acquired deep familiarity with every all-you-can-eat restaurant deal in the greater Sarrià area, and established an all-you-can drink pop-up bar on his balcony. We went to his local Decathlon and bought me some new cycling socks; we watched lower-league Spanish football playoffs on his enormous telly; we assembled the birthday bike that he'd be giving his ten-year-old son Alfie when he returned from a break in France with his mother. In some indefinable way that I couldn't quite put my finger on, all this seemed like an upgrade on cycling all day under a merciless sun. No pliable bidons of hot water to hose into my gob, no humid old pastries, and – unless we got seriously bored – no intimate crevices to smear in medicated cream.

And of course we talked about rona. When I mentioned all the learner drivers I'd seen up at Montjuïc, Adam correctly suggested that most would have been middle aged: an urban demographic who after a lifetime of trams and buses would never again feel comfortable on public transport. By the same token, I realised I'd seen plenty of surprisingly old Barcelonans on e-scooters. Adam had been appalled by my tales of lackadaisical, mask-shy Londoners, and we wondered at the cultural differences that might be in play. Was this country's much keener sense of civic responsibility explained by their enhanced social empathy, a genuine feeling that they really were all in this together? Or was it informed by the legacy of all those decades of dictatorship, when everyone just got used to doing as they were told? Adam felt it was more likely a reaction against the Franco years, at least a nuanced one: in voluntarily following draconian orders that were self-evidently for the common good, the people of Spain were indirectly cocking a snook at all the mindless authoritarian diktats they'd been obliged to adhere to under el Caudillo. Plus, of course, the Civil War and what followed it had endowed a deep tradition of making the best of a truly terrible lot.

On the second day I did something about La Berrendero, which is to say I got someone else to. The bottom-bracket budgie had been possessed by a Dalek for the last couple of hundred kilometres, and changing gear now unleashed a painful metallic cacophony, like a kid in braces eating a Coke can. Adam knew of a bike shop next to Sarrià station; I relieved La Berrendero of her bags and we walked there together.

Unburdening La Berrendero was always a poignant ritual, revealing as it did the slender purposefulness of this machine's natural, race-ready state. It recalled that moment when Jim Bowen pulled back the curtain to taunt a *Bullseye* contestant: 'Let's see what you could have won.' And how I hated putting all the bags back on every morning. Not just because it felt like sticking a roof-rack on a Porsche, but because their obstructive presence made it impossible to mount the bike in graceful motion, with a push-off and a balletically hoisted trailing leg. Instead, I had to hoick a foot over the crossbar and clamber clumsily aboard, like Norman Stanley Fletcher accessing the top bunk.

Adam knows nothing about bikes; I can't speak Spanish. It seemed as if we should be able to mould these two negatives into a positive, but the guy in the bike shop seemed stubbornly unen-lightened by our combined efforts to explain my most pressing mechanical issue. When the words 'il bracketo bottomi' escaped my lips I knew we needed to try a very different tack; I circled a thumb and forefinger to form a small circle, representing the bracket shell, into which I inserted a digit from my other hand, representing the axle. Something about this manual performance seemed unsatisfactory, even when – in retrospect, especially when – I embellished it with a soundtrack of soft shrieks. The bike-shop man, a balding fellow of middle years, looked up from my mime and gazed at me with a look of profound disappoint-ment. '*Mañana*,' he said, in a deep voice, taking La Berrendero by the handlebars and wheeling her slowly away towards his back-room workshop.

CHAPTER 15

'You're not on holiday. This isn't supposed to be fun.' So I told myself two mornings later, juddering down in Adam's apartment lift with my face full of bike. Once again I confronted the weary dread that concluded every out-of-saddle hiatus. At least this time it came with a counterbalance: La Berrendero was reborn. Riding back from the shop the day before, I had laughed out loud at the transformation, smooth and silent as an electric scooter. It was as if the bike had coughed up and spat out a huge hairball of wire wool and gravel. I had laughed almost as loudly when the bald guy presented the bill: a new bottom-bracket bearing, a degreased chain and properly adjusted gears for €29 all in.

I always lost the historical trail in big cities: too many young people, too much change. In consequence, I didn't really ponder Barcelona's unique and significant ordeals in the Civil War until I was riding out of it through a forest of stripy red-and-white factory chimneys. Excuse me while I now ponder the living heck out of them. Because in many ways, Barcelona is a one-stop history-shop for anyone keen to understand why this conflict started, and why the baddies won.

Those chimneys, I realised, embodied both the industrial wealth that set Catalonia apart from Spain's rustic south and west and the workers' movements that took root in the region. The ultra-Catholic provincial landowners who would galvanise Franco's coup were deeply jealous of Catalonia's wealth, and absolutely terrified of its revolutionary radicalism. They'd been burning down churches in Barcelona as far back as 1909. Socialism, and in particular anarchism, were both well entrenched in the region before the war: by 1934, the anarchist CNT boasted over 1.5 million strike-happy members.

When the coup kicked off, Barcelona's revolutionaries got their retaliation in early. As the 1936 Tour de France rolled blithely on, the city's gun shops were being stripped bare, and requisitioned lorries transformed into armoured vehicles with metal plating. Anarchist dockers seized a huge shipment of dynamite and made grenades out of it; print workers piled enormous rolls of news-paper into shell-proof barricades. When, at dawn on 19 July, Franco's rebel generals ordered 5,000 troops to take control of the city, factory sirens across Barcelona sounded the alarm. Almost at once the Nationalists found themselves pelted with homemade bombs and driven into by suicide lorry charges. The resistance came so fast and furious that half the troops never even made it out on to the streets; within two days it was all over. Buenaventura Durruti, history's most prominent anarchist revolutionary, led the final assault on the Atarazanas barracks, a crazy full-frontal charge into machine guns and artillery that would provide a regrettable template for anti-nationalist battle tactics in the years ahead. Six hundred anarchists died and 4,000 were injured in what was a largely pointless display of blind heroism. 'Many of the casualties were unnecessary,' writes Antony Beevor. 'Nevertheless, the courage of that attack passed into anarchist folklore, obscuring the fact that dash and bravery are dangerous substitutes for military science.'

As a moderate, Lluís Companys had long since been sidelined, and with 30,000 of its armed men and women on the streets, the anarchist CNT abruptly found itself in control of Barcelona. A heady few months unfolded: factory workers roared about town in expropriated limos; the formal expression of address – the polite 'you' that remains so weirdly prevalent across much of Europe – was banished; in bars and restaurants, foreign journalists found their tips curtly handed back, 'as this practice corrupts both giver and receiver'. The Ritz was rebranded as the CNT's Gastronomic Unit Number One, a public canteen for the needy. Collective self-management spread all the way down the Republican-held Mediterranean coast, putting 1.8 million industrial and agricultural workers in charge of everything from local bakeries to the Ford factory in Barcelona. It was, by some margin, the biggest anarchist experiment the world has ever known. (Sadly, there is no escaping the fact that this spirited ideology's defining reluctance to take orders lent itself very poorly to winning a civil war, or indeed any bicycle race contested by teams. 'Discipline was almost a crime,' admitted the anarchist writer Diego Abad de Santillán, in an instructive treatise titled *Why We Lost the War*.)

But, as is invariably the case with revolutions, bloodlust and friendly-fire paranoia set in almost at once. A dozen priests at a Barcelona convent were executed on the entirely baseless conviction that they had been shooting at workers from their windows. Five hundred right-wingers were killed in August, most of them on a prison ship tied up in the docks. On a single night in October, forty-four monks were shot dead. And it was in Barcelona that the fatal rift between anarchists and communists first opened up, a civil war within the Civil War that put paid to any hope of defeating Franco.

The Soviet Union had sent its first weapons and 'military advisors' to Spanish Republicans in October 1936, and as Hitler and Mussolini ramped up their aid to Franco, Stalin sought to match them bomb for bomb and spy for spy. By 1937, the Republican government was becoming increasingly concerned – one might say fatally distracted – by Catalonia's anarchist revolution, and figured the Soviets might help them undermine it. Stalin's petrifying Great Purge was then in full murderous flow back home, and he needed little persuasion to tackle another enemy within. I can't tell you how much heavy sighing I did while reading up on the absurd, self-defeating tragedy that ensued. Behold a sadly enduring truth: if there's one thing a hardcore lefty hates more than a fascist, it's another kind of hardcore lefty.

From 1937 onwards, anything bad that happened in Barcelona was blamed on anarchists by communists, and vice versa. In March, an Italian bombing raid that left 1,000 citizens dead kick-started a string of tit-for-tat communist/anarchist assassinations. Both sides forged elaborate documents proving that the other lot were in league with Franco and his foreign fascist allies. High-ranking leaders of both stripes were kidnapped and never seen again. Street battles escalated into full-on armoured engagements; there were even occasional aerial dogfights. For good measure, the Soviets also took on the POUM, a party of 'independent Marxists' that had become increasingly influential – when Orwell pitched up in Spain to fight for the anti-fascist cause, he requested secondment to a POUM unit. But Stalin wasn't big on independent

Marxists. In June 1937, the POUM's leader, Andreu Nin, was arrested, brutally tortured, and executed. Orwell, who was shot through the neck during his time at the front, came to Spain as an out-and-out anti-fascist. He went home as an out-and-out anti-communist.

Anyway, to cut a stupid, horrible long story short, when Franco's troops finally entered Barcelona in January 1939, they met almost no resistance. Two years of infighting had left the city exhausted and demoralised, abetted by a famine that begat pigeon casserole and orange-peel chips. By then over half a million Catalan refugees were already walking north to France, strafed all the way to the border by Hitler's Condor Legion. 'Our pilots have had excellent success,' gloated the Legion's commanding bastard, Wolfram von Richthofen, cousin of the Red Baron and the man who went on to mastermind Hitler's blitzkrieg invasion of Poland. 'They are really getting a taste for it.' The Nationalists who marched into the city were similarly enthused. 'Barcelona is a city which has sinned greatly,' announced their general, 'and now it must be cleansed.' As disappointed as he must surely have been to discover the place all but deserted, his men still managed to find and kill 10,000 people in the first five days of 'liberation'.

Back on the road, heading inland and due west, it was one of those time-warp days when all this history seemed real and tangible, when yesteryear felt like yesterday. The N340 was plaited around a motorway that had opened in the Seventies and sucked away its lifeblood, leaving me alone on aged, weed-pierced tarmac. Every few miles I'd pass the sombre ruin of some art deco garage or hotel, wooing pre-Franco motorists with peeling murals of Cruella de Vil limos and the faded ghosts of Michelin men. And finally, after three weeks and 2,100 kilometres, a raindrop fell on to my left arm. Just the one, mind you: the sky seemed appalled by this lapse, and I watched in awe as it immediately set about banishing every cloud to the furthest horizon. Within minutes, normal service had been resumed, and I was once more traversing the super-sized wheat fields under an imperious sun.

I stayed at a roadside hotel that had survived the cull, a defiantly unreconstructed establishment decorated with silhouettes of finger-wagging beehived women, warning guests off such retro indulgences as smoking in bed and talking in the corridors after 10 p.m. The grand old dear in charge reluctantly permitted me to wheel LB into her office, which boasted two fax machines, then led me up a maze of dusty staircases to another of those special rooms kept in reserve for solitary losers, with an iron-framed sanatorium bed and dead wasps in the bidet. I sluiced them out, filled it up and bunged my bidons in for their overnight soak. Bidons in the bidet: it was always an odious still life. As ever, I told myself it had to be OK, because they were basically the same word. You know – like 'bottle' and 'bottom'.

I drank a can of *tinto de verano* in the bath, then went downstairs and wandered around the bar, waiting for the kitchen to open. The panelled walls were graced with framed newspaper and magazine cuttings; I fired up Google Lens and held my phone to each in turn. The first was an interview with the elderly proprietress, revealing that she'd been working at the hotel since 1965. Her recollections included her father's favourite Civil War story: the hunt for a cache of gold that had supposedly been buried in a nearby village by retreating Republicans. Asked by the interviewer if anyone ever found it, she curtly replied: 'The Republicans were all shot, so it was difficult to know where to start looking.' Another cutting remembered the local children who had supported their families during the Years of Hunger by selling Civil War ordnance they dug up in the fields. 'All the unexploded shells were Russian,' recalled one. 'Most had date stamps from the First World War or even earlier. The Nationalists had German shells that could hit a target 22km away, and they always exploded when they did.' Unamazingly, this line of work cost many children a hand or a foot. I later read that disposal experts are still dealing with a thousand Civil War bombs and grenades every year.

CHAPTER 16

My slimy, wrinkled gloves now ranked as the most appalling items of clothing I had ever put on, certainly since 1978. They looked as if they'd been pulled off the corpse of an Ancient Briton found preserved in a peat bog, and smelled like it too. Whenever my hands passed anywhere near my face, the stench of pickled death brought tears to my eyes and food up my throat. That night I sluiced ten sinkfuls of acrid Bovril out of them, but come morning they still reeked, and were still sodden. I set off with them tied to the bar-bag to dry, but almost straight away had to stop and pull them squelchily back on: changing gear without a padded palm was agony.

I realised that gloves had been a rarity in photos from the 1936 Tour de France – the last gear-less grand tour – but were universal thereafter, just one minor tremor among the seismic changes wrought by the advent of derailleur gears. Though they weren't quite as seismic in Spain: even the top pros couldn't afford a derailleur. Spanish riders would suffer a technological disadvantage that continued for decades, their abysmal domestic earnings compounded by the anti-Franco sanctions that kicked in after the war. Spain was banned from the Tour de France until 1949, and for some years thereafter its riders usually turned up in Paris without a bicycle, knowing that the humdrum yellow service bikes that the organisers would lend them were superior to anything they might have brought over from home. The Spanish-made tubes they were saddled with had to be stretched from the branch of a tree before attempting to force them over the rim, a process that the riders completed using their teeth.

Deep into the 1950s, the principal attraction of racing abroad – along with the copious food – was the opportunity to acquire high-end kit. Plenty of Spaniards raced in France purely to stock up on fancy components they could lucratively flog back home. Even at the Tour-winning height of his success, Federico Bahamontes went everywhere with a big suitcase full of black-market bike bits. 'He had an entire shop in there,' said one fellow Spanish pro. 'He sold us spokes, rims, tubes, the lot. He got them from France and charged a hundred per cent mark-up.'

But the humble origins that inspired such Artful Dodgery also meant that few Spanish riders ever let success go to their heads. The material aspirations that emerge in JB's autobiography are described and fulfilled with endearing modesty: 'The victories I accumulated that season had given me great hope for the future: I would buy some nice furniture.' The only present he ever gave himself was a second-hand Triumph motorcycle, which he bought with his winnings from the 1946 Tour of Catalunya: 'It had telescopic handlebars and cost me 9,000 pesetas. I think somebody had stolen it during the war.' I was also terribly smitten with his down-to-earth stance on celebrity: 'I have to confess that fame can be useful. People are more likely to do things for you if you ask them. Of course you must be alert for those with ulterior motives. But on the whole I prefer to be famous. It makes life easier.'

Such were the reflections that sustained me through a morning of endless apple orchards, as a hot and swirling side wind shoved the bike all over the road. I'd felt a little lonelier since Barcelona, having left two friends behind there: one I'd known for most of my life, and one I'd never met. *El Mundo Deportivo*'s Stage 11 report was topped with an unfamiliar byline, and kicked off in dispiriting style: 'From now until the end, I will be following this third Vuelta a España in place of my colleague Ramón Torres, who is detained in Barcelona by obligations that do not allow him to continue.' Had the Ministry of Education and Leisure tired of those off-message asides, and requested Ramón's substitution? I remembered a few runic mentions in his obituary about 'the official difficulties he endured' and 'issues that had to remain unsaid'. Whatever the reason, from here on EMD's race reporter was Carlos Pardo, who played with a much straighter bat.

At 294 kilometres, the stage from Barcelona to Zaragoza was the second longest of the whole race, and run in the most dreadful heat yet. Ramón would have taken these raw ingredients and cooked them up into a piquant paella, served with rural vignettes and lashings of White Horse vermouth. But Carlos was a meat-and-two-veg kind of guy: 'Botanch damages his handlebars and suffers a delay of three minutes. The sun is strong. At Fraga the riders are applauded by a large crowd.' It felt like that bit in *Good Morning, Vietnam* when Robin Williams is suspended and gets replaced by polka music.

Lleida had been in the news for days, moving in and out of lockdown as the hotspot of Spain's second wave. There were police roadblocks at all the big roundabouts on my way in, each trailing a long queue of motorists waiting to explain their movements, but I was waved through every one without a second glance. Just as well, because whenever I attempted to tell a hotel receptionist or bike-shop worker what I was up to, I realised how horribly irresponsible it sounded: super-spreading Typhoid Timmy scattering deadly sickness in his 4,000-kilometre wake. Hurriedly adding that I'd already had Covid always seemed to alarm rather than reassure. I could understand why. Nobody wanted any contact, no matter how indirect or historic, with this mysterious, death-dealing plague. 'Yeah, I did get bitten by a zombie, but that was ages ago, so I'm probably fine now. Fancy a cuddle?'

There was a lot of Civil War history in Lleida – I was now heading into the anarchist heartlands – but after gawping at the bullet holes that riddled the old city gate, I cracked on. No time to lose if I had any hope of completing this enormo-stage in two days. Especially as the middle bit – the hundred-odd-kilometre section I was about to enter – didn't look like somewhere you wanted to hang around in, on account of it being a desert. Unhelpfully, the last petrol station before the Desierto de los Monegros could only offer me a packet of chocolate waffles and half a litre of Ukrainian-labelled Coca-Cola, a pallid and entirely fizz-free variant.

It kind of crept up on me. The maize and fruit trees thinned, then vanished; I realised that those long, smooth hills around, stippled with khaki shrubs, were vast dunes of sand. Then I scaled a fearsome 8 per cent eminence, tortured all the way to the top by sweataholic flies, and emerged into a bald mesa of overwhelming scale, fifty shades of beige fuck-all. An oncoming lorry driver issued a tiny horn parp as he passed: Good luck, mate; you're going to need it.

Berrendero would never forget what he endured after topping that climb: his autobiographical account of the '41 Vuelta, hitherto threadbare and perfunctory, suddenly comes to vivid life as he recalls it. 'Of that long stage from Barcelona to Zaragoza, I remember nothing but the heat, exhaustion and raging thirst we suffered crossing the Monegros desert – all those endless kilometres of barren, charred hostility.' There's another reason it would have stuck in his mind, though he chose not to mention it: Ezquerra's hopes of victory crashed and burned in the Monegros, a drama that Carlos Pardo inevitably undersold. 'After Lleida, Ezquerra's face denotes some pain. He is attacked by strong stomach cramps, an indisposition that will move him from second place to ninth overall, 20 minutes behind Trueba.'

The tarmac began to soften and gleam. I passed a very derelict motel, sand drifting into its doorless reception. A battered Osborne bull stared me out from the top of a high dune; I squinted through the sun and noted that someone had scrambled up there and sprayed their tag on his dangling ballsack. A desiccating side-gale blew up, like Alex Ferguson bellowing from the touchline after ten pints and a curry. The roadside marker posts quivered; a million hot grains shot-blasted my calves. It began to feel as if every last drop of moisture was being blown clean out of me, a feeling that intensified dramatically when I squeezed the reserve bidon between my crispy lips and heard that drawn-out, desperate suck of death.

It was only half four when I rolled into Bujaraloz, a half-horse town marooned in the sandy scrub. But with 50 kilometres of nothing ahead, I knew I had to stay here: I could either keep my two-days-per-stage dream alive, or myself. 'Mucho calor,' mumbled an old man as I pedalled slowly past his shaded bench in the compact town square. Looking around the houses I realised I was very much back in Castilian Spain – after 800 kilometres of bilingual road signs, separatist slogans and blue-starred Catalan flags, the banners draped over every other balcony were once more striped red and yellow.

The only place with beds to rent was an alleyway bar with upstairs accommodation. It was closed; I sat outside in a shrinking triangle of shade for half an hour before an angry old man opened up and came outside. Clotted strands of sweaty grey hair clung to his balding pate; he wore a grubby facemask under his chin. I found myself unavoidably reminded of Hector Salamanca, the *Breaking Bad* drug lord who must rank as cultural history's most terrifying paralysed mute.

'*Habitacion? Para mi y mi bicicleta?*'

Salamanca looked at La Berrendero as if it was a dead dog, then at me as if I'd just asked him to kiss it better. Twenty minutes later, without the exchange of a single further word, the bike was in a dark stable three streets away, I was stretched out on a bed as soft and broad as a park bench, and my kit was sat in a sink half-full of beige water, its plug-less drainhole blocked with a sock.

Hunger, in its jelly-legged, clammy-browed final form, drove me back out on to the ramshackle streets. Salamanca had wordlessly held up nine fingers when I asked him what time his kitchen opened; that left me three hours to find food or die trying. In mighty heat I shuffled past rows of ancient houses, half of them roofless ruins, the rest proud and immaculate, with the town's solitary shuttered grocery somewhere in between. At length I found myself out on the Bujaraloz bypass, a sad and superfluous feature with all the traffic now miles away on the AP2 motorway. Here, bookended by a pair of abandoned petrol stations, lay a trio of defunct truck-stop restaurants. Horribly, two looked to have closed down very recently; unforgivably, one had a sign outside that boasted of a 24-hour all-you-can-eat buffet, which immediately caused my stomach to make noisy preparations for a phantom feast.

I said bad things in a loud voice, then made my unsteady way back to the bar, tortured all the way by cooking aromas drifting out through the fly curtains and in through my mask. When I walked in the TV weather was on, with a map full of 44s beside the legend CALOR AFRICANO. A digital clock in the corner of the screen told my stomach it still had eighty minutes to wait; I ordered a *tinto de verano* and four packets of peanuts from my balding tormentor, then sat in the corner watching six very old men play cards, and an even older one dropping euro after euro into a fruit machine. They all had their masks under their chins; nowhere else in Spain would I encounter such brazen nonchalance.

Two packets in I sensed there was something not quite right with the peanuts; after three I put my finger on it: they were absolutely disgusting. After finishing the fourth I inspected the packet and saw a sell-by date that had been and gone in 2017. With a shrug I got out my phone and set about my local research, tiny words swimming in and out of focus on the screen. It wasn't a surprise to learn that Bujaraloz had one of the oldest populations in Spain: indeed, it had once been the home of Spain's oldest woman, who died just before my peanuts went off, at the age of 112. A rather headier revelation was the remarkable cameo role Bujaraloz had played in the Civil War's early months. For a spirited few weeks in the summer of 1936, this humble, remote little town was the anarchist capital of the world, occupied by Buenaventura Durruti and 4,000 followers as they regrouped before an intended assault on Zaragoza.

A knuckle rapped my table; I looked up and saw the blank-faced Salamanca aiming a thumb at the dining area. All ten tables were empty, but he had thoughtfully placed a knife and fork on the one in the furthest, darkest corner, right next to a door that my nose forewarned me would lead to the toilet. When he returned I was expecting a menu, but no: he had a huge plate of pork steak and chips in one hand, and a half-full bottle of red wine in the other. Both were slammed wordlessly in front of me and off he went.

In the next half-hour, cramming in forkfuls of meat and fistfuls of chips, I watched Bujaraloz come to life. First in retrospective monochrome, as I scrolled through extraordinary photos of the town's fifteen minutes of anarchic fame, and latterly in the full-colour, surround-sound here and now. Young people started filtering into the bar, couples, small groups, large groups. Mumbling evolved to chatter, then by stages swelled into raucous laughter and shouts. A girl screamed. A glass broke. A huge cheer begat an endless chinking clunk: someone had won the fruit machine jackpot.

When the first tattooed teenager swaggered across the empty dining room towards the toilet he muttered two words as he passed my table. A while later another pair went by and muttered the same thing. Transposing this situation to my homeland, it was only too easy to imagine what two words a young man might murmur to a lone middle-aged stranger who had stationed himself outside a pub toilet. Then a teenage girl passed by and delivered a much clearer rendition of the same mutter, and accompanied it with a little tilt of the head: 'Buen provecho.' I put my knife and fork down and smiled to myself. That had to be the Spanish for 'bon appetit', and a moment's Googling confirmed it. All these loud young people were expressing a polite hope that some random out-of-towner would enjoy his meal. Was this some reflexive superstition, a legacy from the Years of Hunger, when every meal might be your last for a week, especially out here in the desert? I had no idea. But ten minutes later, having cleaned my plate to a veritable chorus of youthful buen provechos, I reeled happily out into the streets, drunk on human kindness and off my tits on pork and chips.

It was dark and warm and very different. Or rather eerily familiar, because as I walked through the dim streets every photographic tableau from those Durruti weeks took shadowy shape before me. There was the hermitage the anarchists requisitioned as an ambulance garage; there, the church they turned into a field hospital; there, the school that was repurposed as, um, a venereal disease clinic, which still stank of medicated ointment when the kids went back after the war. Detecting faint indentations in the wall above a chapel door, I deduced that these were the bullet holes left by Durruti when he test-fired the machine gun that the town's blacksmith had, on request, affixed to his Renault convertible.

As I meandered, I found myself wondering if the whole extraordinary interlude had left an improbable legacy behind in this dusty little town out in the desert. The defiant spurning of masks, the proprietor's proud disregard for the conventions of customer/staff engagement, the raucous young glass-breakers: perhaps all were keepers of the anarchist flame. Then I entered the main square, where old man Mucho Calor had addressed me from his bench, and beheld the backdrop to the most compelling archived images. The arch Durruti's men rolled a piano through on the day of the San Agustín festival, before dancing the night away around it. The wall they parked their unlikeliest war machines against: a line of holiday caravans. And there, centre stage in the square, the double-fronted townhouse that Durruti annexed as his headquarters. That place had seen it all. He delivered his speeches from that balcony. He lined up three members of his militia against that wall, after locals told him they'd stolen a mattress. 'I won't shoot you this time,' he said, sticking the big pistol he always carried back into his waistband, 'but if anything like this happens again, it all ends right here.' When his men frogmarched a fourteen-year-old Falangist POW through that front door, Durruti – who had two Falangist brothers – sat up with the kid all night trying to convert him. (This episode would have made a feel-good cornerstone in any filmed version of Durruti's life, but in reality the boy refused to recant and was shot at dawn.)

As his aforementioned exploits in Barcelona suggested, Durruti was big on showpiece bravery, but rather smaller on hard-nosed tactical nous. He gathered his anarchists – nicknamed the Durruti Column – at Bujaraloz in preparation for an attack on Zaragoza, but in the event the Republicans couldn't agree on a battle plan, and the intended advance gave way to a piecemeal retreat. In fact, almost everything about Durruti's Civil War exploits presaged the stout-hearted, wrong-headed, mutually destructive shambles that came to define Republican combat tactics. Right down to his death in November 1936, aged just forty, in the back of a car driving towards the front line in Madrid. Depending on who you believe, he was shot either by his own accidental hand or by a bodyguard who'd been turned by the Soviets. (The official story blamed a Nationalist sniper – a challenging fit with the powder burns that were found all around the fatal entry wound.)

Durruti is still enjoying a long afterlife as a revolutionary hero, a poster-friendly icon in his leather cap and jacket, with that pistol stuck in his waistband. More than forty years after his death he gave his name to post-punk studenty faves The Durutti Column, even though they spelled his name wrong. Buenaventura Durruti was arguably the most famous anarchist of all time, and indisputably the commander of the largest anarchist rebellion in history. Over half a million people joined his funeral procession in Barcelona, the largest show of public mourning Spain has ever seen. Yet despite this, and all the lingering hero worship, I found absolutely no reference to either man or column in those dark streets. There was a plaque in the square, but it commemorated a sixteenth-century geographer who was born in Bujaraloz. I suppose in a town where people live for a hundred years and memories never die, that kind of history is just a lot less likely to start a fight.

CHAPTER 17

Every evening I collapsed face first on to a hotel mattress and felt relief and achievement wash over me: I'd done it, it was all over. Not once did it feel merely like the end of a day or even a stage, but the definitive conclusion of my two-wheeled life. The last page of a book, not a chapter – so long, cycling, and thanks for all the bum cream. Maybe this was some form of psychological self-defence, shielding me from the outrageous, unreasonable scale of my undertaking. But in unwelcome consequence, every morning always took me a little by surprise: wait, there's more? Fuck sakes. I wish someone had said.

This was very much one of those mornings. In my mind I'd already conquered the Monegros Desert, so it seemed terribly unfair to find so much heated loneliness in front of me, biding its time under a deep-blue sky. For hours, the road ran dead straight across the sandy scrub, a thin grey thread in a huge brown blanket.

It was impossible to believe that the rearing green undulations of the Basque Country lay just half a stage up the road. But at length, trees began to reappear, along with the odd patch of cultivation far off to my left, irrigated by the unseen Ebro: Spain's longest river, and site of the Civil War's longest, largest battle. After the Nationalists cut what remained of the Republic in half at Vinaròs in April 1938, the red team mounted a desperate counteroffensive along those distant banks, their last roll of the dice. In the course of 117 days they pulled out some of their signature foolhardy assaults, inflicting the Nationalists' worst Civil War casualties in the process, but continuous pinpoint bombardments from Nazi field guns and aircraft slowly wore them down, and in November they set off on their final retreat.

I didn't set eyes on the Ebro until I crossed it on my final approach to Zaragoza. New boy Carlos Pardo noted the riders' relief when they spotted the Pilar – the city's high-towered cathedral – from afar, heralding the end of this terrible, broiled stage. One of the best features of any inland Spanish city is its ageless skyline: the Pilar still looked down on the rest of Zaragoza, its four corner towers suggesting a huge upside-down table.

Zaragoza was a second-wave hotspot: the breakfast-news ticker-tape told of 250 new daily cases in the city, and when I stopped at the first après-desert petrol station, a policewoman who had been properly hiding behind a pump leaped out to ticket a motorist who emerged from his car without a mask on. (By way of instructive comparison, in the first six months of the pandemic, Spanish police issued over a million fines for rona-related transgressions. The equivalent UK figure was under 25,000.) When I checked into my bargain Airbnb-style apartment overlooking the cathedral square, the host made me disinfect my hands before and after throwing the keys at me from a good ten feet down his hall.

It was tremendous to have a whole flat to play with, and I endeavoured to make use of every single appliance, including the dishwasher, even giving the hoover a run out after snatching some previous resident's open packet of soap powder out from the under-sink cabinet with excessive euphoria. I staggered back from a supermarket bearing an idiotic surfeit of food and drink, but only after filling the fridge did I wonder how on earth I would ever manage to transfer its entire contents into my stomach before leaving. In the end it proved almost shamefully straightforward, right up to that difficult third melon.

The vast square was resplendent under a mighty late-afternoon sun that gilded the Pilar's towering beige flanks, and sent the sparse citizenry darting across open ground towards the nearest long shadow. The cathedral is named after Our Lady of the Pillar, Jesus's mum on a stick, who very thoughtfully nipped over from Jerusalem to encourage the apostle James while he was preaching in Spain, and even brought along a six-foot column of jasper to stand on once she got there.

Half of Zaragoza seemed to be inside when I walked blinking into the mighty, echoing gloom: perhaps drawn by the delicious drop in Celsius, perhaps by the timeless appeal of faith in a plague. I went in because the other La Berrendero – Mrs JB – was a Pilar by birth. Even in a land full of Angels and Jesuses it seemed like a pretty out-there name for your baby daughter. But a glance through the records informed me that Spain was full of tiny pillars in the decade of Mrs JB's birth: it squeezed into the baby-name top ten, just above Concepcion.

'Here you may kneel and kiss our column.' It was a challenge to maintain appropriate piety when the distanced, one-way queue brought me to a hunk of jasper in a golden porthole and the multi-lingual notice beside it. The little photocopied sign stuck above this didn't help: 'We recommend that at this time you worship our column only. Please do not kiss or touch it.'* I bit my lip and carried on around the back of the altar, where I found that the Civil War had graced the Pilar with its own miracle. There, stuck to a slab of marble, were two large bombs, with a plaque informing visitors that they had failed to explode after falling through the roof during a rare Republican air raid in August 1936. God-fearing locals naturally attributed this to their Lady of the Pillar, though the Russian markings clearly visible on the bomb casings offered an alternative explanation. (I read later that the raid was a freelance effort: a solo Republican pilot borrowed a requisi-tioned Post Office plane from a Barcelona airfield without permis-sion, and almost grazed the cathedral roof when he dropped his bombs – several hundred feet below their minimum detonation height.)

A couple of hours on, sitting at my third-floor window with a glass of wine in my hand and half a melon in my lap, I gazed down at the thin trail of locals walking home across the square. Even in the sombre circumstances I knew I'd see somebody messing about, and sure enough my eye soon alighted on a father and son taking turns to push each other across the flagstones at speed in an old-lady shopping trolley. This was the sort of delightful, carefree spectacle that on so many previous evenings had caused me to wonder just how this country ever had a civil war. But not this time.

---

* The 1918 Spanish flu epidemic offered several cautionary precedents. When the epidemic hit Zafra, home of the killer priest, the bishop defied local health authorities when he encouraged worshippers to honour St Rocco, patron saint of plague and pestilence, by queuing up to kiss his relics for nine straight even-ings. Zafra went on to record the highest death rate in Spain, and one of the highest in Europe.

Because Zaragoza was one of those rare cities where the Civil War's senselessness made sense, or at least came shrouded in tragic inevitability. It was a pious and conservative city – bikinis were banned in the municipal pools until 1970 – yet also a deeply radical one. Durruti's desperation to retake Zaragoza was down to its long-standing allegiance to his cause: the local CNT had 30,000 members, which helped nickname it the 'second city of anarchism'. Perhaps above all, this was a city that boasted a fearsome reputation of proud and defiant self-sacrifice. In 1808, 60,000 Zaragozanos – most armed with nothing more than a knife – laid down their lives defending the city from Napoleon.

Franco was deeply familiar with Zaragoza's bipolar political culture, having spent part of his early career in command of the city's military academy. He paid close interest when, in October 1936, hundreds of young men who had been forcibly conscripted in captured Republican territory across the province of Aragon were barracked at the Zaragoza academy. After 300 had been sworn in, Franco sent word that they could never be trusted in the Nationalist ranks; at dawn the next day, the new recruits were all marched into a field behind the academy and shot dead.

I was on the road early, and with a following wind and a bellyful of fuel I fairly bowled along the Ebro's broad floodplain. The air was cool and the fields smelled fresh, a novel pleasure after weeks of putrid farms simmering in the dog-day sun. Every village was full of little old houses and little old people, sweeping thresholds, filling plastic drums from brass-spouted fountains, forming distanced queues outside pharmacies. As ever, these peaceful, enduring scenes dredged up a few jarring memories from my lockdown evenings with Paul Preston's *The Spanish Holocaust*: passing a sign for Sartaguda, I remembered the terrible massacre that had seen it dubbed the 'Town of Widows'. Across this region, Navarre, it's estimated that 10 per cent of all working-class men were murdered.

My speed nosed steadily up: 27, 29, 32, the easiest and most peaceful kilometres of my ride. The painless accumulation of distance might go against the grain in our current age of hard-driven, climb-centric recreational cycling, but as far as I'm concerned this was what the bike had been invented for: getting places fast under your own effortless steam. I swept into Rioja, my third region of the day, and at once found myself flanked by epic vineyards. The sun belatedly rolled up its sleeves and got to work; I took to dipping my head in the chuckling irrigation channels that ran along every road. Someone later told me that all the clusters of white snails I saw barnacled up lamp-posts and road signs round here were engaged in a sort of anti-hibernation, over-summering at altitude to escape the deadly ground-level heat.

Delio Rodríguez notched another sprint victory stage in Zaragoza, and – spoiler alert! – he would repeat the trick in the following two stages, 12 and 13. Having mildly disgraced myself by taking three days to finish that big desert stage, I figured completing Zaragoza–Logroño in one go would secure atonement. But it all went to shit alongside a half-built motorway, when I found myself squeezed into a narrow strip of temporary tarmac with thousands of enormous lorries. How I came to dread those little vans that passed by with flashing yellow lights on their roofs, astride the runic warning 'ESPECIAL' – outriders for some vast abnormal load about to roar past inches from my skull with a terrifying Stuka shriek: a two-storey house, a trawler, a huge chunk of bridge. This was the scariest cycling I've done outside Russia, and – after a tactical retreat to the earthen verge – the slowest since snow-bound Finland. I threw in the towel at Calahorra, less than 50 kilometres from Logroño. My AVS was down to 25.6kmh for the 140 kilometres covered, but at least, and at last, I had ridden for a whole day above the 1941 Vuelta's 25kmh minimum limit, for once sparing myself the imaginary wrath of Manuel Serdan.

Regret was redoubled when Calahorra revealed itself as the first properly horrible town I had spent a night in. Long ranks of concrete tenements bisected its noisy main thoroughfare, and one of them was home to the town's only guesthouse. By the time the careworn landlady showed up, I'd spent half an hour in her hallway being terrified by a formidably drunk woman who tore off her mask to show me a three-toothed smile, then kept trying to stroke my head.

It wasn't an enormous surprise to find that my room lacked any en suite facilities, which these days seems like a serious infringement of basic human rights. It's pathetic that it should, and I slightly hated myself for even thinking it, for feeling like a prisoner as I wandered down a corridor with a towel round my waist for the first time in several years. Then I entered the windowless cell that was the shared bathroom, and immediately began transferring all this hatred, and much more besides, to other people: to the previous occupant for their disgraceful ablutions, to the landlady for filling a bottle of liquid soap with retina-melting antiviral gel, to whoever turned the bathroom light off from the switch in the corridor when I was halfway through a tepid shower.

I can't really explain it, but I came out of that bathroom determined to wallow in Calahorra's dreadfulness. If there was nowhere nice to stay, there would be nothing nice to eat, and nobody nice to meet. So off I went to the supermarket over the road, returning with a big bag of ice, a litre of TDV and half a kilogram of pork scratchings, and spent the next three hours out on my grubby little balcony with a waste-bin ice bucket, watching cars roar by.

*

I read somewhere that there is a strong correlation between premature death and losing your temper with things over which you have no control. This is manifestly cobblers, or I would never have survived fifteen minutes alone with a headwind. I always take them personally, and on my gale-faced, clench-jawed approach to Logroño I understood why: the effect of this invisible foe was identical to the ageing process, surreptitiously sapping your strength and slowing you down, turning up the resistance wheel on the exercise bike of life. It didn't help that in my hurry to put Calahorra behind me I'd foregone breakfast, and would be playing calorific catch-up all day.

Logroño was where JB completed his compulsory military service in 1933, and where he resourcefully parlayed his electrical skills to help secure a professional cycling licence: officers who had their homes rewired gratefully signed the forms, and allowed him ample time off for training and competition. I had my own history with the town: sixteen years earlier, I had walked through Logroño with a donkey called Shinto, en route to Santiago de Compostela. For days my attention had been magnetically drawn to a particular type of greenery spilling over the hard shoulder, but only now, on familiar territory, did I understand why: it was wild alfalfa, Shinto's drug of choice, which I was forever failing to yank his snout out of. Pedalling down half-remembered streets, my eyes began to prickle, then gently overflowed, as I traversed a downtown junction: this was the backdrop to an image of Shinto and me that ranks as the second most iconic photograph ever taken on a zebra crossing.

Mired in nostalgia, I completely forgot to eat lunch or locate the original stage finish line, pedalling straight out of town and on to Stage 13. Almost at once the terrain turned lumpy, and I found myself going against its grain, up and over every hefty, vine-striped hill. Once again the afternoon heat seemed to transcend its elemental constraints and acquire an actual physical form, a sweaty, fat toddler hanging on to my shoulders, then wetting himself.

Quick and dirty petrol-station fare is never a wise long-distance bet, particularly if you go too hard on the taurine. After ingesting a can of Monster Energy the size of a tennis-ball tube I began to oscillate horribly, super-human up one hill, sub-human up the next, my heart dancing to some very strange rhythms. I'm not surprised that the manufacturers swerve some of the lairier side-effects in their advertising, but any properly responsible commercial for an enormous container of carbonated stimulant really should incorporate a clear warning: 'CAUTION: organs may burst clean out of chest. If affected do not operate bicycle.'

I doubt Berrendero was a doper. In his French years he might plausibly have dabbled, given how much of it went on there: in 1930, Henri Desgrange felt obliged to issue a diktat reminding Tour riders that they would have to supply their own drugs. But in those days, dope was seriously heavy shit, quite literally not for the faint hearted: you tautened tired muscles with strychnine, turbo-charged your cardio-vascular system with nitroglycerine and killed pain with ether. 'You could always smell ether in the bunch near the end,' remembered 1937 Tour winner Roger Lapébie. 'It used to be taken in a little bottle called a *topette*.' The combined effects of stuff like this were inevitably alarming. After the Belgian rider Gaston Rebry won Stage 19 of the 1932 Tour by a ridiculous nine minutes, he had to be dragged off his bike by strong arms: 'He raved as if he had a severe fever, shouting that he had to ride to Paris. He did not recognise his own wife, and wildly struck out left and right.' Onlookers were reminded that they'd seen his manager, a notorious 'mixer', hand him a number of small aluminium bottles at the start. Rebry would die from heart failure at the age of forty-eight.

Amphetamines would hit the pro scene in a big way after the war, but just as Spanish riders struggled to source and afford decent equipment, they were likely left out of the speed loop. It's a stretch and a half to imagine that anyone in the 1941 Vuelta had access to pharmaceutical performance enhancement, when they barely had access to food. After retirement, Berrendero would make regular dark references to contemporary practices, with the bitter disillusionment of someone who always rode clean. 'These days you see riders burst away and then blow up,' he told a journalist in 1975. 'They're taking all sorts of stuff, they're in it up to their elbows. That's why they're so inconsistent. Cycling feels like a stranger to me now. I don't want to know anything about bikes other than the ones I sell in the shop. I only find out who's won the Tour de France when some customer tells me.' (Yeah, right.)

Two hours north of Logroño, my road attached itself to the broad, smoothly meandering Ebro, parting ways just outside Miranda da Ebro, where the Nazis built and ran the concentration camp that would incarcerate more than 70,000 prisoners: Republican POWs, International Brigadistas and refugees from Vichy France – many of them Jews fleeing the Holocaust. It was still up and running in 1947, the last camp standing in Spain, though in the post-war period it largely served as a hostel for escaped Nazis, many of whom would be granted free passage to South America.

Then I turned north-east, and before me stood the green and grey mountains that define Vizcaya, the Basque Country, land of Ks and Zs and steady drizzle. What an absurd contrast there was between the orderly, sun-soaked ranks of vines and sunflowers I had just left behind, and the wild, jagged vertical mess that now glared down from under leaden clouds. Jools had made his name in these big wet hills, and I didn't want to let him down.

Except I did, and almost at once. There was another motorway to avoid, and Komoot decided that the only way to avoid it, even in road-mode, was to slide and slither for miles up a steep gravel farm track with a stripe of skanky grass down its middle. The back wheel scrabbled for purchase; I fell off twice at low speed, in the process welcoming a thousand shards of stone into my shoes. I'd been running on Monster fumes for a while, and now felt my internal fuel gauge flick down to zero.

At the last petrol station I'd stopped at, the man at the till had persuaded me to buy a third maxi-sized Snickers bar in order to receive a complimentary box of Twix sticks. With my body hollowed out and my brain full of drugs, I now clumsily yanked the top off my bar-bag and extracted this bounty in grateful, trembling hands. Cardboard was torn asunder and I beheld my prize: a beige plastic pot. I flipped its lid and was presented with less food than I had anticipated – 100 per cent less. The man in the petrol station had done something bad: he had given me a reusable coffee cup. I vowed at once to make it less reusable, and did so with immense underfoot gusto and a valley-filling roar. I stamped and swore and stamped and raved and kept on stamping until I had nothing left to give.

It was a performance worthy of Gaston Rebry, and one I would swiftly regret. Bullets of gravel were now embedded deep into the sole of my right foot, but of more immediate concern were the two figures that emerged just up the trail when the dusts of fury cleared. A young man was holding the hand of a small boy who I suppose was his son, both stock-still and expressionless, as if posing for a Victorian photographer. I bent down, collected the larger shards of caramel plastic and inserted them carefully into my right-hand front jersey pocket. Then I remounted and creaked onwards, acknowledging the rigid pair with an awkward tilt of the head as I passed.

Vitoria-Gasteiz was plain Vitoria in 1941, as it would be until Franco kicked the bucket and the Basque capital went double-barrelled with its native name. As I rode through the town centre it became clear that I was now in a very different Spain – so different that it was, in fact, Germany. The grey skies, the slate roofs, the Gothic churches and four-square, granite-faced apartment blocks all imparted a stolidly North European ambience, as indeed did the general sense of tidiness, order and quiet prosperity. Gone were the under-limbed beggars; gone, too, was *tinto de verano*, swept from the menus by an appalling regional fixation with mouldy, sour cider, ludicrously dispensed from head height.

Walking into my hotel room I beheld my first duvet since leaving home; shortly afterwards I reacquainted myself with chilly night air. This place even ran on North European time: at 7 p.m. the streets were thronged and the restaurants fully, wonderfully, open for life-giving business. A good thing too, as stumbling about these prim, trim squares with a carton of gazpacho wouldn't have gone down well with the smart and sombre citizens. I sat down outside an Italian restaurant and ate a pizza, and then another pizza, still struggling to understand how I had experienced such an abrupt and comprehensive overhaul of my environment. The weather, the language, the architecture, the food, the drink and every other socio-cultural trapping had all changed beyond recognition; the landscape was painted from an entirely new palette, and built on a very different scale. I had somehow bridged these two worlds in a single day, and I had done it on an old pushbike.

CHAPTER 18

Berrendero loved the Basque Country. In his autobiography, the memory of its 'vivid, picturesque hills' moves him to rare expressive heights: 'For us Castilians, accustomed to barren, straw-coloured fields, these seemed like fantasy landscapes, like storybook illustrations. Moments of romantic contemplation do not often visit the professional cyclist, but I did think how happy my "Pili" and I would be in one of those beautiful country houses.' Ahh. Then, predictably and rather pleasingly, he immediately punctures the mood: 'However I did not come to the Basque Country to contemplate, but to fight. So let us continue.' That's more like it.

If you're asking me, JB's affection for the region was informed less by its bucolic splendour than the career-launching glory it brought him. He lined up at the start of the 1935 Tour of the Basque Country in Bilbao as a self-supported, teamless no-hoper, and a rather weary one at that: not only had he ridden all the way there from Madrid, en route he'd stopped off in Vitoria to compete in a tough one-day race. (Punctures did for his hopes there, though it wasn't all bad: 'I saw Ezquerra, the race favourite, grab his bicycle by the handlebars and saddle and throw it into a field, the typical signature of his withdrawal.')

Berrendero had never ridden a stage race in his life, and the Tour of the Basque Country was – and remains – a pretty big deal. As well as every top Spaniard, he'd be up against some high-class foreigners, most notably Gino Bartali, cycling's new superstar and a future double Tour winner. Jools only had the tyres he rode on and two spares, both half-worn; he would spend every night repatching all four. Unable to afford the Champion derailleurs fitted to his rivals' machines, he had fashioned his own three-sprocket shift system back in Madrid – a terrifying lash-up operated by pulling the chain around with his fingers on the move. 'To everyone else I was just some poor devil trying his luck, a total nobody.'

Some enduring themes emerge in JB's account of the remarkable days that followed. The boundless self-confidence: 'Having passed all the other leading climbers, I ride up to the leader – no less than the great Bartali. I think: "Why not?", and attack him.' The baiting of the foreigners: 'Vicente Trueba and I follow two Italians up the long valley, without taking our turns at the front. They are furious and start to make threats, so with clear gestures, we tell them that if they knock either of us down, they will be knifed that evening.' And, of course, a great big slap-up Ezquerra hate-fest.

The Basque rider was the local hero, and after Berrendero overtook him in the classification he found himself subjected to all sorts of chicanery: a mysterious two-minute penalty, the random annulment of mountain points, 'everything always for the benefit of Ezquerra and my detriment'. Watching the crowd push Ezquerra all the way up an especially tough climb, Berrendero began to cultivate the prodigious resentment that would power him to so many victories. 'That night I slept with an inner rage, and the next day I went to war.' It worked: he soon moved up to third, behind Bartali and another Italian. From then on, as a matter of apparent routine, he went to bed furious and woke up coldly resolute. 'The conspiracy against me was now obvious: I lined up at the start with a face like thunder … I understood that Ezquerra would try anything to snatch my position, but I was now determined to keep it at any cost.'

It went down to the wire in dramatic fashion. In the tour's final kilometres, the peloton was speeding through the outskirts of Bilbao when, at 40kmh, Berrendero's bike collapsed beneath him. 'My frame is broken! I jump off my useless bike, and manage to swap it with a spectator, who hands me a heavy machine with mudguards. In desperation I set off in pursuit of my fiercest adversaries: my own compatriots, who had multiplied the pace as soon as they saw my predicament. Expending my last energies I finally catch the lead group just before the line, to the frank disgust of many.'

JB had held on to third, finishing as the best-place Spaniard, but before he stepped on to the Bilbao podium the referees announced his pending disqualification. His purported broken frame was in fact a mere puncture, they insisted: insufficient grounds for a bike swap under the rules. For good measure, the organiser told him that unless he could provide proof within twenty-four hours, he wouldn't get a penny in prize money. That meant finding his broken bike, swapped for that sit-up-and-begger in Las Arenas, a few miles out of town. Having made a rare friend – very usefully a policeman – JB would spend half the night and all the next morning roaming both sides of the estuary that cleaves Bilbao in two, knocking on doors, talking to kids playing football in the street, handing over coins in exchange for information. In Baracaldo, a mother gave a shifty response to his questions about a broken bike; the policeman flashed his badge, barged in, and found JB's stricken steed behind her son's bedroom door.

An hour later Jools carried his bike into the organiser's office. 'My first intention would have been to break over his head what was left of the machine; but he agreed and apologised, and everything was settled. I was paid my winnings, which amounted to 2,800 pesetas. And so this troubled event was over, my first stage race, the race that made my name. For the first time but by no means the last, I had scored a resounding triumph over my compatriots, despite their best efforts to thwart me.' That's my boy!

Berrendero had started the Tour of the Basque Country as a no-mark, and finished it as the angry young star of Spanish cycling. Indeed, as a golden grand tour prospect: he'd gone toe to toe with Gino Bartali, who would later namecheck JB as one of his toughest opponents. Jools was promptly signed up as a BH rider, and knew that his life would never be the same again. 'How things changed with that victory!' he wrote in *Mis Glorias y Memorias*. 'I was overwhelmed by all the congratulations, and walked about like a peacock with an open tail.' Before the race, newspapers were always getting his name wrong. But there would be no more Julio Barrendero from now on.

The 1941 riders were delighted to find themselves in the Basque Country: better food, smoother roads, much more bearable weather. 'After a supply control in Vitoria with eggs, fruit and all manner of sandwiches, the peloton's spirits rise,' writes Carlos, 'and with a light drizzle in the air, it is much easier to maintain a good pace.' The crowds were bigger too: this was proper cycling country, the region that built all the bikes in Spain, and hosted most of the big races.

An enduring regional enthusiasm was apparent when I went into a bar for breakfast and saw four policemen watching highlights of the previous day's Tour of Burgos: the first cycling action I'd seen on telly in nine months. Regrettably, its incentive value was rather compromised by the day's endlessly repeated principal highlight: the crash that left a Dutch rider one finger short of a gloveful.

But there were indeed an awful lot of cyclists out and about, and an awful lot less heat. I shivered out of Vitoria under grey skies, viewing Spain through unshaded eyes for the first time. Overnight rain blessed my jersey with its first spattery brown backstripe, and a record ninety minutes elapsed before First Cleft Trickle – a good eighty-four beyond the habitual FCT. After sweeping past a trio of team-shirt granddads I got a bit carried away, burning half my breakfast on a series of doomed pursuits. It's always the way: whenever I'm overtaken by a cyclist, of any age or gender, on any type of bike, I simply cannot stop myself trying to get on that wheel. But because I don't get off on bullying children and pensioners, no matter what that judge said, nor on humiliated exhaustion, it never ends well. Nevertheless it is a reflex I seem powerless to restrain, perhaps because it is the only thing I ever do on a bike that unites me with the professionals. Every time a lone grand-tour escapee is swept up by his pursuers, I watch his vigorous, brief, forlorn effort to tag on to them, then nod in hard-bitten fraternity and think: Been there, mate.

Mighty wooded eminences reared up on all sides, like the stands of some vast green stadium, and presently the road veered north to face the mightiest: the Aizkorri massif, home to the highest peaks in a peaky region, their summits lost in mist. I pedalled through hunkered-down villages built for winter, all heavy dark wood and steep roofs, places where the Hispanic had completely surrendered to the Teutonic. Sonorous church bells instead of dismal flat clonks; ranks of dainty little recycling bins; the whiff of baking bread in place of roadkill and hot crap. The tables outside every bar were thronged with elderly patrons, but nobody was washing their breakfast down with alcohol. Even the tap water was now unrecognisable, a cool, clear refreshment after weeks of tepid, cloudy chlorine with all the allure of a late-afternoon swig from the swimming-pool foot trough.

And of course there was that utterly alien language, declaiming itself on road signs that I could only hope to obey via Google Lens: KONTUZ meant warning, EMAN BIDEA advised me to give way, and OINEZKOEN ALDERDIA IGANDE JAJEGUNETAN was the signal to prepare for a dignified candle-day work aspect. Most European vocabularies share at least some common ground in everyday essentials, but I had now entered a world where *Astelehana* meant Monday and bicycle was *txirringa*. When I stopped at a roadside bar and ordered a *bocadillo jamón*, the proprietor looked at me as if I'd just asked for a bag of hair and a spoon.

Cut off from the outside world by vast mountains, the Basque Country has always done things its own way. It was one of the last places in Europe to be Christianised, and its mad language is thought to have pre-Neolithic roots (schoolteachers are given two years' paid leave to master it). I knew rona had impacted the Basque Country much less gravely than the regions I'd just passed through, and wondered if this might be down to that North-European-style social reserve: Basques aren't nearly as huggy or communal as other Spaniards. (In fact, the disparity in infection rates was probably as much to do with the rearing geography that walls off northern Spain, because the shadow of Covid would seem markedly less dark across this whole corner of the country.)

Anyway, that palpable sense of otherness makes it extremely easy to understand why a Basque separatist movement should have developed. Franco's ban on speaking Basque (and Catalan) in public helped ensure that ETA would thrive murderously during his dictatorship, and as a symbol of his 'One Spain' doctrine, the Vuelta was a regular target when it passed through. In 1967, ETA sprinkled nails and oil all over the steepling Sollube descent, causing dozens of crashes; the year after, a roadside bomb went off on the Puerto de Urbasa just before the peloton cycled by. Shots were fired during the 1977 Bilbao stage, sparking a response by police machine-gunners that left a seventy-eight-year-old man dead. In 1978, the concluding time trial in San Sebastián had to be called off after the first riders were pelted with everything from bottles to earth, and the 1979 Vuelta was very nearly cancelled in response to ETA threats. It would be thirty-three years before the organisers dared route the race through the Basque Country, following ETA's 2011 ceasefire.

The villages petered out and I nosed into the big dark hills, reacquainting myself with deciduous trees as mossy-trunked oaks and birches crowded out the pines. My programmed route's compacted squiggling had the look of drawn-out punishment, but as it gloriously transpired, the pass sneaked between the peaks at 700 metres, meaning most of those hairpins were downhill: for days I'd been surreptitiously accumulating altitude, and that morning had started out from Vitoria at 500 metres. The second half of my day was thus spent swishing down to sea level through some fairly hideous industrial towns, all drawn to this mountain valley a hundred years ago by the hydro-electric potential. A railway plaited my road all the way, forever passing above or below, its evocative presence surely a distraction for Jools as the 1941 peloton swept through. The Ferrovía Madrid–Irun, as umpteen rusty signs identified it, had hosted more than its share of defining episodes in his life story, from that springboard-to-glory trip to the 1936 Tour in Ezquerra's awkward company, to the fateful return trip that was so cruelly cut short at its Pyrenean terminus three years later.

'*Campeon! Campeon!*'

The mocking tribute from a youthful bus-stop gathering was still in my ears when I leaned round a corner and there it lay, far below, fringed with stacks of containers and a forest of cranes: the Atlantic Ocean. I waited for some portentous reflection to coalesce in my mind, but all it could muster was: No punctures since the Med #FuckYeah #NoDescendNoSwell. After a helter-skelter final plummet, undertaken at incautious speed through jockeying traffic, I hit the Kursaal, San Sebastián's principal promenade and the Stage 12 finish straight. The Falangist rag *Azul* damned the day's racing as 'vulgar and monotonous', castigating the riders for arriving in San Sebastián an hour behind schedule – Manuel Serdan docked half the prize money as punishment – but the stage came to life on that enormous, twisty descent, with multiple punctures and escapes before Delio Rodríguez once more asserted himself in the final metres, in front of a large crowd.

In 1941 San Sebastián was the most fashionable seaside resort in Spain, the favoured escape for wealthy Madrileños fleeing the capital's dreadful heat. Later that summer, JB and Pilar took their first ever holiday here: a double celebration that marked his birthday and what he called 'my rebirth', as he'd just cheated death in the worst accident of his career. Two weeks after the Vuelta, Berrendero was shooting downhill towards the finish line in the Tour of the North, a three-day race ending in Bilbao. He briefly turned to shout encouragement to his old (and, let's face it, only) mate, Fermín Trueba; 'When I turn my head forward, I see a wall of rock in front of my face: there is brutal contact and a bolt of black lightning, then nothing ... I regain consciousness in the back of a car, with blood smearing my vision, then at once break free from my rescuers, jump out and get back on my bike. Although it only has one crank left I speed downhill to the finish, where my wife is waiting: she is horrified by my appearance.'

It was an incident that resurrected Berrendero's worst professional fears. As improbable as it may seem, this hard bastard had always been a nervous descender. Remember all his mountain-top refreshment breaks in the Tour? He told the French press that all those 'silly stops' for beer, brandy and hot coffee were enjoyed in moments of indulgent weakness: 'These col summit bars are so tempting, and so strategically placed!' But that was cobblers. In truth, he stopped to wait for company on the descent. The Spanish team could hardly forget that in the previous year's Tour, their compatriot Francisco Cepeda had lost his life coming down the Galibier, plunging off the road and into a ravine. It was a tragedy that haunted Berrendero in particular, one repeatedly referenced in his life story. 'I would rather kill myself riding up a mountain,' he concluded, 'than die coming down one.' In consequence of what *El Tour de 1936* calls 'Berrendero's panic attacks', he repeatedly lost big minutes to the top Tour aces who sped past him on the twisty downhills.

That horrific smash in the Tour of the North brought it all back. In his autobiography he admits the accident 'could easily have cost me my life'. But sometimes a man's got to do what a man's got to do. 'I don't remember how I finished in the general classification, but by finishing the race I was able to push Ezquerra into third place in the mountains prize.'

San Sebastián is blessed with three seafronts, and I cruised along them all wondering which of the lovely old stucco-fronted hotels might have welcomed Pili, Jools and his two black eyes. And as I wondered, my thoughts turned to a slightly awkward inter-personal episode from JB's years in France, which I suppose needs addressing.

For a glowering grumpy guts, Berrendero was a surprisingly kissy kind of guy. His autobiographical account of the 1936 Tour is front-loaded with a lot of puckering up, and back-loaded with even more. On the podium in the Parc des Princes, as he's still rubbing away his tears, 'a beautiful golden blonde steps up and covers me in kisses … kisses like great, burning suns. What is it with these French girls? I was stunned – but I returned them, as you can see in the photo below.' And there he is in his sweaty jersey, still clutching the podium bouquet, planting his lips very enthusiastically to the cheek of a smartly turned-out platinum blonde.

I mean, OK, he's engaged to his childhood sweetheart and all that, but you're not King of the Mountains every day, and, well – that's France for you. Right? Not really, as it turns out. A few pages later, the slack I'd cut him was rapidly yanked tight. 'My Pili was still in my heart, but I will confess that many tried to gain entrance, and this spontaneous blonde would occupy my attention for quite a while.'

The next year, finding himself back in the Parc des Princes at the end of a minor race, he spots the spontaneous blonde again. 'It might have been a simple coincidence, but I saw possibilities in the look she gave me … since we Spaniards have a bit of spirit, I snatched two carnations from the winner's bouquet and presented them to her. It was the beginning of an adventure that lasted some time.'

Almost two years, in fact. She's around for the rest of 1937: 'I have never been a Don Juan, but surely few men could resist such a temptation. After all, I needed to relieve my heartache.' She's there in 1938: 'Things got hot. She was a girl of good standing, and of good financial fortune, she was also pretty; she was … well, enough.' When JB does finally break it off later that year, it's only because he's too busy training, racing and helping to run the bike shop in Pau. 'I had very little time left to play love … The blonde was very upset … She passed into history.'

Spain has always been a patriarchal society, and in those days – indeed, deep into the 1980s – the domestic balance of power was hopelessly skewed. A wife required her husband's permission to apply for a job or open a bank account. If a woman committed adultery it was always a crime; a man would be absolved unless the infidelity went on in the family home or he moved in with his mistress. 'A wife has no rights over her own body,' a Francoist school textbook informed its young readers. 'On marriage she gives up those rights to her husband.' As the brazen presence of so many *club alternes* demonstrates, extra-marital action is still considered something of a male human right. So back in 1936, or indeed in 1949 when *Mis Glorias y Memorias* came out, Jools must have felt that this French fling would earn him nothing but approving, blokey winks. After all, he and Pilar weren't even married at the time.

But the affair itself isn't really the issue. What freaked me out, to a degree that caused the words WTF DUDE? to appear along-side the relevant Google Lens translation, was the manner of its revelation. 'So that is the story of my little dalliance – one that my Pili, who is now my wife, will learn about only when she reads this book in the peace of our home.' Seriously, mate? This is how you're telling her? In print, below a photo of you snogging your French bird? While 'your Pili' was under siege in Madrid, eating sawdust bread and orange peel? Unbelievable. I couldn't begin to understand it.

At first I wondered if his publishers (Perez del Hoyo of 56, Avenida José Antonio Primo de Rivera, Madrid) might have encouraged him to throw in a bit of spice. But this would imply a degree of editorial input that seems wholly incompatible with the finished work: much as I love it, *Mis Glorias y Memorias* is a book that manages the rare trick of being both short yet aimlessly rambling, with glaring omissions and a carefree approach to accuracy. After completely ignoring his 1942 Vuelta victory, the author includes a glossary of *palmarès* that states he won the 1943 Vuelta and finished second in the 1944 edition – both years in which there was no Tour of Spain. Indeed, many of JB's *memorias* were just a bit too *glorias*: his fourth place in the 1937 Tour de France mountains competition becomes second, and in the same category in 1938 he promotes himself from sixth to fourth.

As I pedalled up the San Sebastián seafront, more dramatic explanations suggested themselves. What if Jools was being blackmailed? Or at least what if he felt threatened, worried that if he didn't tell Pilar, someone else might? Let's not forget that Ezquerra and Cañardo were there while he was knocking about with his spontaneous blonde. Their great enemy publishes his life story, but – oh dear! – it rather looks as if he's left something out! I don't know. It's all very weird, and just a little sad.

Pilar, of course, never spoke about this, or indeed anything else. In all the press stories and profiles I read, she makes only one appearance: a 1979 interview in *AS* magazine conducted chez Berrendero features two photos of an apple-cheeked, rather matronly Pilar. 'She sits there very quietly,' notes the journalist, 'only chipping in with the occasional "bien" as he holds forth about his career.' (Sample quote: 'I did it all myself.') JB's chuntering rundown of his miserable professional earnings and impecunious retirement lifestyle inspires a rare interruption: 'Julián doesn't drink or smoke. He has no vices except hunting.' Yeah – hunting girls and kissing them up good. Well, there we are. It was a man's world. 'When you are married, you must never confront your husband,' a Franco-era Church guide advised newly-wed women. 'When he gets angry, you will shut up; when he shouts, lower your head without reply; when he demands, you will cede.' Beyond the fact that Pilar died shortly before her husband, I found out nothing else about her.

On I rolled. Better to remember Pili and Jools in happier times, strolling hand in hand past that bandstand and those dome-roofed old casinos, perhaps into this hinterland maze of alleys full of shops that time forgot. I stood transfixed by a double-fronted mill-iners that the two of them might just have popped into, its windows clustered with boaters, pith helmets and hats of similarly ques-tionable appeal to anybody under the age of ninety-five.

There was even a certain retro appeal in lugging La Berrendero up three flights of stairs to access my guesthouse, at least until, on the landlady's stern instruction, I had to wheel it into my polystyrene-tiled bed cell. This would be the first time we'd slept together, my spontaneous bike and I, so a little awkwardness was inevitable. In truth, at the end of every day I was more than happy to see the back of her, to enjoy the respite of some cool, clean, peaceful me-time after all those filthy, desperate, sweaty hours of us-time. Also, without wishing to sound unnecessarily blunt, in the final analysis it was just a bike, a wheeled conveyance, a machine. So when I was pretty sure she was asleep, I crept out and nipped down to the seafront.

Great big cliffy hills reared up all around, one of them topped with a massive floodlit Jesus. Masts bobbed in the marina, and at 8 p.m. the sands were still thronged. I sat down with a beer, watching the sky bruise and darken, and the beaches slowly empty as the Atlantic tide crept in. Life was good, I kept telling myself, trying to forget that the beer had cost me €7, and that the 1941 Vuelta was about to go vertical on my ass.

CHAPTER 19

The native popularity of Spain's northern shore still depends on its breeze-cooled summers, so it only seemed fair to learn from the breakfast weatherwoman that I would be riding along it, and more pertinently steeply up it, in what was forecast to be the hottest day the Basque coast had experienced in more than sixty years.

The sun was already cracking its knuckles as I ascended the enormous bluffs that hem in every coastal city around these parts, softening me up with fierce little jabs of heat when it poked through the low banks of mist. By ten, the dappled corridor of oaks and sycamores the N634 weaved through felt hot and heavy as a rainforest, and for better or worse it was self-evidently the true and original 1941 road – narrow, twisty and crumbling at the edges.

There were umpteen cyclists, all dismayingly proficient, showing me a clean pair of heels and glistening, hairless legs as they eased smoothly past on carbon-fibre dream machines. A chunky-calved couple sped by, the husband punching a wife-sized hole through the air, and with an effort I managed to catch her slipstream. I hung on for a good few kilometres, long enough to complete a depressing study of respective cadence rates and sprocket ratios: going uphill, they completed two breezy pedal revs for every one I agonisingly ground out; going downhill, it was the precise reverse. More deflating still, they never went anywhere near their smallest or biggest rear sprockets, in contrast to the binary approach that forced me into the lowest possible gear for even the gentlest climb, and the highest for any downward slope.

There was a lot of steep greenery to conquer; a lot of old-school resorts and ports to swoop madly into and grovel up out of, trailing a funeral cortège of motorhomes and cement trucks. Whenever the clifftop trees parted, a muscular prospect opened up, generally incorporating some dramatic rock formation crashing into the glittery waves below. And all the while the heat built and built, delivered by a billion-watt hairdryer that blew my helmet right back after the road turned inland. Birds, hitherto very chirpily active, were shocked into sudden silence by these fire-breathing gusts. I drained my second bidon and thought of Juan Gimeno, whose retirement that morning was cruelly attributed to 'an excess of drinking water' by the dutiful and on-message Carlos Pardo.

It was a grim, parched haul up to Eibar, Spain's erstwhile bike capital, another unlovely collection of smutted industrial structures improbably crammed into an Alpine valley. When JB opened his shop, almost every bicycle he sold would have been built here, but sadly none are today: BH decamped to Vitoria in 1959, and fifteen years later Orbea moved a few miles up the valley. I stopped at a petrol station to guzzle fluid, taking my ease on the butane-bottle cage that was a feature of every such establishment, and had become my standard forecourt arse-parker. The manager

came out with some stickers to upgrade the mask-entry requirement from 'recommended' to 'obligatory' on his glass doors; a
chemist sign up the road told me it was 42 degrees, par for my daft
course down south, but rarely charted Celsius territory up here.

The landscape levered itself up into some properly huge hills,
all topped with wind turbines, like birthday candles on a horrible
green cake. After Amorebieta I laboured up a broad and busy road
of heavy gradient, bullying my agonised gurn into an approximation of mildly brow-furrowing curiosity, so that approaching motorists might think I was, say, trying to identify the call of a distant
water fowl, rather than dying a million sweaty deaths. But soon,
and inevitably, my face collapsed into its habitual slack-jawed,
gasping grimace. That morning, I noticed in the bathroom mirror
that my smile had changed colour, from weathered magnolia to
pure brilliant white: I had actually bleached my front teeth by
baring them to the sun all day, Rooney to Clooney in a month.

I have previously suggested that portions of the 1941 Vuelta
route appear to have been dictated by propaganda. But there can
be no argument, no doubt, about the conspicuous deviation that
Stage 13 underwent as it approached Bilbao, veering dramatically
northwards off the N634. The only credible motive: a determination to steer the race through a town whose destruction had come
to symbolise the Civil War's merciless horror, not just within Spain
but right across the world. 'Did you do this?' asked a Gestapo
officer, pointing at a photo of Picasso's *Guernica* after barging his
way into the artist's Parisian apartment in 1940. 'No,' replied
Picasso, 'you did.'

26 April 1937 was market day in Guernica, and its ancient
streets were thronged with farmers and the livestock they had
come to trade. When, just after four thirty, the church bell rang to
warn of an air raid, nobody was too concerned: in the words of

historian César Vidal, 'Guernica was a town that until then had maintained its distance from the convulsions of war'. Small wonder that panic broke out when a Dornier from Germany's Condor Legion appeared in the sky, blossoming into blind terror after it dropped several bombs on its way past. But Guernica's ordeal had only just begun. As citizens rushed about tending to the wounded, an entire squadron of Heinkel 111s flew in and dumped death all over the town. Survivors heard a further wave of incoming aircraft as they fled into the fields: Condor Legion fighters flying low, strafing everything that moved – women, children, livestock, nuns from the hospital. A new, heavier engine note then heralded the arrival of three squadrons of Junkers 52 bombers, which for the next two and a half hours flew in coordinated relays over the town, systematically obliterating it with aerial ordnance: 250kg monster bombs, anti-personnel twenty-pounders, incendiaries in glinting aluminium tubes. Burning animals stampeded madly through the devastation; whole families were crushed to death in their cellars as buildings collapsed.

In the course of an afternoon, Guernica was reduced to a smouldering skeleton. An accurate estimate of the casualties was stymied by the old maxim that history is written by the victors: Franco would always insist that retreating communists had burned Guernica down, and as late as 1970 the Francoist press were stubbornly telling the world that only twelve people had died there. The true toll lies rather closer to the Basque government's casualty figures: 1,654 dead and 889 wounded, together comprising a third of the town's population.

The burning of Guernica would single-handedly shift global public opinion, which even in many democracies – Britain and the US conspicuous among them – had remained stubbornly ambivalent (distilled rationale: Falangism bad, communism worse). Not that this made any meaningful difference to foreign policy, because in 1937 nobody wanted to get involved in a proxy war against Hitler and Mussolini, especially not on Stalin's side. Horrifically, Guernica's most significant legacy wasn't sympathy for its victims, but the triumphant vindication of its perpetrators. In one day, Hitler's air force had shown how war would henceforth be fought, unleashing the first sustained and coordinated aerial assault in history. Carpet bombing, blitzkrieg, firestorms – all the airborne tools and tactics that would soon cause so much murderous devastation across the world first rained down on this little Basque hill town. '60 tons of bombs dropped in 2 mins,' wrote the Condor Legion's gleeful commander von Richthofen in his diary.*

Guernica was a ghastly proving ground for Hitler's Luftwaffe; for Nationalists it had little strategic relevance. Antony Beevor has called the town's obliteration 'a major experiment in aerial terrorism': Franco's principal concern was destroying the morale of the Republicans defending Bilbao, and crushing the dream of Basque separatism. Because Guernica had been a hallowed site to Basques for over five hundred years, hosting regional parliaments under an oak tree to which Wordsworth composed an ode. It was at Guernica, beneath that tree, where Basque autonomy was first declared in the Civil War's early months.

By routing the 1941 Vuelta through these deeply symbolic ruins, Franco's regime hoped to stamp out the lingering flames of separatist sentiment. A warning from history and all that: just four years on, the town's reconstruction would have barely begun. Of course,

---

* The slab-sided, three-engined Junkers 52s that did most of the damage in Guernica had also delivered 15,000 of Franco's troops and mercenaries from North Africa to Spain in the coup's first days – the first major airlift in history. Hitler remarked later that Franco should honour the plane with a monument, as it had proved so pivotal in his victory.

none of the race reports make any mention of the Vuelta's passage through Guernica, but then the entire coverage had been a master-class in dissembling, ignoring dead elephants in every room. Half the towns in Spain were full of scorched rubble even five years later, as that 1946 Vuelta film had shown. Yet aside from that Stage 1 photo caption, obliquely referencing 'the glorious ruins of the University', *El Mundo Deportivo*'s extensive daily coverage contains not a single mention of the conflict or its stark and lingering aftermath.

I entered Guernica through its portent-sapping Aldi belt, then cycled through empty streets of increasing antiquity to the colon-naded marketplace. This was ground zero; I gazed around the silent square with immense sadness. I had never been to Guer-nica, but its tragedy was rooted within me: the legacy of a thou-sand youthful mornings spent staring at the huge framed print of Picasso's masterpiece that hung in my school's assembly hall – the only picture on those walls that wasn't a dead headmaster.

I pushed La Berrendero up to the peace park just above the town, all steep grass and concrete doves, and gazed across the wandering roofs below and the great green hills beyond. It looked like some sleepy Cotswold market town, if the Cotswolds were vast and lonely and you could grow bananas in them. How could such an awful thing have happened in such a placid, pretty place? How could those German airmen, foreigners with no skin in the game, have looked at this painstakingly blameless scene through their bomb-sights and thought, Yep, everyone down there needs to die, right now? There had been moments on my journey when I fancied that living through this pandemic was my generation's war; I thought about these moments now, and wanted to take my brain out and half-volley it into a concrete dove.

I refilled my bidons from a brass-spouted public fountain, then scrolled wearily through the route ahead. It was gone 4 p.m., and Komoot reckoned we were four hours from Bilbao. That would make this my longest day in the saddle, and the 1941 Vuelta's steepest challenge still stood in my way. With the celestial fan-heater now on turbo mode, I was blown north to the port of Bermeo, where they do something that smells of plasticine, summoning a sweaty half-laugh as I thought of the local who shot down an Italian warplane here with his pistol.*Then I turned south again, into the solar storm, and began winding uphill, dread knotting my innards. At once my satnav phone overheated and went black, but it didn't really matter: there was only one road over that ghastly coniferous wall ahead, and I was already on it. The last commercial outpost was a garden centre, and as I toiled past I thought how very much I would like to stop there for an extended visit, in fact to hide for a really long time amongst its sheds and shrubs, living on hose water and bird seed.

The Vuelta a España has of late developed a reputation for climbs of absurd extremity, 20-per-centers such as the infamous Angliru that bring riders to the wobbly, slo-mo brink of humiliation. What fun I've had over the years seeing world-class professionals reduced to fifty-year-old Tim Moores, and how much I was now regretting all that stockpiled karma. The Sollube is no Angliru,

---

* Unlike Hitler, Mussolini would never demand repayment from Franco for his military assistance. All wee Benito wanted in exchange for his contribution was to be taken seriously as one of the big boys – an aim whose hopeless ambition is revealed in pertinent vignettes of the Italian contribution I underlined in Antony Beevor's *The Battle for Spain*: 'seized by panic and fled'; 'the Fiat Ansaldo miniature tank'; 'bombed the wrong town'; 'found to have nothing wrong under their bandages'; 'three of their aircraft crashed on the way'.

but for JB's generation, on their three-speed dreadnoughts, this was as serious as the steep shit ever got.

I was in trouble before the holiday homes had petered out – all over the bike, and not in a good way; in fact, in the dribbly, loose-jawed, bile-throated worst way of all. At the final hamlet a many-generationed family of picnickers gave me a seated ovation from their Formica table, which I managed to acknowledge without too much sick coming out of my nose. Perhaps, after all, there was a reason why professional cyclists fuelled up for their last climb of the day with a couple of energy bars, rather than stopping at a petrol station for a massive tub of Russian salad.

I'd already taken off my helmet; whenever I made the mistake of looking up, the brim of my JB cap did its empathetic best to censor the scene, cutting a big crescent out of the worst bit. But there were no good bits from now on. The road shrank to a wandering stripe of weathered and ever-steeper tarmac, hemmed in by giant bracken and spindly trunks. Corrosive sweat coursed into my eyes, modulating each exhalation into a weary moan of anguish. Why had my own excretions turned on me? It had to be age. The cold-pressed, extra-virgin perspiration of youthful summers past now curdled to granddad's rancid body whey.

Higher, cooler air brought my satnav phone back to life; through heavy lids and a skein of tears, I watched the gradient crank up to double figures as my speed slipped into the singles. If there'd been enough road I might at least have weaved about to diminish the gradient, but there wasn't, and all I could do was stand up and force that preposterous lowest gear ever so slowly down and round, down and round, my legs trembling helplessly under the load, like a novice weightlifter about to do himself an ugly mischief.

My left foot fell out of its toe clip, which henceforth scraped along the cracked asphalt as I wobbled on. A heavy, burning agony spread across my shoulder blades, like a red-hot girder rammed through the sleeves of my jersey. I inched around a corner and saw the road hurl itself straight up a steepling bank of Christmas trees, at an angle flagrantly above the 10 per cent Komoot was now displaying. It was a vista that shot-blasted the last crumbs of morale clean out of my living soul, yet somehow I kept at it, running on muscle memory, locked in a death-watch dirge, 8.7kmh, unsteady as she goes.

As few as three months later I emerged into a benign plateau of farms and gently rolling pastures, then creaked to a halt at a little crossroads. Komoot confirmed that I'd reached the top of the Sollube, but there were none of the usual accessories – no heavily graffitied summit sign, no cairn of stones with a ski pole stuck in the top – just a stack of dented recycling bins and a wonky notice-board detailing municipal collection schedules. Not quite the roof of the world that I'd hoped for, and possibly even deserved.

On 26 June 1941, this crossroads would have been a rather live-lier place, packed with Basques who had come to cheer on their local hero. Federico Ezquerra, as you may remember, wasn't just a proud Basque but a principled Republican, and a man of his word. It was he who 'suffered a grave moral crisis' after the Spanish Tour de France team was told that civil war had broken out, and vowed to win the following day's stage in defiant tribute. And who did just that, then nobly shunned the podium champagne. So when Ezquerra said he'd be first over the line in his home stage, nobody doubted he meant it.

'The riders have been rolling easy for some days,' writes Carlos Pardo, 'but when they reached the dark green slopes of the Sollube, the race exploded.' At least, bits of it did: Ezquerra, JB and Trueba steamed off into that 10 per cent hell, leaving the rest for dead (I knew I could rely on The Swiss Watch, who 'complained about his stomach and rode badly'). The condensed facts: Ezquerra tops the Sollube just ahead of JB; the peloton regroups on the descent to Bilbao; Ezquerra breaks clear in the last metres and takes the stage win amidst great civic delight. The subscript: Ezquerra now poses no threat in the GC, and as much as Jools would like nothing more than humiliating the man he loved to hate in his own back-yard, it wouldn't be worth the risk. The crowds he saw pushing Ezquerra up the Sollube in the 1935 Tour of the Basque Country would merrily push the other way if they saw a rival leading the field. And he wouldn't want to spend another night in Bilbao knocking on doors to try to find his bike. Carlos Pardo all but spells it out: 'For once, the Galician Delio Rodríguez does not take the sprint: he seems to have little interest in spoiling the party for Ezquerra, who is a sporting idol in this region and who therefore wins the stage without having to try too hard.'

It was all downhill to Bilbao; I flung La Berrendero at the farms far below, hot wind shrieking, hot brakes creaking. By stages a profound fatigue began to weigh me down, rounding my shoul-ders, bowing my neck, putting lead in my legs. In a way it felt good, a souvenir trophy of all that hard, hot toil: Carlos Pardo had called this the 'princess stage', the second toughest, and I was going to do it in a single day.

But then it began to feel much less good, because it wasn't all downhill to Bilbao. In the course of that single day I had somehow forgotten the endless ranks of vast hills that girdle every town on the Basque coast. Traffic was now building around me, and the road kept going up, that fiery tempest roaring all the while, now in my face, now up my arse. I had no food and, more vitally, no fluid. Almost at once I sensed I was beginning to lose control, of bike and mind. It all started to feel like a video game, or more compel-lingly one of those marble-run roller coasters, in which I was a helpless, runaway participant with no influence over my own direction or destiny. This was almost precisely where JB ran face-first into a wall of rock and nearly died. But in common with almost everything else, I wasn't aware of it at the time.

I found myself weaving into deep and sultry countryside, and wondered if I might be going the wrong way, dimly recognising that I couldn't now summon the wherewithal to check my route and find out. One minute I was at the edge of a seething six-laner, pedalling woodenly up a hard shoulder through deep drifts of crispy leaves; then, abruptly and mysteriously, it was back into the darkening hills, just me and my empty head on a rising, falling road to nowhere. If somebody had offered me a gentle, level ride in to Bilbao, I'd have bitten their hand off. Then eaten it, and sucked the life-giving blood from the stump.

It began to seem as if everything was draining out of me, every last drop of vital energy, every memory; in fact, everything but a sort of drunken rage. This lent a touch of colour to the final stages of my ride, such as I remember them: slapping a bus window, very loudly advising two red lights and an electric scooterist to fuck off, blowing a thirty-second raspberry at the digital temperature display which told me that at 8.08 p.m. it was still 37 degrees.

By some rare miracle of forward planning for which I shall be forever grateful, at Guernica I had pre-booked myself a Bilbao hotel, and pre-programmed Komoot to lead me to its door. The courteous receptionist spoke reasonable English, which she'd no doubt been waiting an extremely long time to dust off. After care-lessly bundling La Berrendero into a big cupboard full of bog rolls and beer crates, I braced a forearm against her Plexiglas screen and stood there swaying gently as she lamented highest heat weather after one thousand nine hundred forty-seven, a declar-ation neatly counterpointed by a skittering clatter from out in the street: I turned my dull head to see an enormous restaurant parasol being propelled down the middle of the road on its side by the final Saharan blasts. When I turned back she was cheerfully running through the many facilities that her establishment was regrettably now unable to offer, on account of Covid state of situation: centre of fitness, cleaning of cloths, cleaning of shoe. 'So if you will need blanket or coffee—' I cut her short with a trembling hand. 'Now I must go,' I croaked robotically, and lurched away towards the lift.

I had gone up the Sollube on the hottest day in seventy years, and smashed my daily record by a good 15 kilometres, but pride came diluted with melancholy. I still had it, but only just, and it was dribbling away. Was there an age limit to burned-out, brain-dead total exhaustion? If so, when would I hit it? It was all I could do to claw off my shoes before keeling over on to the bed.

Perhaps, I thought, there comes a time when you're no longer physically able to push yourself too far, when your creaking limbs can't carry you into the red zone. Or perhaps wisdom kicks in, some inner voice of experience that pipes up before you overdo it, a wise old head gently overruling a buggered old body: 'Come on, gramps, what say we put that thing back in the shed? I hear e-bikes have really come on in the last few years. Also, I'm afraid you just shat yourself.'

CHAPTER 20

If five-times Tour winner Miguel Induráin is the most famous Basque cyclist, then Vicente Blanco – the first Spaniard to compete in the Tour de France – must rank as the most extraordinary. Blanco was nicknamed El Cojo – The Lame – on account of his absent feet, lost in separate industrial accidents. In 1908 he bought his first bike with the compensation money, and won his first race by pedalling madly away on his stumps to the earliest checkpoint, where he signed in before craftily snapping the tips off all the pencils. In the summer of 1910, hearing that a quarter of the field had just pulled out of the forthcoming Tour de France (having learned that the race would, for the first time, be going over mountains), El Cojo declared an intent to make up the numbers. Two problems: the race was starting in five days, and he couldn't afford the train fare to Paris. No matter. He got on his bike in Bilbao, pumped those stumps for 1,100 kilometres, and made it to the French capital just in time. Impressively, without a wink of sleep, El Cojo completed the first stage: 272 kilometres to Roubaix. Sadly he did so outside the time limit, and was disqualified. 'I could not compete with those well-fed beasts,' he said later. Yet he came back to a hero's welcome, and extraordinarily evolved into a properly great cyclist, twice winning Spain's national championship.

I learned about El Cojo's footless exploits while sitting up in bed: the 1941 riders had a rest day in Bilbao, and so did I. Despite my monumental fatigue, I had slept terribly, tormented through the night by a pedestrian crossing that filled my first-floor room with piercing beeps and flashing green light every minute or so. Every forty-seven seconds, to be precise. That's how bad it was.

This wasn't my first time in the city, though memories of the previous visit are a little cloudy, on account of the intervening years – all fifty-three of them. In truth, even my family's more senior contingent are still trying to forget this ill-fated holiday, which began and ended with a car-ferry voyage on the new Southampton–Bilbao service: six days of violent seasickness bookending a week of tent-bound infant fever, after my two elder siblings and I contracted German measles at the Laughing Whale campsite outside Barcelona.

I only retain a single snapshot of 1967 Bilbao, but it's both vivid and compelling. I'm looking through the back-seat window of my dad's Singer Gazelle as we waited at what must have been a border control at Bilbao docks, my view filled by a uniformed man in a funny hat holding a big gun across his chest. For a three-year-old on his first trip beyond the Home Counties, this was mind-blowing stuff. I'd never seen an actual gun, and here was a huge one, just inches from my face. That three-cornered hat was a doozy too. I didn't have much of a frame of reference at that age, but Spain was clearly a very different place to Swinging London. Much later, decades later, I took stock of a strange, disturbing truth: in common with so many Brits, my first overseas holiday was spent in a military dictatorship.

Foreigners who rode the Vuelta in Franco's peak years were similarly unsettled by the oppressive authoritarianism. Ian Brown, who rode for the Great Britain team in the 1955 Vuelta – the first after a five-year absence – remembered it as 'bloody miserable'. 'There were all these guys standing around with guns, nobody looked happy.' Riding past a concrete building, 'massive, maybe half a kilometre long', Brown spotted a long line of men all chained together. 'I asked a Spanish rider, "What's that?" and he said, "You didn't see anything."'

Half a century after my infant debut, I groggily set out to explore Bilbao on slow, unsteady legs. There was almost nobody about – the receptionist had told me it was a holiday of the public. Restaurateurs were rounding up gale-dispersed outside furniture; little trucks hosed the broad pavements with disinfectant. After breakfast I blundered across the Hotel Carlton, a grand stucco mansion where Carlos Pardo had conducted some extremely lame rest-day interviews, but it was closed until further notice.

The 1941 boys had become accustomed to spending their afternoons off getting lavishly pissed-up at some out-of-town bodega in Ramón's gregarious company, but not this time. The compulsory official outing in Bilbao was very much of a piece with the Guernica detour: a nose-rubbing, triumphalist tour of the elaborate Civil War defences that had completely failed to keep Bilbao out of Franco's hands. 'We pay a sightseeing visit to the historic Ring of Iron,' reports the ever-compliant Carlos, 'a local Maginot line that was overpowered by the heroism of Nationalist troops, writing a noble chapter in the history of our great patriotic crusade.' Woah there. It almost sounds as if he's taking the piss. God alone knows how Ezquerra in particular would have felt being forced to inspect all those bunkers and trenches, constructed in a righteous communal frenzy by the people of Bilbao – women, children, pensioners – then mercilessly nullified by Nazi bombers and artillery in less than forty-eight hours. It was another of those pathetic tragedies that seemed to epitomise the entire war.

Bilbao, like most northern cities, didn't suffer as badly as the rest of Spain in the late 1930s and early '40s: the restaurants and bars stayed open, people dressed well, nobody ate cats. It was, and remains, the wealthiest metropolis in Spain's wealthiest region, a long reign of prosperity spanned by its glorious cast-iron railway station and the gung-ho, wack-job Guggenheim Museum. Shuffling down those quiet streets, peeking through the odd window, I detected a very particular urban vibe that set Bilbao distinctly apart from every other Spanish city I'd been through: this was a place where you might pay €23 for a deconstructed lasagne, and – sorry, mate – watch an arthouse film instead of football, while wearing a white kimono instead of cargo shorts.

And though the shuttered shops and deserted pavements should have tarred every scene with the rona brush, somehow it just felt like what it was: a bank holiday. Everyone remained dutifully on-message, of course – the receptionist gently ticked me off for contravening the hotel's one-way system, which decreed that you went up in the lift and came down by the stairs. But just as this region was spared the worst of the Years of Hunger – and, with some notably horrific exceptions, the worst of the Civil War – so it had escaped the most terrible ravages of Covid. The Basque Country, Cantabria and Galicia – the three coastal provinces I would spend the next thousand kilometres in – recorded fewer deaths between them than the single district of Valencia, itself an also-ran next to Catalonia and Madrid, where almost half of Spain's Covid victims died.

All day the heat dwindled and the sky darkened; the fabled Basque *xirimiri*, a thin drizzle fondly referenced in Carlos's race reports and JB's autobiography, began to speckle the pavements as I returned to the hotel after a ruinous Greek salad and chips. After what had come before and what lay ahead, an early night was vital.

I relieved the rather bemused receptionist of three blankets, then went up to my room and slung them all from my curtain rail. This Ring of Wool proved a surprisingly effective beep-muffler, and muted the green light that had strobed across my ceiling the night before to a softly throbbing glow. I got into bed with a phone in each hand, and having reprogrammed Stage 13 for the purposes of Road Cycling, scrolled through my archived Google Lens screen captures of *El Mundo Deportivo*'s front pages.

There it was: 29 June 1941. An extraordinary declamation ran across the bottom, spanning all four columns: 'TO AVENGE SPAIN! TO JOIN EUROPE'S GREAT CHALLENGE! LET US ENLIST IN THE VOLUNTEER BRIGADES TO FIGHT SOVIET COMMUNISM!' Across the top, the headline that had made me burst out laughing the first time Google Lens offered it up now tolled out in the pulsing green light: 'BILBAO-SANTANDER – THE STAGE OF MAXIMUM HARDNESS'.

CHAPTER 21

The *xirimiri*, pronounced shirry-mirry, hung in the air like aerosol spray as I hauled La Berrendero over Bilbao's encircling eminences. For the first time I had dredged out the big wad of ziplock bags from the depths of my saddlebag: sheathing my jam-packed possessions in a few extra microns of waterproof plastic meant a fight to the death with every strap and buckle. For a couple of hours the road roller-coastered west, overlooking a grey sea clustered with fuzzy supertankers, occasionally diving into an old-school, old-people resort where having fun on a rainy day meant queuing up for fresh crabs or almost getting knocked down by a foreign cyclist taking a short cut across the market square.

A sign told me I'd left the Basque Country behind, though its habitual weather came along for the ride. Komoot steered us inland, on to a road that identified itself as a *ruta ciclista*: almost at once, a guy in a skinsuit shot past with 'Ride of the Valkyries' blaring from a little speaker on his handlebars. There were plenty of reducers to soften me up for the main event, the road twisting up hill and down green, damp dale, now flanked by ancient stone walls, now by eucalyptus plantations whose peeling, russet trunks were a close match to my forearms. A tragic scattering of drizzle-misted, semi-derelict towns marked the way, every one looked down on by a Victorian chimney, and dominated by the ruin of some turreted mansion: respectively the brickworks that had built the whole place and the home of its owner, or so I was later told.

Two young-ish cyclists caught up and sat on my wheel; I didn't know how long they'd been there, but when I turned round to acknowledge them, the one at the front put a finger to his lips and said, with a wink, 'Please, mister – no talk!' The pair had evidently endured extensive exposure to the running commentary that leaked helplessly from my lips all day in the saddle, which by this stage of the journey typically comprised an imbecilic stream of consciousness. I forced out a half-laugh and turned my head back, feeling its front half redden as I tried to remember what inanities they might have overheard. On cue, one of them launched into a wayward hum, interspersed with giggles, that I was able to identify as an approximate rendition of the chorus of 'Chatty, Chatty' by Toots & the Maytals. Yes, there we had it – I had encouraged myself up the previous hill with an improvised ditty that married this tune to my own masterful reworking of the default Basque weather phenomenon. 'Shitty pissy, shitty pissy, shitty pissy,' I had sung, loud and long. 'Shitty pissy, shitty pissy, shitty pissy.'

I rolled sombrely onwards, ears aflame, accompanied by sporadic bursts of rearward laughter. Why didn't they just overtake? They were half my age and had clearly caught up with ease. I pedalled slower and slower, and then stopped, freewheeling until I could hear their poorly repressed guffaws right behind my shoulder. Then I stood up in the saddle, farted prodigiously, sat back down and hammered away up the wet tarmac. I never saw them again. In fact, I didn't see another cyclist all day. A mile up the road a sign announced the end of the *ruta ciclista*, a warning that the recreational fun was over, that shit was about to get real.

The verdant highlands had been closing in for a while, and with their craggy troll-fortress crests could no longer be dismissed as hills by even the most cocksure traveller. Carlos described the cols that defined the stage of maximum hardness as the 'trio of magistrates that would pass judgement on this race', and in Komoot's gradient profile the group suggested a wonky three-peak circus tent, leaping waywardly to the heavens. But when I looked up a while later they were nowhere to be seen, cut off at the shoulders by a fat blanket of cloud.

I stopped at Arredondo, a village at the foot of the first magistrate, to load up on carbs at a bar heaving with regulars. A rather bleary old man outside nodded at my jersey, plucking at his own thin T-shirt and puffing out his cheeks, by way of commiseration with its dead-weight wooliness. When at length my *bocadillo jamón* was placed before me, the barmaid laid it down with a compassionate smile: unbidden, she had accessorised it with three fat slices of cheese and a small hill of *patatas bravas*. As a kind-hearted local gesture, this rather trumped that repeatedly issued by the old man and his friends: I quickly connected their red eyes with the cloud of herbal fumes that hung over their table, out of which an arm would occasionally appear proffering the browned mouth-end of an enormous crooked spliff, disappearing back into it amid much phlegmy cackling when I shook my head. It was clear that I'd entered a different Spain, a realm of lawless rustics where Covid might never have happened.

Leaden with calories, I traded helmet for cap and remounted, clunking and grating into bottom gear with funereal resignation, aware it would be some time before I troubled the levers again. Round the corner stood the sign giving me the bad news: 'PUERTO DEL ASON – ABIERTO'. The stage of maximum hardness was open for business. Just after it another: 'A 12k, 682m.' I had a stab at the maths before my brain filled up with pain, fear and exhaustion. Was that around 6 per cent? If so, it seemed doable; though after the Sollube so did anything. And in truth, these were probably ideal conditions for climbing: cool, a light drizzle, very few witnesses.

I savoured the benign intro, following a gently chuckling stream beneath birch trees full of bird twitter, and doing my best to unremember the law of averages: every easy kilometre down here meant a brutal one up there. Not that there was an up there any more: when the trees parted I saw that everything ahead and above was enveloped in thick mist. A car drove past with its headlights on. Then came a man on a horse. I was given a good-natured race up the road by a goat and a silent, lolloping St Bernard, and won.

Why must all good things come to an end? What a miserable maxim that is. But there we are, just letting nice stuff keep on happening is apparently never an option, so the road veered away from the river, narrowed to a single track and ploughed resolutely up the valley's left-hand flank. Cows grazed on impossibly pitched pastures around me. Once or twice the mist thinned above and something popped out to goad and bully me from on high: an enormous cliff of cork-like rock, or some ghastly squiggle of hairpins, tightly packed as a Wall's Viennetta.

I was only a quarter of the way up, and already gasping for breath, when mist began to wisp across the road. Komoot told me I was on a 9 per cent slope, and then it told me no more: when I tried to wipe all the drops of cloud off the screen my phone went nuts, closing down the satnav app and playing the introduction to a podcast about the firebombing of Tokyo. I yanked it from its mount and shoved it in my back pocket.

By stages I realised I was tracing forlorn little esses across the tarmac, in the hope of moderating the gradient. My arms began pulling back and up on the bars at the bottom of every strained pedal stroke, which seemed like an extremely unhelpful demonstration of some rudimentary law of physics. Every good cyclist has an equal and opposite shit cyclist. I kept telling myself that I was nonetheless gaining height with every turn of the pedals, that these were all metres in the bank, or at least centimetres, that they were mine to keep. The mist briefly parted; how I wished it hadn't. Below me tolled a sheer-flanked plunging void, a vertical canyon of the sort that attracts death-centric idiots in flying-squirrel suits. Far above towered a great wall of grass and granite, like a colossal dam presiding over this awful vista.

I was up into the big hairpins when the cloud closed in for good. In a moment my world shrank to a few foggy feet of narrow asphalt fore and aft, with nothing out there beyond the wooden crash barrier but the muffled clonks of distant livestock bells. An estate car slowly approached from behind; as it drew alongside I saw two young faces examine me from the front seat with evident concern, before turning to engage in conversation as they drove on. 'Darling, do you think that man's all right? He looks really old.'

The road topped out beside a sign that told me I'd made it: 'COLLADO DE ASON ALTITUD 682m'. The air was now saturated with cold mist; I dismounted by the summit benches to extract and don my yellow rain jacket for the very first time. I don't own any protection against foul weather, on account of a lifelong determination never to ride a bike in it, so this was one of my friend Matthew's cast-offs. I saw now why he had stopped wearing it: it had a massive tear in the back and looked really stupid, like something a barber might wrap round your shoulders before he got to work.

'Señor?'

I turned and saw a man I recognised as one half of the couple who had driven past me a few hairpins back. He was standing amid wispy cloud by his car, in a small head-of-the-pass parking area. Then he said something in a questioning tone, something I might have understood at least a bit of an hour back down the road.

'Lo siento, soy Ingles.' Sorry, I'm English. This hopeless, shameful phrase now came out of my mouth more than any other, a rude and humiliating non-answer to almost every question.

'Ah ... ' He shrugged uncertainly, and as I watched him open his door and climb back in I suddenly knew what he'd been asking: if I wanted a lift. I remounted, wondering how I would have reacted if he'd offered me a ride up at the bottom of this mountain, rather than – a little weirdly – at the top. I was still wondering when, after a kilometre or so of chilly, misted descent, I juddered to a squeaky halt at a lonely little junction. The left fork wandered gently down out of the mist. The right marched straight up into its soupy cold soul. A sign beside this horrible option read: 'PUERTO DE LA SIA, ABIERTO, A 8km1200m.'

The name of this col rang a dreadful, ghostly bell from my lockdown route-mapping. I extracted my satnav phone, wiped its screen with a hankie and beheld grim confirmation. That big green dam I'd just ridden up had borne the definitive look of this climb's last line of defence, but it absolutely wasn't. I'd only done half of it, and from here the road got steeper. And wetter, and colder.

A man with an enormous black umbrella over his head was standing beside the third bend up, scanning the befogged slopes below. I supposed he must have been a farmer. As I creaked towards him he turned and his old eyes widened. A stubby brown finger was waggled sternly at me; an urgent voice said a great many words, in a tone of obvious discouragement. 'Lo siento, soy Ingles,' I said as I passed slowly by, eliciting a look of utter bafflement, then a short bark of harsh laughter that was half-swallowed by the mist.

What was I doing? An enduring theme from the misty, lonesome depths and heights of every ride I've ever done is a perennial hope that some good-hearted witness would flag me down, wrap a big blanket round my shuddering shoulders and usher me gently into a warm and waiting car. 'That's quite enough of all that nonsense,' they'd say, with their kind and gentle eyes. But it had just happened twice, sort of, and I'd brushed both Samaritans aside.

It was way too wet for Komoot; I was flying blind through the fog, surveying what was left of the world through slitted eyes, the grubby crescent moon of my cap's peak bejewelled with drops of liquid mist. Rarely have I felt so vulnerable and alone on a bicycle. The mighty droning thrum of unseen wind turbines tolled ominously from above; soon I could see no further than the next snowplough pole sticking out of the roadside ahead. Carlos Pardo had procured a single memorable quote in his Bilbao rest-day interviews, and it now surfaced to the top of my mind, unbidden, and floated there: 'No evil lasts a hundred years.' I'd love to say that this tenacious mantra was one of JB's, but no: these were the words that Federico Ezquerra spurred himself on with. And they did me proud, because very soon afterwards, I rounded a lefthander and saw a little roadside monument up ahead, then, just beyond it, a brown sign with words and numbers on. The head of the pass.

I stumbled off the bike, gazed blankly around, then got out my phone camera and shot a video. I don't know why. It's just fog and the muffled sound of ragged panting, interspersed with the elegiac words 'shitting fucksticks'. Then I propped the bike against the col marker, and shuffled back to the monument. There was a plaque on it, inevitably graced with a poem. I looked at it through stupid, dead eyes for far too long. I can only assume I was succumbing to that ageless, universal urge to take stock atop a conquered eminence – an instinct even Jools couldn't resist when he got to the top of all those Tour climbs. That habit might have cost him a stage win; it almost cost me a lot more.

I knew I was in trouble almost as soon as I remounted. The fog was even thicker on this side; I swooped into the first fuzzy hairpin and felt the first frigid shudder. I was cold, very cold, and with an endless mist-bound plunge ahead of me there would be no opportunity to generate warmth. Braking for the second bend set off another shrieking brain klaxon. In 3,000 bone-dry and largely pan-flat kilometres I had never once had cause to reacquaint myself with the headline idiosyncrasy of period bicycle brakes. Doing so now, I discovered – or rather remembered – that moisture did something to them: it made them not work. I squeezed the levers and nothing happened. I squeezed them harder, much harder – so hard that I thought something would buckle or go *sproing* and that would be it. It was like the moment James Bond or Cary Grant or someone drives over a lofty brow with the Riviera twinkling below and discovers that their brakes have been sabotaged. With the apex almost upon me, I felt a little speed being scrubbed away, just enough to get me round and out with only a brief excursion into the road's gravelled periphery, and the brambles that overhung it.

So it went on all the way down, my voluminous barber's gown flapping and slapping like a sail in a storm. The road began to dry out a little, but the chattered sigh of relief that this forced through my gritted teeth soon evolved into a shuddery shriek: my frozen fists were cramping up. No, no, no-no-nonononono. A deer pranced high over the roadside fence right in front of me, then skittered messily over the other side with a crash of vegetation and a terrible grunt of distress. This was absolute madness: I wanted to stop, I had to stop, but those useless claws at the end of my arms wouldn't let me. Like some insidious poison, the cramp began to spread up my wrists, soon infecting my whole clenched torso. I cornered with rigid, desperate stabs and yanks, fighting the handlebars, all over the road, aware that any oncoming vehicle would be the last thing I ever saw. Somewhere inside, very deep inside, I realised that this was what Farmer Umbrella and that couple in the estate car had been so concerned about. Not the physical rigours of the climb, but the frozen, fog-bound perils of the descent.

Then, all at once, the mist vanished, the road flattened, and there I was rolling down a broad plateau dotted with tractors and barns, whimpering grateful expletives and realising I'd just cheated death in a cloth cap, with my helmet still clipped to the saddlebag.

I have a feeling I was rather happier to see the sign for Espinosa de los Monteros than JB would have been. For me it was the only place with beds near the halfway point of the stage of maximum hardness; for him it was a concentration camp, the one he'd been locked up in for two months before being sent to Rota. I juddered to a halt by the broad main square, then pushed La Berrendero across it with lifeless wrists, my feet meeting the cobbles without registering the slightest sensation.

My ancient guesthouse was right beside the big, dour church; the landlady's eyes widened above her facemask as she opened the door and assessed my condition.

'Puerto de la Sia,' I croaked, by way of explanation.

'*Descanso, descanso!*'

I knew what that meant, at least. Rest, rest. Franco had a ministry for it and they organised bike races.

My room was a tiny, damp chamber, only big enough to swing a cat if you really hated cats. For the first and only time on my trip I wanted more indoor heat: everything I unpacked fell through numb, trembling fingers, and my feet had actually shrunk, the shoes that usually dug into them hanging off at the heel.

I defrosted in the shower for a good twenty minutes, then went out into the square, giving my fleece top its debut. A great throng of people had mysteriously appeared, the older element packing the al fresco bar tables while the juniors stood in a long, loud queue outside the sweet shop. My Bilbao receptionist told me her family had a country house near Espinosa, and the multi-generational groups around seemed consistent with a holiday gathering of the clans: they certainly didn't look like mountain-dwelling locals, in spotless puffer jackets with Ray-Bans propped on their coiffured heads.

The site of the Espinosa camp had eluded my research, and with my faculties restored via two platefuls of steaming, deep-fried *croquetas* I wondered who I might ask, and how I might ask them. It was a plan that didn't survive my post-prandial tour of the square. Standing before the church's sombre façade I saw a black iron symbol embedded prominently into the limestone, with a list of names inscribed beside it. That Falangist yoke-and-arrows motif was the first survivor I had encountered, and the first name, in strident capitals, was JOSE ANTONIO PRIMO DE RIVERA. Beneath, in smaller letters, were a dozen others, presumably local Falangists slain in combat.

While failing to locate the Espinosa camp back at home, I had come across an online newspaper story about a mass exhumation that had taken place in the town a few years previously. Acting on information very belatedly received, a forensic team had excavated the pavement outside a row of 1960s houses on a street heading out of Espinosa. The photos showed a hole full of skeletons, some with shoes on and a few tatters of muddy clothing, victims of an extrajudicial 'walk' one dawn in October 1936. But when I looked at the scene on Google Street View, there was no memorial at the site: no plaque, no stone, no nothing. The pavement, the garden wall and even the little red gate that interrupted it – all uprooted and demolished during the search – had been fastidiously returned to their original condition, with not a single trace that they had ever been disturbed. It was as if the townspeople who disappeared that morning – nine men, four women, aged from sixteen to sixty-four – had been forgotten all over again, this time for good. And yet the names of the men who might very plausibly have killed them were still emblazoned up there on the front wall of the church. I stood and stared until my teeth began to chatter. Then I shuffled blankly across the square to my guesthouse, beset by conflicting urges: to sleep for a million years, and to get the fuck out of this place at once.

CHAPTER 22

'The queen stage of this race was a trial by fire and ice, as hard and relentless as the mountains it traversed, a fierce battle between two men who fought it out with an intensity beyond anything we have yet witnessed.' I know what you're thinking, but no – Ezquerra was dropped on the Puerto de la Sia, and though he later recovered, this would be a straight showdown between JB and Fermín Trueba, his teammate and friend, with no quarter given.

Such a brutal, ruthless close-quarter exchange of friendly fire flies in the face of every long-established code of cycling conduct, but as we have seen, Spanish riders played by their own rules back then. And for once, Jools didn't even start it. Descending the Puerto de la Sia – the road I almost died on, once more 'cloaked in mist and glacial temperatures' – he suffers his third puncture of the day, but Trueba, running alongside him, doesn't stop. Indeed, as Carlos says, 'the little man from Torrelavega presses on alone, riding hard to take full advantage'. In fairness, it was his right. Trueba, remember, had been leading the race since Malaga, and started out in Bilbao that morning with a minute and a half advantage over Berrendero. And this was his territory: Torrelavega, where he'd been raised, was right next to Santander, where the stage finished, and Fermín had been cheered over the fog-topped Sia by 'more than 50 hikers who have walked a good fifteen kilometres to be there'. Over two minutes elapsed before Berrendero emerged through the mist.

Doña Fatalidad really had it in for JB that day, flicking his nose until it bled. He had cut Trueba's lead to a minute by the foot of the Puerto de la Braguia, third and last of Carlos Pardo's magistrates, when he punctured once again. 'We see Berrendero crying in rage in the face of his misfortune,' writes Carlos. While he puts on his last spare, Delio Rodríguez catches up and hands JB one of his own tubulars. Just as well. 'After barely forty metres, Berrendero suffers yet another puncture – his fifth of the day – and loses another minute changing tyres. We watch him pedal bravely away up the empty road ahead.' By the time JB crossed the top of the Braguia, he trailed Trueba by eight minutes forty on the stage, and more than ten minutes overall – with the finish at Santander just 40 kilometres away, most of them downhill. The stage of maximum hardness had done its worst: those three magistrates had summoned Berrendero to the bench, turned their backs, raised their robes and farted. As a race, the 1941 Vuelta was surely over.

I made a rather arresting discovery while pumping up my tyres outside the guesthouse: the rear sported a great scar that ran around almost its full circumference, at points spreading into an open wound where corded fabric peeked through parted rubber. Even by my impressive historic standards of negligence, this seemed a remarkable oversight: here was damage that must have been shriekingly apparent for days, possibly even since the gravelly misadventures that surely catalysed it. With a start I realised that the evening before I had gone down a big wet mountain with one tyre down to its cords. The secondary realisation that I was about to go down a bigger, wetter one incited a full-on dry retch.

But mine is a very particular kind of hamster-hearted cowardice, one that comes seasoned with a pinch of fatalism and a great big wristy splash of bone idleness. Without making any effort to confirm it, and steered largely by my desire to leave the place behind me, I decided Espinosa didn't look like the kind of town that would have a bike shop, and with a shrug I rode away, back towards those green-black, fog-crowned peaks.

My first challenge was a climb that Carlos dismissed as 'a small hill', which rather undersold an ascent into the clouds that at gasping, dreadful length topped out at 1,166 metres. The garish purple heather alongside me had vanished into thick air well before the summit. This morning mist was distinctly colder: on went the barber's gown, and I seriously debated getting my Merkels out, before concluding that on the descent they'd get snagged in the chain, then yanked viciously down to my ankles en route to one of those undignified, sympathy-sapping deaths I so feared, perhaps topped off with a cameo from the defrosting cow pats that clotted the road.

I rode straight over the top without stopping, keen to preserve at least some body heat and finger-function for the descent, which I knew fell twice as far as the road that had taken me down the Sia. Speed built and my sodden period components struggled to shift it. The first insinuations of cramp began to fuse my fingers; horrific plane-window views burst out through pockets in the mist – tiny farmhouses, handkerchief fields, a squiggly thread of tarmac. Shimmering beads of moisture clung to my phone screen; all I could make out was that my speed began with a 6, and in an attempt to restore legibility I swept a clumsy wet glove across it. Komoot at once disappeared; an American lady began to speak. 'Here is the information for your recipe,' she told me.

Terror-wise, I was now introduced to a new kid on the block: under hard braking at high speed, my front wheel began to tremble, then shimmy, then wobble, and to do all these with increasing violence and lateral exaggeration, like a snaking caravan about to jackknife. The only way to make it stop was to release the front brake lever, a remedy that in the circumstances I wasn't absolutely mad keen on. Still, at least it gave me something to think about that wasn't the bare threads of my rear tyre. Yet again I felt myself giving in to a superior enemy, to forces that were so obviously beyond my control.

With the world a juddering blur, the road began to straighten out and settle down. Mist was now mixed with woodsmoke; roofs appeared ahead. One of them, I presently discovered, sat on top of a bar.* I dismounted like a rusty robot and went in, shivering uncontrollably. Only now did I realise that my passage through the clouds had left me utterly sodden, from head to squelching toe. '*Café solo*,' I chattered at the old guy behind the counter. He held my gaze and gave me a prompting look: Anything else? It took a while but I got there. '*Y un brandy.*'

He smiled and raised a finger, then plucked out a little balloon glass and unscrewed the Osborne Veterano. Spanish bars never have measures: the man or woman behind the counter just tilts

---

* Of course there was a bar. There is always a bar. Spain is home to 280,000 of them, more than the rest of Western Europe combined.

the bottle in accordance with their mood, or more usually yours. It had long been apparent that the second glass of wine I ordered was always significantly fuller than the first, and served with a wink: Hey, Miguel, looks like we got us a toper. Anyway, this old feller knew the score. Through heavy lids I watched him dispense a good two inches of brown spirit – a quadruple at the very least, and it wasn't yet eleven. I drank it extremely slowly at a table by the steamed-up window, water pooling at my feet. This was the setting for the grimmest photographic self-portrait I have ever taken, the pouchy, bloodshot ghost of Cycling Yet To Come.

The route at once turned to face the Puerto de la Braguia, and as my numb feet pressed down hard on the pedals I detected something extremely peculiar: in place of dread there was relief. For the first time in my entire life, I was glad to be riding a bike uphill. How good it felt as my cold limbs warmed with expended effort, as I stood proudly aloft in the saddle and motored steadily up the third magistrate's great green curves. As I write this paragraph its alcoholic predecessor looms large, but at the time I honestly didn't make any connection: touchingly, I truly believed that after decades of hating hills like a big baby, I had finally come of age as a cyclist. Oh well.

When JB went over the Braguia almost nine minutes behind Trueba, he would have looked ahead at the valley below – the wandering patchwork of flat fields, the clusters of roofs and cars and gathered spectators – and understood that the steep stuff was over, and with it any reasonable hope. Every bike rider who has ever lived knows how easy it is to win or lose long minutes in the mountains. Attempting to recoup it in serious quantities on the flat is a fool's errand.

But JB had nothing to lose, unless you include his teammate Fermín Trueba's potential future cooperation and friendship. Who knows what hatred fuelled him this time, as he put his head down and hammered away towards Santander. Even a man blessed with such a tight competitive focus could hardly have been unaffected by the proximity of Espinosa, where he'd been banged up in a camp just a couple of years previously. Perhaps that bunged a few old enmities into his inner spite-furnace. Or perhaps he was just hating on *Doña Fatalidad*, who had shat on him from an especially great height that day.

At any rate, JB's extraordinary performance on the run in to Santander jerked Carlos Pardo's ponderous, police-statement prose into life. 'With enormous courage and tremendous determination, Berrendero fought to reduce his enormous disadvantage on the descent, throwing himself explosively and indefatigably into the forty kilometres that separated the last slope from the finish line.' He reeled in a group containing Delio and Ezquerra, going straight through and pulling them all along behind him. Fermín Trueba probably had no idea what was going on back down the road, but with the Vuelta right there for the taking you can't imagine he'd have been hanging about. He crossed the line in Santander, then watched and waited as his GC lead grew. But not for very long. Two minutes nine seconds later JB's group came in. Berrendero had somehow made up more than six minutes in those 40 kilometres, and though he now trailed Trueba by over three minutes, the race was far from over. Carlos Pardo wheeled out an appealing native metaphor: 'As for the outcome of this Third Vuelta a España, the ball is still on the roof.'

El Mundo Deportivo's readership were unaccustomed to reading nice things about the grumpy Madrileño, but this was no time for churlishness. 'Berrendero fights against everything,' wrote Carlos, 'against time, against mountain slopes, against frailties and crises, yet he is a man who knows how to overcome them all, even adversity itself.' I have been rather rude about Carlos Pardo's journalism. But I'm not sure anyone has composed such an insightful encapsulation of the man who won the 1941 Vuelta a España.

Seventy-nine years later I rolled along that same valley, the air balmy, the trees palmy. It seemed like a month since I'd last seen a petrol station, or a seagull, or a *glorieta*, and being drunk I greeted them all like long-lost friends. Within an hour, my foggy, frozen, fear-fuddled mountain ordeals seemed distant and unreal, a weird flash-frame aberration in a ten-volume tale of cloudless plains. It was all too much to deal with. To try to get my head back I kept reminding myself that this was where JB won the Vuelta, or at least didn't lose it, and that I really ought to put in a token tribute effort. But instead, I stopped at a bar and had a big steak, two bowls of *patatas bravas* and half a bottle of red wine.

Santander, previously known to me only for its shit bank – the manager of my local branch once cheerfully dialled the call centre in Bangalore then handed me the receiver – was a city that exuded old money and deep conservatism. The twin seafronts, arranged either side of a huge rock that most of the city is ludicrously perched on, were clustered with venerable hotels and grand villas. An awful lot of balconies had Spanish flags draped over them, and riding under a motorway I saw my first Falangist graffiti: 'F FRANCO CAUDILLO DE ESPAÑA'. A few people had tried to cross it out; several others had sprayed over their attempts, emboldening the words in thick black letters. I'd read and been severally informed that this was the most right-wing city in Spain: as late as 2007 the streets were still cluttered with Francoist plaques and statues. 'In Santander, even the whores and beggars are rightists,' commented one local writer.

This might help explain the unusually snotty reception I received when I booked myself into an unusually pretentious seafront hotel. 'Bicycle no, you must put in street,' said the receptionist, eyes cold above her mask. 'Bicycle yes,' I countered, patting La Berrendero's saddle, then wiping the icky wet warmth off on my jersey. 'This is an important machine from history.' A derisive snort burst through her surgical fabric. She had my freshly photocopied passport in her hand, and I watched her scan it. 'Maybe bad people take your bicycle in … Sheeping Norton.' (Well, come on, we're all born somewhere.) 'In Santander is safe.' Our eyes met, and didn't blink. Without a word, I plucked my passport from her fingers and the keycard from her desk, then marched La Berrendero through the open doors of the tiny lift. I kept waiting for a cry of angry protest but it never came, no doubt because the receptionist was too busy enjoying my humiliating contortions. When at last the doors met, squeaking and scraping against flesh and metal all the way, a cubist portrait graced their mirrored backs: *Man in Lift with Bicycle Necklace*.

Spain was now deep into its tourist season, and with the ongoing dearth of foreigners to feed and house, the service industry's brave-faced, show-must-go-on determination and good cheer had at last begun to crumble. Even quite large hotels seemed to be down to a single member of staff – the same pair of eyes who checked me in would invariably serve breakfast and push a broom down the corridor – and some had begun to fall apart. Lifts didn't work; hot water emerged in a reluctant dribble; shower brackets were broken and sink plugs had gone missing. Most unusually in this placid country, tempers were starting to fray. A couple of days up the road

I walked into the breakfast room to find the waitress going full Fawlty on an elderly couple of North European appearance: 'First you say toast, now you say croissant. You want croissant, you pay three euros and you wait thirty minutes. Understand?' It might have been a regional thing, but of late I had begun to note that beds were being made with a violence that spoke of passive-aggressive guest punishment, the sheets tucked in with such taut, compressive brutality that it felt like forcing my way into a plate-steel sleeping bag. 'You will get in that bed and you will STAY IN THAT BED.'

I'm guessing that Santander's Franco-friendly political culture lay behind the hostility that characterised provincial coverage of the stage of maximum hardness. 'Today's racing has been distinguished by its lethargy,' began one report, a perverse distortion of the dramatic facts. This sort of chuntering had been more or less the official line since the start, communicated by the Falangist press and race referee Manuel Serdan, doubtlessly prompted by the generals who ran the Department of Education and Leisure. In their world, the riders were perennially too slow and too thirsty, forever failing to showcase Spanish virility and endurance. If this race was to set any kind of example to the nation, such indolence must be punished.

Serdan had begun docking a proportion of the stage prize money as a matter of routine, but his ultimate sanction against sloth was a race against the clock. The team time trial scheduled for Stage 15 would be the first *contra reloj* in Vuelta history, and Serdan had been smelling the riders' fear since the start: no shirking, no hiding, no tourist-paced rolls through the countryside. He'd been threatening to hit the peloton with an impromptu time trial ever since Seville, in briefings duly reported by Ramón Torres: 'We were told that as a result of today's low average speed, part of tomorrow's stage would be run against the clock. At the last minute the race referee decided against it.'

Stage 15 was an act of cruel and unusual punishment in its own right. Fresh from their triple-col suffering, the eighteen survivors were faced with a pitiless split stage: 192 kilometres into the wind up the very lumpy coast from Santander to Gijón in the morning, then to kill the afternoon, a 58-kilometre team time trial down to Oviedo. Only as they lined up on Santander's blowy seafront did Manuel give them the bad news, no doubt with a great big smile. 'We learned that the stage against the clock was to be run individually,' reported Carlos, 'and not by teams, as had been the original intention.' No drafting, no breathers, just full-gas, balls-out solo suffering from gun to tape. In all honesty, given the total collapse of the Vuelta's official team structure, it's hard to see what choice Serdan had. Julián Berrendero must have been secretly delighted. He wouldn't have to spend all afternoon riding with Federico Ezquerra, and now had a decent chance of pinching some big minutes off Fermín Trueba.

Vicariously afflicted by Manuel's brutal relentlessness, in the morning I rode clean out of Santander without doing anything about my shredded rear tyre. How it retained any air at all was quite the mystery. At least if it abruptly stopped doing so, on these roads I'd be inconvenienced rather than hurled to a misty death. That said, my westward coast route did roll over some extremely irksome terrain, its tireless up-and-downery poorly compensated by the Cornwall-pattern scenery, wonderful as it doubtless was with all its cliffs and coves. All morning the miles failed to fly by, over a brow at 9kmh, down at 49, rinse and repeat. I just couldn't get into any kind of rhythm, in body or mind: every train of thought was eased into the buffers by brain-draining uphill fatigue, or flung off the rails on some rattling, runaway descent.

My plight was compounded by La Berrendero's ratcheting reluctance to change gear. Even on day one, back in Madrid, I'd been slightly dismayed to discover that the dainty, Merckxian flicks of thumb and forefinger that my imagination had decreed for this procedure fell some way sort of the rustic, blunt-force reality. The passing of 3,000 kilometres, many of them richly gravelled, had done nothing to improve the situation. Getting the rear derailleur to move in the important direction – the one that provided uphill assistance – now demanded the full weight of my body, applied through the meat of my palm on to that tiny lever. Without gloves I'd now be seeing my days out with 'CAMPAGNOLO' embossed backwards into my right hand.

I went through Torrelavega, Fermín Trueba's hometown, where, in accordance with one of cycling's loveliest traditions, the 1941 peloton called a quick truce to facilitate a family reunion, starring The Flea himself: 'Trueba's brother Vicente, and one of their sisters, ride along with us for a few kilometres, an occasion captured by all the photographers who follow the race.' It wasn't hard to see why Fermín and The Flea had been so very keen to get on their bikes and keep going: Torrelavega was almost fascinatingly unlovely, cluttered with aged, belching industrial plants that put me in mind of a Stalinist five-year plan. How very wonderful to ride a mile up the road and find yourself in glorious, fecund countryside, particularly if you were really good at cycling and didn't mind the oscillating scenery. I now watched with some fascination as my left-hand horizon levered itself extravagantly aloft: those huge and hazy treeless hunks were the Picos de Europa, a range that earned its name five hundred years ago as the first sight of Europe for ships returning from the Americas. It was a prospect that might have forced me off the road to vomit with foreboding, but instead I cheerily flicked them the Vs. In defiance of every accepted norm of grand-tour route planning, the 1941 Vuelta very splendidly resisted the temptation to throw itself up those great green fuckers, despite tracking the range for its entire length.

Ribadesella was a small and very traditional Spanish resort, and in the maze of old streets behind the seafront I bagged a hotel room with one of those enclosed glass balconies that stuck out over the road, like a bolt-on Victorian conservatory. This solarium dried my kit in minutes, allowing it plenty of time to prepare for what would be its principal role in my life: sucking up every nocturnal cough and mumble from the street below and amplifying it into a sonic maelstrom to be blasted directly at the pillow end of my bed.

Like so many of the towns along this coast, Ribadesella seemed to cater for well-heeled families from down south who had been coming here year after year, and were happy to pay through their solid-gold arses for the privilege. I spent more on that hotel room than I had on any of its predecessors, and it wasn't at all nice: the sink had a big jagged hole in the rim, as if the King of Masculinity had done something silly on it. All day I'd been gawping at monstrous refreshment bills, while some cocksure paterfamilias in an ironed Lacoste prepared to settle up with a fat wad of fifties pulled flamboyantly from his shorts pocket. The seafront restaurant I ended up in that night seethed with such characters, meaning there was nobody to exchange horrified looks with when I opened the menu. Nobody except the waitress, who very wonderfully garnished my €25 bowl of fish soup with three enormous bread rolls, then another two after she caught me scooping out the last smears from the butter bowl with my coffee spoon.

I never met Jaime's dad, but it's a fair bet he's got a big bulge in his back pocket and a wife who irons his polo shirts. This young man introduced himself to me the following morning, as I stood beside La Berrendero in a socially distanced queue outside Dani Bikes – a shop whose flagrant proximity to my hotel prevented me from riding my abused and sickly steed gaily out of Ribadesella as precedent demanded. I watched as Jaime began to assess La Berrendero with wide and hungry eyes, providing a commentary in the flawless English he had acquired during a year's study in Dublin. 'This is so cool, you have the complete original group set,' he murmured through his mask, seeing beauty beneath all that mud and oil. 'Everything correct, the Campagnolo components, hubs, levers, hoods … so rare to find.' He shook his head in happy disbelief, then suddenly leaned forward, jabbing a hand at the front of the frame. 'And those lugs! Oh man, so beautiful.' I nodded, relieved that my expression was concealed under fabric, so Jaime couldn't see me wondering what the fuck a lug was. The more I wore my mask, the more I came to appreciate its unintended benefits. When I mouthed abuse right into that Santander receptionist's face, it felt like Harry Potter having his first giddy go with the invisibility cloak.

For a fellow in his twentieth summer, Jaime was extraordinarily well informed about road bicycles deep into their autumn years: he got out his phone and showed me some of the nine vintage machines he kept back home in Alicante (he didn't say it, but as well as fleeing the August heat, I imagine his family also came here to get away from all the Brits and Germans). But Jaime's was a passion that began and ended with old metal – when I ran my finger up the name on my down tube, all I got was yet another apologetic shrug. In hope more than expectation, I started to talk about the 1941 Vuelta, and my passage around it, but Jaime only had eyes for my lugs, and seemed to have turned his ears off. (Before you write in, I now know what the fuck a lug is.)

The eponymous proprietor of Dani Bikes was either terribly shy or petrified of infection, or perhaps completely naked: all I saw of him was a hairy forearm, which emerged through the workshop door and pulled La Berrendero inside by the handlebars, while Jaime shouted out my maintenance requests. Ten minutes later my bike was pushed out of Dani's lair with a new rear tyre, a new rear gear cable, and a bill sellotaped to the crossbar. I settled up with the woman behind the shop counter: it was less than I'd paid for that bowl of soup.

I thanked young Jaime and bid him farewell, then set out across the long, low bridge that took the N632 across a wide estuary and out of Ribadesella. Jaime told me his family had been spending their summers here for generations, and now I saw why: around me sprawled a sumptuous, sun-drenched panorama, 360 full degrees of silver sand and palm-fringed turquoise water, presided over by the imperious Picos de Europa. Yet it was a struggle to focus my appreciation, for the natural world holds little interest to the long-distance cyclist with freshly buttered, friction-free gears to play with. I would love to describe the pleasure this gave me that morning, but having made a list of all the relevant adjectives it's probably best that I don't.

The road twisted up the coast, passing through dappled villages that began to feel more and more like the ones I'd pulled my poor donkey through, from the pagoda-roofed corn cribs to the clumsy, persistent horseflies I was forever splattering on his flanks. Blue and yellow scallops began popping up on walls and road signs, demarcating this as one of the umpteen pilgrim routes that these days congregate on Santiago, spreading the Camino load. To my slight amazement, I began to pass little knots of actual pilgrims, who I could only assume had found alternatives to the triple-bunk, rona-farm dormitories that I slept in all those years before.

In a nation of ageless landscapes, these were perhaps the most eternal to date. I rode through a village where old women stooped over a medieval-style communal laundry. I passed a wizened, nut-brown farmer tossing hay on to a horse-cart with a pitchfork, and watching him remembered my favourite Stage 15 snapshot: 'Cyclists frequently dismount to drink milk, which in this region is excellent. There are two ways to obtain it: you ask a farmer, or you milk a cow, as Cayetano Martín has been doing all day to the general amusement of his fellow riders and all of us who follow the race.'

Lost in bucolic, sepia-tinted daydreams, I rolled into Gijón just before 1 p.m. I liked the place even before I saw its majestic beach, or any of the comely old squares that lay behind it: the city's native pronunciation was an exact reproduction of the noise Shinto issued when we met up every morning, and that was good enough for me. As I worked through a fat *tortilla* sarnie and two litres of water under the arches that lined the Plaza Mayor, I realised that the 1941 boys and I had been playing the same game: all that udder-pulling japery and my own ruminative donkstalgia were useful distractions from the looming afternoon punishment of riding as fast as you possibly could for 58 kilometres.

Plotting the route of the Gijón–Oviedo time trial had proved especially fiddlesome. Large chunks of it had been overlaid with motorways, and getting the distance anywhere near 58 kilometres meant taking a lot of sketchy shortcuts – most of them too sketchy for the Google Street View camera cars. Still, I jabbed Komoot's BEGIN NAVIGATION button with high hopes. The 1941 boys had almost 200 kilometres in their legs when the clock started; my warm-up from Ribadesella was a mere 70. And 58 kilometres seemed about my full-gas level: that lockdown loop to Chertsey was only slightly shorter, and before I left I'd been averaging 25 round it. Whisper it, but that would have been good enough for third last in the 1941 TT, neck and neck with The Swiss Watch.

Almost at once, barrelling up a busy downtown four-laner, I found myself duking it out with a facemasked pizza porter on a fixie and an indomitable old-timer on a beaten-up mountain bike. The lead swapped hands a dozen times as the buses and lorries weaved around, taking turns to baulk us. This was the most sustained battle of my entire tour to date, and I emerged victorious, albeit by exploiting the Spanish cyclist's curious native reluctance to overtake lines of stationary traffic.

I was bang on it as the buildings began to thin around me, head down, taking *glorieta*s in an apex-clipping straight line, swishing through red lights. A slightly terrifying gyratory system took me around and above Gijón's outlying heavy industries, and then I was out in the hills. And the wind. And the sun.

Carlos Pardo's time-trial report runs to 158 words. No doubt he had to dash out his copy in order to make the morning paper, but for a stage of such defining import, it comes across as more than a little cursory. And more than a little bitter and begrudging. 'Our car follows Berrendero,' he writes, 'who pushes very hard in the first 40 kilometres, passing several other riders. In Lugones, taking his time against that of Trueba, we see that he is five minutes ahead. Well, Berrendero is now the race leader on the road. In the final kilometres he begins to tire, but though Fermín cuts into his advantage a little it is not enough to prevent the cherished *maillot blanco* passing to Berrendero.' Fuck sakes, Carlos. Is that it? The greatest cycling all-rounder Spain had ever produced has just taken a pretty decisive lead in your national grand tour – a lead he last held on its first day – and that's the best you can manage? Once again I could only wonder why. Was it a Madrid/Barcelona thing? Fear of praising a man who'd been banged up as a traitor? Or was Berrendero just too hard to love, too selfish, too silent, too bloody grumpy? I really don't know. Maybe JB went to the EMD office party one year and got off with everyone's sisters.

How deeply I would love to expand such speculations, perhaps in the form of a 900-verse poem, because back on the road my own time trial was turning into a story I'd rather not tell. Carlos hadn't mentioned any kind of inclines in his report – though the suspiciously low average speed should perhaps have forewarned me – but by Luanco, less than a third of the way in, my thighs were trembling with protracted uphill effort. What was going on? I'd been surprising myself all morning with a new-found facility to scale impressive heights without even noticing: whenever I'd caught a glimpse of glittering sea through the roadside eucalyptus trees, it was gratifyingly further beneath me than expected. Looking back, I appear to have made a causal connection between this and the rejuvenated slickness of my gear changes, which, however nonsensical, had set in as an established fact by the time I rode out of Gijón. What a tragedy, what a perplexing injustice, to find this imbecilic non-theory being torn up and eaten.

I pushed on, pushed hard, trying to channel Berrendero's furious determination as portrayed in that 1936 Tour report, clenching my teeth, glaring at the tarmac, crushing the pedals. With the last physical reserves gurgling down my inner sluices, all I had left was will-power. In extremis, I summoned the internal sporting commentaries that have helped me through so many in-saddle crises; imagine my dismay when even these turned traitor. 'At Luanco, taking Moore's time against that of The Swiss Watch, we see that he is already thirteen minutes behind. Near Aviles he descends to swell, and his shorts fall down.'

Everything was going wrong. My chain fell off for the very first time, jamming itself between crank and frame in a manner that denied me a safe and graceful halt. Komoot lost its head in the industrial outskirts of Aviles, leading me up a canal between dark satanic mills, then over several pedestrian footbridges with massive zigzag stairs at either end. But even as I slid deep into ridicule, I wouldn't give up. With the bike over my shoulder I half-ran, half-fell down that last staircase, sustaining umpteen abrasions that I didn't even notice for several hours, when I turned on the shower taps and screamed the hotel down.

The road out of Aviles took me to a very bad place: a steep and green place, with a motorway on stilts a thousand miles above my head. I passed four apple pastries from bar-bag to mouth, and two from mouth to road. I saw a donkey that wasn't a donkey; that was in fact a six-foot concrete bollard. I felt my bleary gaze drop down to the tarmac, and all the glinting bits of glass and metal that winked at me from its extremity, and found myself steering towards them, praying for a pop and a hiss that would bring this misery to an end.

When Oviedo at last appeared, I wasn't in the least surprised to see it perched on an enormous hill. I got to the top feeling sad and beaten and strange, stopping the clock beneath the first hotel sign I saw. 'What a Tour!' Fuck you, Komoot. A while later – a really big while, like right now as I'm writing this up – I would reappraise my average speed: 22.2kmh, abysmal as it sounds, would in fact have been good enough for second-last place (this is not the time to imagine the catastrophes that must have befallen Isidro Bejarano, who rolled in fifty-three minutes behind The Swiss Watch). But at the time, I pushed La Berrendero across a strip-lit foyer, shaking wrists round filthy bars, not knowing whether to vomit or cry. Just a few hours before, rolling over the sunny coastal hills and up Gijón's well-peopled esplanade, I had bloody loved cycling. Now I absolutely despised it.

'I'm sorry,' said the receptionist, 'but you cannot take your bicycle into your room.'

'I don't want to take it into my room,' I said, in a cracked monotone. 'I want to throw it off your roof.'

CHAPTER 23

As had been apparent on my undulating death march into Oviedo, there would be no easy way out of the city. Riding past its residential outposts twelve hours later, a grand king-of-the-castle vista opened beneath me, as if someone had laid a lovely green bedspread over the land, but being Spanish had then tucked it in way too tight, causing a lot of enormous granite outcrops to rip through the fabric. But the sky was blue and the breeze was cool: in weather terms, this would be one of those rare Goldilocks days. I filled my lungs and pedalled forth with vigour, marvelling yet again at a miraculous overnight reinvention. Battle after battle had been lost, but still I fought the war.

On scabrous tarmac I bumped and juddered down ravines of corky rock, then up through silent hill villages, scanning the square for bald brown heads and San Miguel parasols, harbingers of local refreshment. A lazy river spanned by medieval arches; an extremely old woman in wellingtons leading a cow down a lane. The twenty-first century was a remote and fleeting presence, whooshing high above on a motorway viaduct or, in that typically native fashion, despoiling some distant valley with a thicket of belching industrial chimneys. I rode for hours without seeing a soul under seventy, yet everyone was up and at it, going about their aged business with a stubborn sense of purpose, shuffling doggedly across the street with huge bags of shopping, pushing barrows of firewood, filling jerrycans from a town-square stand pipe. With all due respect to the fabled benefits of the Mediterranean diet, this is really why so many rural Spaniards make it into three figures: from cradle to grave, they are just unstoppably active.

For the 1941 riders, this was pretty much a day off, 98 kilometres of trundling relief after the mountains and that ghastly split-stage time trial. Delio Rodríguez won the sprint into Luarca, leading a bunch that was two riders short: The Swiss Watch was now locked in *lanterne-rouge* combat with Martín Santos, a cyclist competing in the second and final professional race of his career. This pair trailed Berrendero by more than six hours on the general classification, and their tortoise-on-tortoise showdown would go right down to the saggy, rusting wire.

Predictably enough, the sailing was rather less plain for me. 'Nobody can tell us why this little hill is a puntable crest,' wrote Carlos Pardo of the ascent to La Espina. I wish he'd asked me. It stuck out in Komoot's stage profile like a pointy-eared ogre, 13 lonely kilometres up to its twin peaks and a pockmarked, bone-shaking 20 back down, a combo that along with the protracted absence of food meant I wobbled into the first petrol station in a state of some disarray. There, in the shadow of a refuelling tractor, I struggled to ingest four bags of cheese puffs. It was all the apologetic attendant could offer me to eat, and as I wanly crunched through smelly handfuls of air and yellow dust, it felt as if the process was expending more calories than it replaced. I should have asked him to chew them up and spit the slurry into my mouth, like a loving mother bird.

Luarca was a sweet little town, a cluster of white walls and pantiles hunkered beneath an encirclement of mighty cliffs. It was the smallest *ville d'etape* the 1941 Vuelta had yet visited, a bijou resort that then as now moonlighted as a fishing village. Rather breathless from the spiritual rigours of my final approach down Luarca's vertical cobbled alleys, I rolled around a compact harbour full of glittering water and colourful wooden boats, peering into the exorbitant shabby-chic seafood restaurants that lined it. Down towards the beach, smartly dressed little girls and their parents watched whooping sons and brothers jump off the sea wall into the Atlantic.

Once again I simply couldn't picture such a peaceful, happy place being ravaged by murderous civil conflict, and for once I was almost right. In his war diary, a Nationalist officer who had been stationed in Luarca wrote that he'd been ordered very much against his will to attend the dawn execution of eleven local men. 'But when the rifles were fired, instead of falling to the ground all the men ran away, with their hands still tied behind their backs.' As was apparently common, the firing squad had anaesthetised themselves by drinking through the night: all their shots missed, and several of the intended victims made good their escape. The officer recorded that six months later, he bumped into one of them while on leave in Oviedo. 'He told me his case had been reviewed, and that he had been acquitted.' Almost five weeks in and with 3,500 kilometres under my wheels, I had finally found a Civil War story with a happy ending. Happier than my own farewell to Luarca, it has to be said, which saw me ride away from another semi-feral guesthouse in the town's darker, cheaper hinterland with a mysterious souvenir: a saddle full of ants.

The coast road was full of amateur pelotons, which meant a busy morning for my hands: as well as exchanging waves with every oncomer, I had of late developed a habit of treating all overtakers to a flamboyant gear-change, snaking fingers down between my legs to make it plain that I was being handicapped by ancient machinery. As a bonus, anyone coming up behind during the first hour got a front-row view, with impressive audio accompaniment, of a man who really hates insects scooping loads of them out of his crack.

I crossed a huge estuary on a bridge that delivered me into Galicia, a province that immediately let my bottom know that it had better things to spend its money on than highway mainten-ance. After Ribadeo the careworn N634 bent inland, the morning mist burned off, and I found myself alone in a hilly, humid nowhere, brow after big green brow of unmanned countryside. When would I learn? Every time I emerged from one of these vast rural voids, parched and dizzy with malnourishment, I vowed to never again find myself so foolishly under-provisioned. As a man with extensive pilgrim-based experience of Galicia's embarrass-ment of town-free backwoods, this time I had even less of an excuse than usual.

At least I was in good company, because Galicia's foodless emptiness incited the worst *pájara* that Julián Berrendero would ever endure – a memory so traumatically vivid he devoted five pages of his slender autobiography to it. Nearing the end of Stage 2 in the 1935 Tour of Galicia, JB finds he has 'consumed every last atom of food, even the crumbs in my pockets'. With the sun setting, his eyelids droop, 'more through hunger than fatigue', and the next thing he knows he's waking up on his back by the side of the road: *el hombre del mazo,* the man with the hammer, had smacked him unconscious. 'I must have passed out in the saddle and fallen. The rest of the peloton was nowhere to be seen, and I did not have the strength to get back on the bike and chase them.' As he's lying there a car pulls up: 'It was my *soigneur* Carlos, carrying bread, fruit and all sorts. I sat up, grabbed the whole lot from his hands and devoured it like a hungry wolf.' Revitalised, JB sets off in pursuit. But then it all goes a bit me: succumbing to a raging thirst, 'the bride to my hunger', he drops his bike and runs down to a stream, meeting a herd of angry bulls who chase him round a darkening field. 'Eventually two cowherds appeared and pulled their beasts away, laughing at my predicament. They clearly knew nothing of any bicycle tour of Galicia, and seemed to believe that I was not in my right mind.'

Berrendero would eventually roll in ten minutes down on the day. But of course he wound up winning that tour, and by an enormous fifteen-minute margin. Even more satisfyingly, en route he would destroy a certain Basque rival. 'On Stage 3, Fermín Trueba and I gave Federico Ezquerra a battle without quarter. Both of us, though especially me, had an account to settle, and this time our rival had no local supporters to aid and abet him. When he escaped we chased him down, then rode him right off our wheels. After he eventually crossed the line, Ezquerra told everyone he'd suffered with punctures. But that was just his story. We all saw he was exhausted, because of what we had done to him. When he didn't turn up at the start the next morning, we knew we had won our battle.' This really was the hate that kept on hating, the little electric hate-hare that JB chased around the track throughout his career. Every one of his major stage-race victories incorporated the humiliating destruction of Federico Ezquerra. With the exception of the 1942 Vuelta, in which Ezquerra did not compete, offering one possible explanation as to why this event is deemed unworthy of mention in Berrendero's autobiography.

Before succumbing to the full bonk, the malnourished cyclist first finds his head emptied of all useful thought. As the empty road meandered forth, boredom kicked in, and kicked in hard. I ran through several loud interpretations of whatever that God-awful Robbie Williams song was, performing it in the manner of Kraftwerk, then Jarvis Cocker, and at ragged length a drunken, yodelling Winston Churchill. There was an iron-throated Spanish oral exercise, during which I informed the trees and the tarmac that there was much heat and a red roundabout, two ham sandwiches and a son of a whore please. Finally, after staring at my front wheel for a very long time in vacant silence, I found myself drawn into something close to a hypnotic trance. The wheel slipped out of focus, a blur of grey and glinting chrome; my eyes widened and glazed. Having done so accidentally several times in the act of changing gear, I watched with helpless detachment as I now deliberately jabbed my right-hand index finger into the revolving spokes. A chorus of shrill jeers swelled from the hillside as my agonised yelp died away: the crickets were back.

At last, some walls and roofs hoved into view. Vilamar was a settlement of few buildings, but one, praise be, was a bar. I pulled in and clumsily prodded Komoot: I'd covered 76 kilometres, and all I'd had since breakfast was a petrol-station Snickers. A hazy scroll through the route ahead suggested this bar would be my last nutritional opportunity for some hours.

'*Cambiarte camiseta!*'

A round of unvarnished laughter broke out as I made my unsteady way to the counter. I turned to see four dusty, fat-nosed men, who had doubtless arrived on the two bulldozers that were parked outside. They were jabbing merrily at their chests, and I deduced that after a lengthy respite, my Espanyol shirt was once again the object of comic derision. I eased my mask down and smiled back, then bent my head with the intention of kissing the badge, by way of banterous rejoinder. But something went wrong between my brain and my mouth, and instead I stuck out my tongue – an enormous, prehensile protuberance with the shameful ability to insert itself deep up my nostrils – and gave the crest a great big lick.

The laughter tailed uncertainly away; I directed my attention, such as it was, to the proprietress, now eyeing me warily from behind the bar.

'Para comer?'

My well-worn request for food was met by a slow shrug and a slight furrowing of the brow.

'Tortilla? Bocadillo?'

The proprietress carefully shook her head, and waved a hand across the little tray of savoury nibbles that even the grottiest Spanish bar will serve you with a drink. Seven cocktail sticks, each speared through a dice-sized cube of bread and a pound-coin roundel of chorizo. I ordered an *agua grande* and two bottles of Kas Limon, but as these were placed on the bar before me alongside a tiny saucer with a single skewered snack upon it, I felt calorific desire swell into ugly, primal need.

'Todos – todos para mi,' I blurted. Not a question, but a statement of desperate intent: I wasn't asking if I could have the other six nibbles, just telling her that I was going to. Without waiting for a response, I gathered my refreshments in one arm, then with the other tipped my solo snack back from whence it came and snatched up the tray. Tunnel vision had set in: I bore my perilous load towards the door with reckless haste, back-heeled it ajar, then laid everything to rest on the nearest outside table with a terrific clatter. Before I knew it there were seven empty cocktail sticks on the tray; not long after, three empty bottles stood alongside. But there could be no getaway: in Spain you never pay when you order, only when you're finished. I needn't have worried. The bulldozer boys looked frankly alarmed when I came back in, and the proprietress silently counted out an awful lot more change than I'd expected: she didn't charge me a cent for cleaning out her nibbles. 'Lo siento, soy Ingles,' I mumbled on my way out.

It's said that fortune favours the brave, but only by people who haven't seen fortune ripping its kit off for the rude and grasping. How deeply grateful I was for that requisitioned road fuel, as a sultry afternoon took me up some relentless, muggy inclines. None were deemed worthy of mention in Carlos's Stage 17 report, not even the one that Komoot reckoned went uphill for 16 whole kilometres, with gradients that touched 12 per cent. When someone told me before I left that I was about to ride round the second most mountainous country in Europe, I nodded flintily, thinking: Don't be daft. Spain? Beachy, deserty, rain-on-the-plain Spain? But I was finding out the hard way that they were right. I've just learned that there is only one road in the United Kingdom that goes uphill for more than 10 kilometres. In the course of three days I'd ridden up half a dozen.

After 123 kilometres, with the wobbly cold sweats upon me once more, I came to Vilalba. The town didn't look up to much, but it was home to a parador – one of those grand old castles and palaces that the Spanish began converting into upscale hotels back in the pre-Franco age. I'd always fancied staying in one, and looking up at that glorious hexagonal tower I wondered if now might be the time. Then I got my phone out, established that they'd just slashed their room rates in half, and stopped wondering.

Regrettably, the tower rooms were under reconstruction, but with no more than a slight quiver of revulsion the receptionist offered me a suite in the adjoining wing. Entering a fancy hotel room always seemed to bring on an especially severe bout of the self-pitying mumble-swears, as if only now, in counterpoint to all this comfort and luxury, could whatever miserable ordeal I had just survived be placed in its properly heroic context. I drank two minibar beers in the bath, muttering compound profanity into a mound of scented foam, then fell asleep in it.

CHAPTER 24

'Good morning, ladies and gentlemen, now that I have your attention I'd like to introduce you all to my genitals.' Striding into a hotel breakfast room in Lycra shorts always felt like a statement, one that seemed way too bold for that time of day. There would be unease and sometimes visible sadness, sagging shoulders and wincing faces that turned back to their pastries with diminished enthusiasm. The typically modest total of fellow guests made these entrances more conspicuous and thus somehow more excruciating, and at the genteel and sombre Vilalba Parador I recorded peak breakfast groin shame.

What a very different place the dining hall seemed in the cold light of morning. The night before I had cut a reasonable dash in my Merkels and linen shirt, seated at a vast table for one amid a scattering of socially distanced elderly diners. Admittedly this impression took rather a hit when I ordered a whole bottle of wine, a request the waiter made me repeat twice in case anyone missed it, and chose to accompany it with chorizo and beans, a keenly priced option whose very existence he seemed appalled by when I pointed it out to him in the menu's peasanty depths.

Anyway, I probably won't stay at a parador again. In truth, there was something a bit prissy about the place, with its linen foot doilies on the floor beside the bed, and something just a little naff: all that reproduction ironmongery and dark furniture put me in mind of a 1930s Hollywood castle, somewhere Errol Flynn ought to be swinging through on a black chandelier. Plus, during the night my pants and one sock blew off the laundry line I'd rigged up outside my window, and via some process that has doubtless earned me a lifetime ban, ended up in a little plastic bag that the receptionist silently handed over when I came out of the breakfast room.

The seventeen surviving riders had rolled out of Luarca with diminished zeal, succumbing to a lethargic fatalism that would infect the following few stages. Berrendero's lead over Trueba was only sixty-four seconds, but nobody seriously expected an attack from his wingman – certainly not before the Navacerrada, the vast climb the riders would face on the final stage. The ennui was reflected in the press coverage, which devoted far more column inches and significantly greater enthusiasm to Hitler's advances through Soviet territory. Carlos Pardo's reports wither to threadbare statements of fact – he didn't even bother filing any copy at all for Stage 17 – and the Falangist papers' perennial denunciations of monotony and sloth were for once fully justified.

In *Mis Glorias y Memorias*, JB admits these stages were 'countryside rides, contested with little energy', and doesn't sound aggrieved that 'in punishment for our lack of combativity, half of the prize money was withdrawn'. As race leader, it was hardly up to him to force the pace. The race jury had to investigate claims that several riders had been taking tows from a truck – diplomatically finding insufficient evidence – and day after day the peloton trundled up to the finish well behind schedule, with nobody mounting a serious challenge to Delio Rodríguez in the final sprints. With six consecutive wins – he had also romped home first in the time trial – Delio was on his way to setting a record of twelve stage victories in a single grand tour, an extraordinary achievement that has only been bettered once, when Freddy Maertens took thirteen at the 1977 Vuelta.

In empathy, or perhaps in glorious tribute to my burgeoning prowess and stamina, my own retracing of the 1941 race now settled into an approximation of comfortable routine. I was still doing a stage every two days; still tackling thick heat and big hills; still careering madly down the cliffs towards the sparkling sea and a boulevard finish, ready to dismay another hotelier and despoil one more gracious square with my stained *alpargatas* and a malodorous carton of cold red soup. But for once, I did it all without farce or drama. I always had enough to eat and drink, and with Komoot finally brought to heel, those off-piste misadventures were a thing of the past. La Berrendero was on pretty good form, bar a reluctance to engage high gear at the time of my choosing, preferring to do so of its own accord with an abruptness that generally introduced my testicles to the saddle with immense force. The only other conspicuous physical discomfort I now endured was the pinpoint of pure and perfect armour-piercing agony that randomly lasered the outside top edge of my left little toe: possibly some sort of invisible bunion, or maybe gout. The cramps were gone, that incandescent girder had been prised off my shoulder blades, and my leathered exoskeleton was now impervious to sun. It had taken us five weeks, but my bike and I were finally on a roll.

And though it would be offensively inaccurate to contend that the *guerra civil* left this far-flung corner of Spain alone – 1,600 people were executed by Falangist hit squads in A Coruña alone during the second half of 1936, and local fishermen would be finding bodies in their nets for months after – Galicia had an easier war than most parts of Spain. There was very little fighting here, and not many lefties to murder. Apart from anything else, this was Franco's manor: he'd been born and raised in the Galician port of Ferrol, where a twenty-foot bronze statue of him on a horse stood in the main square until 2002. They seem pretty at ease with their past. Franco's former Minister of Information, Manuel Fraga, served as Galicia's regional president until 2005.

After A Coruña, I rode through Santiago de Compostela, down steep stone alleys alive with the echoing tippy-tap of walking sticks and a tangible air of emotional anticipation. I'd been passing pilgrims in increasing numbers for some days – once gloriously reeling in and spitting out a trio on e-bikes – but found myself flabbergasted by the sheer volume of rucksacked scallop-danglers being funnelled into Santiago's ancient finishing straight. Despite the substantial current disincentive, there were ten times more than there had been when I cajoled Shinto down these claustrophobic passageways and into the broad, tilting Praza do Obradoiro. Out there, between the magnificent façades of the cathedral and the world's oldest hotel, the flagstones were dense with selfie sticks and overwhelmed pilgrims, some dazed and confused, others weeping uncontrollably or clasped in desperate embrace, facemask to facemask. I confess to a little moment of my own, here, where one broiled afternoon sixteen years before, blinking away tears of fulfilment and mourning a companionship that was soon to be severed for ever, I stooped to bag up a final heap of steaming road apples.

I pressed on southwards, past oncoming pilgrims, over Roman bridges, tagging on to weekend club pelotons with no more than a light mist of lactic acid hissing out through my leg pores. Except for a couple of afternoons spent tootling around at rickety vintage bike rallies, I have never ridden in a big group of cyclists. Quite the adventure, isn't it? All that jockeying about, all that clicking of gears and huffing and puffing, the warning fingers jabbed at potholes and drain covers, the urgent mutters bidding Granddad Twat Helmet to piss off. (I'm joking, of course. At least I hope I am – my Galician isn't up to much.) Spanish cyclists had by now firmly established themselves as the most fraternal two-wheelers I have ever shared a road with: almost every single one of them raised a chin or a few fingers in greeting, and some went much further. My ride-by exchanges with fellow touring cyclists, rare as they were, now edged towards mania, with Viking roars and stand-up salutes, fists punched high into the sky.

It took me a while to realise that these fleeting encounters represented my only contact with like-minded people, and that their blossoming hysteria was down to me and me alone, the clumsy, desperate interactions of a man who craves companionship but has been apart from society for too long. I may not have put it like this to any of those cyclists, but it somehow felt rather like that bit in *Midnight Express* when Billy's girlfriend comes to visit him in his Turkish prison, and instead of the sensitive reunion she has imagined, he gets her to pull her top up while he knocks one out.

In truth, I had been wandering away from the accepted norms of human conduct for some time. Mosquitoes, mercifully absent in the arid south, were now routine bedroom companions, and each evening, post shower, I would hunt down every last one of them, *alpargata* in one hand, towel in the other, with a psychotic, fully nude intensity that would have made me a very unpopular roommate. In this it was compatible with a growing roster of odious solitary endeavours, not least my chorizo-powered 'belch yourself thin' diet.

And that wasn't all. There's no way of not making this sound a bit odd, and indeed definitively pathetic, but I had begun to befriend the inanimate cornerstones of my life on the road: my kit, my bottles, my laundry line and clothes pegs. We were all in this together, brothers in arms. One evening, I found myself talking to my shorts as I wrung them out in the bath before the towel-rolling stage of the drying process. 'OK, fellas, what do you fancy – the one I've already used, or the one I've already used twice?' It felt like only a matter of time before they answered back, though that night they restricted themselves to a weary groan. Still, at least I didn't give anything a name. Except my Merkels, obviously. Oh, and Daddy Three Bags, the triple-wrapped king of the ziplocks that was home to my passport and charging cables. And who could forget Stubby and El Gordo, that cheeky little-and-large bidon double act? Or, indeed, Edward Picklehands, the vinegar string-backs that all those retching receptionists could have grown to love, if only they'd known their heart-rending back story.

The 1941 riders rode into the Balaidos stadium in Vigo to meet a crowd that had been there since morning, clapping dutifully along to 'a procession of little girl and boy cyclists' and other such totalitarian tedium, organised and overseen by the Ministry of Education and Leisure's regional inspector. As it had across most of Galicia, Franco's coup faced only token resistance in Vigo, though that didn't prevent a brutally repressive aftermath: seven young men were shot dead for listening to a Madrid radio station, and another for passing unfavourable comment on the Nationalist war effort. It's quite possible that the peloton might have spotted a Nazi U-boat or two refuelling in Vigo's dockyard – anyone who sat through all 418 hours of *Das Boot* may remember U-96 dropping in here (fun fact: more time has now elapsed since that film was made in 1981 than the gap between the depicted events and its release). Along with his División Azul, now on its way to the eastern front, this was the only conspicuous show of support Franco ever accorded Hitler.

I found the city hunkered under a bank of fog that blotted out the top half of its lofty suspension bridge, and wisped dramatically around the endless quaysides, with their enormous bill-posted warnings against off-quota crab fishing. The grey-washed conditions did no favours to the art nouveau mansions that ghosted by on my run-in, or indeed to the Balaídos stadium I semi-sprinted up to, a mothballed citadel of steel and concrete. Still, Vigo was inarguably doing a great job of being massively colder than Madrid, thereby fulfilling the seasonal brief that was once again its big summer draw. Indeed, it had indirectly brought me here, or at least brought me here much earlier in the day than I would normally have arrived at a stage destination. By prior arrangement, I was to pass the afternoon and evening with a Madrileño whose family have been spending their cool Julys on this part of the Galician coast for many decades.

I waited for Rodrigo outside my port-side hotel in a state of mild unease, running through the half-remembered protocols of polite social introduction. Merkels freshly wiped down, dab of Savlon behind the ears, bidon gaffer-taped to forehead – was there anything else? Rodrigo and I had been put in contact by my parents' very wonderful carer, Rebecca, who had come to know his family during a year spent in Madrid with her own. In the course of a brief exchange of emails, Rodrigo had kindly offered to meet me when I passed through this corner of Galicia – in fact, the family's summer residence lay a few miles down the coast, at Baiona – and I had accepted with grateful alacrity. An extraordinary and deeply thrilling coincidence had emerged during our correspondence: Rod, as he liked to be known, had been brought up in Madrid's Chamberí district, and told me of several formative weekends spent in Berrendero's shop, having his troublesome bike attended to in the great man's presence.

A black Peugeot pulled up and a cheery fellow of late middle years raised an expectant eyebrow. Rod was a doctor whose spoken English matched the excellence of his written output, and during the drive to Baiona he held forth entertainingly on everything from cava to Columbus. Well, almost everything. As a Madrid-based medic, this year Rod hadn't just come up here to escape the heat: he'd clearly had more than enough of Covid, and shook his head in haunted silence when I brought it up. No less conspicuous was the JB-shaped hole in our conversation. Every time I tried to fill it, Rod smiled and raised an appeasing hand from the wheel: all in good time.

Baiona was a delightful little resort, at least once the mist burned off and I could see it. Its seafront, looking out through a lot of yacht masts at a vast bay girdled with hills and sand, was busy with Rod-alikes, men of about my age who had done demonstrably better for themselves, wearing lazy smiles and big watches. We strode up to the extraordinary castle that stands guard over the mouth of the bay, traversing three full kilometres of wandering medieval battlements. Far below, Rod pointed out the replica of *La Pinta*, one of the three ships that formed Columbus's plucky fleet, a tubby little ark among the marina's sleek white hulls. *La Pinta* beat the others back home, so when it docked here on 1 March 1493, the people of Baiona became the first to learn of the New World. (You can see how this earth-shattering moment in history might have left a long shadow across such a modest community, so perhaps it isn't surprising that the locals haven't moved far beyond it. Rather brilliantly, Rod told me Baiona still nurtures a deep-seated hatred for Sir Francis Drake, whose rebuffed attempt to take the town in 1585 is celebrated annually. 'Here he is always *Il Pirata Drake*.')*

Then we walked down through the old town, past charmingly homespun restaurants with terrifyingly priced menus, and came to a little church. My gaze snagged on a symbol hewn into its wall, just above head height: another Falangist yoke and arrows, would you believe it, beside another dedication to José Antonio Primo de Rivera. Rod had just told me his wife came to worship here every week, and when the priest emerged he greeted him like the old friend he clearly was. But when I pointed out the inscription, Rod expressed bemusement: 'Strange,' he said, stroking his chin. 'We never notice this before.'

We met up with Rod's wife and one of their daughters, both as chipper and charming as he, then meandered through the facemasked alleys to their favourite seafood place. I was almost bursting with Julián-based expectation by now, and perhaps Rod could sense it, because as soon as we all had our knees under the table he coughed gently, turned to me and said: 'So – Berrrrrenderrrrro.'

After all the quizzical shrugs this name had elicited – not a single flicker of recognition, I now realised, since I'd left Biketown on day one – how thrilling, how Trump-slappingly splendid, to hear at length, and in English, from a man who didn't just know about Julián Berrendero, but had actually met him. 'I was a young

---

* Columbus's last descendant, the Duke of Veragua, was kidnapped and shot dead by a communist hit squad in Madrid on 16 September 1936.

boy, not a teenager, so we are in the first years of the 1970s. My friends and me we had these really old bicycles, of BH brand, with those, what you say, metal rods for brake, no cable. So when we have some problem we take to the Berrendero shop in Chamberí. It was not a tidy place; the main business was repairing old bikes, not selling new ones. He was always there, also his nephew, who did the repair. "Hey, boy, come here and fix the tyre of this kid, let's do it, hurry up."' I smiled: that's my man. 'So, anyway, I remember Berrendero always fine, always kind and good to us kids, but always ... *serious*.'

Rod sat back, nodded slowly, and took a sip of wine. Was that it?

'Serious ... in what way? Did he ever talk about his career, or um ... ?'

'With me? Never.'

Oh well. I suppose I shouldn't have expected more. I'm not sure I could have told you half as much about any shopkeeper who might have served me a few times half a century ago. Apart from maybe Ron Lutz, who ran the newsagent opposite my school, and who sold single cigarettes to small children, and whose daughter was briefly in *Grange Hill*, and who once gave me my change while holding a cigar, leaving a scar that still decorates the palm of my right hand.

'But with my father, many times.'

And with these heady words, our conversation reversed dramatically out of its dead end. As my Merkels slithered around the seat in excitement, Rod revealed that his father, a gregarious corporate executive and a big cycling fan, had spent hours talking to the great man in his shop, and in the café-bar next door, long enough to consider him a friend. 'People always had confidence in my father, he was like that. He came with me to pay for the new tyre, or the brakes, the chain, whatever, and he start to talk with

Berrendero, so – you win this race, you win that race, let's have a coffee. This is how it was. They would talk and talk.'

'About races?'

'About everything. About what happen when Berrendero come back to Spain and he go to the jail.'

I probably gulped. The waitress appeared, and Rod masterfully drew out the suspense with an extensive order that seemed to cover the full spectrum of Baiona's marine bounty. This interlude brought welcome respite for Rod's wife and daughter, who had been doing their admirable best to maintain polite interest in our man-chat.

'You know, I cannot remember exactly how my father says it, but Berrendero tells to him that he did not believe he would go in prison. He thinks when he return from *Francia* he can make some arrangement with the *régimen*. Of course, it was not so fine in the camp, not so pleasant. I know he never talks of it interviews, not never.'

And afterwards? In Rod's retelling, accompanied by the fitful slurp and clatter of shellfish consumption, Berrendero came to terms with his painful past, or had at least done so by the time he spoke about it with Rod's father, thirty years on. 'He wasn't an angry man any more about what happened to him. He tell to my father he just finish on the wrong side, if you like he bet on the loser. But Berrendero was not a political person, not at all.'

I'd figured as much. All the same, it was mildly astounding to hear that JB had put a photo of himself with Franco up on the shop wall. 'A really big one, I think from a reception after he wins the *Vuelta ciclista* the second time. They are shaking hands. It's a smart political move. Most people then would do this if they could, good for business, good to show the *régimen* you don't have no problems with Franco.'

Rod dropped me off in Vigo a couple of hours later; I thanked him for his many kindnesses, and the revelations I was still struggling to process. How desperate that Berrendero, robbed of a big chunk of his professional prime, should find himself obliged to show such public respect for the dictator who stole it. In truth, he had little choice: as Antony Beevor notes, 'those regarded as politically unreliable were not allowed to open a shop'. And how tragic that this abasement should seem so banal, so inevitable, to those like Rod who'd been born into Franco's Spain. Even now, in common with everyone else I'd tried to raise it with, he still politely sidestepped the Civil War. An attempted conversation on our drive back never got off the ground, and I was still a little freaked out at how his family had managed to gaze straight through the Falangist symbol that had stared them in the face for all those years. Not for the first time on this trip, I went to sleep thinking: Thank fuck we got this civil-war shit out of our system three hundred years before I was born.

CHAPTER 25

'Ourense? Oh, it's not so far.'

The night before, Rodrigo's daughter had dismissed the journey to my next intended destination with a car driver's typical airiness: 125 kilometres is an irrelevance to the right-minded majority who would never contemplate covering it under their own steam. Somehow this nonchalance rubbed off on me, exacerbated by a stupidly premature end-of-term mood. The road out of Vigo suddenly felt like the home straight: I was turning the corner, leaving the sea behind for good, setting course for Madrid. For good measure, that morning I tapped into my last tube of Savlon, hurling its predecessor into the hotel bin with the gusto of a rider offloading a bidon on the run-in.

In consequence, I set out in an unhelpful frame of mind, feeling that I could just sort of turn up and sign those 125 kilometres off, without the bothersome need to ride them. It was a fantasy that curdled dismally as I hauled La Berrendero over Vigo's precipitous geographical defences, lungs aflame and breakfast reversing up my gullet. There were 500 miles still ahead of me, I now groggily accepted, and they clearly didn't intend to go down without a fight.

Hopes of a decent daily average speed died on their arse well before lunch. Carlos Pardo's perfunctory Stage 19 report made no mention of climbs, yet having started out at sea level I found myself up above 1,000 metres, that respiratory orchestra once again tripping over itself in a ragged, off-beat mess of rasps and gurgles. With the Atlantic breeze now far behind, the inland heat grew and kept growing, its durability expressed in the dead brown hills around, and, more dramatically, by the helicopters that flew overhead all morning, ferrying big buckets of water towards distant billows of smoke.

A brief lull in the topography took me through Ponteareas, hometown of the Rodríguez clan, and another of those startlingly hideous settlements that brotherloads of cyclists couldn't wait to get out of. At the 1945 Vuelta, Delio would claim victory over an ageing Berrendero by a whopping half-hour, and five years later, his brothers Emilio and Manolo made grand-tour history by finishing first and second. I'd wanted to pay homage to this remarkable family with a full-tilt sprint through the bankrupt furniture showrooms and mid-rise apartment blocks, but it all went wrong on the endless *glorietas* between them. Then it was back into the sun-dried hills, my dull gaze scanning one more forgotten road, one more vast and vacant panorama.

The new-case Covid graphs were now soaring straight up every TV screen, and rules were being tightened hard. In Vigo I found that each of my hotel coat hangers wore a removable set of plastic shoulder pads, to facilitate inter-guest sterilisation. Local lockdowns were spreading across the north, and restrictions on cross-regional travel threatened to undo my mission right at the last. Every receptionist now handed me a big form to fill in, asking where I'd just come from and where I was off to next. That first question was always a poser: where *had* I just come from? In Ourense I had to rewind through what seemed like several days of road-recall before I found myself back at Vigo. It was the same story at Verín the night after.

Even now these two towns are merged in my mind, which seems a bit daft as Ourense was a pretty big place built right up the side of a huge hill, and Verín was both pan-flat and tiny. But they both emitted the same poignant vibe, faraway towns that had been left to their own devices for an awfully long time, the wealth of centuries past evident in the grand old townhouses that had shed their roofs and windows, and now stood in mournful vigil over a sad and desperate present. Some neighbourhoods had been almost entirely abandoned; at times it felt like exploring a Victorian Pompeii.

In the afternoon sun's brutal last hurrah, I walked down street after baking, desolate street, eventually taking my ease outside a bar in my hotel square, then drip-feeding *tinto de verano* into my hollowed frame, hoping the kitchen opened before my brain drowned. A couple of hours later, snoring at a hotel ceiling, I'd be drawn from slumber by a chorus of chatter and chinks that swelled and swelled, until I stumbled to the window and looked out at a seething, garrulous crowd of drinkers and promenaders filling the square beneath. Where had all these people been hiding, and why had they waited until ten thirty to break cover? And on a Monday. Or a Tuesday. Even at eleven the waiters were still taking orders from new arrivals.

Not for the first time, I struggled to square this nation's hard-focused war on Covid with their helpless addiction to congregating en masse. On both nights I saw a lot of backs being slapped, and a fair few hugs. They just could not stop themselves. Even Julián Berrendero, that irretrievably miserable git, had been upgraded via Rodrigo's revelations into a discreetly affable old geezer, hiding his light under a grumpy bushel. It was now much easier to picture him down there in those bustling, full-contact travesties of social distancing, gruffly patting a few shoulders, jabbing the odd rival in the spleen.

Verín was by some margin this Vuelta's smallest *ville d'étape*, and its least engaging. I'd slept in the town's only hotel – in truth, a bar with a few upstairs rooms – and when I Googled 'things to do in Verín', all that came up was some winery half an hour's drive away and a Romanesque church 8 kilometres back down the road. The mystery of the riders' overnight halt here was only resolved when I consulted the map over breakfast: there was absolutely nowhere else they could have stopped, for miles and miles around. Consulting the route of Stage 20, my way ahead, it seemed I would face a record-breaking 160 kilometres swathe of Galician fuck-all before arriving at a town that might plausibly accommodate me.

It was a challenge that the conditions would redouble. Dispatching a huge quadrant of *tortilla* in my bar, I stared at the overhead TV that for once had nothing to say about plague: the screen was full of cars and wheelie bins being tossed through towns on frothing brown torrents, and sad farmers wandering through ruined fields. Shortly afterwards, following the small, round proprietor to the lock-up garage La Berrendero had slept in, I surveyed the aftermath of a nocturnal calamity that had somehow failed to rouse me. Shattered roofing tiles and shards of window box lay strewn up the wet pavements; one of Verín's rare surviving shops had had its awning shredded; a big iron drain cover lay upside down beside an open hole in the road, presumably expelled by a rising fountain of flood water. 'Is bad today for bicycle,' said the bar owner as I hitched on my bags. 'Have a nice travel.'

I watched him walk away, and felt an enormous raindrop impact the top of my head, heavy as a pebble. My hand was poised over a bin, holding the can of TDV that I hadn't got around to drinking the night before. After brief reconsideration, I popped the top and downed it in one.

At 301 kilometres, Stage 20 was the longest in the race. But Carlos Pardo's report glossed over the first two-thirds of it, thereby failing once more to forewarn me of an absolutely enormous climb. Almost straight out of Verín I found myself toiling up the Cordillera Cantabrica, the mountains that hem Galicia in, weaving through stuff that the storm had ripped off trees or sluiced down hillsides. Presently I entered the apocalyptic aftermath of a recent forest fire, inching up through an acrid wasteland of charred stumps, the gutter full of cinders and melted roadside marker posts. I passed an incinerated wild boar; my phone coverage expired.

As I neared the thousand-metre mark, the cinders gave way to great drifts of unthawed hail, some of the stones as big as marbles. You may gather from this that it was cold. Bitterly so: my fleece went on, then the barber's gown, and, at shuddersome length, my facemask, as a stand-in snood. When the rain solidified my every extremity went numb. Except the one I really wanted to: my left little toe, by now transforming each slow-mo upstroke into a miniature hell.

The mist that had smeared out the peaks above surreptitiously wafted down to meet me, and as I approached the first of three thousand-metre cols it swallowed the world whole. Somewhere down in that void lay the motorway that everyone else was on, drumming their fingers lightly on nice warm steering wheels as they smoothly reeled in the miles. Far above, I rolled stiffly over a terrifying bridge that disappeared into the fog, like some portal to the other side. It didn't seem right, or fair, that all this should be happening to me near the top right-hand corner of Portugal, in August.

The final fog-topped fucker took me to 1,380 metres, the highest I'd been since the Alto de los Leones back on day one. My relief when the road tilted down was short lived: in an instant, the light sleet evolved into shotgun blasts of iced rain. With my eyes puckered to a tight, protective squint, I approached the first corner. Oh yeah, I thought, my brakes aren't going to work. Just as well the front wheel's starting to shimmy and there's storm-strewn gravel all over the road.

I shot out through the last bank of mist and found myself streaking towards a bleak plateau, its clumps of deserty vegetation rendered monochrome by all that scurrying greyness. The bars juddered viciously in my hands, as if I was attempting to restrain an unruly spin drier. Then, just as the road flattened out, my feet were abruptly locked into a mad rotary frenzy, with a violence that quickly threw them out of the toe clips. What the naked, freaking flip was happening? Breathing hard, I looked down and saw the pedals spinning madly, with a sense of frenzied, runaway purpose that I felt no wish to interrupt. With my legs splayed wide out of harm's way, like a kid riding through a puddle, I braked to a wobbly halt.

There was clearly something awry in the rear-hub department, an issue with the freewheel that I could only hope would respond very well to clueless staring and a stout shake. The one-bed town of Tábara was still 30 kilometres down the empty road; I tentatively remounted, and placed a foot gingerly on the pedal. It span on demand, and stopped when I did. OK. Off I rolled, muttering encouragement, wheedled praise and threats to the silver bicycle beneath me, telling La Berrendero that it was better than this, that it couldn't let me down, not now, not so near to the end, and that if it did I might regretfully have to consider legal action.

It worked, for a bit. Ten minutes later, after a muffled crunching twang from somewhere deep within, the cranks once again took control of their own destiny and began pushing my feet round. It was as if the bicycle I had come to know so well was now a stranger, an enemy, possessed by some fixed-wheel ghost rider. If only I'd ridden a fixie more than once in my life, and if only I hadn't fallen off twice while doing it.

After a couple of miles I regained control; after a couple more I lost it. It was like that all the way to Tábara, another sad and unkempt place condemned to a slow death when a motorway stole its life-giving traffic. I was so relieved to have made it, and so utterly drained by a hundred steep miles of freezing fog and fear, that I couldn't have cared less. My eyes barely registered the great drifts of litter piled up across the floor of the bar-hostel I blundered into, nor was my nose much interested in the wave of dung and death that greeted it when the sullen landlady kicked open the tractor shed that La Berrendero would be pondering its deficiencies in overnight.

I'd learned by now that the Spanish hospitality trade likes its lifts small and bouncy, but nothing I had experienced to date could compete with the bungee coffin of Tábara. Arrival at the second floor involved a double rebound that took me halfway up to the third, then halfway back down to the first. If there'd been any head room I'd have really hurt myself. Again I endured it with weary stoicism, just as I did when the cold tap in my room dispensed a fluid that even after ten minutes didn't get any less warm or yellow. It was now three days since my laundry gel had run out, and in traditional endgame fashion I'd been making do with hotel shampoo. But all this place could offer, for man and kit alike, was a doll's house sliver of Lux. I let out a tiny sigh, then showered twice, once with all my clothes on and once without.

Sensory awareness slowly returned as I sat in the bar downstairs, ankle-deep in peanut shells and crisp packets, waiting for the kitchen to open. Halfway through a tumbler of white wine I realised it was truly horrible; I finished it all the same, then filled the empty glass from the *agua grande* I'd ordered with it. When the sullen landlady next passed by, I asked for a glass of red and watched her eyes narrow. '*No blanco?*' In one angry movement she grabbed my glass full of water and stomped off through the rubbish to the bar. Watching her hurl its contents furiously into the sink I realised what was happening: she had mistaken my glass of water for an untouched glass of white wine, believing I had capriciously changed my mind.

In the linguistic circumstances there was nothing to be done about it. Nor would there be half an hour later, when she stood over me with hands on hips, glaring at the bowl of half-eaten stew I had pushed to the far end of my table. To be fair, I did prepare an explanation, and had it ready to go on my phone in a Google Translate box. 'Why is there tripe in my bean stew? It is the food of Satan.' But by now the bar had filled up with horny-handed old locals who didn't seem likely to take my side in a fight. '*Lo siento, soy Ingles,*' I said, dropping a €10 note on the table and heading off to pit my bubbling innards against the lift.

CHAPTER 26

The 1941 boys seemed to be working to rule: stages 18, 19 and 20 were the slowest of the race, all run at an average speed well below the 25kmh prize-money cut off. Even the press seemed to have gone past caring. When I noticed a conspicuous absence in the Stage 19 general classification, finding an explanation meant digging into JB's autobiography: 'Federico Ezquerra did not make the start line at Vigo. He was sick and had boils.' If only they'd had emojis back then.

The reporters finally broke their yawn-enforced two-day silence when the riders reached Zamora, 200 kilometres into this fear-some enormo-stage. 'The III Vuelta a España enters our city three hours behind schedule,' grumbled the local Falangist rag, *Diario de Zamora*. 'But despite this, a large crowd is still gathered to greet the riders as they help themselves to a feast laid on by the Ministry of Education and Leisure.' Carlos Pardo, wandering among the face-stuffing peloton with his notebook, seems amazed to discover what I had just found out for myself. The riders hadn't been soft pedalling: they weren't late because they were lazy, but because this stage was a total bastard.

'Race leader Berrendero assures me it has been a tough morning, one of the toughest of the race ... Escuriet, his mouth full of fruit, shouts at us with difficulty and some feeling: "Don't talk to me! I've only had six punctures." He says "only", because some have suffered 13. The rest of the competitors seem extraordinarily fatigued, in part because of the poor state of the roads, some of the worst they have tackled.' (A tally at the end of the stage would reveal that the sixteen surviving riders had endured no fewer than eighty-three punctures between them.) He doesn't even get a decent quote out of The Swiss Watch. 'And finally, we approach the rider in the red jersey with a white cross on it, as he is devouring a formidable beef sandwich. We ask him how he is going, in his native French, but he just looks at us and says "Oui," before returning to his lunch.'

In the morning I at least thought about attending to the free-wheel issue. How shameful to recall that my very expensive ultra-light tools had been taken out of their bag only twice: to assemble Alfie's birthday bike, and in a failed attempt to prise a detached jersey button from the depths of a bidet plughole. But the exploded diagrams I looked at on my phone were starkly terrifying; I set off for Zamora, two hours south and home to the nearest bike shops, hoping for the best.

As it was, The Bad Thing only happened once en route, a brief and manageable spell of demonic appropriation on the dead-straight, dead-quiet road south. Cloudless sky and sunflowered flatlands: it was as if Galicia had never happened. Just before Zamora I rejoined the N630, the road that had taken me right through Extremadura all those weeks before. The end was nigh. And the Civil War horrors were back.

One especially appalling tale from Zamora's repression seemed to aggregate every dreadful theme. When war broke out, Ramón Sender – a well-known radical and novelist – joined the Republican ranks and sent his wife Amparo Barayón from Madrid back to Zamora, her home town, along with their two young children, thinking the family would be safer there. But in August she was arrested and her children sent to an orphanage; two months later, for the crime of having married in a civil ceremony, she was shot dead. It transpired that Barayón was betrayed by her own brother-in-law, and had been refused absolution by the priest who heard her final confession. Her executioner: one Segundo Viloria, a former suitor whose advances she had rejected. By then, both of Barayón's brothers had been executed, and all three siblings were later posthumously sued for damages by Franco's Commission for Political Responsibilities. Sender, who later fled to the US, never spoke about any of this, not even to the couple's own children. Like Berrendero, like almost everyone I'd tried to speak to about the Civil War, he thought it best just to bottle it all up.

The bike shop I went to overlooked the broad and lazy river that runs through Zamora. I explained my woes to a small man in overalls who spoke a bit of English, enough to tell me he had no idea who Julián Berrendero was, and that he would send me a text when my bike was ready for collection.

It felt very odd wandering about in my kit, sweaty and a bit dishevelled, all dressed up and nothing to ride. I ate a tub of tuna salad on the steps of a supermarket; I murmured the chant about a famously wayward striker who shared his surname with this city and briefly played for Spurs, sung to the tune of 'That's Amore': 'When the ball hits your head and you're sat in row Z, that's Zamora.' Then I sat on a shady bench by the river, watching the kayaks go by, and began idly scrolling through the Stage 20 race data.

Not only was Verín–Valladolid the slowest stage of the race, at an average speed of 22.73kmh I learned that it still ranked as the slowest stage in Vuelta history. This was my sort of stat. I fired up Komoot on my phone and established that I had covered the first 200 kilometres of Stage 20, many of them very steeply uphill, at an average of 20.9kmh. I had another 100 kilometres, on largely flat roads, to get it above 22.73. Was it doable? I stared out across the sun-dappled water with hope in my heart, daring to dream small.

'Your *bici* has some wrong things.' I looked at the bike guy's open face, thinking: So *that's* why I brought it into this bicycle-repair shop. I knew there had to be a reason. 'Too many wrong things.' He waved his hands helplessly at La Berrendero's every significant part. 'I can't do nothing.' A happy shrug and a big, blithe smile. 'Please, ten euro.'

It was two and a half hours since I'd left the bike with him, and it was exactly where I'd left it, propped up against a stack of boxes in the corner. Hating him and hating myself, I extracted two sweaty fives from my back-right jersey pocket, handing them over with a face purged of all expression. It was now almost 3 p.m. I pushed La Berrendero out on to the towpath and got going.

It was due east to Valladolid, on a crumbly old road that ran through cornfields and the occasional comatose village. The freewheel was behaving itself; I gradually wound up the speed. At long last I had a Berrendero-pattern hatred to spur me on. Just picturing the bike guy's stupid, useless grin had a noticeably positive influence on my cadence. Soon I upped the ante with some choice alterations to make that grin more hateable still, removing a couple of front teeth and dangling a pendulous string of idiot's drool from one corner. Just look at him. What a wanker.

I was steaming past a huge old sugar refinery – can't be many of those with their own on-site church – when my non-navigational phone buzzed in a rear pocket. I took it out and read it on the move. 'I am sorry I cannot help better.' It was the bike-shop guy. A follow-up pinged in at once. 'Good travel to the end of your return.' It took me a while to get it: from lap to tour to revolution, 'vuelta' had many different translations, and that was another.

Fuck sakes. In a final act of selfish malevolence, this apologetic, conciliatory monster had siphoned away all my hate-fuel. I swiped through Komoot's screens: my AVS had risen to 21.9, and there were 50 kilometres to go. Feebly unimpressive as my target might be, I was hell-bent on hitting it, and success now depended on my own internal resources. At reckless speed I flung open the bar-bag, hauled out two custard-filled pastries and crammed them both into my mouth. Make way, Castile. Make way for an old man on a shit mission.

I was set fair at 22.6 when my road veered off to join a motorway, leaving me on an access path alongside that decayed in miserable stages to pallid gravel and loose stone. I had very foolishly neglected to reprogram this leg as a road ride, and a panicky scroll through the route told me I'd gone much too far to turn back. There was nothing else for it: I went all in, the back wheel spinning and bucking, the front getting some big speedway energy, throwing up dust as it slid sideways through the bends. Now hemmed in by flesh-slashing bamboo, the trail went on and on, and I felt my reserves ebbing away: riding a road bike on gravel at speed demands a level of concentration and physicality that will swiftly exhaust you from the scalp down. Scrabbling perilously for sustenance, I snatched out another pastry, then hit a big stone and squeezed its hot custard through my bunched fingers.

The bamboo parted; the gravel turned to hard-baked mud and plumb-lined straight through an eternity of maize. This was better. Then it wasn't. Sprinklers were at work, bizarre many-headed hydra-hydrants that whiplashed crazily above me, spewing water ten ways at once. My wheels sank into beige slurry and I took faceful after faceful of musty fluid. After a ridiculous, filthy half-hour, La Berrendero and I finally hit tarmac, slathered in crap and erratic. I grabbed a fistful of jersey and wiped the screen: my AVS had dropped to 22.5, and Valladolid was only 11 kilometres off.

Well, what do you want me to say? Probably not this: I did it. In fact, I pissed all over it. I hammered over a few old stone bridges then flew into the city up a boulevard bike lane, jumping every red light and giving the early-evening traffic no quarter. At 18.50 p.m. I shrieked to a halt halfway up the four-lane Paseo Isabel la Catolica and stopped the clock with a triumphant stab of my right thumb. On 5 July 1941, having broken away from a lead group of ten just outside Valladolid, Julián Berrendero crossed the line here to win his second stage of the race, by thirty seconds. His average speed over 301 kilometres: 22.73kmh. Mine: 22.9. Yes, it had taken me two days, on better roads and with better machinery, but for the first time – the very first time – I felt I had done justice to the man, and to his silver bicycle.

In weary celebration, I booked myself into a showpiece hotel right beside the cathedral, stopping round the corner to brush the worst of the mud off my legs and my bike. My first-floor room had a little balcony overlooking the cathedral's majestic white flanks: in due course, a stream of worshippers and promenaders would be gazing up at – or in two cases loudly deriding – a grubby wet man in his pants, hanging out his grubby wet laundry.

It was a warm and convivial evening, as almost every one of them had been. I dragged my *alpargatas* across a massive tilting square lined with big old churches, an encroaching tide of fully occupied bar tables spilling out across the grey paving. Families and friends of all ages, and nary a foreigner in sight: I realised that the Spain I'd experienced was much the same as the one my grandparents did when they took a caravan round Iberia in the 1950s, only with less fascism.

I finally found an empty seat outside a Greek restaurant just off the square. Over a double souvlaki and chips, I ran through my usual local homework, scrolling down the relevant section of lockdown-research notes. There was much more material now that I'd left Galicia, and none of it was nice. I had rarely viewed a place through kinder eyes following this procedure, and Valladolid looked a little less lovely when I walked back to the hotel. This was no less than the birthplace of Falangism, the city where Primo de Rivera had formed his party in 1931; five years later, it was here that Franco's uprising first succeeded. The railway workers who mounted the only serious resistance were herded into a tram shed and shot; by December 1936, 3,000 citizens had been killed. Most were executed at a sports field near the edge of the city, before large, jeering crowds kept refreshed by coffee and snack stalls. When Giles Tremlett researched *Ghosts of Spain* in 2007, a retired Valladolid butcher was still boasting of all the reds he'd murdered with a bullfighting dagger. There was a predictable symmetry to the 1941 *parcours*: the Vuelta's first stage had ended in Salamanca, Franco's wartime headquarters, and its last would start in the city they called 'the capital of the coup'.

I was in my very lovely bed when Gerardo's reply pinged in. Throughout the ride I had kept him up to speed with my progress, and now, with the end in sight, I'd sent a text seeking to arrange a tragic last appointment: handing over La Berrendero at Biketown in Madrid. Gerardo told me that he was away on holiday, but that the shop would be open until noon on Saturday, then closed until Monday. OK, I thought, before realising it wasn't. Tomorrow would be Friday, and I'd booked a flight home on Sunday. If I took my usual two days to ride the last stage, getting to Madrid by noon on the second of them would mean a pre-dawn start.

I mean, I could have done that. Of course I could. The 1941 boys were often on the road by 6 a.m. But as I lay there, still riding dangerously high on my Stage 20 performance – an almost literally pedestrian achievement, if truth be told – I made a sudden, reckless pledge. The last stage was 198 kilometres, and I would do it in a day.

CHAPTER 27

Moore descends
and swells.

How very strange it had felt as I pulled my kit off the balcony washing line and gathered up my possessions. It was absurd to imagine that my life would soon no longer revolve around these objects and their associated rituals. A day that didn't begin with an arse full of Savlon and didn't end with a bidet full of bidons – what on earth must such a day be like? For the first half of my journey, every evening had felt like a full stop, the end of the road. But I had now built up a relentless momentum, each day in the saddle seamlessly connected to the next by an overnight ellipse. My brain simply could not accommodate the possibility that this groundhog ride would ever finish. It had become what I did. It had become what I was.

Alone in the breakfast room, I tried to put my imminent, crowning task in perspective. On the one hand, I had only ever ridden further than 198 kilometres in a day on a single previous occasion – and that was twenty years before, when I covered the longest stage of the 2000 Tour de France in as few as fifteen hours. But on the other, I was in the fricking zone. After six weeks I had every core skill down to a fine art: the packing, the laundry, the fungal control, even bits of the bicycle riding. I had finally mastered the little tap-dance flick that swung the toe clips into position on the move. USB cables went into their chargers the right way up first time, every time. I could glance at any foodstuff and – as I did now – make an instant, accurate assessment of its kilometric value. These two *tortilla* wedges were good for twenty each; ten a piece for the ham-and-cheese croissant on my plate and the other two down my jersey.

On balance I was feeling pretty punchy about the challenge ahead until, after necking a quadruple espresso, I reprogrammed Komoot for the final time. A great long slice of Stage 21 had been annexed by a motorway, and the shortest tarmac-based detour added a further 29 kilometres to an already exorbitant challenge. And there was more. When I zoomed in on the big spike that leaped up from the otherwise benign route profile, I discovered there was a reason why the Navacerrada had a bit of a rep, why even the useless bike guy in Zamora had puffed out his cheeks when I mentioned it: at 1,880 metres, this vast bastard was hugely higher than anything I'd ridden up yet. The end suddenly seemed much less nigh. I put my phone down on the table, sighed softly, then raised my wan gaze to the overhead telly. With a wink, the weatherman delivered the *coup de grâce*: I'd be riding into the wind all day.

'Madrid? With *bici*? Today?'

The same sympathetic receptionist who had graciously welcomed a man and his filthy bike into her elegant realm the night before now looked at me with anxious eyes. I hadn't revealed my intended destination to show off, at least not entirely: it was more that by sharing it, I would saddle myself with a moral imperative not to throw the towel in halfway. Segovia, at the foot of the Navacerrada, seemed dangerously appealing in that regard.

'Please, it's too much.'

I essayed a flinty gaze and let out a brisk, manful sniff, both compromised by being transmitted above or through a floral facemask. 'Bring it on,' I said, though my tone suggested a preference for taking it far, far away. Then I bullied the helmet over the eccentric contours of my skull, and heaved La Berrendero out through the automatic doors into a blinding sun.

Whoever laid out Valladolid's bike lanes was a road-race fan: they were the first I've ever ridden down with a drop-bar silhouette painted on them. Duly inspired, I went hard at it, recording FCT well before I broached the city limits. It was already gone 9 a.m., hardly the dawn start my outrageous itinerary demanded: this stage would now be a marathon and a sprint.

With the houses behind me, I crested a low brow, felt the wind in my face and looked out across a colossal forest of globular stone pines that would be my home for an extremely long time. Beyond it, high on the horizon, rose a hazy rank of mountains. The Navacerrada, I thought, and narrowed my eyes. But then I realised it couldn't possibly be, unless I had developed the ability to see for 100 miles. A hundred miles! And plenty more where they came from on the other side of the mountain, before the finish in Madrid. What a bewildering scale this whole day was laid out on. After an hour on the road I still had 197 kilometres before me.

I pushed hard through the parallel pines for hours, happy to trade mind-numbing tedium for protection from the sun and the headwind. But as ever, the absence of distracting stimuli soon encouraged all manner of latent ailments to assert themselves. For almost the first time, my heroic arse began to complain quite loudly, and the pedals started digging into my soles like steel Toblerones. And though the freewheel held firm, the front-wheel shimmy was now a constant companion above 25kmh, top gear had left the building, and I'd detected a very slight rough spot in every pedal revolution, a truly vexatious micro-niggle, like a grain of sand in a mouthful of food.

At length, civilisation returned in its most durable Spanish form: silent, far-flung gatherings of ancient little homes and ancient little people. In one of the larger examples, I shrieked to a halt by the San Miguel parasols and rushed inside to refuel: *agua grande*, *café con leche* and 40 kilometres' worth of bread and chorizo. Heading round the town's farewell *glorieta* I was stopped at a police roadblock.

'*Caballero! A dónde vas?*'

'*A Madrid*,' I panted, through a mouthful of bocadillo. '*Directo a Madrid*.' They waved me through. One gave a cheery salute.

The pines pulled back and I rode out into a plain of leather. Ruined Moorish castles looked down from distant bald hilltops; disconsolate, croaky squeals leaked out from scattered pig sheds. My staple backdrop for so many long, hot days, served as ever under a vast blue sky. Sustaining morale had been a perennial challenge across the barren infinities: you always felt you were going nowhere, slowly. This was not the day for such defeatism, so to keep my dander up I adapted a few popular classics to elucidate my most recent physical discomforts, and roared them at the russet emptiness. 'Balls on fire, rolling down the road!' I bellowed raggedly. 'Just notify my next of kin, these balls shall explode!'

Grain fields and sunflowers gradually annexed the roadsides, then, just before 4 p.m., a cathedral tower wobbled up from the Van Gogh prairie. On any previous afternoon I'd have called it a day at Segovia, and to avoid this temptation I engaged tunnel vision and rode straight through it, stopping at a petrol station on the city's southernmost *glorieta* for a splash-and-dash can of Relentless and a trio of Snickers.

There, rearing up through the heat haze behind a road sign for Madrid, stood my last and mightiest puntable crest. *!No Pasaran!* They shall not pass: the stirring Republican slogan that had failed to keep Franco at bay seemed to shout down at me from the top of those misted eminences. With 125 kilometres gone and a further 100 to go, the road up the Navacerrada would be a journey deep into uncharted stamina, to a realm beyond even the sweariest day-end shower mumbles.

Pedalling up to the mountain's pine-covered, steamingly resinous lower slopes, I girded my hot, sore loins with a favourite anecdote that – in some indirect and frankly nonsensical fashion – seemed to cut this awful bastard down to size. In the penultimate stage of the 2003 Vuelta, the notoriously intemperate *directeur sportif* Manolo Saiz was driving up the Navacerrada behind a TV camera motorbike, when he decided its pilot had been helping to pace a rival team. With an angry flick of his steering wheel Saiz forced the bike off the road, then – as the camera rolled, beaming the encounter live into several million Spanish homes – let out a truly exceptional stream of unhinged invective. 'I shit on your mother! I shit on God! I shit on the fucking Virgin! Yes, go on, keep recording. Let everyone know that I'm going to kill you and cut you into little pieces!' He was thrown off the race in the morning. (Five years earlier, Saiz withdrew his team from the Tour de France with similar elan, telling reporters: 'I have stuck my finger up the Tour's arse.')

Anyway, running through Manolo's imaginative way with words duly bought me a bit of time, maybe three minutes of comic distraction as the tarmac pitched up and the spindly red trunks closed in. In fact, I almost felt inspired to jump off my bike and disparage the dozens of motorcyclists who were taking their ease outside a bar in the final village, cheeks puffed out and limbs splayed in weary triumph after riding up and over from Madrid. 'Oh, you poor things! Did you have to twist your little zoom-zoom handles all the way round?'

Altitude was counted out in roadside markers; I felt a surge of excitement when the first informed me I was already at 1,100 metres, though most of it dribbled away after I zoomed in on Komoot's stage profile and noted that Segovia sat just below 900 metres. In the interests of self-confidence I stretched two fingers across the screen and broadened the horrendous stalagmite I was riding up into a gently pitched little bump. A molehill out of a mountain. It looked much better.

Just after 1,200 metres I replenished my bidons at a roadside fountain and swapped helmet for old white cap. My gaze dropped to the tarmac, and surveying my shadow from the neck up I understood that I'd been away for a very long time: big wispy flaps of hair sprung out from either side of the cap, like the mad head feathers of a rockhopper penguin. At 1,300 metres, with the abandon of a man who's just realised he no longer has to eke out his mobile data allowance, I fired up Spotify on the handlebar phone and got some empathetic tunes going: The Stranglers when I stood up in the saddle, the *Enigma Variations* when I slumped back down. I had three tubular custard pastries festering in the sweat-lodge bar-bag, and at 1,400 metres I disconsolately retrieved these pus-filled corpse fingers and prodded them between protesting lips.

The hairpins kicked in hard just before 1,500 metres, ramp after rearing ramp that could only be conquered with a full-beans run-up. No small ask when you're down to your last bean on a 13 per cent gradient. A lorry was huffing and puffing right up my arse; when I glanced down from the upper reaches of the worst switchback, I saw a long queue of vehicles behind it. Please go away, I thought. This wasn't how I wanted Spain to remember me: dying on my last mountain with a tinny Elgar requiem. After 1,600 metres the road straightened out and everyone filed patiently past; I killed Spotify and through red and heavy eyes saw faces of all ages pressed up against windows, appraising me with keen interest and no little amusement, as if the occupants were taking bets on my success or survival.

At 1,700 metres, with my front wheel starting to twitch and wobble, I took a weary mouthful of warm bidon and failed to down it between rasping breaths. With a gurgling choke it all spewed out. When I'd regained a tiny scrap of composure I looked down and saw my phone liberally spattered in fluid; I swept an unsteady glove across it and somehow contrived to both blacken the screen and resurrect Spotify. A single-note riff blared out as I pawed uselessly at the wet glass, followed by two strident female voices: 'My my! At Waterloo Napoleon did surrender.'

Agnetha and Anni-Frid were still at it when a clutch of roofs appeared, astride a tarmac brow. There it was: the last brown sign with a number on it I would pass on this trip, and the biggest number of all. 'PUERTO DE NAVACERRADA 1880m.' I clambered off La Berrendero rather messily by the ski-station restaurant, squeezed in my last energy gel and finally managed to dry the phone into silence. Far, far below, the plains beyond Segovia spread away into a fuzzy forever. I had killed the Navacerrada, cut it into little pieces and shat on its mother. At least I'd certainly have liked to. Still, I hadn't got off to push, hadn't surrendered, hadn't met my destiny in quite a similar way.

The 1941 peloton reached Segovia at 4 p.m., pleasingly the same time as I had, before throwing itself up the Navacerrada with some gusto. Jools had effectively killed off the race for overall victory with the cheeky thirty seconds he bagged on the run in to Valladolid: Trueba was still only a minute and bits behind, but as the beta male to JB's alpha, 'little Fermín' would never have dared try it on, least of all on a stage that ended in Berrendero's home city. There was, in any case, a clear quid pro quo. The two riders shared the lead in the mountains competition, but in that contest too there was only ever going to be one winner.

The reporter from the *Hoja Oficial del Lunes* was touchingly taken in by the battle between the pair after they broke away together up the Navacerrada: 'In the last metres there is a truly formidable fight, in which Trueba passes the summit line with just half a wheel advantage over Berrendero, securing the mountains prize amid great drama.' But Carlos Pardo knew the score. 'Fermín crossed the last scoring col first and so took the Grand Prix of the Mountains, but in truth he was carried up the Navacerrada on his teammate's wings: instead of a true duel between Berrendero and Trueba, we saw a plan played out by team tactics.'

There were 69 kilometres to go; it was 5.45. Truly, madly, deeply grateful that the only way was down, I shakily remounted, light of head and heavy of leg. Cap off; helmet on. Vamos, Hooolián! Vamos, La Berrrrrenderrrrro! The road fell sharply away and one last huge, hot plateau opened up beneath me. After all this time, the lonesome immensity of these desiccated landscapes still freaked me out, yet as I gazed down I knew I would miss them terribly when they were gone, when I was back home in Europe's largest city, with the North Circular Road rushing past the end of my street.

Going up mountains had always been my challenge, and mine alone; on the descents, it was all about the bike. With the first sharp bend upon me I pulled the levers and at once felt the front wheel oscillate violently. The harder I braked, the worse it got; I juddered through the apex like a human tuning fork. There was a stridently terminal feel to this process, a sense that next time the whole bike would wobble itself to destruction. After some of the hairiest hairpins of my life, I realised my only hope was to pull the rear lever hard in right down the mountain, straights and all. At first this was no more than a frustration; but quite soon, just after a great parade of tall, thin buildings took murky shape ahead and below, my right fist began to fail.

A sign to Alpedrete flashed past: the town I'd spent my first night in, around twenty-nine years previously. Recall of that horrible debut impressed upon me an unwelcome truth. Although the way from here to Madrid was predominantly downhill, it was far from exclusively so, and this time I was doing it with 200 kilometres in my legs. Sure enough, I soon found myself back in deep and undulating countryside; the requirement to pedal, and pedal hard, quickly spooned up the last dregs of my physical and mental faculties. When the road swooped down to the first big *glorieta*, my right hand did what it could to scrub off speed, while my left forearm braced itself across the top of the bars. I have no idea what this appendage thought it was playing at, but the resultant imbalance very nearly brought me to grief.

The traffic steadily thickened around me. Big-city motorists are always far more selfish and intolerant than their provincial cousins, and I was in no fit state to mix it with all the pusher-inners and edger-outers. My feet felt like toeless stumps, my right hand had shut up shop, and by stages my whole trunk locked itself in a weird hunch. The deathly cold sweats of extreme calorific deficit trickled down my temples. I drained the big bidon and felt it slip from my feeble fingers en route back to its cage. That's El Gordo for you, always the joker. He did it again a mile up the road.

Quite soon I was little more than a detached observer. Oh, here comes a deeply inset drain cover. But that's going to hurt when I fail to take any evasive action. Why, yes – yes it did. And look at all this sand piled up in the gutter! I really shouldn't be riding straight through it. Was that a red light? I suppose it must have been, what with all these honking cars shooting about. At one point, riding up a central-reservation bike lane, I crashed straight through a knee-high hedge rather than make any attempt to negotiate an onerous dog-leg crossing.

The sun was now setting behind me; I lethargically pursued my 50-foot shadow towards the glinting glass towers of Madrid. Half-remembered scenes from my outward ride passed by in a dim blur: Las Rozas, Majadahonda, places whose significance in Civil War history and the career of a Madrileño cycling legend now rang only a dull and distant bell.

Back in my garden all those months ago, I had indulged myself with a little freelance addition to Stage 21's endgame: a detour up to the Parque del Oeste, a big swathe of urban green where most local bike races finished back then. It was here in 1935 that JB won the Castile Championship, despite an ugly fall on the Nava-cerrada that made a horrible mess of his left knee. His parents had come to watch him together for the first time, still nursing a deep scepticism about the plausibility of a career in cycling. All that evaporated at the finish line, in a scene Jools describes with rare and affecting fondness. 'When my mother hugged me, there were tears in her eyes. I heard my father shout, with the full strength of his lungs, "That's my son! That's my son!"' There's a sweet little photograph of the trio in his book, proud parents standing either side of their boy on his bike, old arms round young shoulders. His nut-brown dad is in his saggy Sunday best; his tiny mum looks about ninety-four.

It was quite the tipping point. His father became JB's biggest fan, and 'Señor Martín' was soon a regular sight at the finish line, toting an enormous wineskin with the family name emblazoned on it. 'Whenever I won, my excitable and generous father would offer the wineskin to all and sundry; more than once I received this treasured prize from his hands.' There's a photo of that scene in *Mis Glorias y Memorias*, too: Señor Martín, a gregarious, treble-chinned old bloke in a beret with a big bag of booze, seems an improbable genetic source of his son's furious intensity.

It's the last picture in the book. On the penultimate stage of the 1948 Vuelta, JB – sixth overall and set fair to improve – was leading the race into Leon when one of the official motorcyclists rode up alongside.

'Have you heard the news?' he shouted.

'What news?'

'Your father's dead.'

It was certainly a less sensitive age. Utterly devastated, Berrendero quit the race and rushed back to Madrid. 'I had left my father in perfect health, and cried uncontrollably at this shocking tragedy. He had become my most passionate supporter. My morale was completely shattered. That would be my last Tour of Spain, and what a terrible end.' Of the seven Vueltas he entered – first twice, second twice, and two mountain prizes – this was the only one he didn't finish. Indeed, it was the first time he'd ever abandoned any race. Three weeks later, fulfilling a contractual obligation under duress, he rode the Tour of Portugal, finished fifth, and at the age of thirty-six hung up his handlebars. That, at least, is how his career ends in *Mis Glorias y Memorias*, published at the start of 1949.

How dearly I had wished to honour all these poignant remembrances, here on the long, green avenue where JB's censorious, bike-hiding parents so joyfully threw their lot in with him. But as I weaved ashenly up the Paseo de Camoens, finished off by a short, sharp climb up to it from a river I don't even remember crossing, my head had been emptied of all thought. All those hours before, hammering out of Valladolid, it had felt as if the heroic import of my mission must be screamingly apparent, as if I was exuding a sparkly glow, like some powered-up Super Mario, which would compel motorists to afford me a wide and respectful berth and salute in awe as I shot past. Now I felt invisible, hollowed out and worn away into nothing. My eyes dully registered Franco's scabby victory arch, sickly yellow in the dying sun. Just beyond it, a digital sign by a bus shelter told me it was 20.55, and 35 degrees.

I hadn't realised how steep Madrid was on day one, or possibly my factory-fresh legs just hadn't noticed. No getting away from it now. The way up through University City was pitiless, a mini Montjuïc that wound steeply between deserted faculties on a road full of leaves. Just past 7 p.m. on 6 July 1941, four riders steamed up this hill – straight through the 'glorious ruins' that *El Mundo Deportivo* had described on Stage 1 – and into the Estadio Metropolitano, where a packed crowd had been waiting for three hours.

Vicente Carretero and José Jabardo had caught JB and Trueba on the Navacerrada descent; Carretero would cross the line first, after a one-lap sprint round the stadium track. Just under half an hour later, The Swiss Watch came in, sixteenth and last. Overall he was a full six hours down on Berrendero, but despite his worst efforts, TSW would tragically be denied the *lanterne rouge*: Martín Santos sat fifty minutes further back, in an upside-down class of his own.

As the local hero, Berrendero would have been cheered to the rafters as he rounded the stadium; Señor Martín, waiting with his wineskin, was in for a busy time. But JB's account of his victorious homecoming is beyond muted. In place of bouquets and tears, all we get is a bluntly cynical audit of success. 'So the III Tour of Spain ended with a great and overwhelming victory for our coalition. I won the overall classification. Trueba was "King of the Mountains" and second in the GC. Delio won twelve stages and was fourth overall. Martín won a stage and placed seventh.'

He couldn't celebrate, because he couldn't stop thinking of the what-ifs. What if it had been the Tour de France; what if he hadn't just sacrificed his sporting prime in a prison camp. 'Had this collaborative triumph taken place in the Tour, we could have lived very nicely on our winnings for eight or ten years. The money we earned here was barely enough for one.' (The official tally of prize cash, 'with all fines deducted', revealed that JB won the equivalent of around £12,000 in today's money; The Swiss Watch went home with £650.) A bit of a moot point, mind you: if this Vuelta had been a Tour, he knew it would have ended in tears. 'Despite the triumph, my powers were clearly diminished. If, after my enforced 18-month retirement, I'd had to race the Tour instead of the Vuelta, it would have been a humiliating disaster.'

Nor could Carlos Pardo muster much passion for JB's victory. 'Berrendero's triumph is deserved,' he writes, baldly. 'He was the most complete rider in the race.' His final report makes grim reading, in truth: it is little more than a torrent of shit-eating regime worship. 'The Ministry of Education and Leisure can be given the highest praise for overcoming every difficulty in making this event a beautiful success. Everything else – the classifications, the racing incidents, all of it – must take second place to their achievement. The abiding memory is of a wonderful tour that united the symbols of Falangism and sporting endeavour, bringing every Spanish region together in a true display of fraternity and patriotism that honours those who organised it.' It could have been written by General Moscardó himself. Maybe it was.

The Estadio Metropolitano was demolished in the 1960s to make way for a university expansion and several institutional buildings. I had pinpointed its site as the Calle Beatriz de Bobadilla, a thoroughfare that Komoot now steered me onto. Even in my diminished state I could see this was no place for a chequered flag, a drab parade of twelve-floor concrete blocks on either side of a broad avenue where cars were parked in neat diagonal ranks. There wasn't a soul in sight. A medical centre; the headquarters of the Nuclear Safety Council; a sliver of park behind locked gates. With a final rending shriek of brakes I came to a halt by the park railings, and jabbed 'Finish and save' for the last time. Komoot's verdict shone bright in the gloaming. 'What a tour!' It was 9.17 p.m.: I'd ridden 225 kilometres in a shade under eleven hours, 4,534 kilometres in exactly six weeks. I leaned La Berrendero on the railings, then sat down against them and raised two frail arms. A cat darted past my feet and stopped to stare at me from under a small hedge. 'Moore descends and swells,' I told it.

Madrid, lightly subdued when I'd left it, was now a doornail-dead ghost town. I steered the unlit La Berrendero down dark and empty streets, reanimated by three cans of Fanta purchased at the first open shop I passed. The first open hotel was a soulless, guestless many-floored block manned by a dead-eyed receptionist, who instead of bowing before me and my bike in unworthy reverence shooed the two of us off to the lift with an appalling flick of the wrist. 'Go, take *bici* to room.' So be it. One last bicycle necklace, on this our farewell evening.

All those bacchanalian finish-line celebrations I'd concocted to help me through the bad times had lost their lustre; in truth, as I lay flat out on the bed, I could barely remember what they'd been. Alcohol seemed like a terrible idea, not least because I had absolutely no interest in eating, lost in a land way beyond hunger. It had gone eleven, and with a pallid half-smile I acknowledged the irony: this was the first time I could have dined out on Spanish time. In the voice recordings I made that evening I sound tiny and broken and absolutely pitiful, like Simba trying to rouse his dead father.

In weary reflex I reached for my phone to check the forecast, then realised there was no need. Weather, executive producer of forty-two dawn-to-dusk sagas, had now gone back to its day job, just a peripheral influence on gardening and picnics. At vacant length, I stumbled into the shower, looking down at my numb feet and wondering when I would next clog a plughole with bits of road and countryside. And I still feel sorry for the faithful old retainers I didn't say a proper farewell to that night, acknowledging that their noble work was done. The clothes pegs and drying line, abruptly redundant, left alone in their little bags. Edward Pickle-hands, flung into the saddlebag and forgotten. After one hell of a farewell gig, I'd broken up the band. Though I might as well tell you now that Stubby and El Gordo have watched over me throughout the writing process, sat there on top of my monitor, chipping in with the odd synonym for heat or nausea.

Ride, eat, sleep: my life had become a wanky wall-art slogan. I'd got into a groove, which through endless repetition had worn down into a rut; then, mile by mile and day by day, into a hole that now seemed too deep to climb out of. I didn't mind at all. It was so cosy, down in the only home I now knew. How fitting that La Berrendero should be here in my hole tonight, so to speak, up against the wardrobe, filthy but fetching in the soft glow of the bedside light. What a trooper. Forty-five and still up for anything. A front-wheel shimmy and a freewheel wobble: mere footnotes in a rapturous end-of-tour report. I was in particular awe of all those Campagnolo components, which had performed with a doughty resilience not typically expected from pretty Italian machinery. Not once had I adjusted the gears or brakes, even though I definitely should have. The spoke key and chain-link remover, in heavy rotation on my last two rides, had never come out to play. Over 4,534 kilometres, not a single bolt or screw had worked loose. My maintenance schedule in full: twenty drops of oil.

No, La Berrendero hadn't let me down. But I had let her down. A Campagnolo-stamped pedal cap had vanished. One of the decorative B-for-Berrendero handlebar plugs was gaffer-taped in place, having shed its retaining clips on some Navarran roadside. The right-hand toe strap hung by a thread. But worse than any of this, much worse, was a mutilation so deeply shameful that I have chosen not to confess it until now, though the scars had been horribly apparent for weeks. It was the reason I took solace in the sprinkler-wrought Valladolid mud that spattered La Berrendero's silver frame so liberally. Because beneath that mud, something terrible was happening.

In the form of his surname, or its initial, Julián Berrendero was celebrated eleven times on this bicycle. Or he had been when I left Biketown. Since then, the desert heat, the mountain mists of Cantabria and Galicia and my own clumsy feet and hands had conspired to deface this great name. To scuff, buff and otherwise adulterate its bright-yellow component letters, so that other, less great names were now celebrated underneath all that mud, people like BERRI and DERC and ENDER. Not one of the nine full surnames had survived intact. Every time I carried La Berrendero into a lift or up a staircase, tiny flakes of yellow decal would come off on my gloves. Each clumsy clamber on or off the bike left a similar legacy on my shoes.

In the course of my ride around his homeland, I had met only one man to whom the name Julián Berrendero meant anything. This great champion was fading from the nation's consciousness, and as I lay there, still wired on adrenalin and residual stimulants, I was possessed of a melodramatic conviction that I had, quite literally, just erased him for good.

CHAPTER 28

Julián Berrendero's 1948 retirement didn't last long. News that the Spanish were being invited to the 1949 Tour de France after an eleven-year absence stirred a comeback clamour: Federico Ezquerra had hung up his wheels in 1943, a year after Mariano Cañardo, making Jools the only plausible representative with any Tour experience. At thirty-seven he knew it would be tough – even Fermín Trueba, two years his junior, had long since retired – but the temptation of one last Tour proved too hard to resist. When the six-strong Spanish team was announced, Berrendero topped the list as its leader.

Preparations got off to a reasonable start when JB finished a solid eighteenth in the Dauphiné-Libéré, then as now the Tour's traditional warm-up. But when the peloton rolled out of Paris three weeks later, Berrendero's worst fears were swiftly realised. On the first day of his own first Tour, the insane pace and relentless attacks had left him shell-shocked; thirteen years later, he listened as a new generation of Spanish cyclists cried themselves to sleep. 'We had never been in a race like that, with more than 100 riders,' said Bernardo Ruiz. 'Back home you had a starting peloton of 30 at most.' Even five years on, there were only twenty-three professional cyclists in Spain. Most of them still rode to races, Ruiz revealed, covering 'seven or eight hundred kilometres at a time' because they couldn't afford the train.

The team was a man down after Stage 1, when Bernardo Capo, a podium finisher in the 1948 Vuelta, trailed in outside the time limit. Berrendero had wheezed over the line 114th out of 120, and things would barely improve: his best finish in the next three stages was 79th. No teammate fared much better.

In their defence, the Spanish had rubbish bikes and rubbish support. The riders had been asked to pay for all their own expenses. Their DS was stone deaf. The 75kg of sugar that the Spanish Cycling Federation had supplied to help keep them going mysteriously vanished: rationing was then ongoing throughout Europe, and it's presumed the team management flogged it to black marketeers. And of course, a lot of their rivals were now on amphetamines – this was the Tour that Fausto Coppi, a big fan of 'la bomba', would win by a country mile.

Stage 5 of the 1949 Tour, 283 kilometres of gently rolling hills from Rouen to St Malo, would go down as a day of shame for Spanish cycling. When Dalmacio Langarica's gears broke after just 80 kilometres, his teammates dutifully waited with him. But the deaf DS at the team-car wheel didn't pick up on the urgency, and an excruciating thirty-eight minutes elapsed before he tootled up to his stricken charges. Berrendero and three others abandoned on the spot; the final Spaniard would retire the following morning.

Being let back into the world's largest annual sporting event had been a real coup for Franco, and he had even persuaded the Tour organisers to route a stage through Spain – a huge step in the push to bring his pariah nation in from the cold. Now there wouldn't be a single Spanish rider left when the race came through San Sebastián. For a regime that had trumpeted its return to the Tour as an international showcase for Francoist virtues, the humiliation was too much to bear.

The Spanish press ripped into the riders for their perceived lack of grit and gumption. 'Dwarves of the road' was amongst the many withering headlines. 'These men are not cyclists!' thundered *Marca*. 'How can you give that name to slackers who go slower than a goods train, indeed barely above walking pace?' Berrendero, who prided himself on his no-surrender determination – defined himself by it, in truth – must have died a thousand deaths reading the coverage. An abandonment, just the second of his career, and in the biggest race on earth. And once more he stood accused of betraying his nation.

After their return to Spain, the Tour team was summoned by sports minister General Moscardó – yes, that General Moscardó, who'd ordered his own son to die like a man at the 1936 siege of the Alcázar, then overseen several hundred retaliatory murders. 'He said only two sentences,' recalled Berrendero many years later. "'If you were too slow, then you must have been tired. So take a year off to recover.'" The whole team had their racing licences revoked for twelve months; at Berrendero's age, that was that. The regime that had stolen his sporting prime would also bring an extraordinary career to a degrading end.

This sorry fate, with which I reacquainted myself over two successive breakfasts at a café by the hotel, sat heavily upon me as I steered La Berrendero through the bright and silent bank-holiday streets of Chamberí. For our final journey I'd stripped the bike of its bags and racks, leaving them back in the hotel room along with my unwashed kit. *Alpargatas* in the toe straps; Merkels sliding about on the saddle. I hit the Calle General Álvarez de Castro and coasted to a halt on the little *glorieta* at its conclusion.

A familiar scene spread out around me, one I had surveyed so many times through Google Street View's all-seeing eye. A circle of stolid seven-floor apartment blocks with small shops and café-bars on the ground floor, arranged around a neatly tended miniature park that filled the *glorieta*'s hub. On screen, and now in the sunny real world, it looked like a place where respectable old people lived quiet and blameless lives. But only one thing had drawn me here for so many virtual visits, and it had vanished. There was the bar that Rodrigo's dad had sat outside with Berrendero, right next to his shop. So where had the shop gone?

I was aware, from my own research and Gerardo's first email, that Bicicletas Berrendero – bequeathed by JB to the nephew who had run it for him since the late Seventies – had closed its doors for the last time a few months before I left. A mothballed website still carried a farewell message about the owner's retirement and a liquidation sale. But sad as this failure was, it also seemed frankly overdue. Along with the shop, nephew Juan appeared to have inherited the full set of unfortunate Berrendero character traits. None were a good fit with the customer-service environment, as the extraordinary parade of one-star Google reviews confirmed.

'Terrible experience! The proprietor seemed angry with me for some reason. I went in for a spare part and he told me my bike was a "Neanderthal piece of shit".'

'They make you feel like they are doing you a favour. I was served by a guy in his 40s who almost kicked me out of the shop. Then an older man came up and he was even worse.'

'Rude and arrogant. It is sad that a shop with so many years of supposed experience should treat its customers with such contempt and superiority.'

'I dealt with a very unkind gentleman, or rather an unpleasant one, who instead of treating his customer in a correct and empathetic manner had a tone of voice that suggested I was bothering him, and that he was also offended by my ignorance.'

'I went in to ask about some bicycle spoke keys, and it seems I must have entered with a balaclava and a gun, because the treatment they gave me was criminal. I do not understand how a business that treats its customers this way can survive. I thought that the previous reviews must be multiple misunderstandings, but I can assure you that they are totally truthful and precise.'

Reading these heavily modified my regret at being denied an over-the-counter audience with an actual Berrendero. As an ignorant Englishman I would surely have incurred the wrath of Juan, particularly after turning up with a Neanderthal piece of shit, even if it had bits of his name on it. But my sorrow endured, because on Street View, Bicicletas Berrendero lived on in spirit: a blue awning with that fabled name across it in bold yellow capitals, and a little plaque set into the wall by the shop's front door, bearing the bike-wheel coat of arms that still decorated my head tube, in diminished form. Now there was nothing.

It was a while before I spotted shadowy grey outlines on the wall, one tracing the outline of an absent awning, the other a ghostly silhouette of a bike-wheel crest. So there it was: the shop door that JB had stood outside in so many newspaper photos, the door my bike had been wheeled out through, now glazed with frosted glass, as was the former shop window alongside. The only signage was a sticker warning of video surveillance. Following on from my decal calamity, it seemed as if the name Berrendero was being systematically scrubbed from the record. I felt my eyes prickle.

Two slightly nervous old dears in facemasks emerged from the door of the neighbouring apartments.

'Berrendero?' I asked, tilting my head at the frosted glass.

'*Quita la casa*,' mumbled one as they walked past without stopping. Left the building, I thought. Checked out. But when I did an online translation, the top match was 'repossessed'.

Five years after his ignominious retirement, and an effective second *depuración*, Berrendero was returned to the official cycling fold. In the run-up to the 1954 Tour, he accepted an offer from the Spanish federation to serve as national *directeur sportif*. 'Good luck to Berrendero,' said *El Mundo Deportivo*. 'As the most complete Spanish cyclist of all time, he deserves this.' But, as whoever wrote those words would surely have been aware, it is difficult to imagine anyone more abysmally ill-suited to a role in team management than old Loney McLonewolf. JB himself would later admit he'd detested the job: 'I never feel comfortable in command. I got bored and irritated. Can you believe I had riders asking to have their bikes cleaned? In my day you cleaned your own bike. And you were your own DS.' Perhaps, in the circumstances, he simply felt unable to turn the authorities down.

It wasn't entirely disastrous: Federico Bahamontes would win the King of the Mountains prize at his first attempt, just as his boss had done eighteen years before. But the Spanish riders didn't have many kind words for Berrendero. Some claimed that his most decisive contribution was removing all the cherries from their table at the presentation dinner, in the obscure conviction they might catch dysentery from them. Bahamontes remembered leading the race up a col on a bike with several bust spokes, and stopping at the top to wait for a new wheel. By the time JB showed up in the team car, his star rider had lost an enormous fourteen-minute advantage over the field. 'I was furious with him,' said Bahamontes.

A part of me wonders if some kind of subconscious sabotage was at work. JB had a blanket disregard for the new generation that echoed the low opinion he'd nurtured for his own contemporaries. I just cannot see him wanting Bahamontes to do better than he had himself. 'Would you think badly of me if I said Bahamontes had the good fortune to be riding in an era without many great climbers?' he told an interviewer some years later. 'Don't ask me any more about him, I don't want to cause offence.' The only cyclist Berrendero ever expressed any admiration for was Eddy Merckx, who rather wonderfully reminded JB of himself. 'The big names get carried by their teams. Even Coppi only had to ride hard for two days in a race. Merckx suffers. He has to do it all on his own.'

When the Vuelta returned after a five-year absence in 1955, Jools was installed as the Spanish 'A' squad's DS. His charges would obediently mirror the total absence of tactical cohesion and team discipline that had comprised his own professional experience. As one of them bluntly put it: 'We ate together, we slept together, but when we got on our bikes it was just: "last one to the finish is a poof".' A journalist following the race was so appalled by the disarray that he secretly stepped in as de facto team boss, driving up the road to bring renegade A-team breakaways to heel. Berrendero himself received a public warning for 'gossiping to the press instead of instructing his team'. The 1955 Vuelta A team was perhaps the strongest squad of Spanish cyclists ever assembled, containing riders who would finish first, third and fifth in forthcoming Tours de France. But courtesy of JB's reverse alchemy, the race was won by an unexceptional Frenchman, with Italians taking nine of the fifteen stages.

That should have been the end of this dalliance in management, especially after Dalmacio Langarica – last seen suffering that fateful breakdown in France – took up the DS reins and steered Federico Bahamontes to Spain's first Tour victory in 1959. But in 1960, JB was very surprisingly offered another shot at the Tour. Even more surprisingly he accepted, perhaps lured by a conspicuous name on the Spanish team sheet: his own nephew, José Herrero Berrendero, brother of Juan, who had been racing for five years without notable success.

Anyway, it was an absolute shambles. Langarica had learned how to indulge and mollycoddle the moody and sometimes childish Bahamontes, but JB would rather have died. In likely consequence, the pre-race favourite abruptly abandoned during the second stage, for no apparent reason beyond a total lack of motivation. 'I've no idea what's wrong with him,' Berrendero told a journalist. 'It seems our diva just had an attack of nerves.' No Spaniard would finish that Tour in the top ten. For good measure, his nephew came in as the *lanterne rouge*. Two years later José Herrero retired, still only twenty-eight, without a single career win to his name.

That really was that. JB withdrew from professional cycling, and went back to his shop. The interviews from this period showcase that forensic grasp of financial detail, and a wounded bitterness in regard to the paltry sums under discussion. 'After 16 years in the saddle I retired with 200,000 pesetas [perhaps £50,000 in today's money]. And that includes the value of my house. It's basically nothing. So I still work from 8 in the morning until 9 at night, and lead a humble life.'

In September 1964, a new Berrendero suddenly popped up in my chronological trawl of the newspaper archives, under the headline: 'Big pools win for Berrendero's brother.' The story beneath revealed that Juan Berrendero – father of both aforementioned nephews – had scooped a 500,000-peseta prize. 'I think I'll take my wife to the Canaries,' Juan told the paper. 'But I've got six children, and I've only told one of them so far. He's already asking for a TV and a fridge!' I could almost hear JB's howls of rage and frustration as I read on. While Julián was killing himself on a bike for half a million kilometres – his own career-total estimate – Juan had been pottering about for the water board, just like their father. Now, out of the blue, he had won more than twice as much money as his illustrious, long-suffering brother had ever earned. And he had six kids! And one of them was a pro cyclist! It must have been almost too much to bear.

At sixty-five, Julián Berrendero at last began to take things easy. He spent less time at the shop, leaving Juan Junior in charge, and indulged his passion for hunting. The press coverage thinned out, but I came across some eye-catching interviews. One, in a 1986 edition of *El Mundo Deportivo*, was a three-way conversation between Berrendero, Bahamontes and JB's old mate, Fermín Trueba. It starts with some mild bantz, when Berrendero gets out a photo of a recent haul of quail. 'Where did you buy them then?' asks Trueba, with a smile playing around his lips. Then things kick off.

The tone is set. Bahamontes, sat between the pair, acts as referee.

'Your problem is that you lack courage,' says Berrendero. 'You always did.'

Fermín is quick to reply: 'I beat you more than once! Get a load of this guy. What about that time in the Madrid Championships when you had a big *pájara* and I caught you?'

'If you could only catch me when I had a *pájara*, what does that say about you?'

Trueba, the only friend JB ever had in cycling, was then seventy-one; JB was seventy-four. They'd known each other for fifty years. How dearly I wanted to frame this to-do as no more than blokeish ribbing between old mates.

Berrendero's final interview appeared in the July 1995 edition of *Epoca* magazine. He was eighty-three by then, and in the accompanying photo – as ever posing outside the shop door with his hands on the bars of a Berrendero bike – he doesn't look great. Those deep-set eyes are now sunken, and his skin has a yellowish tint. Most conspicuously, his right foot is encased in a big white plastic boot. 'A car recently ran over his foot,' explains the interviewer. '"If it weren't for that," Berrendero says angrily, "I'd be winning veterans races right now and everything."'

We learn that he has recently lost his wife, Pilar. He touches on his time in the camps, mentioning the breakfast miracle at Rota, without naming Captain Llona. There is discussion of that hated nickname, which for the first and only time he actually utters in full. 'This "black man with the blue eyes" business, that was a silly invention of the French. What can I say, I'm a brunette by birth and I take the sun better than most.' Very movingly, he shows the interviewer a photo that he has kept in his wallet for fifty years. '"Amazing, look at this! I had four punctures that day and barely lost any time."' There is no further explanation. I want to believe it was taken on the stage of maximum hardness in 1941, when he made that miraculous comeback.

And then, right at the end, the interviewer asks: 'So who is the winner of the war of words between you and Fermín Trueba?'

I moved my phone camera down the page with some foreboding, and waited for Google Lens to do its stuff.

'I never lie. Fermín has been saying he once beat me by eight minutes, but he never even beat me by one. He couldn't take eight minutes out of me over a whole season! We've been companions and friends all our lives, but now we have fallen out.'

The sorrow aroused by these words swelled into the very bleakest melancholy when I read Berrendero's response to the interviewer's final question. 'So Julián, who do you want to thank for their support in the cycling world?'

'Do me a favour and print this in large letters: nobody.'

A month later, Julián Berrendero, the last champion cyclist of the Republican era, succumbed to heart failure in a Madrid hospital. The obituaries I found seemed sadly perfunctory. *El Mundo Deportivo* offered little more than a brief rundown of his biggest victories, and glossed over the camp years with startling indifference: 'After the civil war, Berrendero won the 1941 Vuelta a España, a feat he repeated in 1942.' I had to wonder if the *pacto del olvido* was at work. Almost sixty years on, even in death, Julián Berrendero still carried too much baggage, his ordeals under a long-dead dictator still too painful and divisive to discuss, best left unremembered.

He was buried in San Agustín del Guadalix, his birthplace, where a street had already been renamed in his honour. In Berrendero's last interview, he said the mayor had promised him a sports centre, but it never materialised. Riding around Spain I'd seen lesser cyclists celebrated with far greater enthusiasm. I remembered passing a big sports complex named after Fernando Escartín on my way into Zaragoza. Escartín was a decent rider, but he never won a grand tour and had no apparent connection with the city. He wasn't even dead. A single street in a small village seemed a poor return for such a great champion; this difficult man with his difficult past had been swept under the carpet. I took a last look at the ghost of Bicicletas Berrendero, then slipped an *alpargata* into a toe strap and pedalled slowly away.

It was 13 kilometres to Biketown, and I took them easy, gliding north-west up the quiet boulevards. Out through the banking district's glass towers with a warm breeze at my back, and into narrower, steeper, hotter streets I had laboured up one bright blue morning six weeks before. I did my best to savour La Berrendero's unladen pace and grace, race-ready at last, when my race was run. The brakes were much more effective with so much less weight to pull to a halt, not least the 7 kilos of body fat I later established had been left behind on the roads of Spain. There suddenly seemed like an awful lot of stuff I ought to appreciate while I still had the chance. I even found myself trying to embed that sound-track in my memory bank, the lollystick-on-railings thrum of poorly adjusted Campagnolos, the painful shriek of rubber block on grimy Mavic.

I crested a long, steep bridge that passed over a gyratory system, and on the coasting descent, with a grating clack, the pedals lurched into life and began pushing my feet around. After 300 obedient kilometres, the freewheel had stuck. In panicked reflex I kicked back, hard: a faint metallic commotion issued from the rear hub, like a modest win on the world's smallest fruit machine, and normal service was resumed. Alarm melted into relief, and then something close to awe. Vamos, Julián! In these final moments, he had made his spectral presence felt. Well, it was that sort of day.

I had to take a moment to compose myself before turning into the wide, empty street that was home to Biketown. This would be the first time I had finished one of these enormo-rides and not taken the bike back with me. It was a prospect that caused my regrets to express themselves in a fashion well suited to sunglasses. But in the event I had plenty of time to come to terms with this impending tragedy: when I wheeled La Berrendero up to the shop it was dark, empty and locked. I messaged Gerardo; he replied at once saying he'd forgotten that it was a national holiday, and would make some calls. A text arrived a minute later: Antonio, the English-speaking friend who had been there to wave me off, would be along in a bit to pick up the bike. I wheeled La Berrendero into a sliver of shade, then sat down next to her and waited.

What, in all honesty, would JB have thought of my ride? I'd love to have looked him in his bright blue eyes and said: 'I did it, Don Julián. I bloody well did it.' He might have been impressed. He might have been flattered. He might have laughed in my face. Anyway, I had excelled myself. That's all you can hope for. And perhaps he'd have cut me some slack, because I was cutting some for him.

That final falling-out with his only friend had convinced me there was something behind all the bile and bitterness, that his tireless antagonism was more than just an overdeveloped competitive streak. It seemed obvious, really. The hatred was pure projection. He could never say a word against the regime that had stolen his best years, and brought his career to a humiliating end. That was the hate that dare not speak its name. But it had to go somewhere, so it went to Federico Ezquerra, and Mariano Cañardo, and *Doña Fatalidad*. And when nobody else was left, it went to Fermín Trueba.

Twenty minutes later, a smart black Volvo SUV pulled up and a facemasked Antonio emerged, wearing Ray-Bans and an ironed blue Lacoste. It was all very responsible and restrained: after a polite nod, we tapped elbows, and he retreated to a safe social distance. Antonio was no hugger. But he was self-evidently an extremely nice man, who waved away my gratitude and any suggestion that he might have had better things to do on a bank holiday.

'Please,' he said. 'Our pleasure is in your legs.'

I knew what he meant. It was a day of rare praise, and Antonio's memorable tribute made a perfect companion to the messages I'd received as I'd waited for him. From Gerardo: 'A strong hug, you're a big guy.' From Rodrigo, in reply to a text about my last-stage marathon. '225km is too much for even professionals! You are great!!!'

'Don't forget my arms,' I said, and yanked up a T-shirt sleeve to show him my tan line: a band of creamy white atop toasted Berrendero brown, like a pint of Guinness. His eyes widened and a bark of laughter burst through his mask. Feeling I'd softened him up, I gravely and sincerely apologised for La Berrendero's abused condition.

'Is kilometres.' He shrugged. Antonio seemed entirely unconcerned, as would Gerardo after I sent him a lengthy email debrief full of appreciation and remorse. I suppose, as experienced cyclists, they hardly expected a bike to return unblemished from such an enormous journey. 'You have nothing to worry about,' wrote Gerardo. 'La Berrendero is perfect with one more beautiful story to tell.'

'You are so lucky with the time,' said Antonio, swinging La Berrendero into his boot with practised grace. 'Now Covid is coming back, the situation for your adventure is much more difficult.' How very true that was. Writing these words in the midst of an interminable third lockdown, I still can't quite believe it. Somehow I'd sneaked out of the country between waves of infection and slipped in a cheeky 4,500-kilometre Spanish bike ride.

I leaned into the Volvo and patted that dusty, scarred top tube. Then a boot slammed, a door clunked, and an engine roared into life. In a moment I was alone, on an empty street outside a padlocked shop, feeling traumatised and utterly bereft. An extraordinary chapter in my life had just come to an end, but instead of tenderly and respectfully turning the page, it felt as if the book had been snatched from my hands and flung over a wall.

'His full name José Luis Navares González.' During my ride, I'd messaged Gerardo three times asking what he could tell me about La Berrendero's original owner. Now, in reply to the fourth, he obliged. 'We meet him in Javi's shop, he was a great fan of cycling. He bought this special bicycle at the shop of Berrendero, and he give to us, because, as he said: "You understand the valour of this man."'

I pocketed the phone, puffed out my brown cheeks and gazed at the distant, dusky mountains. José Luis Navares González, I hear you.

ACKNOWLEDGEMENTS

Thanks to Gerardo Suárez, Javi and Antonio; Stefan Padberg, Asociación para la Recuperación de la Memoria Histórica, Rebecca Sewell, Dr Rodrigo Rial, Charmian Inman, John Perring, Arlene Peters, Geoff Cumming, Georgia Garrett, Rachel Cugnoni, Joe Pickering, Sally Sargeant, Alison Tulett and Steven Appleby.

penguin.co.uk/vintage